The Comp... *Guide to* Sexual Fulfilment

Your Questions Answered

DR PHILIP CAUTHERY & DR ANDREW STANWAY

with FAYE COOPER

VERMILION
LONDON

Published in 1992 by Vermilion
an imprint of Ebury Press
Random House
20 Vauxhall Bridge Road
London SW1V 2SA

Eighth impression 1992

British Library Cataloguing in Publication Data

Cauthery, Philip
    The complete guide to sexual fulfilment:
    your questions answered.
    1. Sex
    I. Title   II. Stanway, Andrew
    III. Cooper, Faye
    306.7   HQ21

ISBN 0 09 177051 3

Designed by Tony Fahy for Phoebe Phillips Editions
Cartoons by Bill Belcher
Illustrations by Malcolm Barter
Photographs courtesy of Barnabys Picture Library
Film stills courtesy of the National Film Archive of
the British Film Institute

Photoset by Service Filmsetting Limited
Richmond House, Richmond Grove
Longsight, Manchester

Printed and bound in Great Britain
by Butler & Tanner Ltd, Frome and London

CONTENTS

ABOUT THE AUTHORS

Dr Philip Cauthery MB, ChB, DPH first became interested in the psychosexual aspects of adolescent medicine in 1965 when he started working as a Student Health physician after 16 years in the Royal Air Force Medical Service. In 1967 he participated in the creation of contraceptive services for the unmarried in Birmingham and he has always been a pioneer for women's rights to contraception and abortion. His interest in sex education led him to start a series of public lectures at the University of Aston under the title 'Know Thyself'. The texts of these lectures were published as the *Fundamentals of Sex* (W. H. Allen) in 1971. In 1973 he wrote *Student Health* which is largely concerned with the psychological problems of adolescence. He has worked as an adviser and as a participant in many radio and TV programmes. He regularly contributes to the medical press on psychosexual topics and was for six years the editorial adviser on psychosexual medicine to *Parents* magazine, writing and answering letters about sexual problems. His most recent book, co-authored with Drs Andrew and Penny Stanway, was *The Complete Book of Love and Sex: A Guide for All the Family*, published to wide critical acclaim in 1983. Dr Cauthery is married and has two children in their twenties.

Dr Andrew Stanway MB, MRCP practised medicine on the Professorial Medical Unit at King's Hospital in London before leaving to edit medical journals for doctors for five years. In 1973 he started a medical film company making educational and documentary films for doctors, dentists, health-care professionals and TV around the world. He has written 18 books including *A Dictionary of Operations*; *Taking the Rough with the Smooth*; *The Boots Book of First Aid*; *Overcoming Depression*; *Why Us? – A Guide for Infertile Couples*; *Alternative Medicine – A Guide to Natural Therapies*, *Prevention is Better* ... and four titles with his wife, Dr Penny Stanway, about family life including *Breast is Best*, an international bestseller about breastfeeding, *The Baby and Child Book* and *The Complete Book of Love and Sex: A Guide for All the Family*, with Dr Philip Cauthery. His books on depression and infertility took him further into the area of sexual problems and their effects on people's lives, and he has since become increasingly active clinically in this field.

After studying Social Science at Leeds University, *Faye Cooper* worked as a social worker specialising in fostering and adoption. She went on to train as a Marriage Guidance Counsellor and worked with the Sheffield Marriage Guidance Council for 11 years. Research work with a Consultant Psychiatrist into the effects of mental illness on family function and the marriage relationship led to her employment by the NHS in a newly founded Sexual and Marital Difficulties Clinic. Faye Cooper lectures to medical and professional groups and is a founder member and Honorary Secretary of the Association of Sexual and Marital Therapists. Faye is married and has three adult children.

INTRODUCTION

Very few of us get the best we could out of either love or sex. Just why this is so will become clear as we go along – but the reasons are complex and involve many factors in our own past and present and in our choice of partner.

A few people are only too aware that they and their relationship are unfulfilling, the cause of frustration and difficulty, or even despair. Others get along pretty well most of the time, with just the occasional difficulty that rocks the boat. Even in the worst situations, though, things are rarely as hopeless as they seem – and if we really want to, we can learn from our defeats and disappointments and do better. Problems, troubles or difficulties all contain a seed of hope; this book is about encouraging the growth of these seeds.

When we think about physical illnesses, our knowledge of what constitutes good health mainly comes from the study of diseases or abnormalities. By discovering their causes we can learn how to treat them, and how to prevent their occurrence in the first place. The same is true for the hidden beliefs and attitudes which produce the dis-eases which can distort our closest emotional and sexual relationships.

We can all benefit from having experienced bad times and difficulties but only if through them we discover how to understand ourselves and our partner.

It's also sensible to learn from the experiences and problems of others. After all, there's no sense in making mistakes which could be prevented with a little knowledge and a few words of advice.

The traditional male complaint is that women only see sex in the context of love and romance, while women complain that men are 'only interested in one thing'. This is because our culture programmes us to believe that men are basically emotionless, caring only about physical sex, and that women are only interested in love and feelings and don't much care for physical sex. We hope this book shows how harmful such stereotypes are and helps the reader, male or female, to get more out of *both*.

We have organized the contents of the book so as to be helpful as possible if you are trying to cope with a practical problem by yourself. This involves three basic stages; first, understanding the basics (Part One of the book); second, doing something about it (Part Two) and, lastly, answering any questions that all this raises (Part Three). Of course these all overlap, but we have tried to ensure that no matter where you turn to there will be relevant information.

We hope the book will give you additional knowledge, increased confidence, and most of all, loving sex, and sexual love.

UNDERSTANDING THE BASICS

SEX AND SOCIETY

Throughout history and in all cultures today people have always found it necessary to make rules to regulate and control sexual expression. Obviously the ways that have been used and the exact nature of the restrictions have varied enormously both from place to place and even within any one country over the years. Often such restrictions on sexual expression are tied closely to religion, but this is by no means always so.

Because sex is so powerful a drive most of us agree that some rules are necessary – the trouble is that as society changes – and it is changing very fast almost everywhere in the world – the rules that govern both personal and social sexuality change too. Until this century the average person's idea about what was acceptable and what wasn't had been based on classical Judaeo-Christian teachings in the western world. Today, though, things are rather different as the traditional rules are eroded and new secular – as opposed to religious – concepts of morals take their place.

All of this plays an increasingly important part in people's sexual and relationship problems because the new order not only creates problems of its own but questions the traditional solutions to sexual difficulties.

Before looking at the specific sex problems that are the result of social factors let's briefly look at the changing social scene that so affects all our thoughts on this subject.

Social changes that have affected sexuality

Although 95% of adults in the West are, or have been, married, marital breakdown is now extremely widespread. Some surveys suggest that as few as 1 in 10 couples are 'happily' married and a survey in 1983 conducted among 'conservative and romantic' women found that 40% of them accepted before marriage that their marriage might not last. Approximately 1 in 3 marriages ends in divorce so they have every reason to be wary about their own marital future. But why should this be?

There are two sets of social factors that are playing a part in marital dissatisfaction and eventual breakdown – general ones and specific ones.

Probably the greatest single general social factor is the changing role of women in society. Not only have women become increasingly independent financially as a result of going out to work but they have also become more equal in other ways. No longer are women so completely dependent on men. It is easier to support oneself, with or without the help of the State. This has also been helped by smaller families. Single-parent families do, of course, have considerable financial difficulties, but it is possible to cope, and so escape from an unrewarding marriage that would have to have been endured years ago.

But in addition to this, marriage itself has changed from being an institution to a demanding, inter-personal relationship. Classical, stereotypical marital roles and notions of what men and women 'ought' to be are changing. Younger husbands see themselves less and less as the natural head of the family (partly because the State takes over certain of their traditional responsibilities), and more responsibilities are generally shared. Couples today share their lives and their feelings in a way which would have amazed their great-grandparents, but this has hazards as well as benefits. Today's married couples are often far *too* closely involved with each other's feelings, living as they do in a nuclear family with neither friends nor an extended family with whom to share life's stresses and burdens.

As a result each demands so much that neither can cope. They are trying to be all things to each other – friend, therapist, lover, father-figure, mother-figure, partner in work, householder, and so on. It is obvious that no two people could possibly be perfect for each other in all these areas. It is probably true, though not necessarily very helpful, to say that many couples would be happier if the role definitions *were* clearer.

Marriage and change

Then, too, today's successful marriage will last for 50 years or so. This is a new phenomenon that results directly from our longer lifespan. At the time of Christ the average person died at about 30, so even allowing for early marriages a couple seldom lived long together. Even as recently as 1911, the average marriage only lasted for 28 years. Women today are also having fewer children, and this leaves them free of the traditional burden of childbearing by around the age of 30–35. Allowing for years at home looking after the babies and young children, these women are back in open society looking for jobs, company, interests and fulfilment. Working women have more opportunity to meet members of the opposite sex than do their sisters who stay at home who may have more time to dream or think about it, but fewer contacts.

Then there are certain risk factors that seem to make sex problems more likely from day one. Studies show that marriages entered into when the woman is under the age of 20 fare very badly, with divorce rates 2 or 3 times the *normal* divorce rate. This increases still further if the man is under 20, too. Premarital pregnancy is a bad starter, with hasty marriages having an exceptionally bad outlook, especially if the couple marries late or near to the birth. A combination of young marriage and a premarital pregnancy is almost doomed to failure.

So preparation for marriage, often considered to be stuffy and unnecessary, really pays off. An enjoyable engagement period bodes well for a good marriage – in fact it may be the only pre-marital way of being able to fortell how happy (or otherwise) a marriage will be. Unfortunately many young couples short-cut the courtship and engagement stages of their relationship and never really discover the truth about one another until it is too late.

Older couples

Clearly in such a brief review we can only scratch the surface of the vast scientific and sociological evidence available about society and the man-woman relationship, and their sexual life. For many, the new order of things has come as a body blow, and some are disorientated socially and sexually. Conditioning as children has told them to believe certain things, yet today's society appears to be saying something very different. This in itself can produce profound sexual identity problems within a couple. The husband, keen to appear modern may well want his wife to be the same and perhaps even behave sexually as if she were 20 or so years younger – in short to be a woman of the '80s. She in turn might not be able to do so because her childhood conditioning is so powerful that she still thinks of sex as 'something a man does to a woman in private'. On the other side, women who see the new interest in female sexuality and sexual expression as a vindication of their hidden desires may drag their reluctant husbands down the liberated path kicking and screaming. What, he wonders, has happened to the innocent little virgin he met all those years ago? The answer, of course, is that she may never have been as sexless as he took her for; she has simply begun to assert her own sexual needs.

But sex is a unique subject in the human experience. It is at one and the same time a basic human drive, like eating and drinking, yet it involves another person. Whilst eating and drinking with others adds to the pleasure of satisfying the basic bodily needs and is often linked with social ritual, sex involves another person in a much more personal and intimate way, which in turn involves society as a whole.

Sexual deprivation and how to cope

Society generally accepts the myth that most people are leading happy (or tolerable) lives with a sexual component that satisfies them most of the time. Unfortunately, this is not so. The reality is that there are millions of people, including the young, the old, the separated and divorced, and the widowed who have no satisfactory sex life and this is often, for them, a very real and insuperable problem. Add to this the millions of married people who are deprived of sex for part or even all of their married lives and it's easy to see that sexual deprivation is enormously widespread, even in our so-called permissive society.

Society has very strong views on how sexual deprivation, inside or outside marriage, should be handled. But before looking at the solutions to the problem let's see who the sexually deprived actually are.

The young

Youngsters reach the genital stage of their psychosexual development in their early teens in our culture, yet we have so arranged things that we don't marry until our mid-20s. This means that for most normal, healthy young people their heterosexual drives are frustrated for a dozen or so years. Of course, this doesn't mean that most children or even very young adults are necessarily mature enough emotionally and psychologically to embark on a meaningful and enjoyable sex life; they are not. But biologically the drives are there and demand some form of satisfaction.

Laws governing the age of consent are vital to protect the very young from premature intercourse, often at the exploitative hands of an older person of the same or the opposite sex, but by definition almost, this means that some perfectly mature girls will be unable to have intercourse legally whilst others who are nowhere near ready will have the act sanctioned by law. There is no glib answer to this because laws have to reflect averages and 16 is a workable age in our culture. When it comes to boys the question is even more difficult because some 16-year-old boys haven't even begun to mature genitally.

But just because sex is *legal* at 16 doesn't for a moment mean that western society sanctions pre-marital sex as the norm. On the contrary – all our cultural conditioning, even today, suggests that a woman should be a virgin when she marries – and ideally, so should a man. The average girl today loses her virginity at about the age of 18 and fewer than 1 in 10 girls walk up the aisle a virgin. So clearly for young girls today their biological drives overcome their cultural conditioning. This is their way of reducing sexual deprivation to a minimum.

Sexual deprivation among young women, then, is less of a problem than it was. This is not true for young men, some of whom have such poor social skills and are so wary of girls, whom they may have been conditioned into seeing as hunters interested only in monetary support, that they cannot talk to a girl long enough to get to know her, let alone enough to satisfy their sexual drives and appetites. It's worth pointing out here that a man's sexual drives are at their highest point at around the age of 18 or 19 – after this his appetite falls very slowly over the years. So among young men there is often a very considerable amount of sexual deprivation, even though many are sexually active from time to time.

The divorced, separated and bereaved

Although some people callously imagine this group of people are having a wonderful time when they are 'back on the market' again, the truth is often entirely different. Most experience a combination of the following: emotional disturbance, anger, a sense of rejection, depression, suicidal thoughts, physical and mental illness and guilt, after the loss of a spouse through death or divorce. They may not even feel much like sex for a year or more, and some lose interest for much longer. Gradually, the drive comes back, but then they have to be confronted. Especially among older women, this creates a deep well of sexual deprivation. There are millions of widowed women over the age of 60 who will never have a sex partner again, and many of them will live without sex for the equivalent of up to half their married lives. A very real problem, but the subject is almost unmentionable, although our culture places such an emphasis on sex for the young.

Deprivation within marriage

It would at first sight seem unlikely that sexual deprivation was common within marriage. After all, an important reason that most people get married is to enjoy a sex life together as part of their relationship.

This is certainly often true, but, as with so many matters to do with sex, the apparently obvious is not always the way things are. In fact, there is probably more sexual deprivation within marriage than there is outside it. But how can this be?

The circumstances and reasons for sexual deprivation within marriage are many and complex, and the following list can only mention the most commonplace ones. Most couples will experience one or more of them during their married life together and for many they will be the most pressing sexual problem they ever have.

To start at the beginning, *non-consummation* of the marriage will result in deprivation for either or both partners. Whilst non-consummation (never having had intercourse) is relatively rare, when it does occur it may or may not be very distressing for one or both partners. The story is usually of one or both unconciously colluding to avoid intercourse because of their fears and wishes. A marriage that hasn't been consummated isn't technically a marriage in law but this is usually of little concern to the couple. Such marriages almost always need skilled professional help when the problem comes to light – often when a baby is wanted.

Illness, be it mental or physical is often a cause of sexual deprivation. We lose interest in sex when we feel ill or anxious. But these are perfectly normal reactions to easily perceived medical conditions.

Far more difficult are the mental and psychological conditions that produce sexual problems (see page 87). The commonest by far is depression. One of the first casualties of depression is one's sex life and this is a well-recognized symptom of the condition. Some women, however, try to ward off early signs of depression by excessive sexual activity. Since depression is the commonest psychiatric illness by far (especially in women) this alone accounts for many hundreds of thousands of individuals' sexual deprivation. In this case it is the spouse of the depressed person who is deprived and often not just of sex.

Depressed people themselves don't usually say they are deprived – they are far too miserable to bother about sex. This has negative effects on other areas of the relationship apart from sex, of course, and all of this can add up to produce a very troubled couple.

More difficult still for those who have to deal with the sexual consequences of ill health (mental or physical) are those individuals who use a minor but real complaint as a reason to get out of sex altogether. 'My husband's so considerate – he knows my arthritis is terrible' and other similar remarks are commonplace in such couples. An inhibited individual who never was very keen on sex or thought it a necessary evil of marriage, rather like paying the mortgage, latches on to the smallest physical ailment and uses it as a way out of sex. Needless to say this can raise very ambivalent feelings in their partner who doesn't want to appear disbelieving but is doubtful that the physical symptoms can possibly be sufficient to account for the unwillingness to have sex.

Babies are a major source of sexual deprivation in the younger married couple. Today's obstetrician rarely advises against sex during pregnancy (except around the 12th week if there is a history of miscarriages or perhaps during the last month) so this source of deprivation is thankfully a thing of the past. After childbirth, though, many couples keep away from sex for weeks or months, and many women simply don't feel very sexy if they're up awake at night with their baby. Tiredness, pre-occupation with being a good mother, adapting to the new maternal role, problems with breastfeeding, pain from an episiotomy, a fear of damaging her genitals (especially if she had any

form of operative delivery), fear of infection, fear of pregnancy, general anxiety and a host of other things can all make the weeks after childbirth a time of deprivation for the couple. This need not be the case, but it often is.

The *menopause* is often a time of sexual deprivation for both men and women. A man's wife has often invested so much of her sexuality in the care of their children that when they all leave home and she stops having periods she sees her sexual life as completed. Many such women unconsciously believe that sex is only for babies and that now they can no longer have them they have no need (or right) to be sexually active.

A reduced level of sexual activity further increases the natural vaginal dryness which can occur quite normally as a result of falling levels of oestrogen in her body after the menopause and before they know where they are the couple has a real, 'medical' problem on which to blame her withdrawal from the sexual scene. The man is thus sexually deprived and is especially vulnerable at this age to extra-marital affairs which further confirm the woman's feeling of withdrawal. Some simple lubricating jelly or a hormone cream can often solve the physical problems so the outlook needn't be as bleak as it seems. A woman who doesn't take these simple steps may have a vagina that is so sore that she avoids sex. It is probably true that the average woman who is having sex only rarely or infrequently will be even more

The understandable distractions of pregnancy and babies can lead to neglect of the marital relationship unless care is taken to guard against it

likely to stop entirely after the menopause.

Gynaecological operations are common-place. In women over the age of 25 hysterectomy is the second commonest operation after a D & C. In the US more than a quarter of a million women lose their uterus each year. We look at this more on page 326.

Mismatched needs and desires are considered on page 255.

Absence of one partner. With modern life organized the way it is many couples are parted for at least some of the time, and for many people this is a way of life. Merchant seamen, those in prison, export business-men, long distance drivers, shift workers and many others simply aren't around at home enough of the time or at the right time of day to be able to sleep with their wives or even to have sex with them. Many other couples see each other only at weekends effectively because the hus-band comes home from work too late and goes straight to sleep, perhaps after watch-ing some television. Many thousands of couples quite quickly evolve such a sexu-ally deprived way of life and are totally in-active sexually during the week.

Secret divorce is very common indeed. About 1 in 3 marriages end in actual divorce but probably as many again persist unsatisfactorily. There are no studies of which we are aware that have assessed marriages according to whether the couple still sleep together but clinical experience shows that almost a quarter of teenagers, when asked, say that their parents sleep in separate rooms. Many couples stay together for social, religious, financial or family reasons when to all intents and purposes they are divorced in all but name. Usually one or both will be sexually deprived.

Emotional immaturity is unfortunately very common, especially in men. Many such individuals can't hold a relationship together for long no matter how suitable their partner is and sex often suffers. Such people need professional help.

Ageing. As a man gets older he needs increasing amounts of excitement and stimulation to obtain and sustain an erec-tion. All can be well if he has an under-standing and willing wife who is able and prepared to stimulate him more as the years go by. However, many women, especially in the older age group, are so inhibited about such things that they can't bring themselves to do what is necessary. In this type of problem it's simply a matter of factual knowlege and goodwill.

Deviancy is a small problem numeri-cally but is often very difficult to cope with and treat. Some individuals have such strange sexual needs as a result of their upbringing and other influences that they can't find many (or indeed any) people with whom they can have satisfactory sex. Extreme forms of sexual deviation are always genuinely sad for this very reason. Just imagine being able to satisfy your hunger by eating only one or two ex-tremely rare foods, served only by a hand-ful of restaurants in the whole country, and you'll be able to sense the deprivation of such people.

One of the commonest variations of this problem is based on the common clinical finding that a less than psychosexually mature person will always want to relate to individuals of the same chronological age as his or her *psychosexual* age. So it is that an older woman may well take up with a younger man or a teenager because psychosexually this is where she is frozen in time. Some older men are similarly turned on by schoolgirls or women dressed as schoolgirls. They can't cope with real women of their own age who are, for various reasons, too threatening and 'adult' sexually for them. The spouses of such people are often deprived because they don't match up to their partner's needs for sex. Often such marriages persist for years with the deficient partner seeking his or her preferred form of sex outside when the pressures get too great.

When it comes to dealing with sexual deprivation we are all different and the individual with a relatively low sex drive (or high inhbition level) will find deprivation easier to cope with. An individual to whom sex is an important and regular feature of life will, on the other hand, find even short-term deprivation quite intolerable and will become bad tempered, sleep badly and feel edgy much of the time. Many people when deprived of sex turn their dissatisfaction or even frank anger onto their partner, who is made out to be permanently at fault.

This, the commonest of all sex problems – affecting as it does millions of individuals at any one time both within and outside marriage – is ill-understood, except by professionals working in the area, because people's ideas of 'deprivation' and its importance vary so greatly. One person's deprivation could well be a veritable orgy of excess to another, so it's often impossible to find a willing ear when one has such a problem.

Solutions

Let's look now at the possible solutions which have, for the most part, been used since recorded history. We aren't suggesting that any or all are suitable for any

particular problem, but simply that they are all used by people from time to time in their lives.

Given the sort of society we live in it is hardly surprising that the only entirely socially acceptable answer to sexual deprivation is *celibacy*. Although celibacy is a somewhat unfashionable concept today, this has not always been so. There are people who have willingly given up sex for spiritual and religious reasons, but in addition, surprisingly large numbers of quite normal everyday folk lived celibate lives. In the days when large households had several servants most of them would have remained unmarried and virginal (or nearly so) for life. Certain jobs stipulated that the person be unmarried, and marriage could be a bar to promotion in domestic service.

Today things are different, but many people are just as sexually deprived as the socially induced celibates were.

So for many people today, especially the widowed elderly, whose ideas are traditional, and whose opportunities for meeting the opposite sex are few, enforced celibacy is a real way of life. Many, if not most, would probably rather not be celibate but their moral views leave them little option. They channel their activities and energies elsewhere, often into good works, grandchildren, looking after animals and so on. For some this will be a welcome relief from a lifetime of sexual activity reluctantly undertaken as part of their marital duties, or undertaken with a partner for whom they felt little sexually but didn't or couldn't leave.

However, most, if not all, celibates masturbate a few times a year and many have sex dreams with or without orgasm. Even many of those who choose celibacy (rather than have it thrust upon them) masturbate from time to time.

Celibacy then is the readily chosen path of a very few (for whom sex is not a 'problem' so we won't discuss them in this book) and a reluctantly accepted path for very many more. Western culture can easily cope with this answer to sexual deprivation but other solutions aren't as easy to accept; perhaps the most common and acceptable is sublimation.

Sublimation is a psychological manoeuvre in which prohibited sexual and other instinctual energies, which cannot therefore be used directly, are displaced into more acceptable activities (see page 297).

Women often sublimate their sexual drives to areas of interest close to the home, such as children, housework, caring for animals, caring for others, doing good works, looking after grandchildren and so on. In this way their needs to be wanted, loved and to receive affection and praise can be answered in a culturally acceptable way that does not involve genital sex.

Men tend to sublimate their sex drives into activities away from home (though many a DIY fanatic is undoubtedly sublimating his sexual appetite in a acceptable and even laudable way). So they build businesses; travel, work constantly and enjoy sports.

Most of this goes on at the unconscious level, of course. For some, the cause and effect will be very obvious. They see their lack of sex life at home as proving they are unloved or are thought of as an unsatisfactory lover and so quite consciously try to promote themselves in other areas of life in which they *can* shine.

Many men become so absorbed in meeting their need for achievement that they neglect their emotional oportunities with their wives and both partners lose out as a result. The hardworking husband who does this earns the praise of a society in which hard work is prized but his relationship with his wife might well be disastrous.

The woman who devotes herself excessively to the care of her children and to good works also gains social approval, yet it can also damage her relationship. If they are more concerned about what the rest of the world thinks than about their relationship, both partners can live alongside each other in a form of marital charade which the outside world perceives as the ideal marriage.

Of course, the activities into which people sublimate their sexual drives are necessary and valuable, but it helps to understand that if these activities become an end in themselves, they can be an escape from the dissatisfaction of a one-to-one relationship.

Some people become celibate simply by being too busy to have time for sex.

Of course it would be foolish and wrong to suggest that all hardworking men or very busy women are sublimating their sex drives – in fact the opposite is often the case. Very active individuals also tend to be active sexually – a busy sex life is just a part of their busy lives generally. However, an excessive concentration on any one area of life to the exclusion of one's partner should flash warning lights and needs sorting out with or without the help of a professional. We all sublimate a part of our powerful drives to non-sexual activities; it is a matter of degree. The next step is:

Retreat from sex, or its total repression. These individuals cross sex off their life's agenda. They avoid all references to sex; try not to acknowledge its presence in the world around them; avoid their sexual feelings and urges most of their lives and can always find something else that's more important to do than to have or even think about sex in any form. Within marriage this can be a disastrous form of sexual deprivation for the partner who almost never shares his or her spouse's retreat from sex. Such a retreat can occur as a slow slide downhill. As they retreat, these individuals even stop masturbating and rarely have sexy dreams, until eventually they live virtually sexless lives.

But few people can repress or sublimate their sexual urges totally and the majority still have some form of sexual outlet, if only once or twice a year.

Masturbation is probably the commonest solution to sexual deprivation at all ages. Although it has been (mistakenly) condemned since Biblical times, it is an almost universal practice in people of all ages from the cradle to the grave. More than 95% of men admit to masturbating from time to time and almost 90% of women do so too. It is a safe, reliable and enjoyable alternative to intercourse. Many patients say how they 'would have gone mad' if it weren't for masturbation, at various periods during their lives, even during marriage but it is much more than simply a safety valve. It is often through masturbation that a young person can relieve his or her sexual tensions and learn about his or her own body's sexual responses in a way that will be useful to them later in their one-to-one relationship.

For most people masturbation is a 'second best' activity – when intercourse is not possible – but this doesn't mean that it should be ignored. The 'sex or nothing'

attitude has killed more marriages than we care to relate. Masturbation, lovingly performed by a partner, can be every bit as caring and loving as intercourse itself. Even being held by one's partner and cuddled while one masturbates oneself is a close and sharing alternative to intercourse and protects the one-to-one bond until the reason for the temporary sexual deprivation is over.

Masturbation is, of course, the main form of sexual expression for the single, bereaved, widowed, divorced and separated and all those without a partner either permanently or temporarily. Many couples are loving enough to use masturbation as a support during temporary sexual deprivation but still look to intercourse as their main form of sexual expression.

But masturbation has another valuable role to play in marriage. In one sense, given that we are all potentially promiscuous, we are all at least to some extent sexually deprived *because* we are married, as usually we can't have intercourse with everyone we fancy. Masturbation is the way that these natural promiscuous drives can be contained – to the eventual benefit of the one-to-one relationship. Although Jesus said that to lust after someone was much the same as actually committing adultery with him or her and in psychological terms he was absolutely right, in practical terms it's a lot safer and helps protect marriages and families to fantasize about someone rather than to go off and have an affair with them.

So masturbation can be a solitary and even lonely pursuit closely linked to fantasies outside a couple's sex life; a loving part of one's everyday sex life; a crutch to rest on in lean sexual times or a retreat from the anxieties of life.

Affairs are one of the commonest responses to sexual deprivation within marriage – although to be fair, many individuals will have already tried many or most of the manoeuvres we've already discussed before resorting to an affair.

Affairs are said to be increasingly common, though all the statistics about how common they are must be misleading because they tend to be under-reported in surveys. The impression of clinicians working in this field, however, is that women are as likely, or nearly as likely, as men to be, or to have been, in such relationships and that possibly by the age of say 55 around three-quarters of married individuals will have been involved in one or more affairs even if they haven't ended in actual intercourse. In fantasy, if not in fact, virtually everyone will have had several.

Paradoxically, a few people find a kind of sexual refuge in marriage and have little practical sexual interest in other members of the opposite sex but for most, marriage does not reduce this attraction. The attraction may be expressed only in fantasy, friendship or flirtation with limited sexual aims but it is still there. A few immature people are incapable of making serious attempts at sexual commitment in *any* relationship and so affairs continue regardless of marriage. Some people, by divorcing and remarrying, perhaps several times, 'legalize' their affairs in a way that would not have been really possible in the past, except for rather special cases such as Henry VIII.

A few couples who feel they can't tolerate the sexual restrictions of marriage reach an agreement or 'contract' which specifies that extramarital relationships are acceptable within certain constraints and rules. Sometimes a condition of such an agreement is that the partner be informed although many people say the opposite in that they don't mind their partner having such relationships provided they *don't* know. Either way it is, perhaps, a better alternative than repeated divorce, especially if the individuals believe that their relationship is worth preserving. In several western cultures it has been considered to be socially acceptable for a man to have a mistress and for his wife to accept it as a fact of life. Today, the true mistress is a rare creature but men (and increasingly women) who find one sex partner for life insufficient sometimes look outside marriage for this variety.

It is scarcely surprising that affairs are as common as they are today because in the absence of any culturally acceptable way of coping with sexual deprivation within marriage and the need for sexual adventure and variety over a married lifetime, many people are likely to seek alternatives as a way around the problem.

An affair may simply be an adventure or a refuge and never meant to replace a marital relationship – in fact, individuals may say that they want *both* the new partner *and* their spouse. Of course, a few of those having affairs are either consciously or unconsciously on the lookout for a new partner because of underlying dissatisfactions in their marriage.

There is also the concept of the 'ideal' partner. Although we know that we are far from perfect ourselves, and so shouldn't expect it in others. This expectation is harmful because perfection is not found in this world.

A difficulty in any affair is that in our culture marriage includes the promise that the relationship will be sexually exclusive.

Is she speaking to the butcher about his bill . . . or is she having an affair?

In an age of efficient contraception old objections about reproductive (and inheritance) confusion which would have resulted from extramarital sex have lost some of their validity. They have not lost all of it as is shown by the fact that a substantial proportion of married women seeking an abortion do so because they are pregnant by someone other than their husband. Increasingly, however, marriage is seen as a relationship which doesn't necessarily confer exclusive ownership rights on the partners, and 'good' sex is seen as something of a right.

So we can see how various the motives are for the start of an affair; the search for an ideal love; curiosity (especially in those who had little or no experience before marriage); a poor sexual self-esteem for whatever cause; sexual boredom; experimentation; revenge; reassurance; testing of the partner's love and so on. Promiscuity as such is, perhaps surprisingly, not a frequent cause, although an unfulfilled sexual need is. Travel, holidays, being away from home, alcohol and parties all provide opportunities for intimacy to occur, although these usually lead to only brief relationships.

When the relationship becomes more than sexual, it might turn into a full-blown love-affair. This can be a real disadvantage. A man or woman may start by seeking sex, and end up in a complex interpersonal relationship that finally wrecks the marriage. Given that sex is so complex a human pastime, it's dangerous to imagine that one could easily pick it up, uncontaminated by emotions, and come out sexually satisfied and walk away. On the contrary; in an unconscious effort to reduce guilt men and women often emphasize the love aspect of such a relationship. If either believes that it is only possible to love one person at a time, then divorce may be the end result. So the original relationship may be destroyed, only to be replaced by one which is not much better and may even be worse.

If both parties involved in an affair make their intentions clear at the start, such situations can sometimes be avoided. Too often men mislead women by showing more emotion than they really feel, so as to get them to agree to sex, and women mislead men by behaving more sexually than they really feel so as to establish an emotional relationship. Greater honesty between the sexes could avoid many such unhappy outcomes.

Affairs are usually secret, and the first realization that a partner may be involved can lead to destructive suspicion. But sometimes a partner who can't physically have intercourse may, out of consideration, urge the other to have an extramarital relationship rather than see him or her permanently sexually deprived. Sometimes the intentions are not so honourable, such as a wish to have the partner reveal in minute detail what happened, as a form of vicarious sexual pleasure.

An extension of this is wife-swapping, on a casual or a permanent basis. This is a poor term because it is sometimes the wife who is the instigator. This could be called a joint affair because the husband and wife are both involved. It can also lead to jealousy on both sides. It is not surprising that wife-swapping is often so destructive to relationships.

For some people the very secrecy of an affair is part of its attraction – they say they find 'naughty' sex more satisfying than 'legal' sex because they are more inhibited with the person they love.

Perhaps the biggest dilemma facing the person who is having an affair is whether or not to tell their partner. There are no easy answers to this but it's probably wise to err on the side of discretion. It may make *you* feel good (or even self-righteous) but it can have a devastating effect on a partner who, especially if it comes as a surprise, may react more dramatically than you imagined. Some people even use confession as a way to get revenge on their partner. Few people really want their confession to be accepted with equanimity – simply because it seems to show that he or she doesn't care. Yet deception, secrecy, lying and subterfuge are the prices one has to pay to keep an affair secret, and for many these outweigh any advantages.

Prostitution can teach us several valuable lessons if only because prostitutes are the sexual outlets for many problems and are a way that some people cope with sexual deprivation.

Often, the man is paying the prostitute not so much for sex as for freedom from emotional complications and anonymity. Also, when having sex with a prostitute a man isn't bothered about revealing his needs and doesn't worry so much about performance failure. A prostitute may also meet his needs to exhibit himself or to watch her exhibiting herself and for many such men prostitutes meet their needs for sexual variety that they can't get within their marriages.

So, for example, some men pay the woman to tie him up, gag him, humiliate him or dominate him. Others want her to dress in special clothes and/or to dress in women's clothes themselves.

The main question is why such men should feel they have to satisfy their unfulfilled sexual needs in this way. There are two main reasons. First, many wives are too inhibited to join in such games and second, many men see their wives as too 'nice' to even approach about such things because they unconsciously equate them with their mothers who were negative about sex during their childhood. Such men are simply afraid to reveal their 'dirty' needs.

A new phenomena to many is the male prostitute: we should not be so surprised by the concept, because there have always been men who have clung to rich women for financial advantages. 'Escorts' available by the hour for social and sexual companionship are less common, but they fulfill many of the same needs: an outlet for sex without emotional demands, or for desires which may be hidden from a woman's conventional partner. They also supply the additional role of an acceptable social partner on occasions when a woman feels she needs one. By and large, though, women do not have to pay men in order to get what they want sexually and this is why formalized male prostitution is less common than female prostitution.

Few men going to prostitutes want only 'straight' sex – most want oral sex or some kind of activity they find difficult to obtain at home.

Some men can function only within a sexual context in which love and affection don't intrude.

The attitude of nice and wicked women is carried through into the average marital bedroom, and most men don't think of asking their partners to fulfil any of their even mildly 'abnormal' needs. The irony is that the wives often complain that their men are unadventurous and boring. Obviously some men have very deviant sexual needs that are almost impossible to be catered for by ordinary women, and such damaged individuals will have to resort to a specialist prostitute who will accommodate them, at a specialist price.

The would-be lover
So far we have looked at the sexual deprivation resulting from all kinds of causes and we have examined some possible answers. But there is also a very different social problem – people who are simply so socially unskilled that they can't get their first foot on the ladder to form a relationship with someone of the opposite sex. In short, they are cripplingly shy.

The following table should be of help to those who can't even find the ladder! It is based on many years of experience of helping those who are too shy to get started. Remember this condition can affect people of any age, intelligence, education or job but this table will be most useful for young men.

1 Get hold of a good book on overcoming shyness or on social skills training.

2 Join a local skills training group. These are available all over the country and are very reasonably priced. Your general practitioner, marriage guidance counsel-

lor, local MIND group or local paper will be sources of information.

3   Take every opportunity of talking to men or women in every possible social setting.

Always go to shop assistants, bank clerks and so on, of the opposite sex and indulge in minor social pleasantries. Try going for a whole week talking only to the opposite sex in such situations.

4   Always say just a sentence or two *more* than is absolutely necessary to achieve the purpose of your conversation. In this way you'll get more confident.

5   Smile in a friendly but un-threatening way.

6   In general, if you are pleasant to someone they will usually be pleasant to you, and this will gradually built-up your self-confidence.

7   Try to think of the opposite sex as being pleasant company rather than being rejecting, critical and frightening.

8   Forget any ideas about sex objects. Pretend that the subject of sex isn't involved at all. Try to relate simply as human beings.

9   Men still usually have to ask a girl out. Don't lay your self-esteem on the line to be trodden down, especially in the early days. Not 'Will you go out with me to the pop concert on Saturday?' but something like 'There's a pop concert on Saturday, I'm going, would you like me to get you a ticket too?' If she then says 'no', she may simply not like the group that was playing. You can usually tell from the way she refuses if this is really so, and can try again another time.

10   Remember that there is no reason why every girl you ask out should say 'yes'. After all, if the tables were turned you wouldn't be happy to go out with every girl who asked, would you? You don't like all girls, so why should all girls like you?

11   Both men and women can get involved in clubs and other social or sports activities that also involve the opposite sex. Things that allow you to express your personality are best. Drama groups, sports activities, dancing lessons and many others are good because by meeting people who share your interests you're much more likely to meet someone with whom you'll get on. An evening class is often a good meeting place – you'll have something in common right from the start.

12   Still a good bet are singles clubs and holidays. The best ideas are singles holidays with specialist interests such as skiing, painting, sailing, photography and so on. Once again you'll meet like-minded people which will give you a head start. Clubs and pubs, wine bars and discos, are not usually very good for meeting the opposite sex in a meaningful way.

13   Marriage bureaux and friendship clubs can be really good but some are a rip-off, charging a handsome fee for poor results and poor matchings. The best ones do fairly deep interviews and really match their couples. Bureaux are ideal for very busy people who simply can't make the time to scan a wide field. This is especially true of many people in their late 20s and 30s or even the 'available-again' widowed, divorced and separated. Many such people find the shelves pretty bare and their expectations rather higher than average, both of which make 'shopping' for a partner much more difficult.

Becoming this intimate with a member of the opposite sex will seem like scaling the north face of the Eiger to some, but if you are guided by this list of hints you'll be amazed how quickly you progress

14 Advertising *can* be highly successful but be sure to word your advert very carefully and truthfully. Always state what you want first and then say clearly and simply what you have to offer. Several responsible newspapers and magazines carry such ads and the most amazing cross section of the population use them. There are also some magazines that specialize in this type of advertising.

15 Lastly, try to become a more interesting person in yourself. Think about others more rather than being concerned all the time about what you think they think of you; and do things for other people. When you do talk, don't talk endlessly about yourself, treat other people as interesting and valued individuals. Rather than acting out a role you think you should be playing, try to be yourself and remember that what other people think of you is up to them. Whatever your faults some people will love you for them. The basic truth is that if you like people they will like you. If, however, you are fearful, over-critical, over-submissive, excessively self-conscious or self-preoccupied, you may need professional help. Many of these attitudes can be reversed with help and the change can revolutionize your life.

HOW THE SEX ORGANS WORK

Even in today's so-called permissive society there is still ignorance about the structure and function of the sex organs. Sometimes ignorance leads to real sex problems but more commonly it produces dissatisfaction or fears of abnormality. It can also be a sign that the person doesn't want to know about it, and this can be more serious. For example, a man who has been married for many years and claims to be very keen on women and sex may never have had a good look at a vulva and is unaware of the existence of the clitoris in spite of all that is written about it in the media. Without realising it he is avoiding sex. Because of unconscious fears he doesn't want to know too much about women and their genitals.

In any case these are in our culture, 'private' parts of the body – the average person doesn't know what other people's genitals are like in detail and this leads all too often to feelings of abnormality and inferiority.

A woman's sex organs

A woman's primary sex organs are both internal and external and with her legs closed there is very little to see except for a triangle of pubic hair.

When she opens her legs various structures become visible. First, and most obvious, are the two, large, fleshy folds that are covered on the outer surface with hair. These are known as the labia majora (large lips) and they, unless held apart, or the legs are widely opened, hide all the other structures of the vulva.

If these outer, large lips are parted, two smaller lips are seen inside them. They meet at the front to form a little hood-like structure that covers the clitoris. The clitoris is a small rounded organ which becomes erect during sexual excitement, but otherwise it can be quite difficult to find. Its head is firm to the touch and about the size of a small pea. The shaft, which is fixed to the pubic bone underneath, is a thin cylinder which can be rolled under the fingers. Most women get maximum sexual sensations from stimulation of the clitoral area directly with fingers or a vibrator and describe the sensations this produces as very different from those produced from stimulating the vagina. Because it is so sensitive many women find too direct stimulation of the clitoris, especially the tip, unpleasant and so prefer to massage the surrounding area.

Moving backwards a little towards the vaginal opening one comes to the tiny opening of the urethra (urinary passage) that leads from the bladder. This is hardly visible in many women but lies immediately in front of the vaginal opening. In

Finding the G-Spot

What is the G-spot?

It is a sensitive area in some men and women situated below the base of the bladder at the top of the urinary passage. It is felt in the front wall of a woman's vagina and in the front wall of a man's rectum within his prostate gland. When stimulated the G-spot is exquisitely exciting and produces orgasms of a totally different nature from those produced by clitoral or penile stimulation.

Not everyone has a G-spot and its existence is somewhat controversial. If you don't have one it doesn't mean you are deficient in some way.

Finding a woman's G-spot

A woman can find her own G-spot and so can her lover.

Here's how to do it:

● Get into a position in which you can feel inside your vagina easily; this is usually best when sitting or squatting.

● Put one or two fingers inside and stimulate the front wall of the vagina. This usually produces a desire to urinate at first but if you have already urinated you'll know that you won't do any more and can carry on until you get used to this new sensation.

● If you have any difficulty finding the area that's most sensitive inside the vagina press one hand over the very lowest part of your tummy at the same time as stimulating the front vaginal wall.

● As you continue stroking you'll prob-

ably notice some pleasant sensations in your uterus, especially if you are already sexually aroused when you start the G-spot search. Experiment with this area just as you once did with your clitoris and find what's best.

If trying to find this area with your partner:

● Lie on the bed face down and with your hips on a pillow or two.

● Ask your partner to insert two fingers (palm down) into your vagina and then to explore the front wall until you can feel him stimulating your G-spot. You can move your pelvis to make the stimulation all the better for you. Later get him to insert his penis and ask him to use that to give you exciting sensations there. He will feel the spot about two thirds of the way up the front wall of the vagina between the pubic bone in front and the cervix at the top.

● You'll probably notice that the sensations resulting from G-spot stimulation are totally different from those produced by clitoral stimulation. Most women say that the orgasms they experience are deeper, involve more of their body and seem to be very uterus-centred.

● Once you have found the G-spot you or your lover can stimulate it during foreplay or in rear-entry love-making positions.

Finding a man's G-spot

A man's G-spot is deep in his prostate gland.

Here's how to find it.

- Lie the man down face down on the bed with a couple of pillows under his hips.

- Lubricate one or two fingers very well and insert them into his rectum palm downwards. You'll feel the prostate as a firm mass the size of a large walnut. Stroke it with your fingers under his direction until he says it feels best. An alternative position is with the man on his back with his legs drawn right up. The prostate is then felt on the front wall of the rectum.

- Keep on stroking until he ejaculates. Many men ejaculate without having an erection in these circumstances but the sense of relief is just as great, if not greater, than when he has an erection too.

Some women like their G-spot stimulated using a vibrator.

fact the urethra runs in the front wall of the vagina at its outermost part.

The most obvious structure to be seen when the large lips are held apart is the vaginal opening itself. This opening is usually closed because the vaginal walls lie next to one another unless something is placed in the vagina to part them. The opening of the vagina is usually surrounded by small tags of skin which are the remains of the hymen, a thin, tough membrane that partially covers the opening until it is broken. The tags can be quite long but never cause sexual problems. The inner lips (labia minora) are sometimes rather enlarged.

Moving backwards still further is an area between the back of the vagina and the anus called the perineum. This area is packed with muscles and is that which is cut during an episiotomy to let a baby out more easily. Since 90% or so of first births are 'assisted' in this way a scar in the perineum is now the norm in women who have had a baby. This usually does little or nothing to hinder their sexual functioning and enjoyment in the long term, but in the short term it certainly does hurt, and can slow down the return to sexual activity for some time after the birth. In some women it provides an unconscious excuse for the long-term avoidance of intercourse.

All these structures are easily seen in a mirror. The next stage in understanding the structure of a woman's sex organs is to put a finger or two inside the vagina.

The vagina is only a potential space, it is not a cavity that is present all the time as many people believe. Gently insert one finger and feel its walls. As you put your finger further in you'll realize that the vagina has an S-bend – it goes upwards at first and then turns to run backwards and finally upwards. Around three inches inside you'll be able to feel a firm knob-like structure with a dimple in the centre. This is the cervix or the mouth of the womb (uterus). Sweep one or two fingers around inside the vagina and you can see how different the vagina and the cervix feel.

The next and final exploratory stage is to run your finger(s) along the front wall of the vagina to feel the urethra and to see if any particular place feels exceptionally pleasant and stimulating. In some women about two thirds of the way up the front wall of the vagina is a very sensitive and exciting area called the G-spot (named after a gynaecologist called Gräfenberg). This area becomes swollen and very sexually exciting in some women to produce a distinct vaginally-centred orgasm which they say feels different from that resulting from clitoral stimulation.

While the fingers are still inside the vagina contract the muscles of your pelvis as if trying to stop passing water. These are the pubococcygeus muscles. Women who train their muscles so that they can tighten them firmly at will may have easier and more pleasurable orgasms and men find their contraction around the penis highly enjoyable during intercourse.

The external genitals of a woman and the vaginal fluids that are produced quite normally all the time have a characteristic scent and contain substances called pheromones that can affect male behaviour. In some women these natural fluids become profuse enough to stain their pants at certain times of the month (usually around ovulation). These secretions are usually colourless and pleasant-smelling (if the woman's level of personal hygiene is good) and certainly should cause no concern. The consistency and smell changes from one part of a woman's cycle to another in a way which is characteristic of her sexual cycle.

Although most couples don't think of them as such, a woman's breasts are an intrinsic part of her sexual organs – indeed some women have orgasms from nipple stimulation alone and about half of all women find breast play and nipple stimulation pleasant and sexually arousing. The degree of pleasure often varies throughout any individual woman's menstural cycle and pre-menstrually some women don't want their breasts touched at all. It makes sense for a woman to get to know the feel and appearance of her breasts so that she can notice any changes that occur at once and report anything that concerns her to her doctor.

What happens during sexual arousal?

The main change that occurs is an increased blood flow to all the sexual organs, including the breasts. This results in the swelling of all of a woman's pelvic and sexual organs.

The first physical signs of sexual excitement are that the nipples erect. The breasts swell and the veins on the breast skin become more easily visible. In three out of four women there may be a sex flush – a faint measles-like rash which spreads over the abdomen, chest and neck.

The next signs are that the vulva swells and the inner lips especially become engorged with blood making them appear darker in colour and slightly swollen. At the same time the vagina begins to expand in length and fluid 'sweats' from its walls

to lubricate the vaginal cavity. Some of this fluid may appear at the vaginal opening and may even flow quite profusely over the lips and the vulva generally. The amount of this fluid varies greatly from woman to woman and even in the same woman, depending on her state of sexual arousal. As arousal proceeds the clitoris enlarges with increased blood flow. In some women the clitoris swells to more than twice its resting size and in others it hardly changes in size at all. As the woman enters the next, plateau phase, of sexual arousal the shaft and tip of the clitoris curl up under the foreskin of the organ and it appears that the clitoris has all but disappeared.

At this stage the outer lips swell more and become darker in colour and open up the vulval area a little. The woman's body is now becoming excited, her muscles tense and her uterus pulled upwards as the vagina relaxes and opens up at its top end so enlarging the vaginal cavity.

Further breast swelling occurs, the woman sweats, her heart beats faster, her breathing gets faster and her body starts to twitch. The first signs of twitching are often in the toes and feet or the wall of her abdomen makes fluttering movements.

As she reaches orgasm her body may arch, her muscles may tense, her face may draw into a grimace and she may cry out or make a noise of some kind. Her vagina, pubic muscles and uterus all contract ryhthmically and the whole body may be thrown into spasms. Some women who are especially restrained, shy or inhibited show very few outward signs of body movement, and make no noise. The response of any one woman during an orgasm depends greatly on her personality type, her previous sexual experiences, her mood on that day, her level of excitement, how acceptable she believes her sexuality to be to her partner and the intensity of the occasion. Once the contractions of the pelvic muscles, uterus and vagina stop, she calms down but is capable of having another orgasm within a minute or two. Some women can have several orgasms one after the other but many say that one is enough and have no need for more. Some women can have 50 or more orgasms at a session (usually of masturbation) but most have between 1 and 3. How many a woman has depends on her previous experience, her partner's ability and his willingness to continue stimulating her, and of course, her desire to have more.

What happens after an orgasm varies greatly from woman to woman but slowly over the next hour or so her body usually returns to normal. She may feel sleepy and doze off to sleep, or feel invigorated depending on the time of day and her emotions at the time.

A man's sex organs

Because almost all of a man's sex organs lie outside his body and are thus easily visible and felt many people imagine the male system to be simpler than that of the female. This is not so and there is still a lot that is unknown about the structure and functions of the male genitals.

The penis is a tube-like structure at the base of the abdomen. Although it looks like one tube, it is in fact three. As you look down on the penis from the top there are two visible tubular masses of tissue under the skin called the corpora cavernosa. They're called cavernosa because they're cavernous in structure and can swell to accommodate large volumes of blood. The third cylindrical structure in the penis lies on the under-surface and is called the corpus spongisoum. It ends in a bulbous swelling (the glans) which forms the sensitive tip of the penis.

The three cylindrical parts swell when a man becomes sexually aroused and an erection occurs because more blood flows into the penis than is allowed to flow out. The penis has to swell and become rigid to fulfil its sexual function – that of placing semen high up in the vagina near the cervix.

The urethra is the tube that carries urine from the bladder to the outside, and terminates at the tip of the penis in a small, slit-like opening. Semen comes out of this same opening, so the urethra has a dual urinary and sexual function in men but not in women. Because the urethra runs through the corpus spongiosum it is compressed and virtually shut off while the penis is erect. This is why it is difficult for a man to pass water when he has a full erection. The shut-off point is above the level at which sperms enter the urethra from the vasa deferentia so that urine is 'held back' but semen is allowed through. Certain medical disorders and some drugs can so alter this muscular mechanism that the affected man ejaculates semen into his bladder instead of down the urethra (this is called retrograde ejaculation).

The shaft of the penis is covered with darkened, loose skin which looks rather delicate and thin and this skin continues below over the scrotum (the pouch that contains the testes) as a more wrinkled, thicker and hairier covering. The skin protrudes over the tip of the penis as the

Above: The external genitals of a woman. Middle: Cross-section through the pelvis of a woman. Below: Cross-section through the pelvis of a man

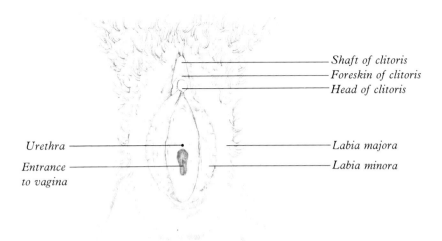

Shaft of clitoris
Foreskin of clitoris
Head of clitoris

Urethra

Entrance
to vagina

Labia majora
Labia minora

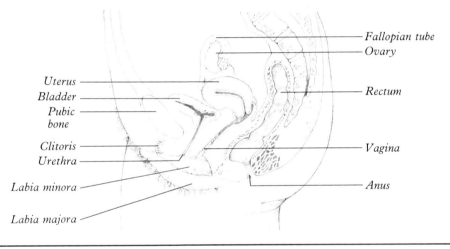

Fallopian tube
Ovary

Uterus
Bladder
Pubic
bone

Rectum

Clitoris
Urethra

Vagina

Labia minora

Anus

Labia majora

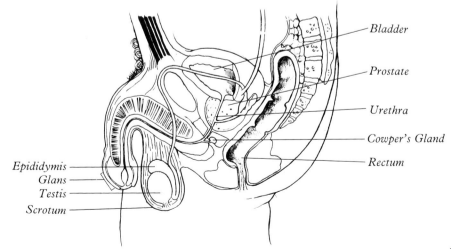

Bladder

Prostate

Urethra

Cowper's Gland

Epididymis
Glans
Testis
Scrotum

Rectum

foreskin. A sensitive band of skin, called the fraenum, connects the lower surface of the glans to the foreskin. If stimulated it will arouse a man very quickly.

Just as women are concerned about the size of their breasts, men worry about their penis size. Women, however, are much less concerned about the size of men's penises than men imagine they are. Research in the past few years shows that there is no relationship between flaccid (unerect) size and the final erect size, and in any case, there is no evidence that, on balance, women like big penises better than small ones. The vagina adapts to fit any size, only the outer third of the vagina is really sensitive. One New York survey of sexually experienced women indicated that they did not find large penises particularly exciting. Women who are not sure of their own anatomy actually dislike the idea of being stretched, and other women may genuinely find a large penis painful.

The scrotum is a bag of sensitive skin, sparsely covered with hairs, inside which are the sperm-producing organs, the testes. The height of the testes is controlled by the cremasteric muscles. The skin of the scrotum is composed of several layers, the most important of which is muscular. This layer of dartos muscles, as they are called, acts in conjunction with the cremasteric muscles as a heat-regulating mechanism which helps keep the testes at exactly the right temperature. This is important because normal sperm development can only occur if the testes are maintained at a temperature of about 2–3° lower than that of the core of the body. Cold (and also fear) cause the dartos and cremasteric muscles to contract and so draw the testes nearer to the body thereby

making them warmer. A mass of veins surrounds the artery that supplies the testis on each side, producing a counter-current heat-loss system that loses heat from the artery to the veins. In this way the testes get blood at a lower temperature than that supplied to the rest of the body. When warm the muscles relax and the testes then descend well away from the body and so become cooler.

The formation of sperms in the testis takes about nine weeks. After passing through the tubules in the testis, the sperms are collected in the epididymis where they mature and become able to move on their own. They enter the vas deferens, a fine, muscular tube, and travel along this, up out of the scrotum into the abdominal cavity. It is the bottom end of the vas deferens on each side that is cut and tied off in men undergoing vasectomy. The vasa deferentia gently milk the sperms along by muscular action to their upper ends where they widen to form the ampullae. Beyond the ampullae are two blind bags off the vasa deferentia called the seminal vesicles, which produce a sugar called fructose which is the fuel sperms need to enable them to live on their long journey to fertilize an egg.

The prostate gland lies at the base of the bladder and surrounds the first part of the urethra. The prostate produces substances which act as a vehicle for the sperms, supply them with nutrients and

RACE YOU
TO THE TOP

buffer them against attack from acid vaginal secretions. It is because it needs to counteract acid vaginal secretions that semen is so alkaline.

Beyond the prostate is a pair of small glands called Cowper's glands. These add a small amount of lubricant to the seminal fluid before ejaculation takes place as excitement mounts. Rather less than 10 per cent of the volume of any ejaculate is composed of fluid from the testes and epididymis; about 80 per cent comes from the seminal vesicles and the remaining 10 per cent from the prostate.

The whole process of maturation of a sperm from the day that it starts in the testis to the day it is ejaculated takes about three months, most of which time is spent in the epididymis while the sperm matures. Sperms then, unlike a woman's eggs, are being produced all the time. Even if a man ejaculates frequently more sperm

are produced all the time, so there is no point holding back on any form of sexual activity for fear of running out.

What happens during sexual arousal?

When a man is aroused, messages travel along nerves to his genitals via the spinal cord. These nervous impulses shut off the return of blood flow from the penis, damming up blood in the cavities of the organ. This makes it swell and harden and alters the position from a limp downward-hanging organ to an upward, rigid, rod-like one. This is called an erection.

No man can order an erection – the control of erections occurs at the unconscious level, though, of course, conscious thoughts can provoke or hinder an erection depending on the appropriateness of the time and place. Many even quite sexually experienced women don't realize that a man can't order his penis to erect, and are frustrated or even offended if it does not happen. But a single word said in the right way can switch on the penis control centres in the brain and his limp penis can be transformed in seconds to an erect state. Because the trigger mechanisms for erection control are so fine (though this is less true in teenagers and young men) they can also lose an erection at the slightest hint of noise, disturbance, or an off-putting remark or action from their partner. These basic physiological facts put men at a distinct disadvantage because although a woman can take part in sexual intercourse even if she is hardly aroused and perhaps not enjoying it very much, a man has to be highly aroused if he is to be able to penetrate her at all. This is undoubtedly why it is that men have so many more performance fears than do women. A woman can fake willingness but a man cannot.

Whilst a penis is erecting changes are taking place elsewhere in a man's body too. His heartbeat quickens, his pupils enlarge, his blood pressure rises, his breathing quickens, his nostrils flare, his muscles become tense, he sweats a little and he feels sexual tension mounting inside him. About one man in four has a sex-flush. During this excitement phase his scrotum becomes more tense and thick and the testes are drawn up tightly to his body.

Up to this stage a man, if no longer stimulated, can return to his resting non-excited stage. Of course he'll feel let down but will feel normal again within minutes. More often though he'll go onto the next stage and have an orgasm.

During the next, plateau phase, the penis swells even more, its tip becomes purplish-blue and the contents of the scrotum increase in size. From here onwards it becomes more difficult to return to normal until the man has an orgasm.

At orgasm itself a man feels that he has no choice *but* to ejaculate. His pelvic muscles contract, as do all the muscles which form part of his genital organs, and semen is spurted out of the end of his penis. Often, especially in younger men, a small, first portion emerges with force and can travel a considerable distance. This produces a unique sensation deep down inside the pelvis as the prostate gland (previously engorged with fluid) discharges its contents into the first part of the urethra. A series of four or five contractions follows at a rate of one every 0.8 seconds each producing a smaller volume of semen than before until all the semen-carrying tubes are empty. Eventually the contractions cease and the man relaxes. His penis returns quickly to its normal size and he may feel sleepy.

Unless he is very young, is particularly aroused, or emotionally intense, a man may need several hours to recover before he can become aroused again. By and large this 'refractory time' increases with age. Some boys can have repeated orgasms just like women, but few men past their 20s can do this regularly. There is no harm in ejaculating several times a day, but it can be tiring.

How a knowledge of male sexual arousal can help your sex life

The hardness and size of a man's erection is a pretty good barometer of his sexual arousal level but a man can show all the other signs of arousal and yet have a very poor erection. This can come about if he is tired, not really ready for sex or if he is impotent. Inserting the penis in this half-erect state can, if the woman is keen and active with cuddling, kissing and pelvic movements, soon make it become the fully erect organ they both want. So a poor erection need not necessarily mean the end of a love-making session. Most penises respond to oral love-play in this state and are soon ready to perform.

Many women find it difficult to know when their partner is about to ejaculate and indeed it can be difficult to tell in some men. Most penises undergo a final enlargement just before ejaculation and the man becomes totally 'lost' to his environment and will have an intense expression on his face in the few seconds preceeding ejaculation. Some women find that they can tell how excited their man is by feeling his testes. If they are tight up against the body they know he's nearly ready to come – but this isn't a universal rule.

Just as many women complain that their partners go straight for their clitoris or breasts so too, some men say that they'd like their partner to stimulate and tease non-genital areas of their bodies to make them more aroused or more quickly aroused. A man's nipples, scrotum, testes, anus or the area between anus and penis can be pleasurable if handled properly and massaging the 'root' of a man's penis may make him come very quickly. On the other hand some men complain that their woman doesn't stimulate their penis enough, or even at all, and yet others claim that such stimulation over-excites them. Some men are shy about asking for what they want and others are wary about telling their partner when she does something he doesn't like for fear of offending her or putting her off doing anything. In other words, men can be just as tricky about these matters as can any woman.

A note of caution

At any stage of foreplay some fluid may appear at the opening of a man's penis. This usually means he's pretty aroused whatever the size of his penis. As this fluid can contain sperms it's wise to treat it as if it were semen or the woman could theoretically get pregnant.

Making the most of what you've got: Increasing penis size

There is no evidence that anything you do to your penis once you are fully grown in fact increases its size. If you have a rare hormone deficiency condition then testosterone, the male hormone, will increase penis size but not otherwise. There are no pills, creams or potions that will increase penis size but anything that gives you a better quality erection can appear to increase its size. This is probably how penis enlargers on sale at sex shops work – as they seem to for some men at least.

Increasing your staying power

Young men and adolescent boys often ejaculate very quickly, from lack of experience and control. However, even healthy, normal men, may ejaculate sooner than they or their partner would like, especially when they have had a period of abstinence from sex. The excitement that builds up can quickly trigger the ejaculation reflexes, so reasonable frequency is essential if you are to enjoy good ejaculatory control and high quality orgasms. This means having sex frequently and masturbating or getting your partner to masturbate you if necessary. You can practise the following exercises which we have found to be valuable:

Masturbation training in progress

1 With or without the help of erotic reading matter or a sexy video raise your level of sexual arousal to the state where you want to masturbate.

2 Masturbate until you feel you are just about to start having an orgasm, and then stop, if necessary by squeezing your penis with your thumb on one side of its head and three fingers on the other. Squeeze around the rim of the head just enough to make your level of excitement subside and when your penis is floppy again re-arouse it.

3 Keep on with this cycle until you have produced 5–10 erections and let them subside or until a certain time, such as say 10 minutes, you have set yourself has elapsed.

4 Read, work, or do something else for a while and completely forget your erection exercises. Then return to repeat the procedure a few times again.

5 When you choose to do so masturbate to orgasm and really immerse yourself in the feelings.

6 After some practice the exercise can be repeated with the additional application of baby oil to the penis.

This exercise is valuable because it achieves several things:

◆　It proves that just because you have an erection you don't have to ejaculate.

◆　It enables you to become totally confident that, under these controlled circumstances at least, you can ejaculate *when you want to.*

◆　It may improve the quality of your erections and train you to sustain them and have more powerful orgasms.

◆　It will give you confidence that when your partner next caresses you or when you have sex with her you'll be able to last much longer to your joint satisfaction.

These exercises can also be done as a couple, seeing how long the man can go without ejaculating. Or you can practise alone to astound her with your new-found skills.

Some couples play games involving hanging things (such as small towels) on the man's penis in an effort to build up the supporting pelvic muscles and there's no doubt that muscular fitness generally helps a man's sexual performance.

How a knowledge of female sexual arousal can help your sex life

Looking at the vulva, touching it and putting fingers into the vagina can all help you know how aroused the woman is. The vulva of a depressed woman looks depressed itself, and fine perspiration occurs around the vulva of an anxious woman. An aroused vulva looks red and swollen, and the clitoris may also be visibly enlarged. Lubrication of the vagina is also a very good sign that a woman is aroused and is the equivalent stage of arousal to a man with an erection. However, some very inhibited women claim to be unaware of arousal even when they are very wet.

Breast changes too give good clues to a woman's sexual excitement level. At first the nipples erect as she becomes aroused but many women's nipples erect at the slightest touch or even as cold air gets to them so this may not be a reliable sign of true arousal. As the arousal stage progresses many women's nipples appear to lose their erection as the breasts themselves swell. A woman who has a sex flush during the peak of arousal loses it quickly at orgasm. This can be helpful because many women dislike being asked if they have reached orgasm, and this can be a valuable sign. Similarly, the breast swelling goes soon after orgasm and makes it seem that the nipples have erected again.

The man who is experienced with his partner can tell exactly where she is in her arousal cycle at any one time and this must help prevent some of the many misunderstandings about poor timing that are so common in bed. Many women complain that their husbands are too insensitive to their arousal (or lack of it) but there is really no excuse for this if the man takes a little trouble. Women too could help themselves by being more communicative about their arousal level. A couple who are really in tune with one another can pace themselves during intercourse so that both get the best possible pleasure out of it.

Vaginal control

Few women make full use of their vaginal muscles and many have not learned to control them at all. This is a shame since it gives the man an intense sensation and improves the quality of woman's orgasm. Rhythmic contractions of the muscles with nothing in the vagina can give some women an orgasm. For many couples the ideal is for the woman to contract as the penis moves inwards. Control can be learned by doing regular exercises.

Pelvic muscle exercises

1   During urination stop and start the flow until with practise you can do it easily. The muscles you are using are those that can be used to advantage during intercourse. Once you've mastered this technique you're ready to start the pelvic exercises proper.

2   Tighten and relax your pelvic muscles, holding them in the tight (contracted) position for several seconds, then relax them. See how long you can keep them in the contracted state and try to increase the time as the weeks go by.

3   Tighten and relax the muscles quickly in a sort of fluttering way. This will gradually increase your muscle control.

4   Pull up your entire vaginal area as if your vagina were a 'pump' drawing up water, then force the water out of the 'pump'. This exercise uses abdominal wall muscles too.

If you put two fingers inside your vagina (or get your partner to) you can gauge how well you are progressing. Early on you'll feel hardly any grip at all if your pelvic muscles are weak but as the weeks go by you'll be amazed how firmly you'll grip your fingers. A few women use a vibrator (without turning it on) to practice squeezing on and when muscle control is good they find they can control the depth of penetration of the vibrator without using

their hands, slowly letting it slip out of their vagina in a controlled way. Repeating this exercise with the blunt end of a pencil is a severe test.

All of this is very good training for intercourse. For the real enthusiast there are various commercial gadgets for measuring pelvic muscle strength and for developing muscle power. If you think you'd like to try one discuss it with your doctor but most women get on perfectly well with the exercises we've discussed.

These pelvic exercises are valuable to any couple but are especially useful after a baby when the pelvic muscles are understandably lax after stretching to let the baby out, and should be taught routinely to all post-natal mothers. You can do them in the car, while washing up or in the queue at the supermarket but if you're one of those women who are turned on by doing them just beware of the self-satisfied smile or people will think you're odd! They are best undertaken on a routine basis such as 10 contractions every hour. Pelvic muscle exercises are also recommended to any pre-orgasmic woman as a start to getting her on the road to having orgasms. A couple can also build these exercises into their love-lives. Many a pleasant hour can be spent finding ways of measuring a woman's progress!

Breast size

Probably the most important sexual symbol in the Western world today is a woman's breasts yet a study of 300 women found that 75% were dissatisfied with their breasts in one way or another. A few women with extremely large breasts are unhappy about them, but the majority of women complain that their breasts are too small or are of unequal size.

The severe test of pelvic muscle control. After inserting the blunt end of a pencil a couple of inches into her vagina, the woman is removing it whilst trying to hold onto the pencil firmly with her vaginal muscles

When it comes to breast enlargement there is little that can be done that is proven to be effective unless you are prepared and happy to have surgery. Do-it-yourself breast enlargement techniques that are claimed to work include self-hypnosis; regular cold water splashes; special creams to be massaged into the breast (some contain hormones); breast massage with semen and swallowing semen. Probably the best way of apparently enlarging your breasts is to do arm exer-cises that increase the bulk of the chest muscles under the breasts.

Self-hypnosis using properly designed records and tapes can be useful and several studies have found that the results last for months. Cold water splashes certainly erect the nipples and make the skin of the breasts go taut but this effect is very short-lived and no clinical trials have found the result is long-lasting. Hormone-containing creams can work, but many women (and most doctors) believe that the oestrogens in the creams can be absorbed through the skin and could be hazardous. There are many anecdotes but no clinical studies, which claim that breasts can be enlarged by massaging them with semen or by having regular oral sex and swallowing the semen! It is dubious that such methods work on any grounds that science currently knows but it could be that such women are simply aroused much of the time because such of practices and we saw on page 27 that a woman's breasts enlarge when she is aroused.

Men may well notice big-busted women in the street but most say that breast size is of little real importance. Small breasts are just as erotic for most men as large ones. Small-breasted women are as likely to obtain pleasure from their breasts as are larger-breasted women. Of course, any woman who feels badly about her breasts will not feel at ease during lovemaking because of *her* views of her body's shortcomings or because of what she imagines her partner thinks. This can produce problems. Such a woman may not want to undress in front of her man and may prevent him from caressing her breasts during love-making. This can be very frustrating for the man, especially if he doesn't share her negative views about her breasts.

The more you do it the better it gets

Sex, like any other skill, improves with practice and benefits from continuous experimentation. A lot of people complain that their sex lives are boring or even a dead loss yet they put a little or no effort into improving things and fondly imagine that making love a couple of times a month will guarantee them a rewarding, if infrequent, sex life.

Unfortunately, this isn't so and most couples who really enjoy sex make love a lot. The advantages of frequent sex are:

◆ It keeps both partners sexually keyed up most of the time so that they are more receptive to each other when either wants sex.

◆ It becomes a pleasurable 'habit' rather than a planned 'event'. This has an important advantage in that the occasional failure or poor-quality sexual experience (which occur all the time in even the best relationships) is accommodated because the couple know that tomorrow or the next day it will be enjoyable again.

◆ It is an outward sign of affection and love for your partner – feelings which may not be easy or practical to demonstrate in other ways. We can't give each other presents or flowers every day but we can give ourselves.

◆ It keeps the bond strong between the couple so that because they are relatively satisfied *within* the relationship they are far less likely to look elsewhere for sexual variation or fulfilment. The couple that makes love frequently and to their joint satisfaction stays together, works well together and can weather the storms of life better.

◆ If the couple are trying to start a baby frequent sex is helpful. It is surprising how many couples attending infertility clinics are making love once a month or less. Given that most women are only able to conceive in the few days around the middle of their cycle (about day 15) frequent sex is important *then* if at no other time.

◆ It gives a couple increased opportunities to experiment and enlarge their love-making skills and repertoire. The couple who make love once a month or so will probably aim for the 'safest' positions, love-play and so on so as not to reduce their chances of successful and enjoyable sex. The couple that makes love on most days are more likely to experiment, if only because doing the same thing 20 times a month gets boring, however pleasant it is. This experimentation opens new doors for them. Some older couples say that they are still discovering new techniques, pleasure spots, ways of arousing each other and so on even after 20 or 30 years of marriage. Dullness sets in if each time you make love you have so much invested in the event that you go for the lowest possible 'safe' level of activity you can cope with.

◆ Almost all surveys show that both men and women today want more good sex than they are currently getting, so stepping up your intercourse rate will probably please your partner even if he or she hasn't actually declared him or herself to be wanting more.

◆ It makes communication easier on other matters in life. The couple who can communicate well in bed (as they learn self-less love-making) tend to talk to each other openly about other things too. They agree with each other more than they row and when there *are* disagreements in life about family, work or domestic matters they feel better able to accommodate the other's point of view.

◆ Good intercourse can be a way of recovering from a row and a way of saying 'I'm sorry' gracefully.

◆ Regular intercourse can be used to say 'I love you' rather than simply 'I want sex with you'. It also says things like 'Thank you for being so nice', 'I need you', 'Thank you for being good at sex with me'.

◆ Regular intercourse is a superb bonus to the friendship that should be at the heart of every man-woman relationship. To waste, misuse, reject or harm our sexual relationship is a real mistake. In the ancient world Aphrodite, the goddess of love, punished people who behaved in this way!

Some common questions about the sex organs and how they work

Q Why is it that when my husband tries to make love to me my vagina is so dry?

A One possible explanation is because he hasn't spent enough time caressing you, or caressing you correctly, first. Most women take a few minutes to become sexually aroused and to start producing vaginal lubrication and this is speeded up greatly if the man caresses (kisses or strokes) the sensitive parts of her body. Almost anywhere on a woman's body can arouse her sexually if properly caressed by the right man but the most sensitive areas are her lips, tongue, ears, neck, shoulders, back, breasts, abdomen, buttocks and thighs. The order varies quite a lot from woman to woman of course. Quite a few women actually have orgasms from persistent caressing of any one of these areas and some women find foot massage highly erotic and arousing.

You need to find out, either alone or with your husband, what *does* make you lubricate and then to incorporate whatever this is into your love-play. Other possible explanations for poor lubrication are discussed elsewhere in the book.

Q My wife often complains about the way I handle her breasts. Is there a right way?

A The simple answer is to ask her and if she's sensible she'll tell you but generally speaking it's the nipple and the areola (the pink or reddish-brown flat ring around the nipple) that most women like to have stimulated. Some women prefer stimulation to the whole breast. Most men find out pretty quickly by trial and error what their woman likes, provided of course that the woman says what is best. Those women who complain about the way their men handle their breasts may have never given their man a guided tour, or specific instructions, on the grounds that he should 'know' what to do.

Gentle stroking of the breasts – especially from below upwards – is pleasant for most women but the greatest turn-on for some is undoubtedly kissing, licking and sucking the nipples. Other women greatly enjoy having almost all of their breast taken into their man's mouth. Hard sucking can be painful and it's best to keep your teeth out of the way unless she likes being gently bitten. Most women like gentle but repeated nipple stimulation and some

even have orgasms from such stimulation alone. Such love play will arouse about half of all women and get their vaginal lubrication going.

Don't forget that what a woman likes with regard to breast play will vary from time to time in the month. Her breasts may become more tender, heavy and swollen as her period approaches, and stimulation of almost any kind may be unwelcome.

Q My wife says that me stimulating her urinary opening gives her nearly as much pleasure as rubbing her clitoris. Is there any harm in this?

A No there isn't provided your finger is clean and hasn't been in or near her anus. Remember that a woman's urinary pasage is very short indeed and bacteria travel up it quickly especially when massaged up the tube by a penis or fingers during love-making.

Needless to say nothing should ever be inserted into the opening because it could be sucked up into the bladder.

Q I have read lots of sex books but in spite of everything I have read I still think my vagina is small. What can I do about it?

A Perhaps you experience pain or discomfort on intercourse and find vaginal examinations at the doctor's painful. The fact is that almost any vagina will accommodate almost any size of penis. The reason you think you are 'small' is that you involuntarily contract the muscles around your vagina. You need to relax more while love-making and especially at the moment of penetration and your partner needs to learn to spend more time arousing you so that you lubricate a lot before he enters you. Perhaps you should get used to very gradually increasing numbers of fingers inside you as you get more aroused so that you become used to the sensation of your vaginal walls being stretched during love-play. You could do this yourself while you masturbate until you get used to your muscles relaxing as something enters you. A vibrator can be a good training device too either alone or during love-play. Experiment with what seems nice to you. Take things gently and be satisfied with small improvements week by week.

Q   When I put fingers inside my wife's vagina during love-play she seems to be very turned on if I play with her cervix. Is this safe?

A   Yes it is provided your fingernails are short.

Women's cervices vary enormously in their sensitivity. Some seem to be rich in nerves and others almost anaesthetic. Some women greatly enjoy having their cervix played with and such women like very deep penetration during intercourse as the penis tip pushes on their cervix. Some men say that after their wife has had a full hysterectomy a lot of *their* pleasure goes from intercourse because the cervix has gone and they then receive less sensation to the tip of their penis.

Obviously your wife enjoys her cervix being stimulated but even so take it easy. If what ever you do causes pain or discomfort stop at once and advise her to see her doctor. A few women enjoy quite vigorous movement of their cervix because this moves the body of the womb around. This can be exceptionally exciting for a woman

if you do it just as she climaxes.

None of these games with the cervix is advisable during pregnancy. ⁔

Q   My husband hasn't been circumcised and his foreskin doesn't pull back well. Is there any danger in this? I notice it hurts quite a lot at times when we're making love.

A   Some men who haven't been circumcised have a foreskin which never pulls back fully as it should. Often they masturbate by massaging the head of the penis with the skin forward instead of pulling it back.

The problems are three-fold. First, cheesy white material called smegma accumulates under the foreskin and this can irritate the penis tip, making it more liable to become cancerous and even possibly cause cancer of the cervix in the partner of such a man. Second, the man may have pain or discomfort as he has an erection and third, his penis will be difficult to wash and keep clean which isn't very pleasant aesthetically for his partner especially in oral sex.

Some men can stretch the hole in their foreskin themselves over a period of weeks but most will need to be circumcised. This is a simple operation and clears up the problem for good.

Q   I very much like having my testes squeezed during sex but wonder if it will do any harm?

A   No it won't provided your partner doesn't squeeze too hard. Remember that as you reach the plateau (high excitement) phase of arousal pain sensations become dulled. This makes it easy for your partner to squeeze the testes really hard and possibly even to damage them without your being aware of it. If ever you feel any pain in the sides of your abdomen or in your groins it's a sign that she's squeezing too hard.

Firm squeezing which increases in pressure until the man ejaculates is a favourite of a few men but others enjoy their testis 'popped' between finger and thumb in an unpredictable and teasing way. Some men simply enjoy being massaged and others prefer their scrotum to be stroked or lightly scratched or cupped by the woman's hand.

Q When I masturbate him my husband has his best orgasms if I massage his prostate with a finger in his bottom. Could I do any harm in doing this?

A No it's very unlikely you could harm him – assuming your nails aren't long that is! Stimulation of the prostate is extremely pleasurable for some men. The prostate is the equivalent of the G-spot in a woman. For some men this produces very powerful sexual sensations and they ejaculate considerable distances as a result.

Your husband is lucky having a wife who will indulge in this intensely exciting form of love-play because many women refuse. One of their main arguments is that it is messy putting a finger in a man's bottom and this can but need not be true. A way round this is to use a latex finger stall (available at chemists to cover a finger that has a wound on it and needs to be kept waterproof) which is then washed and re-used. Under normal circumstances the lower part of the rectum is usually empty anyway so there is no problem.

Q I only ever have a single orgasm either when I masturbate or during sex yet I read everywhere about multi-orgasmic women and many of my girl-friends have several orgasms. Am I normal?

A Yes, you certainly are. Lots of women are just like you and have one perfectly satisfactory and satisfying orgasm at a time. Almost one in 7 women though find one orgasm simply not enough and don't feel satisfied unless they have several. Why this should be isn't known but there are two possible explanations. First, it could be that during adolescence the multi-orgasmic woman was stimulating herself a lot and so has become used to a very high level of excitation and multiple climaxes. Second, it could be that all women are endowed with the potential for many orgasms but that most, because of the negative unconscious feelings that they have about sex, don't go on to enjoy as many as they could. Some women who *do* later progress to multiple orgasms say that they felt before that one was 'enough' and talked as if orgasms should be limited in some way. Such women are often found to put brakes on other pleasure areas of their lives. Perhaps they have been brought up to believe that sex is naughty, sinful or dirty (even though these notions may well lie deep in their unconscious) so that they eventually ration the pleasurable feelings they get from sex.

Having said all this having multiple orgasms isn't necessarily so great. *You* have the advantage that when you have had a climax you feel totally relaxed and relieved (like a man does) but a multi-orgasmic woman will feel she needs to go on to have more.

Most men find the multi-orgasmic

woman flattering because it makes them appear fantastic lovers but this is rarely true.

It's also probably worth pointing out that 'more' doesn't necessarily mean 'better'. Multi-orgasmic women have very different experiences but most say that their first orgasm is often not the best. Such women disagree as to which *is* the best and it seems to vary even within any one women from session to session. Many single-orgasm women have such a fulfilling orgasm that they can't even imagine anything 'better'. Who is to argue with them?

Finally, don't forget that many women have two very different sorts of climax.

One is produced by stimulating the clitoris and the other by stimulating the vagina including (if she has one) the G-spot. Such women tell of a normal, clitorally-induced orgasm being produced by their partner or themselves caressing their clitoris in the usual way and then of a very different, much deeper and more satisfying sensation (definitely an orgasm too) that is produced when their partner penetrates them in intercourse. Such women regularly enjoy a kind of double orgasm rather than multiple orgasms as such.

Q   I seem to be able to have orgasms from lots of types of stimulation not just from my clitoris. My husband thinks I'm a nymphomaniac – am I?

A   Your husband should consider himself lucky – most men would envy him. Research over recent years has proved what most women have know for centuries – that they are much more arousable and more generally 'sexy' than are men. Therapists with a clinical experience in the field are no longer amazed at anything a woman says about her ability to become aroused and experience orgasms. Women can experience orgasms over the phone, by fantasy, when riding a bicycle, when combing their hair, when passing water and during a thousand and one other unlikely pastimes. This amazes men whose repertoire is for the most part extremely limited by comparison.

Some women are so highly-tuned sexually that almost anything turns them on, especially at certain times of the month. It's difficult to know whether this is one end of the normal spectrum of sexiness which starts at the 'difficult-to-arouse' and ends with women like yourself or whether all women have the potential to be aroused by a wide range of activities (both mental and physical) yet have been conditioned out of them by their sexually repressive (sex-negative) upbringing. There is probably a little of both at work. Whatever the cause, you and your husband should enjoy your sexuality.

Q   Why is it that – if as the sex books say – ejaculation is simply a physiological event orgasms feel so different from one time to another?

A   At orgasm fluids produced by the seminal vesicles, the prostate gland and to a much lesser extent the testes shoot with

considerable force into the first part of the urinary passage which lies within the prostate gland. The walls of the tube contain muscles which are triggered into powerful contractions. The force with which these contractions occur varies from day to day even within any one man and so produces different types of sensation from ejaculation to ejaculation. Why this should be isn't known but undoubtedly the man's hormonal emotional and psychological state plays an important part. A really hard erection (when the circumstances are just right) usually goes along with a satisfying ejaculation and most men's ejaculatory enjoyment is related to the frequency at which they are having sex or masturbating. Possibly men enjoy the sensations more after a short period of abstinence.

It is also interesting to point out that men don't need to have an erection to ejaculate. An example of this is the premature ejaculator who is avoiding intercourse. The accomapnying orgasm is usually very weak.

Incidentally if you've had a vasectomy – and millions of men now have, ejaculatory sensations are exactly the same. Only a tiny percentage of the fluid ejaculated comes from the testes – well over 90% comes from higher up and is totally unaffected by the vas deferens being tied off.

SEX AND HORMONES

How hormones affect our sex lives

Although many people with a sex problem – or with a partner with one – assume that 'it's something to do with his/her hormones' this is rarely the case. Hormones play a vital, if ill-understood, role in human sexuality but there is as yet little real evidence that they have any important part to play in sexual disorders or difficulties.

Let's first look at the basics. A woman's monthly cycle is regulated by the ebb and flow of various hormones and this has a variable affect on her desire for and enjoyment of sex. Most women say that they feel at there most sexy just before or after a period yet the hormone profiles are very different. Some women claim to want sex most actually *during* a period and yet others at around the time of ovulation (day 15 of their cycle).

The trouble is that there are so many variables when it comes to the desire for and enjoyment of sex that it's almost impossible to do controlled studies with objective, measurable end-points. After all, it's very difficult to rate orgasm capacity or enjoyment on scales from 1–10 and there are certainly no ways of measuring 'sexiness' or sexual pleasure.

The contraceptive pill has on numerous occasions been cited as a cause of a poor sex drive in women but the situation is ex-

tremely complex because psychosexual factors come into play. A woman who uses a totally safe method of contraception, and then goes off sex, could simply be rejecting sex because it has no deep, primitive purpose for her – to get pregnant – and it is only when there is the possibility or likelihood of getting pregnant that she can enjoy sex. For such women sex is for babies, and sex purely for pleasure without even the possibility of a baby at the end of it all, is unacceptable.

In both men and women an interest in and an appetite for sex seems to be the result of the hormone testosterone. This

Intercourse positions for the inventive couple

A   Both partners standing, the woman's legs apart; shallow penetration. They can see and kiss each other to caress and stimulate, he to touch her breasts, she to hold his scrotum.

B   He standing, she with her legs round his waist; deep penetration. They can see and kiss each other, and he can reach her anus. But it is tiring, and stimulation is mainly through her pelvic muscles.

C   He is standing behind her; deep penetration. He can hold her breasts, caress her clitoris, and stimulate the front wall of the vagina. Full stroke movement, useful for inexperienced women to come to orgasm.

D   He is standing while she is on a stool; deep penetration. He can caress her breasts, clitoris and anus, she can reach back to hold his scrotum. The full stroke movement can stimulate the front wall of the vagina.

E   He is standing while she is bent over; deep penetration. This is tiring for her, but he can reach her breasts and anus, and his penis stimulates the front wall of the vagina.

F He stands in front of her lying half on the bed; shallow penetration, and good during pregnancy. They can see each other and kiss, and he can reach her clitoris and her breasts and see her vulva, and she can touch much of his body.

G She sits on him facing him; deep penetration. She can be very active if her feet can touch the floor; they can kiss and caress most of each other's body, and she can help herself to reach orgasm by controlling the speed and depth of penetration.

H She sits facing away from him; deep penetration. He can touch her breasts, clitoris and G-spot (with his penis). She can hold his scrotum, and can control the speed and direction of movement.

I She sits sideways on a chair; penetration is shallow. This is slightly awkward for both, and tiring, but they can see each other and kiss, and he can stimulate the clitoris and she can reach his scrotum. Movement is dependent mostly on her pelvic muscles.

J She sits facing him in a deep armchair; deep penetration. They can see each other, kiss and caress, and she can control movement – useful when she has problems reaching orgasm.

K She kneels facing away from him; shallow penetration. This is comfortable during pregnancy; he can stimulate her G-spot and anus, and she can move gently to help control orgasm with her pelvic muscles.

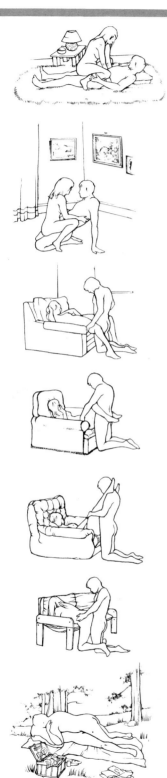

L She squats over him, legs either side; deep penetration. She can move, although it is tiring unless she is reasonably fit. They can see and caress each other, he can raise his head to see her vulva, she can control movement and thus orgasm.

M Fairly complicated; he is kneeling, leaning back, she sits on his penis; deep penetration. They can see and kiss each other and, although it is tiring, she can control movement enough to help her reach her orgasm.

N He is kneeling in front of the armchair; she could be on a low table or bed; shallow penetration. They can see each other, caress and kiss. It is comfortable during pregnancy.

O The same as N except that her feet are pulled up and held around his waist; deep penetration. Special points are that it is more difficult to kiss, although they can still see each other.

P Same as above, except her legs are now over his shoulders; deep penetration. It is a good position because partners can come to orgasm with only slight movement to achieve full penetration. Good for conceiving.

Q He kneels behind her; she can be supported by a chair or bed, or simply by her hands; deep penetration. he can reach her anus, and they can enjoy long stokes of the penis.

R He lies on top between her open legs; shallow penetration. They can kiss, she can caress him, and reach his anus. This is good for new partners, and for conception, and they can achieve full penetration with little movement.

S   As above, but her legs are closed with his legs on either side; very shallow penetration, otherwise as above.

T   Very similar to R and S, except that by lifting himself up they can see each other better, and her open legs and bent knees allow deeper penetration.

U   Another variation on R, this time her legs are pulled up to lock ankles round his neck. They cannot kiss, but penetration is deep and so it is good for conception.

V   She lies face down, legs apart, he lies on top of her taking his weight on his hands; shallow penetration. Stimulates front wall of vagina, also allowing man full stroke movement.

W   They lie tucked into each other, facing the same way, he is behind; deep penetration with relatively slight movement. Good when the man is tired or has been ill.

X   A similar position although she turns back slightly to open her legs and let the top one go over him; deep penetration, with slight movement. This is comfortable during pregnancy.

Y   On sides, facing each other, he lies knees bent between her legs; usually shallow penetration. They can kiss and caress each other.

Z   On her back, legs up and apart, he lies at right angles to her buttocks; medium penetration. Good for conception and during pregnancy.

circulates in varying amounts in both sexes, although there is less in women than in men. In men there is no clear reproductive hormonal cycle as is the case with the female hormones in women. Testosterone given to women certainly does make them more sexy, but it also produces hair growth in the beard area, stops their periods and reduces breast size if the dose is large. Studies of sexually unresponsive women have found that those given testosterone have sex more often and enjoy it more than they did before taking the drug.

But it's not just testosterone that affects women sexually. Oestrogen too seems to play a role. Women whose ovaries have been removed usually suffer from a poor sex drive and a dry vagina – indeed their symptoms are similar to those seen in menopausal women. Of course there's a psychological element in both cases, but when oestrogen is given as a drug these same women regain their normally lubricating vaginas. And this may improve their sexual morale.

Prolactin, a hormone produced by the pituitary gland in the brain also seems to be involved in libido control in both sexes. In women who have a condition in which too much of this hormone is produced loss of libido is a major problem. This can be cured by opposing the hormone with a drug called bromocriptine which returns libido to normal. Prolactin is normally produced in large amounts during breastfeeding which raises (but doesn't answer) questions about the whole subject of a woman's sex drive being turned off (prolactin does this) soon after birth and during the breastfeeding period. Many women say that they feel completely disinterested in sex after a baby – could this be

why? This is not easy to answer, because as prolactin levels rise, so do testosterone levels. Perhaps the anti-libidinal actions of prolactin are balanced out in normal women by 'sex-positive' testosterone. Anyway, the conflicting studies of some women finding breastfeeding a very sexy business and others going off sex for some weeks or months are likely to be explained *not* by hormonal changes at all but by psychological attitudes. We simply don't know enough about the subject.

Testosterone

Endocrinologists (doctors who specialize in hormone disorders) are very loathe to commit themselves on the subject of hormones and sex. Certainly they are happy to describe what happens in normal people, and in those who have abnormally high or low levels of certain hormones, but because as a breed they tend to be precise scientists they are frustrated because of the lack of ways of measuring sex drive and the pleasure of sex. One study using a potent sex-hormone 'proved' that it caused a rise in sex drive – until the experiment was repeated using saline when exactly the same increase in sex drive was found. Certainly it's true that a few men with impotence have a low testosterone level but the vast majority of men with sex problems have perfectly normal hormones as far as can be judged at the moment. It does appear that men who are not having orgasms have lower testosterone levels than those who are but this is the result and not the cause of the reduced activity.

If you are a man you can tell whether you *are* seriously deficient in testosterone (due to a gross abnormality and so could definitely be helped by replacement therapy) by the following signs:

- Your skin is soft and finely wrinkled like that of an older woman.

- Your beard grows poorly (you need to shave only every third day or less)

- You have a poor sex drive (rarely thinking about sex and rarely having an erection)

- Body hair didn't develop much at puberty

- Your testes have never grown and are not much bigger than a large pea

Of all of these poor beard growth is probably the best indicator. But unless you have real evidence of reduced testosterone (from the above signs and by a doctor measuring blood levels of the hormone) there really is no point going onto the hormone as a medicine.

In many animal species the female only becomes sexually aroused and is welcoming (or indeed attractive) to a male when she is 'on heat' or in oestrous. This is due to oestrogen production having risen. Men and women have no such season for intercourse and can desire and enjoy sex at any time of the month or year. We have pointed out already that some women feel at their sexiest around ovulation time but far more feel most interested in sex around period time when conception is *least* likely. This could possibly be a way that Nature limits population growth in Man or of course it could reflect the common desire to avoid pregnancy.

A few women, however, appear to ovulate either from intense sexual excitement or during extreme stress. Several studies have found that more women get pregnant when their man returns home after a long period of time away than could possibly be explained by the women happening to be at the ovulation stage in their cycle. In fact 'bunny rabbit ovulation' is probably much more common than the medical profession gives credit for and many of those working in this field see the results of it fairly frequently.

Ovulation may stop in very obese women and in those who are slimming dramatically and can return very erratically when the fatty slims or the anorexic puts on weight. Very fat women have raised blood levels of oestrogen and testosterone and so *should* be more sexy than average but there is no clinical evidence that this is so. On the contrary, some very fat women so dislike their body image that they feel permanently *less* sexy in a society that is so sold on slim bodies. Alternatively, such women may be oral rather than genital in their psychosexual make-up (page 270).

The role that sex hormones play in male assertiveness and aggression and female submissiveness in sexual matters is a much-debated one. Animal work has found that dosing them with testosterone increases their dominance within a group but the role of oestrogens is not so clear. Oestrogen certainly increases female willingness and desire to copulate and reduces their aggressiveness and competitiveness towards the males around them but this behaviour only seems to affect sexual interactions. Recent rat work, however, suggests that oestrogen seems to have the opposite effect to testosterone in *all* social interactions between rats. The subject is

Overleaf:
This couple in their 50s are now free of their family and are renewing their love and sex life

clearly very complex and needs further study. It's interesting to note in passing that dominant, aggressive, high pressure men, with the personality categorized as type A, have significantly higher levels of testosterone and more heart disease and high blood pressure than do other men. Perhaps women are better off with their low levels of this maleness hormone! Men do produce small quantities of oestrogen which might be protective to their health. Large quantities of oestrogen, though, make men impotent, amongst other effects.

Sexual 'chemistry'

A subject that is little discussed and even less researched is the role of the hormones of one partner on the other. A fascinating paper from the US found that: (i) there was a positive relationship between a man's level of testosterone and his own wife's sex drive (ii) the amount of sexual activity in a couple was determined by the level of the *woman's* testosterone in her blood at the time of ovulation (iii) there was a significant relationship between the woman's pleasure from sex and her average blood testosterone level during any given menstrual cycle and (iv) there was a positive link between a woman's baseline testosterone level and her ability to form interpersonal relationships.

Just how such linkages occur is not understood but it could be that phero-mones play a vital role. Pheromones are chemicals produced by the body of an animal or human which have an effect on the behaviour of its fellows, as a form of communication. They are known to be very important in animal behaviour but their role in human sexuality is more controversial. They are 'smells' which are not consciously recognized by the brain but nevertheless affect the behaviour of others. Pheromones have been widely described in various animal species and recent research has confirmed, not surprisingly, that humans have them too. A substance called androstenone occurs in male sweat and urine and has an attractant effect on women. Similar substances in females called copulins are vaginal phero-mones which attract males. These are produced in increased amounts around the time of ovulation and arouse men most then.

There are other fascinating pheromonal phenomena. For example, women living together (in women's halls of residence, nurses' homes and convents etc) tend to menstruate at the same time after they have been living together for some time. They synchronize with the menstrual cycle of the dominant woman. Even though their menstrual cycles are quite different when the enter the community they tend to synchronize in time. One researcher spread male pheromones on the pillows of nuns' beds and found those nuns' periods were disrupted from the 'norm' of the other nuns. This has been called the 'strange male effect'. It has been reported that telephones sprayed with male pheromones are used more by women than adjacent ones that are not sprayed; and that theatre seats sprayed with male pheromones attract women. Even children can detect the sexual odour of adults and around the age of three sometimes have a distaste for the smell of the same-sex parent and many mothers and babies can identify each other pheromonally.

Many couples tell of their almost tele-pathic powers – each knowing what the other is about to say or is thinking and no one has ever adequately explained such phenomena. Certainly long-established man-woman relationships have an extraordinary depth of communication that goes way beyond what is currently understood. Pheromones may play a part but there are other mechanisms without doubt. We know the function of only about 10 per cent of the human brain – the other 9 tenths is still a mystery. Perhaps a part of the brain communicates with those around us in such a way as to modify the functioning of their endocrine glands and so their sexuality among other things. The thought centres in the brain affect the pituitary gland which in turn controls the production of hormones so the idea is not as odd as it might at first appear. People have talked about 'sexual chemistry' for years but we are still no nearer knowing what if anything it means, or how it works.

Hormones and the menopause

Whilst most of us take puberty and the mainly pleasant results of the hormones that start to be produced in large amounts around this time for granted, once the reverse processes start we are often less happy. For reasons that are not yet understood women today start to ovulate younger and experience the menopause later than did their ancestors as recently as 1–200 years ago. In hunter-gatherer 'primitive' populations in the past and today, a woman would start to menstruate in her late teens and experience the menopause at about the age of 38. Today, the fertile life of a western woman starts at 12 and ends at 50.

The first sign of the onset of the menopause is usually irregular periods. At the menopause a woman stops producing eggs and oestrogen – in fact the levels fall below the oestrogen levels found in most men. Male sex hormone production continues, at least for the first few years after the menopause, which could account for the degree of facial hairiness some women experience at this age. The commonest symptoms of the menopause are hot flushes, vaginal dryness, pain on intercourse, lightheadedness, headaches, muscle and joint aches and pains, dry skin and personality changes such as depression, excitability and loss of confidence. The vast majority of these signs and symptoms can be reversed by giving hormones, under medical care.

Over the age of 50 ischaemic heart disease (heart attacks) becomes much commoner in women and a few women lose their pubic and armpit hair, or have degeneration of the vulva and vagina with vaginal dryness. Women also begin to lose bone strength at the menopause and are more likely than men to suffer fractures.

Men are thought to have a similar but less dramatic 'andropause' in which the symptoms can be remarkably similar to those women have. Common symptoms, according to one study were fatigue, inability to sleep, lack of concentration, loss of self-confidence, muscle and joint pains and headaches. Hot flushes were rare but sweating attacks and chills were common. Some men noticed that their scrotums became withered. Many of the symptoms responded well to testosterone.

Hormones and sexual function

In a man during the excitement phase chemicals are released into the bloodstream from the parasympathetic nervous system. This nervous system deals with the routine day-to-day body functions. The better known sympathetic nervous system produces adrenaline (epine-phrine). This tends to switch off sexual excitement and cause impotence or pre-mature ejaculation in men and vaginal tightness and dryness in women.

Recently a third type of nervous control system has been found to exist in certain organs of the body and in the reproductive and digestive organs in particular. This nervous system releases substances called vasoactive intestinal peptides (VIPs) and it is thus called the VIPergic nervous system. Sexual stimulation produces a marked increase in production of these peptides which remain present (in women at least) for nearly an hour after the stimulation stops. Samples of penile tissue taken from diabetics who were having operations on their penises were found to contain none of these nerves at all. This could explain for the first time why it is that diabetics can have sexual dysfunction problems.

A knowledge of these hormonal stages helps explain why it is that overactivity of the sympathetic nervous system can so easily ruin a love-making session. A noise, worry or anxiety can switch on the sympa-thetic nervous system and kill an erection or tighten the woman's vagina and make it go dry. Excessive sympathetic nervous system stimulation can also be caused by certain drugs and these too kill sexual drive. As sexual excitement progresses too much adrenaline can make a man ejaculate too soon, especially if he is anxious.

In a woman the situation is very parallel but is further complicated because other hormones are released when she becomes sexually excited. The two main ones are prolactin and oxytocin. During all repro-ductive and sexual activities a woman's blood levels of these hormones rise. Oxy-tocin in particular is central to all female sexual functioning from orgasms and in-tercourse to giving birth and breast-feeding. It is released in surges to have profound effects throughout the body. This explains how it is that a woman having an orgasm and a woman giving birth can look and behave similarly. A woman's breathing; the type of involun-tary sounds she makes; her facial expres-sions; the rhythmic contractions of her uterus; the periodic contractions of her abdominal muscles; the loss of conscious awareness of her surroundings as she seems to enter another world; her unusual muscular strength; the outbreak of sweat-ing; the swelling of her vulva; her insensi-tivity to pain and external stimuli at the height of the sensation; the sudden return of awareness on completion of the act; the sense of achievement and contentment after the act; and lastly, the spontaneous demonstration of maternal feelings to-wards the other person involved – her partner or her baby are all features of both an orgasm and a natural labour.

Research has found that uterine func-tion during the second stage of labour is directly linked to a woman's ability to have orgasms during intercourse throughout pregnancy. The women who did have orgasms, according to one study, exper-ienced shorter second stages of labour and were less likely to need forceps.

At first sight this may all seem rather strange or improbable, but a knowledge of female physiology soon solves the mys-tery. First of all it makes sense that the three 'essential' sexual functions of human females, intercourse, childbirth and breastfeeding, be pleasurable or ful-filling or women wouldn't have wanted to continue to repeat them, thereby ensuring the survival of the human race. It could, of course, be argued that childbirth is an inevitable end-product (biologically) of intercourse, and that although the latter had to be enjoyable to some extent, the former could and would usually have been accepted as a means to an end, pleasurable or not – with varying degrees of inhibition and prohibition according to the individual concerned. Breastfeeding is widely experienced by many women as pleasurable, yet this is a largely undiscussed or taboo subject. In a survey we made of 300 women, 64% said that breastfeeding was 'sexually pleasant' or 'sensual', and some said they had orgasms during breastfeeding. Clinical experience shows that once the subject is broached, all but the most inhibited of women are willing to admit that breastfeeding was pleasurable for them, and once 'allowed' to express feelings they'd otherwise feel guilty about, some women frankly admit to sexual excitement and vaginal lubrication when breastfeeding. Many women said that they felt guilty feeling 'so sexy' during breastfeeding and some had even given up because of guilt over this; this applied especially if the baby was a boy.

The link between orgasms, childbirth and breastfeeding is the female hormone called oxytocin as we have seen. This is released in surges in all female sexual activities, and elegant experimental work in animals has found that the same is true for them too. Vaginal stimulation of one ewe whose blood supply has been connected by a tube to that of a second ewe produces milk ejection from the breast of the second animal.

Of 300 women under 50 surveyed, nearly one in five could have an orgasm by breast stimulation alone. A woman's nipples and clitoris are linked in the brain by a network of nerves so that stimulation of one produces arousal in the other. The recent interest in the G-spot has led experts to suggest that those women who experience the passage of the baby's head down the birth canal as intensely pleasurable, could be doing so because of the stimulation of their G-spot.

Hormones and love

Although a lot is known about sex hormones in health and disease very little is known about what actually makes people feel sexy and want to make love. Human beings are enormously complex animals in whom sexual behaviour is modified by the culture in which they find themselves. Psychological factors further modify this sexual arousal and responsiveness. In spite of major technological advances our understanding of the relationship between hormones and human sexual behaviour has progressed very slowly. On the contrary, it could be argued that the more we know, the more ignorant we appear to be in this vital area of our lives.

What *is* certain is that there is no simple hormonal answer to the vast majority of sex problems and that except for a tiny minority of people drugs are not the solution. Similarly, many people imagine that their lack of sex drive (as they see it) must be caused by a hormonal (glandular) problem but this is almost never the case.

So overall it doesn't look as though a knowledge of hormones is going to be of much use to us in the near future and it seems likely that sex will continue to work or not between two people for reasons that are largely beyond measurement even in the best-equipped laboratory.

BARRIERS TO SEXUAL FULFILMENT

Recognizing sexual problems

A sexual problem exists whenever anything interferes with sexual performance or pleasure.

This statement is only twelve words long, and yet it contains the essence of this book. For a start, what does it mean?

If a husband enjoys having intercourse with his wife only rarely – does he have a problem? It's true that there is almost certainly an underlying difficulty which *could* be improved, but if neither is particularly bothered about the situation then perhaps nothing needs to be done.

If you don't enjoy reading an erotic book, does it mean you have a sexual problem? Well, not all erotic themes appeal to everyone; some may arouse a particular individual and turn off another. However, if you become tense when you read *anything* erotic, then you may have a problem, if only that your erotic capacities are impoverished.

If someone becomes anxious when they masturbate – do they have a problem? Anxiety about touching the genitials usually begins in childhood, and might have a harmful effect on sexual development and therefore adult relationships later. It does appear that contrary to much earlier teaching, masturbation is one of the foundations of good intercourse; it has the same relationship that learning to talk has to a later capacity to converse with others. So, excessive anxiety about masturbation could well mean that intercourse will be less successful and pleasurable than it might be.

If someone is so shy, underconfident and timid that they can't form social relationships and, therefore, can't attract a partner, is this a sexual problem? Perhaps the social problem is really psychosexual; a sense of inadequacy about sex has created so many fears and inhibitions that no relationships of any kind are possible.

If a man is impotent with his wife but potent in masturbation or with another woman then the problem obviously isn't with his genitals; they are clearly capable of functioning perfectly well! It *could* be his wife who has the basic problem. Perhaps she was brought up in a way that put her off intercourse or any form of sex. Her sexuality may always have been at a low ebb or held artificially in restraint. We know that submitting to intercourse, as long as the woman is not actively unwilling, is not particularly difficult, but her lack of real excitement may lead to such dryness and perhaps even to such obvious pain on penetration that eventually her husband simply becomes impotent with her. This is an example of a *partner-induced* problem – the woman has the real, if hidden, problem but the man goes first for help.

When the relationship has a problem

If a married couple have to live with their parents they may be so inhibited as a result that although they enjoy intercourse somewhere else, they can't do it or enjoy it at home. Do they have a sexual problem? Of course, places do affect desire and performance. However, if such a couple are ashamed of being overheard, or of leaving tell-tale marks on the sheets, it does suggest that they were brought up to hide their sexual activity. At first, their sexual desires will often overcome these feelings of shame, but their basic anxieties may make the pleasure less than it could be. Later on, when they *can* be alone in a house of their own, they might find problems begin to arise.

If a couple can have intercourse and enjoy it but frequently row, sulk and frustrate each other so that intercourse rarely occurs, do they really have a sex problem? They may have. Many rows, especially those started by the man, can have sexual resentment as an underlying cause. Men do have some control over their orgasms and a resentful one may allow himself to ejaculate prematurely so as to frustrate the woman. On investigation such a man may be found to have hostile attitudes towards all women and so has a *pyschosexual* rather than a *sexual* problem; that is it is in his mind and has to do with his attitudes towards sex and women. Eventually he would be likely to want to punish any woman in a relationship with him. Similarly, some women will not allow themselves to have an orgasm with their husband, in order to

deprive him of the satisfaction it would afford, but they may come easily and repeatedly in an extra-maritial relationship. Does such a woman really have a *sexual* problem? She herself may believe the explanation to be that she loves and wants to please her boy-friend but not her husband. The true explanation is sometimes that she has a potentially disastrous problem because she has been brought up to believe that sex is naughty with the result that illicit sex is the only form which really excites her.

If a couple have so many inhibitions about sex that they each unconsciously selected a partner who would avoid intercourse as far as possible, do they have a sexual problem? The answer, of course, is that each probably has a sexual problem

which would ruin a marriage with a less inhibited partner, but the relationship itself doesn't have a problem. They are well suited to each other sexually, which is ideal unless or until one of them begins to change and needs more sexual fulfilment.

If a couple have fairly frequent and happy intercourse but one of the partners, either the woman or the man, also masturbates a lot, then does he, she or the relationship have a problem? Masturbation is common in both sexes after marriage, and it is often helpful. However, if the reason is that one partner wants intercourse much more often than the other, then although each individual may be 'normal' the relationship *does* have a problem unless the refusing partner usually offers to satisfy the other in some way.

Similarly, if a woman can enjoy intercourse only on her back – but the man can only enjoy a really satisfactory orgasm with her on all fours, then the relationship has an obvious problem.

If a woman can be fully aroused in intercourse only if her man says obscene words to her or if a man must have his partner wearing silk stockings and a suspender belt, do they have a sex problem? If the partner will happily cooperate with such needs then the relationship has no problem but the individual with the unusual desire may possibly be heading towards one, if such a preference becomes an all-consuming need.

What we've done by highlighting a few barriers to sexual fulfilment is to demonstrate that the twelve words of the

Bed can be a bloody battleground but surely it's wiser to use it as a place where we can most easily kiss and make up

Even today, with all our scanty beach clothes and nightwear, this simple image can be as arousing as a completely naked body

initial definition are open to considerable discussion and hide an enormous complexity of human feelings, emotions and behaviour. Few are truly simple – but some of them can be helped in simple ways.

The vocabulary of sex

Although words concerning sex problems are used loosely (in this book, as much as anywhere else) it does help when trying to understand sex problems to distinguish between them.

In most English-speaking countries the word 'sexual' is often used when 'genital' would be more appropriate. The genitals are the organs of generation or reproduction and things which pertain to them are labelled 'genital'. For example, 'oro-genital' activity means mouth-to-genital activity and *'genitality'* means the genital component of sexuality. *'Orality'* is another component of sexuality as expressed, for example, in kissing. For some people, *anality* is yet another part of sexuality because stimulation of the anus adds to their pleasure during intercourse.

One part of the genitals is termed the 'phallus'. In common-or-garden language this means only the penis, and a lighthouse, chimney, statue or pencil may be referred to as 'phallic symbols'. However, during development within the womb a baby of either sex has a protuberance called the 'genital tubercle'. In girls this develops into the clitoris and in boys into the penis. *So technically a phallus may be either a penis or a clitoris.* During one early stage of development (between three and five years) the penis or clitoris is the principal source of sexual interest and pleasure.

Genitals and genitality are only a part of 'sex' and 'sexuality'. Sex is literally the state of being female and producing eggs, or of being male and producing sperms. It involves all that is different between the sexes. 'Sexuality' is the sum total of all the attributes, characteristics, qualities, behaviour and tendencies which result from a person being a member of one sex or the other. It is the sexual side of our personality. Sexuality is infinitely larger and more complex than genitality, and one way or another, affects virtually everything we are and everything we do. Our sexual personalities are infinitely varied. Many features are shared by members of the same sex, but other aspects are as unique to an individual as are his or her own finger-prints.

In spite of the traditional view that men are more influenced by sex; sex and sexuality have a more pervasive role in women than in men, perhaps because of their greater involvement with reproduction. Some women can, for example, have an orgasm simply by thinking; they don't have to stimulate their clitoris or any other part of themselves. Such an activity is thus sexual but not genital – although their genitals show all the signs of sexual arousal. In contrast, we know of only one man who can erect and reach orgasm without physical stimulation. Nocturnal emissions, (wet dreams) may be an example of similar psychic masturbation in men but it is thought more likely that either they stimulate themselves genitally in their sleep or that friction between the erect penis and bedclothes produces the orgasm.

*Any random group will include many people
who suffer from sex problems*

The words *'psychosexual'* and *'psycho-sexuality'* refer more to the mental and emotional aspects of sexuality rather than just to the physical ones. Psychosexual development involves all the stages a human being passes through from mouth-centred pleasure (orality) at birth to genitality in adulthood.

All these words relating to sex tend to be used interchangeably and sometimes rather sloppily but the concepts which underlie them are very different.

Other confusions arise over the terminology applied to sex problems themselves. They may be referred to as 'genital', 'sexual', 'marital' or 'psychosexual', and also as 'difficulties', 'disorders, or 'dysfunctions'. 'Dysfunction' (a medical term meaning not functioning correctly) usually refers to a practical, genital problem including erection and ejaculation difficulties in men and lubrication, penetration and orgasm problems in women. The term emphasises the mechanical aspects of sex, and as we believe such troubles have, or can have, very varied causes, ideally it should be avoided by anyone who really wants to understand the true nature of sexuality.

Who is not fulfilled?

Virtually everyone has a sexual problem or difficulty at some time in their lives, if only because of our culture which is largely negative towards sex. This exerts an effect from childhood onwards. We are almost always restricted and frustrated, at least to some extent, and this usually limits the pleasure of our sexual lives. Of course, some people encounter few such negative influences and can function well, but most are not so lucky, and their sexual lives may be damaged, which in turn can damage or restrict all other aspects of life.

Of course, problems aren't there all the time – they wax and wane, according to other eventualities. These include, for example, the level of current anxiety.

Sexual anxiety in young men, for example, may produce erection difficulties or premature ejaculation in their early attempts at intercourse, just as the muscles which surround a woman's vagina may go into a painful and involuntary spasm, because of her fears, when she first attempts intercourse. These difficulties are only overcome when the level of their desires rises to a point at which their anxieties are exceeded by them.

This type of problem involving the balance of desire and fear can continue throughout life. An inhibited individual may apparently function adequately in intercourse for some years but during this time his or her desires for sex only just exceed his or her fears of it and, although he or she may not realize it, their sexual performance and pleasure may be much less than that of which they are capable.

After therapy, it isn't at all unusual for such people to discover reservoirs of sexual desire and immensely greater pleasures than they had ever previously been aware of.

Many inhibited individuals may never seek treatment because they seem to be adequate. A woman, but more commonly a man, may only encounter real sexual problems early in middle life, perhaps in their forties, and it can seem easier simply to give up. Unless their partner objects and insists on getting help, the problem will never come to light.

Another intermittent problem is the occasional failure. A man may occasionally not be able to erect, or a woman may fail to lubricate. Sometimes such now-and-then difficulties can lead on to persistent problems as the individual or the couple fails again, and anxiety sets in. When we have failed once, we often fear another failure, and we then become so anxious that it actually occurs.

How common are sex problems?

Sexual problems are probably the commonest *dis-eases* in the Western world. But are there really more sex problems around today, or are people simply more aware of sexual difficulties because they have higher expectations than before?

As so many people worry about where they stand, we have summarized three large studies of what people actually do and feel sexually, so as to put many a reader's mind at rest. After all, if you feel that you have a 'problem' because you don't make love every day – join the club to which millions of others belong!

The main findings of a report carried out by *WOMAN* magazine in the UK (1982) Sample: 2,000 married women of all social classes and ages

◆ *3 out of 4 thought that greater openness about sex saves people suffering in private*

◆ *One quarter said they thought that kissing and cuddling were more important than intercourse – more than two thirds thought it was at least equally important*

◆ *More than one third of husbands don't kiss or cuddle as much as their wives would like*

◆ *Three quarters of wives who are completely satisfied with their sexual relationship are married to men who tell them they love them at least once a week, the majority of these, once a day*

◆ *The average couple make love once or twice a week*

◆ *More than one third of wives want more sex*

◆ *One in four wives wishes she had had more sexual experience with other lovers before getting married*

◆ *Three in ten wives admit to having an affair since marriage and one in ten is having one now*

◆ *Two thirds of wives rate their husbands as good or excellent lovers yet . . .*

◆ *Four out of five experience difficulty in becoming sexually aroused*

◆ *Two out of five wives fake orgasms*

◆ *More than half of all wives sometimes make love wishing they weren't*

◆ *More than half of all women say they fantasize. The less often they make love and the less content she is with her marriage and with her husband's performance as a lover the more likely is a wife to fantasize*

◆ *By far the commonest fantasy is substituting a man they know for another lover and imagining him as their dream lover*

◆ *Nearly one third said that their marriages were 1. 'Always been average' 2. 'steadily worse' 3. 'always been poor'. About one fifth claimed that their marriages had 'always been good'*

◆ *Nearly three quarters of wives want to take the sexual lead sometimes*

◆ *Three out of ten like reading erotica to turn them on*

- *One in seven say they use a vibrator*
- *It is more important to husbands that their wives have an orgasm during sex than it is for the wives themselves*
- *Only two out of five couples never have a sex problem with 'wife's lack of interest in sex' being the commonest by far (37%)*
- *Only one third of couples confine their love making to the bedroom*
- *Among wives aged 35 or under more than 9 out of 10 had made love with their husbands before marriage*
- *Only 3 out of 10 couples who thought they had a sex problem sought help of any kind*

The main findings of a survey carried out by *COSMOPOLITAN* magazine and published in the US in January (1980) Sample: 106,000 US women of mainly good education and earning level

---

- *Nearly 70% first had sex with a man between the ages of 16 and 20. One fifth first had sex between the ages of 10 and 15*
- *Three to five times a week is the average frequency of intercourse*
- *Sixty per cent want to make love more often*
- *A third of all women want to make love on the floor (apart from in bed); the next most popular place was on a couch, and the third, on a beach*
- *Four out of five women want to make love with the light on dimly*
- *About half the women wanted foreplay to last about half an hour*
- *Most women take between 2 and 20 minutes to have an orgasm from the onset of stimulation*

- *Seventy per cent sometimes have multiple orgasms – 1 in 10 say they always do*

- *Three quarters of women experience orgasms only by clitoral stimulation*

- *One in 8 regularly have anal sex*

- *Eight in 10 regularly practice fellatio (oral sex to their man)*

- *One quarter masturbate 'several times a week' and a third 'several times a month'*

- *Over a third have sexual fantasies whilst having intercourse and most fantasies are about their partner*

- *Three quarters feel that good sex is possible without love*

- *Just over half admitted to having had an extramarital affair but 4 out of 5 say they wish their partner wouldn't have an affair*

Study of male sexuality by Anthony Pietropinto and Jaqueline Simenauer published as a book 'Beyond the Male Myth' by Signet 1977 Sample: 4,066 men, mainly of above average educational levels but all classes and races

---

- *More than half the men enjoyed hugging and kissing even without sex*

- *Kissing and carressing are the sexual activity that gives most pleasure during foreplay to one third. For one fifth it was touching and sucking their partner's breasts*

- *Nearly half of all men say that they currently find sex more enjoyable than ever*

- *More than a third want their partner to be more active sexually and one fifth would like more oral sex*

- *Half of all men think that marriage with the wife being the only sex partner is the ideal but 1 in 5 think marriage with occasional outside sexual activity best*

- *When it comes to longterm sexual relationships most men wanted 'concern for my needs' and 'sincerity' more than 'a sexy woman'*

- *One in three claim deliberately to delay their orgasm until their partner climaxes*

◆ *Just over half want intercourse between 3 and 7 times a week and 1 in 7 want sex every day*

◆ *The biggest reason by far (apart from love) for getting married is companionship (47%)*

◆ *Most men fantasize about their current partner if they do so at all during masturbation or intercourse*

◆ *Nearly one third of men discuss what they'd like their partner to do as they have sex. About one fifth say they just do what they enjoy*

◆ *When asked what they would like to do more often by far the biggest request was for 'different sexual positions' (more than half) and 'oral sex' (a fifth)*

◆ *Most men (40%) see the sex act as ending when both parties have had an orgasm*

◆ *By far the most irritating thing during sex was 'if the woman seems cold or disinterested' (60%). Nearly half (45%) say that an unresponsive woman turns them off so much that they 'might not be able to complete the sex act'. 'Having an unresponsive woman' was considered by 6 out of 10 men as 'the most unpleasant part of sex!'*

◆ *When asked to say how they felt about today's women the biggest single group replied 'they were too independent'*

Sexual dysfunction in 'normal' couples by Ellen Frank, Coral Anderson & Debora Rubenstein Sample: 100 couples who rated their marriages as 'working well'

In the US a hundred couples were sought who were willing to complete a sex questionnaire, who were not under treatment for any sexual problem and who thought their marriages were working. Church groups, Rotary clubs and the like were approached for volunteers.

The resultant sample was 95% white, over 30% Catholic (as opposed to 10% here in the UK) and overwhelmingly very well educated, especially the men. Educated men make more attempt to delay orgasm in order to give satisfaction to the woman. The high degree of orgasm difficulties found in the women in this survey is therefore surprising.

				Men	Women
	Number			100	100
	Average age			$37\frac{1}{2}$	35
	College education or better			87	73
	Not employed			1	47
Marital satisfaction	Marriage regarded as happy or very happy			83	83
	Would marry same person again			88	89
	Divorce being considered			2	4
	No marital problems or very minor			57	61
Sexual satisfication	Very satisfying			42	40
	Moderately satisfying			43	46
	More satisfying than rest of marital life			24	19
	Gives same satisfaction as rest of married life			60	63
Sexual difficulties	Partner chooses inconvenient time			16	31
	Can't relax			12	47
	Attracted to someone else			21	14
	Too little foreplay			21	38
	Turned off			10	28
	Disinterested			16	35
Sexual dysfunctions	Men		Women		
	Impotence	16	Difficulty getting excited		48
	Premature ejaculation	36	,, maintaining excitement		33
	Retarded ejaculation	4	Reaching orgasm too quickly		11
			Difficulty reaching orgasm		46
			No orgasm		15

Why are sex problems so common?

Not all societies bring up their children with the idea that sex is sinful and dirty. Many have warm and appreciative attitudes which do not see sex as very private or shameful. Children, in consequence, see adult sexual activity, if not actual intercourse, in such communities and so learn naturally in this way. They are not rebuked for being interested, touching their own genitals or playing sex games.

There is less or even no conflict between sex and religion and also sex is less romanticized.

Our culture, on the other hand uses romance constantly to sell all sorts of things, but often contradicts itself by teaching that sex is sinful, dirty or shameful. As a result, a child's natural sexual interest and expression is suppressed, if not by his or her own parents then by others. For some parents the obvious interest their children show in sexuality reminds them of old wounds from their own childhood and may even cause distress about current sexual events in their lives. Whatever the explanation, for many parents their children's emerging sexuality is very difficult to deal with and they react against it (usually quite unconsciously) and as a result try to suppress their children's normal and healthy interest in the subject.

In the mistaken belief that human beings are born with no interest in sex, or have no sexuality until they are told about it, many adults try to control the media, art, literature, public behaviour and – so called – sex education their children are exposed to so as to prevent any 'ideas' reaching them so that they can keep their innocence, until the day they marry, at least. Such a view certainly makes sense if sex is regarded as awful, unwholesome and corrupting, rather than something natural or instinctual. Presumably they believe that if no-one were ever told about sex we would go through life being 'pure' and utterly sexless. The biology of human and animal behaviour simply doesn't bear this out, though to be fair there is a large learned component in most sexual activity, especially in males, as we shall see later.

The absence of accurate information about sex leaves the way open for fantasy, misinterpretation, misunderstandings and pure ignorance to exert their toll of sex problems later.

Our culture does even more harm with its heavy emphasis on the sacredness and special nature of the sexual relationship between people. Some, perhaps many, relationships are established on no better grounds than the fact that initially the couple were willing to copulate with each other. Young women particularly tend to exaggerate their *loving* feelings to reduce their guilt about sexual activities, and so end up by marrying a totally unsuitable person. At first, the genital relationship may be very satisfying to both, but the relationship will break down as the romantic fantasies fade, and the disharmonies between their personalities become apparent.

Apart from such harmful exaggeration, this over-romantic view emphasizes the very aspect of the man-woman relationship which is least likely to hold them together. The emphasis should be on personality and sexuality not genitality. Looked at in this way, the potential for sexual exploration lying within us all is very helpful. It makes us eager to know many members of the opposite sex – and so to gain experience of one's self and others.

In this way the young can learn that the saying 'yes' or 'no' is not the be-all and end-all they have been brought up to believe in. A good relationship which is *not* based solely on genitality is the one sure preventive against later dissatisfaction, disharmony, or even divorce. Unfortunately, so great is our culture's emphasis on genitality, that youngsters see genital activities and their success as paramount.

Too much romance?

Ideally, a man and woman coming to a marriage would be sufficiently experienced to know that their partner will be a true and enduring friend, that they can communicate, and that they understand and appreciate each other in all important areas of their attitudes and personalities. They should know they have the capacity to adjust to any 'faults' in the other and even love them for their faults. Such a couple have the best chance of finding enduring emotional, sexual, genital and social contentment. They may each continue to be attracted to others, but they will be able to be faithful not because it would hurt their partner if they weren't, but because they know that on balance better satisfaction is available at home. Over-romanticizing the relationship and over-emphasizing genitality does nothing but harm by raising expectations which cannot be met, once the heady first few months of living together or marriage are past. As someone has remarked, marriage is one year of flame and twenty years of ashes.

Too often we are led astray by notions of the 'ideal' partner and the 'ideal' relationship. Myths, fairy stories, and modern advertizers don't help much either. Sleeping Beauty evidently knows nothing of life or sex and is totally inert in every way until Prince Charming sees her once, does his stuff, throws her on his horse and gallops off to his castle on the hill to live happily ever after. This must be a morality tale in disguise designed to suppress female sexuality, and yet it is probably the favourite fairy-story of most girls, and in various guises is at the heart of the plot of hundreds of romantic novels. No exchange of any kind between the two was necessary and no effort was needed to make the happy ending; all Prince Charming did was touch the correct bit of her and she sprang to life as the perfect partner and wife. It is all so grossly misleading.

Such stories affect our future expectations about 'love at first sight' being the so-called basis of a happy marriage.

Divorce as a solution

Because so many relationships are unsoundly based from the outset, the relief offered by divorce seems only humane and sensible. However, the very availability of divorce may aggravate the problem by making people less cautious about embarking upon relationships likely to lead to marriage. A degree of scepticism in the first place is far better than the thought that if things go wrong divorce will be easy. Most divorced people fare no better in their second relationship than in their first, so any children involved may suffer without any corresponding benefit to the parents. Many people who are quick to take the opportunity of sampling the greener grass in someone else's field soon realise that it too has to be cultivated and looked after. All too soon they are back into much the same way of life as before but simply with a different partner.

Our cultural pre-occupation with genitality does harm in other ways too. As genital activity is said to belong only to marriage any infidelity may well by definition be seen as an end of the marriage – indeed it *is* a ground for divorce. As in so many other issues which are regarded as moral ones, the net effect of the interventions of moralists is often to promote what they supposedly want to prevent.

Signs of trouble

Disharmonies within a relationship can precipitate all sorts of problems. The

couple may simply say they have 'gone off' each other sexually and that, as a result, intercourse no longer occurs. Sometimes the couple may agree unconsciously to avoid each other, under the guise that they are so busy that they are too tired, or have no time, for sex. A relationship may appear stable, but the woman has stopped having orgasms, and later, perhaps, she will develop pains when intercourse is attempted, or he may become impotent. In yet other cases, the couple may have constant rows, and even continue with some sort of sex life, which is occasionally said to be good. Or the couple may have actually stopped having any joint emotional life or true involvement with each other, and either or both will find they function best genitally in uncommitted relationships. Then one may be in the process of 'deloving' the partner so as to clear the decks for establishing a new relationship, with or without divorce. Another sign of trouble is one partner urging the other to find an extra-marital relationship. This may be a way of suggesting something is missing, or it may be paving the way for an extra-

marital adventure, or a sign that such a relationship already exists.

Religion and sex

We may also be affected by religious prohibitions without realizing it even when we do not subscribe to formal religious creeds. For example, in the days when the Church was fanatically opposed to sex, individuals tried to express their normal sexual needs in ways that relieved their tension whilst not committing a sin. One way was by flagellation which became increasingly common as the anti-sexual fervour of the Church increased in the 11th and 12th centuries. In other words, a form of sexual expression, albeit perverted, was carried out under the disguise of mortifying the flesh i.e. suppressing sexuality. Of course, this was a long time ago but some prostitutes say that there is a considerable demand from men, even today, to be whipped or physically abused in one way or another as a part of the sexual encounter, and some women enjoy sex more if their bottoms are smacked in play before intercourse.

Other cultural influences

Clinical experience shows that many genital, sexual, psychosomatic and marital problems originate in childhood from early relationships, frustrations, bad examples and unhappy experiences. At first sight it might not seem that any of these things could be related to cultural beliefs and that therefore such beliefs can't be held to be solely responsible. However, it's important to bear in mind that all such factors interact, largely within the unconscious mind, often inflaming each other, to produce problems sooner or later.

The sexual scene is complicated. Nearly everyone believes we live in a 'permissive' society in which most individuals are having more sexual intercourse than preceding generations. This is the consequence, it is argued, not only of a change in social attitudes towards sex, indulgence being less shameful than it has been, especially for women, but also of the increased efficiency of contraception.

If all this is so, and everyone is having an increasingly good time sexually, it is difficult to see why there has been such a rise in substitutes for sex such as pornography – real pornography, not just erotica which only increases the desire of the sexes for each other – sex films, especially violent ones, sex shows and so on.

Although it's difficult to be sure, there is evidence that suggests that rates of intercourse within stable relationships may have been, and still are, *falling*! Other evidence seems to suggest that men are increasingly concerned with their ability to satisfy their women sexually. This could be related to the increased openness about women's sexual needs since the '20s and '30s and the detailed interest in genital responses of women in particular during sexual arousal, inspired by the sexual researchers, Masters & Johnson, in the late '60s which is still with us. Contrary to popular belief, even amongst younger husbands, it is men, not women, who still have more influence on the rate of intercourse in a particular relationship. Emotional and other upsets may make a woman refuse but clinical experience shows that women are at least passively willing most of the time.

A possible explanation is that men may have collectively been made more anxious about their skill at intercourse and about their ability to satisfy women. If so, they will be less willing, on balance, to have intercourse. The ultimate truth is, of course, that no-one knows exactly how much sexual activity is occurring in the population or what form it takes. Surveys, even those we quoted on pages 66–71, are based upon subjective responses to possibly-biased questions and so they crucially depend upon the skill with which the questions are framed, the percentage responding, and the honesty of the responses. For example, over the years surveys of masturbation in women indicate that an increasing proportion of women masturbate, but it is much more likely that such surveys are actually measuring the gradually dropping reluctance of women to admit to masturbation.

So the truth may be that society is being more permissive only in the sense that it is not so ashamed of sex as it was in the past, especially when it concerns the sexual interests of women.

Superficially, at least, many men say they dream about having sex with as many women as possible. However, in real life this goal is not so welcome; when a woman makes her sexual intentions clear, a man will often avoid the invitation, preferring to leave the question of his sexual competence in doubt rather than risk a loss of face. The increase in the numbers of 'saunas' in which men are masturbated by women, rather than perform themselves, is possibly another indication of the problem. Of course such services may simply reflect the need that many, perhaps all, men have to play the passive role occasionally – a need which most of their wives are unable to fulfill because they find taking the lead impossibly anxiety-producing.

There is another socially-based difficulty in discussing sex which is usually ignored; there are considerable differences in sexual attitudes, interests and behaviour between individuals in the population and between groups with different backgrounds, but in general it can be said that most women come for help because of their problems in emotional attitudes, and most men because of problems with performance. We all tend to think that the way we and our friends behave is 'normal' but this is often far from the truth. Many people say how astounded they are once they learn intimate details of their friends' lives.

Both at the level of society at large and at the personal level, evidence suggests that sex is far from being the straightforward issue it is usually misrepresented as being. What we think and what we do, both collectively and individually, are subject to many influences, some of which we see and some of which are hidden from ourselves and also from society as a whole.

How do personality, expectations and problems affect our love-life?

For anyone fortunate enough never to have experienced problems in their sexual life it may be difficult to imagine how disruptive and even disastrous they can be. A good relationship between a man and a woman can cope with quite a lot. Yet many people believe that the overall satisfaction they derive from their marriages declines as the years go by. If satisfaction declines it is probable that their level of tolerance declines too. Any actual or even potential sexual problem which exists may then begin to loom larger and larger. Sometimes sex may be knocked down as a bystander. It is difficult, for example, to have intercourse with a partner you detest or with whom you are angry. Sex can also be deliberately used, or misused, as a weapon of war between a disaffected couple or, it may be the unacknowledged, or even unrecognised, cause of a war which is then fought by other means.

If the characteristics of someone's sexuality are very different from their apparent personality then problems will arise sooner or later. For example, a man who seems outgoing, self-assured, confident and successful, but who grovels to specialist prostitutes, begging for forgiveness and requesting them to thrash him, has sexual fantasies probably dating back to childhood which will affect his emotional relationships, even though he may be capable of functioning genitally in a perfectly satisfactory way.

Personality, sexuality and genitality can also be uncomfortably too alike. A man or woman with a mean and parsimonious personality will show the same traits sexually and ends up resenting giving anything, including love. Such a person's partner in turn will gradually withdraw from showing any warmth in the relationship, at least emotionally.

So personality, sexuality, psychosexuality *or* genital factors may be the most important problem in any particular sex problem. More commonly, there is an interplay of many of these variables in both members of the partnership.

Often the past of one of the partners is the prime cause of the problem; this is commonly seen in deviations. The vast majority of these are not the gross, florid, highly abnormal conditions described in some of the Sunday newspapers and the psychiatric textbooks; they are much more subtle and merge with normality, and should really be called borderline deviations. In this form they probably afflict both sexes, but in different forms, and for anatomical and performance reasons are less obvious in women. Their presence in a man affects his performance and response. It's important to distinguish them from sexual enhancers.

Sexual enhancers

Sexual enhancers are activities occurring before or during foreplay, or in intercourse, which maximize sexual response, and pleasure. A man goes to a strip-tease show, returning home in a state of arousal which makes him urgently want sex with his partner. If the strip show has made him more aware of her attractions, then his love-making may please them both more than usual. A woman may read a sexy book during the day, and this may so increase her ardour and her expectancy of his arrival home that her excited and passionate state will greatly please and arouse her partner.

More complicated enhancers may involve the use of such things as special underwear, sexy talk, special games and so on. Another example is oral sex.

Enhancers and the avoidance of intercourse

Oral sex may be, and commonly is these days, an exciting component of foreplay for many couples, but if it is always taken to the point of full satisfaction, intercourse is obviously avoided and the act becomes a deviation. This is true even though many inhibited men and women who get little enjoyment out of intercourse can respond best by having an orgasm while their partner performs fellatio or cunnilingus. They don't realize they are trying to avoid intercourse, they just wish that it would 'work' as well for them. Sometimes the very fact that there is no penis near the vagina allows their unconscious anxiety about intercourse to go away, so they relax and enjoy an orgasm. Some women, of course, respond in the opposite way and cunnilingus makes them more tense. Their upbringing probably emphasized the 'dirtiness' of their genitals.

The use of obscene language, urinary games, wearing special clothes, anal stimulation and so on may all be enhancers or deviations. The point about sex enhancers is that they are of most value when used occasionally and that their routine use will rapidly lead to boredom. With true deviations the desire is to repeat the performance every time. Using the deviation produces maximal satisfaction and its absence leads to dissatisfaction or even a complete disinterest in sexual intercourse. The deviant practice rather than actual intercourse, then becomes the focus of sexual activity.

Some deviants can have intercourse if they use a fantasy of their deviant needs. For example, a homosexual man can have sex with a woman by imagining a homosexual scene.

Working out your partner's fantasies

The simplest way of discovering your partner's fantasies is to ask but there are three practical difficulties.

1   He or she may be unwilling to tell or to tell completely, perhaps out of shame or perhaps for fear of your response.

2   The nature of the fantasies may upset you because it may involve other members of your sex. Obviously, it's important to be encouraging and not to be upset. After all, the information should be of value whatever its nature.

3   Some people repress their fantasies into their unconscious mind because they are too threatening to their peace of mind. Such people say they have no fantasies.

The second method of discovering fantasies involves keeping a close watch on any erotic material or themes which capture your partner's attention. These may not even be overtly sexual but may be to do with situations which simply have sexual possibilities. The material may be found in newspapers, books, magazines TV, films and so on. In a similar way, whenever a partner is particularly aroused or responsive in any given sexual situation it sometimes helps to try to think if anything has occurred which might have caused it. Once you discover arousing themes in this way it usually only takes a little imagination to piece together the underlying fantasy. Although the method sounds cum-

What is the rest of her fantasy and how will it end?

bersome it has proved itself useful in clinical practice and can be used to solve the problem of the partner who appears to be sexually inert – responding to nothing in particular.

Jointly looking at magazines, reading articles about sex and particularly reading correspondence columns about sex problems and practices, can be useful in two ways. Some of them may turn on your partner but, more importantly, it opens up discussions about fantasies. For example, one might then say 'I have often thought about that and would like to try it out'. Even quite a shy partner can be encouraged in these ways.

It's sometimes possible to work out the type of fantasies your partner has from apparently trivial signs. For example, a man who rarely makes sexual advances to his partner but responds eagerly when she does so to him may well have passive fantasies about the woman taking charge. The accompanying tables of surveys of fantasies may be of use in putting two and two together. They're certainly reassuring if only because they show how common fantasies are. Once this type of insight is used it can be extended by testing it out and even discussing the theme with your partner.

Another technique which relies upon indirect clues and which some couples find both stimulating and informative is to take it in turns to tell each other, not something labelled as a fantasy, but simply a sexual story. A variant of this is to pretend they are about to make a sexy film and they outline the story in some detail.

Rank order of the extent to which various themes are arousing to men and women in erotica and imagination

*1 means this theme was most arousing: (From Byrne and Lamberth, 1971)

	Men	Women
Cunnilingus (heterosexual)	1*	1
Group oral sex	2	8
Face-to-face intercourse	3	2
Fellatio (heterosexual)	4	6
Female masturbation	5	7
Nude heterosexual petting	6	3
Intercourse (woman sitting on man)	7	5
Nude female	8	14
Partially clad heterosexual petting	9	4
Nude females petting	10	13
Cunnilingus (homosexual)	11	$9\frac{1}{2}$
Scantily clad female	12	19
Male torturing female	13	15
Female torturing male	14	17
Male masturbation	15	$9\frac{1}{2}$
Fellatio (homosexual)	16	12
Homosexual anal intercourse	17	18
Nude male	18	11
Male in undershorts	19	16

Sexual activities during which women fantasize and the percentage of women doing so

From Talbot, Beech and Vaughan (1980)

Activity	Per cent of women
Self-masturbation	65
Initial part of intercourse	52.5
Foreplay	27.5
To elicit climax during intercourse	27.5
Other sexual activities with a partner (eg oral sex)	25

Types of fantasies used by 40 women during intercourse and other sexual activities

From Talbot, Beech and Vaughan (1980)

Fantasy	Per cent of women	Number of women
Reliving previous experience	45	19
Overpowered/rape	29	12
Sex with more than one partner	21	9
Same-sex fantasies	19	8
Sexual activities with animals	10	4
Observing a sexual act	7	3
Sado-masochistic fantasies	7	3
Being observed during sexual activities	5	2
Incest	2	1
Other	10	4

I'VE NEVER BEEN MUCH OF A ONE FOR SEX

Reasons for use of fantasies and percentage of women giving them

From Talbot, Beech and Vaughan (1980)

Reason	Per cent of women
To increase sexual excitement	59.5
To start sexual excitement	28.5
To increase and start sexual excitement	9.5
To decrease sexual excitement	2.5

Nature, incidence and frequency of erotic fantasies occurring in women in the course of heterosexual activities

From R. Gemme and Connie Wheeler (eds) (1977)   *Incidence (%)*

1	Scene reviving a former sexual encounter	78.8
2	Scene with a different sexual partner	78.8
3	Scene from a sexually-exciting movie seen	71.2
4	Scene in which you embrace male genitals	63.6
5	Scene in which a man embraces your genitals	63.6
6	A romantic scene	60.6
7	Scene in which a seducer excites you sexually	54.5
8	Scene where you are the sex object of several men	50.0
9	Scene where you witness the sexual performance of other persons	50.0
10	Scene where you are tied up while being sexually stimulated by a man.	48.5
11	Scene where an enormous penis penetrates you	42.4
12	Scene where you witness group sex activities	42.4
13	Scene in which you are a victim of aggression	42.4
14	Scene where you pretend to struggle and resist before submitting to a man's sexual advances.	39.4
15	Scene where you find yourself with an imaginary lover	39.4
16	Scene in which you are observed during your sexual performance	37.9
17	Scene where you have sex relations with another woman	34.9
18	Scene where you receive male ejaculation in your mouth	33.3
19	Scene in which you receive anal penetration	31.8
20	Scene where you see yourself with another body	30.3
21	Scene where you see yourself as a prostitute	30.3
22	Scene where you are being fondled by a faceless lover	28.7
23	Scene where your sexual activities are performed in public	27.2
24	Scene in which you yourself are the aggressor	27.2
25	Scene in which you are overpowered and forced to have sex with one or more strangers	22.7
26	Scene in which you are obliged to have sexual relations against your will with someone you know	19.7
27	Scene where you initiate a boy in sexual functions	18.2
28	Scene where you perform actions considered dirty or forbidden	18.2
29	Scene where you are the object of humiliation	15.1
30	Scene where you receive a beating	13.6
31	Scene where you are the sexual partner of an animal	10.6

Which of the following do your fantasies involve?

The Cosmo Report 1981

	Total resp.
Total answering	9679 (100.0)%
Your partner	6871 (70.9)%
Someone else you know	6536 (67.4)%
A celebrity	1638 (16.9)%
A stranger	3669 (37.8)%
Animals	506 (5.2)%
Other	389 (4.0)%

Scene from 'Last Tango in Paris'. How many women subsequently cast themselves in the role of this actress?

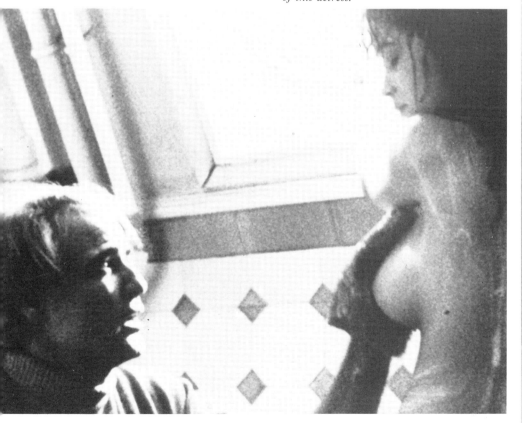

The importance of fantasies

It's clear from all this that the way normality, enhancement and deviation all merge into one another make it difficult to see clear-cut distinctions between them. Everyone, whether they are consciously aware of it or not, is thought to have fantasies from each of these categories.

One of the things that attract some people to each other is the hope that they will each be able to fulfill their fantasies. Usually, the realities of body and gential contact gradually replace the dreams with actual and mutual pleasures. However, if at the beginning, the fantasies are not well-matched, frustration and even the collapse of the relationship may follow before the couple has time to adjust. For example, it appears from clinical experience that many more men have masochistic fantasies than women have sadistic ones. A masochistic man, who wants to be sexually controlled some of the time by women, may well have difficulty in finding a partner who is aroused by such situations. He may end up disillusioned and disinterested in intercourse.

Men are thought to be more likely to use deviant fantasies (in place of intercourse) than are women, perhaps because males depend more on visual stimulation for arousal and fantasies are a form of visual stimulation. Then, too, women have usually hidden their own fantasies, perhaps because they are too shy to reveal them, or are afraid of the cultural rule that women only respond to the sexual needs of men, and don't want to take responsibility for having sexual needs of their own. This undoubtedly leads to frustration, given that their partners are not mind-readers!

Anxiety and sex problems

Borderline deviations are closely allied to sexual dysfunctions. In the latter fear is sufficient to disorganize and disrupt sexual intercourse rather than lead to deviant needs. A man may not erect at all, or he may erect during foreplay, especially if this includes breast play, but as the time approaches for penetration he wilts. Alternatively, he may ejaculate before penetrating, or have unaccountable difficulties in penetration, or he may ejaculate immediately after penetration, or simply lose his erection. The result is that sex is avoided or shortened, and this also reduces the period during which he feels anxious.

Very similar situations are found in women. Some lose their lubrication as the time for penetration approaches or never lubricate at all. Others develop pains during intercourse which may make sex impossible; their menstrual cycle becomes so disorganized that they are bleeding most of the time or they become intolerant of any form of contraception. So intercourse can be avoided without actually having to refuse.

A further complication is that a sexual dysfunction such as impotence, disorders of ejaculation, painful spasm of the vagina on penetration and an inability to have orgasms in intercourse, may show up with one partner but not with another. This may reflect childhood inhibitions when they were threatened with a loss of love as punishment for sexual activities – 'If you don't stop playing with yourself, Mummy won't love you'. In this way dysfunctions may occur later but only with a loved partner. Others, women especially, report that sex is only good in illicit relationships such as pre-maritally or extra-maritally. This is hardly surprising when we remember that girls more than boys are told that sex is naughty. In fact when women want to hit back against society for one reason or another they sometimes do so by being 'naughty' and resort to sexual behaviour of a type they had been brought up to believe is bad; for example, by being promiscuous.

Proving your love

The emotional side of sex is usually, but not always, related to love. Most people's ideal of a good love life includes a good sex life, and sex and love are seen in our society as almost synonymous.

But troubles can arise when it comes to people's ideas about how a 'loving' partner should behave. A man may think of women as intrinsically sexless – only having sex or 'making love' because they are in love, so a sexual refusal amounts (for the man) to a declaration that he is not loved, and if the woman persistently refuses him the belief grows. He may seek revenge in other ways, which leads to a deterioration in the entire relationship. He feels that if the woman loves him she will not only *have* intercourse with him but she will *enjoy* it. If she doesn't, perhaps for reasons that are nothing to do with him but with her upbringing, he often assumes that he is ill-equipped, a poor performer or not worth loving. If the woman needs to masturbate during – or after – intercourse to reach orgasm he may reach the same conclusion even more quickly!

In turn a woman may need to be frequently told she is loved and desirable if she is to function happily in bed. She may not be able to ask directly, because, she argues, this would invalidate the answer, and she is simply too embarrassed to ask anyway.

Instead she begins to test the man's love for her. This might take the form of refusing intercourse to discover whether he cares or not; changing her hair style or buying new clothes to see whether he notices; displaying her body 'accidentally' to see if he is turned on or by making demands for 'goods' to explore her monetary value. Such testing behaviour can produce the wrong answers, and this can lead to conflict.

The effects of rows

When women need to express their feelings of anger in words, men may see the verbal aggression as coming from a hostile and critical mother figure. If he has a poor sense of his male self-esteem (a weak male ego) he is unable to bear criticism or even advice from a woman and as a result shouts at her or even hits her. Either way the man is likely to withdraw while thinking 'if she really loved me she wouldn't say such things'. Part of his love and affection is lost, and a small degree of 'warmth' is removed from the relationship, often for ever, and is invested elsewhere such as in the garden, another woman, work or male friends at the pub or club. This is exactly the opposite of what the woman wanted and the attacks may then become more frequent and more bitter as the entire relationship slides into trouble. Yet ironically rows are simply a form of testing for some women because if they can get their man into a rage it shows he cares at least enough to row.

The movies have given us many unrealistic ideas about love and sex but for sheer realism the biting, searing dialogue of 'Who's Afraid of Virginia Woolf' takes some beating. In the final moments of the film we are suddenly aware of how close pain and anger are to the most tender emotions

For many men the whole business of emotions and rows is tiresome and tedious, and almost any man can gain the instant sympathy of other men by saying that women are generally impossible and especially impossible to understand. But men are often angry, moody, touchy and difficult, infuriating when they run away mentally or physically from a woman who clearly has an important issue to air. Valid emotional concerns often go unrecognized, are ignored or written off as 'silly women's stuff'.

Depression and sex

Sexual problems can cause emotional disturbances and the reverse is certainly true. When marriage and love run into trouble many of us become depressed. Many people lose their desire for sex when they are depressed, and so a sexual problem – disinterest – may come into being where none existed before and worsen the situation.

On the other hand anyone may become depressed for reasons which have nothing to do with their relationship but the partner suffers as a result. People can suffer from recurrent bouts of hidden depression, without displaying any of the usual signs and symptoms of the disease. Because they are apparently bright and cheerful, with the depression appearing as head pains, for example, they may be treated for years for 'migraine' or 'ear-trouble' or similar conditions.

Such a couple came into therapy because of the husband's intermittent attacks of impotence. When the story was finally unravelled, it was clear that his impotence coincided exactly with his wife's bouts of depression, although neither was aware that she was depressed. Somehow, she communicated her lack of sexual interest without being aware of it, and even openly resented his impotence as a criticism of her. The detection and effective treatment of her concealed depression restored his potency, and saved the relationship.

Emotional illness and sex

Sexual problems can be the result of certain psychiatric disorders, and also their cause. For example, anorexia nervosa is thought to be related to a girl or woman's desire to avoid her adult sex-role by returning to pre-puberty. Since the breasts and periods often disappear in girls with this condition it seems a reasonable suggestion although there are many contributing factors, both physical and mental.

Sexual or psychosexual factors are thought to be contributory to many psychiatric disorders. Sexual shame, guilt and anxiety can all affect mental health, personality and behaviour. They can also express themselves psychosomatically – often in the skin. Adolescent girls sometimes develop psoriasis following early sexual experiences of which they feel ashamed. Sexual problems may also show themselves as symptoms in the genital region of both sexes; as contraceptive problems; as infertility or especially as overwhelming fears of sexual disease, especially VD.

Cover-up stories

Almost any complaint, whether real or imagined, can be part of an unconscious desire to avoid sex. A man will blame his backache for his unwillingness to have intercourse. The pain may be resistant to all medical efforts, and he may even exaggerate its severity because, unknown even to himself, he is using it for an ulterior purpose. This phenomenon is technically known as 'secondary gain' – the situation has a hidden, usually unrecognized advantage!

Some men avoid women and sex on the grounds that their penis is small or abnormal in some other respect which would humiliate them. On examination nothing is usually found to be wrong. Women with abnormal fears of penetration often have a distorted view of their vagina, seeing it as far too tiny to take a penis.

In both cases the problem is not genital but psychosexual. It is not sufficient to reassure such men and women of their anatomical normality – the problem goes much deeper and needs sorting out psychosexually rather than anatomically.

How do sexual problems come about?

Very, very few sexual problems are simple, although, they can sometimes be relieved by simple methods. It is like having a temperature. The cause of the temperature may be instantly obvious, for example a chest infection, but often the reason for it is obscure and may be due to one of a thousand conditions. The temperature simply says something is wrong but it doesn't say what.

The majority of failures to find complete sexual fulfilment have three basic causes. The first is to do with the instincts and what happens to the individual in the various stages of his or her psychosexual development. The second is concerned with learning or, more properly, mis-learning, especially during childhood and adolescence and the third is more to do with here-and-now factors, and is thus situational or environmental.

A sexual problem is nearly always the result of the presence of several negative conditions each of which makes its contribution to the final outcome.

General conclusion

From the evidence in this section it's difficult to escape the conclusion that western culture has gone adrift somewhere in its management of the man–woman relationship. The key problem is the prohibitive attitude to sex in all its forms but especially those affecting women. This has diminished the value of the sexes to one another and has reduced the importance of the man-woman relationship in most people's lives. Because these cultural attitudes affect the way we bring up our children the problem looks like being perpetuated from this generation to the next and so on unless we do something about it. The way we currently bring up children makes it almost impossible for them to get the best out of their lives later as adults . . . and we don't just mean genitally.

Given that sex and sexuality in all its forms and guises affects our lives so profoundly it is probably not too much to claim that the future happiness and stability of the western world as we know it depends to a considerable extent on there being a serious review of how men and women live and love together. It is in this context that we have written this book.

DOING SOMETHING ABOUT IT

SEXUAL DIFFICULTIES AND HOW TO OVERCOME THEM

This section of the book looks at the 'plumbing' problems – the physical things that commonly go wrong and what can be done about them. Given that human sexuality is so complex, including as it does, so much more than our genitals, there are all kinds of psychosexual insights in what the reader might think should be a fairly straightforward nuts and bolts chapter. When it comes to sex, the story is often more complicated than it at first appears.

In a close monogamous relationship in which the individuals have invested so much in terms of their personalities, their past families, their fantasies, hopes and aspirations a sexual problem can damage the balance. Many couples weather temporary difficulties because of the strength of their relationship, but such difficulties can also raise much deeper questions – questions which can be painful to ask and even more painful to answer. It is this realization that all might not be what it seems, especially after years of marriage, that makes sexual problems so different from most other things that afflict a relationship. Most of us feel we are not responsible for each other's *medical* wellbeing, but when sexual ills hit a couple, they both have to accept some of the responsiblity, and to work for the cure together.

The bottom line

There are three basic problems each in men and women. In men they either avoid sex completely, fail to get their penis into the vagina or have ejaculation problems when it is inside. Women can obviously avoid sex too, or can be unable to take a penis into the vagina or not enjoy it and remain unsatisfied. All mechanical sex problems are a shade of these six situations and any man or woman can move up and down the scale from avoidance at one end to satisfactory intercourse at the other via the two intermediate stages.

It's also vital to remember that when one partner has a sex problem it usually affects the other. On other occasions the problem is a joint one – it is contributed to by both partners.

Men who avoid sex

Some people avoid sex when ever they can, even for much of their lives. There are men who have sex infrequently, and those who don't even get as far as having any form of genital activity with another person. They may fear rejection or ridicule, perhaps over excessive or imagined shortcomings in the size or shape of their penis or because of deeper fears. Some avoid

women but can fantasize about girls because they are less afraid of them.

Aversion from women, or just not wanting intercourse with them, has many roots. We have looked at the cultural history going back over nearly 2,000 years on pages 74–75. Men whose sex drive has been impaired by other factors can easily be tipped into avoidance by such antisexual cultural attitudes.

Childhood influences leave some men with the, largely unconscious, notions that women, or sometimes just the women they love, are sexless; powerful enough to punish any display of sexual interest in them or their bodies, or so 'pure' that they will reject or punish any suggestion of 'interesting' sexual activities in foreplay. Men brought up in this way eventually see women as sexually boring, or as a mother

The baby is not intruding on this couple. Their lovemaking may have been interrupted but they are still continuing to enjoy each other

figure, with whom sex is forbidden and frightening.

In spite of this such a man may still be able to perform, perhaps with slightly less pleasure and abandonment than he otherwise would, and gradually he may learn that women, or his partner in particular, are only too keen on sex; but it is important to realise that while this might make things better *physically*, his unconscious never learns. His old fears still lurk there, only to reassert themselves under favourable circumstances, perhaps after a row, too much to drink, when he's tired, or even if he wants to punish the woman for a recent irritating offence.

Then he may fail to get an erection, or he may ejaculate prematurely. Most men have enough self-confidence to get over these occasional failures, but in others the problem overwhelms them. All their old unconscious fears come to the surface, especially if the woman is scornful or becomes emotionally upset, accusing him of not loving or wanting her or of having another woman. Even if the woman behaves well, as most do, the man may be so upset that he'll interpret almost anything she says as being against him. For example, if she says 'don't worry, it often happens with men', he can become preoccupied with thoughts about her previous lovers and how they performed. Were they better than him? His old jealousies of his father and brothers may be reactivated too, perhaps with childhood anxieties that his penis is too small. 'Not to worry' – as a type of comforting remark isn't at all helpful because he *will* worry and wants to be taken seriously. Such men are hurt even more if they feel their partner *really* doesn't worry, because clearly he isn't of much value to her sexually!

So he begins to brood on his failure, and starts to fear and expect failure the next time he has sex. This is called secondary anxiety. He concentrates on the performance of his penis, becomes more anxious, and the failure is repeated again. And so it goes on, time after time. He then avoids sex altogether because no one likes to do things at which they fail.

Sex avoidance can also start after a relationship has been established for some time, often years. In the early days a couple enjoy intercourse frequently. Gradually the early excitement dies down, and an underlying problem which has been dormant begins to surface. A common example is the birth of a baby. This can reactivate the man's old anxieties about the wishes he had as a child for his mother. He may then lose all desire for his wife and avoid her sexually. Some men also have difficulty coping with the extra attention and the demands the baby makes on their wife and others are overwhelmed by the new family responsibilities that come with a new baby, especially a first baby.

Impotence

What is it?

First of all we should stress that we are not discussing the occasional failure to erect which any man can experience when he is ill, tired, or simply too worried or too drunk to be aroused. Impotence is a specific condition in which a man, persistently or recurrently, is unable to obtain or maintain an erection of sufficient rigidity or duration to start or complete intercourse. It can have a purely physical basis, or it can be a form of sex avoidance.

The term impotence may also be applied to masturbation. Some men are impotent in intercourse and mutual masturbation but not in self-masturbation. Some who are potent in self-masturbation can only remain so as long as they use a fantasy. Others can only be potent if they have a fantasy of normal heterosexual activity which does not go as far as the woman being naked and of his penis entering the vagina. If, in therapeutic masturbation training, some such men are asked to fantasize penetration they lose their erection and can not complete the act. Quite obviously all these men are unconsciously avoiding normal sex.

When does it happen?

Sexually inexperienced men often suffer from impotence – much to their humiliation. They may soon overcome the problem if only because their desires are so strong, especially when the relationship is a good one. They also become capable of permanently overcoming the fears which caused the impotence in the first place.

Experienced men may find themselves impotent in extramarital or similar situations. Their fears prove stronger than their desires, so sex is avoided. Older men may become impotent after many years of apparently normal performance, as their sex drive sinks below the level of their inhibitions. This can be aggravated by their partner's unwillingness to stimulate their penis and becomes more of a handicap as older men need more stimulation to become erect. An older man can become impotent if his partner is suffering from menopausal symptoms with which she is having difficulty. Both men and women can find it difficult to cope with the problems surrounding their teenage children and *their* emerging sexuality.

Men who have taken risks outside marriage and fear they have caught VD may want to avoid intercourse with their regular partner so as to prevent her catching anything. If his avoidance results in awkward questions being asked, his fear may produce impotence.

A man may be impotent with his regular partner, due to all sorts of negative feelings, but none of these may apply to his extramarital partner, and so he functions well. Some men are impotent only with the woman they love. Fear of adverse comparison with others can also lead to impotence with a particular partner, especially if she often talks about the pleasure she had with previous lovers. The man who has taken his wife back after she has had an affair often feels resentful, and even threatened, and this too can produce impotence.

What happens – or doesn't?

A man who is impotent cannot get an erection (or a full erection), or he may have an erection but loses it as the time for penetration approaches. Some men who unconsciously avoid sex perceive their erection as being insufficiently rigid to penetrate the woman. Their partners often say they are quite hard enough but the man will not be reassured and try. In another form the man gets an erection but loses it at some stage after penetration yet before reaching orgasm.

What causes it?

The problem with any individual impotent man is to decide if some or all of the cause is medical – the result of diseases or drugs. Medical, physical and organic causes are listed below but even if they *are* the main cause, psychological factors may still be important. A physical cause may have triggered off secondary anxiety so making the problem worse than it might otherwise be. Over half of all impotent men believe there is some physical cause for their disability. This is understandable because it spares both his sense of self-esteem and seeing himself as a sexually

When a man is afraid of failure he sees threats everywhere. His partner chatting to a friend about the kids' school or a problem at work can appear to him to be feminine gossip about his impotence

inadequate man and puts the responsibility onto someone else – a doctor – to get him better.

If you are in any doubt that there could be a physical cause for impotence – see a doctor. Once you have a clean bill of health, try to come to terms with the fact that the causes are psychological. Some men keep on avoiding sex by endlessly seeking further medical investigations for a condition which cannot be treated in physical ways. There are some doctors who reinforce the belief that the cause is physical, and even discourage psychological approaches to the problem. This can have the effect of 'writing the man off' sexually because the doctor refuses to believe in a psychological cause, and yet cannot find a physical one of sufficient magnitude to explain it.

Signs that the problem is in the head rather than in the penis are erections during the night; firm erections on waking; the ability to masturbate and erections which happen in other circumstances. If the problem comes and goes it is almost always a sign that the cause is psychological. If impotence starts suddenly the problem is unlikely to be medical unless the onset was associated with an injury, a sudden illness, an operation or the taking of a new medicine or drug. Even then the man may unconsciously be using the event as an excuse. Night erections can be studied scientifically in sleep laboratories, but simple tests can be used at home. These do not measure the rigidity of the erection, which is important, but they do show that the man's penis *can* erect. One trick worth trying is to stick a line of postage stamp edging around the unerect penis; if it has burst in the morning it proves the man had an erection in the night. If a man never has night erections it is likely, but not definite, that there is a physical cause.

Of course, a man who has psychological impotence, or a tendency towards it, may develop a physical illness which then makes the impotence worse!

Examples of some of the causes of impotence

Any number of these causes may be at work at the same time. It is the sum total which creates the impotence.

Physical

● Anything that produces pain – a torn foreskin, short fraenum, or any other penile abnormality

● Diabetes – in some cases

● Arterial disease – e.g. diseases obstructing arteries that supply the penis

● Injuries to the spinal cord

● Disease of the nervous system – some cases of multiple sclerosis; paraplegia etc.

● Operations e.g. lumbar sympathectomy, renal transplants, pelvic sugery for cancer, prostatectomy

● Severe shortage of testosterone e.g. underdeveloped testes

● Disordered hormone production, e.g. hyperprolactinaemia

● Psychiatric illness – e.g. severe depression or obsessional/compulsive neurosis

- Drugs of abuse – e.g. hashish, alcohol, even excessive tobacco

- Medical – e.g. some drugs for high blood pressure, anti-depressants, anti-androgens

- Medical treatment – ECT

Psychodynamic

- Man unconsciously equates partner with mother – therefore she's prohibited, leading to anxiety; may occur especially after first baby.

- Fear of intimacy

- Guilt about sex

- Sees intercourse as aggression

Psychological

- Inability to relax – over-concern with his erection and sexual performance generally

- Depression – leading to loss of sex drive

- Anxiety – e.g. about effects of illness such as a recent heart attack

- Fear – of women, their genitals, their 'pureness', their criticism or assertiveness

- Apprehension – e.g. in affairs, of VD, pregnancy, of possible consequences generally

- Misperceptions of women's sexuality

Behavioural

- Earlier failure – producing secondary anxiety

- Expectation of failure – producing performance anxiety

Biological

- Ageing

- Pheromonal or other influences of partner e.g. depression

- Loss of sex drive – for any cause (see page 248)

Relationship

- Doubts – about sexual acceptability to partner e.g. if she never reaches orgasm or has vaginismus.

- Alienation – e.g. due to personality clashes

- Hostility – desire, usually temporary, not to please or even to punish partner

- Non-compliance – real or assumed, to special needs e.g. clothes, language, dominance

- Boredom – with sex or with partner

Situational

- Possibility of detection – e.g. in parental home; in public place

- Tiredness – perpetual, may also be an avoidance manoeuvre

- Wrong partner

- Latent homosexuality

- Fear of injury to partner – e.g. after baby, operation or any gynaecological disorder

- Demand – by woman for performance

- Temporary stress – e.g. redundancy, moving house, business problems, problems with children

What can we do about it?

If any physical cause, or likely cause, is detected it should be corrected, with medical help as appropriate.

An interested partner, who really wants to help, can be a great ally and the sharing of her observations and possible conclusions can help the man understand what's going on. Some women, out of their own unexpressed guilt, refuse to cooperate on the grounds that because they never refuse intercourse, the fault must be with their man. Some men don't discuss the problem with their partner, or even read a book she suggests could be helpful, because he then sees her as criticizing him.

The ideal solution begins with talking it all over honestly, being careful not to apportion blame.

The next practical step is to stop having intercourse. Even better, the woman can assure him that she doesn't want to expose her lover to the anxieties of intercourse until things get better. Once the threat of intercourse is removed the man can often erect perfectly well in response to physical and/or mental stimulation. In this way he regains confidence in his penis. Next he can learn to be less concerned with its responses by repeated cycles of stimulation and no stimulation so that this confidence in gaining, losing and regaining an erection is increased. See p.105 for the technique.

Courtship behaviour can be substituted for intercourse and, at first, the erotic zones and certainly the genital area should be avoided when cuddling or massaging each other. The emphasis should be on love, closeness, mutual pleasuring, kissing, cuddling, massage and so on. When the genitals are eventually brought into play the initial emphasis should be on touching, looking and exploring, like young children, more than on erection, masturbation and so on. This return to courtship behaviour should be seen as a new beginning in which old mistakes can be avoided. A sensual holiday (see page 189) can be a great help in encouraging such courtship behaviour.

Working, perhaps slowly, on any misconceptions her man has about female sexuality (by revealing her own), a woman can help him overcome his fears and soon he begins to see her as a friend and helper rather than an adversary. Looking at erotic magazines and video films together can be very helpful because this proves to the man that his partner shares his interest in sex. If the woman refuses, on the grounds that such things are boring or dirty, then she runs the risk of appearing to be a mother figure. It's well worthwhile making a conscious effort to avoid all dominant maternalism. On the other hand, suddenly switching to wearing sexy underclothes, for example, and becoming a sex siren can appear to be a demand for performance by the man which may well further worsen his problem. A sensitive couple will find a happy middle path.

Along with all this the man should make an effort to re-establish self-masturbation if he's lost the habit. It need not go as far as orgasm if he doesn't want to but now is the time to overcome old fears, shames and guilts about it. Masturbation fantasies of happy, enjoyable, successful intercourse are helpful. Steps along the route could be re-establishing masturbation, eventually involving the woman in soothing, stroking and encouraging, and finally getting her to do it. This gives the couple a chance to learn that the 'uncontrollable' is in fact

A few seconds of quick, affectionate cuddling can create a glow of pleasure and expectation that lasts for hours

controllable. The use of KY jelly, baby oil or talcum powder increases penile sensitivity and helps offset any small discrepancies between the technique she uses to masturbate him and the one he uses himself. Aids such as vibrators, artificial vaginas, so-called penis-enlargers and erection creams are helpful for a tiny minority and anything that helps *helps* even if only by suggestion. The overall aim is to concentrate on obtaining the best possible pleasure and not on just the penis itself. A watched penis never boils – at least not if it is watched by an anxious man or his anxious partner.

Needless to say, social behaviour such as excessive visits to the pub (especially that 'last' drink), excessive socializing, exces-

sive sport and late-night films on TV should be avoided as they were in the days of original courtship.

Some previously impotent men are so overjoyed at the restoration of their erections that they want to test them out in intercourse at once. This is a mistake. Progress towards intercourse should build up slowly. For tips on how to do this see page 201.

What can anyone else do?

If these methods don't work, or work only for a while, it may be wisest to get a medical opinion. The doctor may prescribe tablets to reduce anxiety and offer specific advice. The man or even the couple may be sent to a specialist for psychotherapy when, depending upon circumstances, an attempt would be made to investigate any unconscious factors that are a part of the problem so as to make the man aware of them. The man's partner would be involved, both to help treatment along by doing joint 'homework' and to deal with any part she may have to play in the problem. Alternatively, the man may be taught to control anxiety and how to relax.

If all else fails and the man is willing, the problem can occasionally be corrected surgically by the insertion of special tubes into the penis. Some such devices make the penis permanently stiff and others are inflatable.

Premature ejaculation

What is it?

Premature ejaculation is another way men unconsciously avoid sex. In many men with sexual problems, erective difficulty and premature ejaculation go together. The man may say he needs so much stimulation to get an erection that he gets so aroused that he ejaculates as soon as he puts his penis into his partner's vagina.

Premature ejaculation may also be the result of simple inexperience, especially in young men. In general, it is easier to recognize than to define. As a result, the 'experts' have had a field day. Sometimes it is defined in terms of the woman's response – the man fails to last long enough for the woman to have an orgasm on half of all occasions they have sex. This is unfair because some women take a very long time to reach orgasm and sometimes never have one during intercourse, and secondly a couple may be poor at foreplay so the woman is never sufficiently aroused before penetration to reach orgasm within a reasonable time. The fault is with her not being aroused rather than the capacity of the man to last as such. However, it's also true to say that men who fear they may lose their erection if they spend too long in foreplay go for quick penetration as soon as they are erect, and that men who have a tendency towards premature ejaculation often try to shorten foreplay because they fear that prolonging it will reduce their staying power even further.

Sometimes premature ejaculation is defined in terms of the number of thrusts (say 10 or 15) the man makes during intercourse before he ejaculates. This is also rather unsatisfactory, because it is arbitrarily based on the time the penis is in the vagina. Some couples, at least occasionally, greatly enjoy a passionate 'quickie' in which intercourse may last as short as a minute or so but the man experiences a fully developed orgasm and the woman may say she has several. Another difficulty with such definitions is that the man and the woman may differ widely in their estimates of the number of thrusts, or of the time it takes for the men to ejaculate.

So there really is no hard and fast definition of premature ejaculation – it is simply a term used to describe a condition in which the man ejaculates too soon for his or his partner's liking. Interestingly, some women complain that *they* come too quickly, but as often with woman's sexuality this is a very little discussed subject. In the survey we report on page 70, 11% of contented wives said that they had orgasms too soon for their liking.

Ejaculation can also occur prematurely whenever the sexual act being undertaken produces excessive anxiety. So it can happen in masturbation, mutual masturbation and fellatio, as well as in ordinary intercourse. A man who is capable with his wife may suffer from premature ejaculation when he attempts extramarital sex.

Premature ejaculation, like impotence, can be primary or secondary. Primary means that the condition has been present since the start of the person's sex life and secondary implies that the condition started after a period of normal functioning. In primary premature ejaculation cases there is often no trouble with erections and the man's sex drive is often high. He may, however, start to avoid intercourse to protect his ego from the consequences of failure. Secondary cases are frequently associated with erection difficulties and a loss of sex drive. Sometimes they start quite suddenly, often following a sexual setback, but more often the onset of the condition is hard to pin-point. In some instances, ejaculation may occur without any form of stimulation to the penis, when a man places himself voluntarily in a sexual situation he wants but of which he is also afraid. This happens occasionally in extramarital sexual encounters – especially with prostitutes.

What happens or doesn't

The ejaculation which is premature can occur before the penis erects, at the moment of penetration or immediately afterwards. Where the man has never succeeded in having an orgasm in the vagina penetration may be difficult and ejaculation often occurs as he fumbles about while trying to insert his penis. He

has cut short the full response cycle by ejaculating too early. In some instances the orgasm he experiences is so poor that he is unsure whether he has ejaculated or not. Perhaps, more accurately, he doesn't want to know. In the same way the premature ejaculator may overlook or be unable to recognize the sensations that immediately precede ejaculation and which warn other men to reduce stimulation temporarily if they want to prolong their performance.

What causes it?

Kinsey found that the time from penetration to ejaculation was two minutes or less in 75% of men. Copulation is a brief business for many animals and this, as well as the anxiety shown by the males of some species, is understandable biologically because they are vulnerable to attack while copulating. It could be argued that if ejaculation were too easy to control it might not occur at all, which is not in the interests of reproduction. It could therefore be argued that premature ejaculation is 'normal' and men only learn to control and prolong their time to ejaculation to please their partner. Sex, in which the man is unconcerned about the woman's satisfaction is frowned upon today but by doing so we put pressure on those men who come quickly after penetration. The Victorian gentleman's justification was, no doubt, that the sooner intercourse was over the better for the 'nice' woman. Many men today, more or less unconsciously, still equate intercourse with an assault. Such background notions are often found in premature ejaculators when they are explored in therapy.

On the other hand, so concerned are

some men today with their woman's satisfaction that they can't enjoy intercourse unless the woman has an orgasm. They make intercourse very anxious for themselves and their partner by continuously asking her if she has come yet. Obviously this is counter-productive for both of them. He should unobtrusively note her physiological responses, such as in her breasts, and not arouse her self-consciousness. In any case, the real question in his mind is not so much about the woman's satisfaction but a more selfish one about his own manliness, that is, his capacity to give his woman an orgasm with his penis which he sees as being a sign of real masculinity.

A further dimension can be that just as he believes a woman who really loves him will always want him, he may also believe that such a woman will experience at least one orgasm during intercourse with him. In fact, he is using his staying power as a measure of other factors in the relationship, and this in itself can have a detrimental effect. As in some cases of impotence, the performance of the penis is carrying more of a psychological burden than it can bear.

The most widely accepted theory today is that some men are unable to learn to control ejaculation and that this group are the true premature ejaculators as opposed to those men who are simply quick or early ejaculators. The distinction between them can be a fine one but the true premature ejaculator gets little real pleasure from his orgasm in intercourse.

For whatever reason, the premature ejaculator either can not sense, ignores, or fails to act on the preliminary feelings that other men experience, warning them that they have reached the point of no return.

These warning feelings are something like mini-orgasms, and possibly the premature ejaculator lets-go at this early stage. He experiences it as the 'over-excitement' which some premature ejaculators report, but the real underlying cause may be the anxiety or other emotions that lead to an unconscious desire to avoid or shorten intercourse.

Just as rapid masturbation, perhaps out of a sense of guilt, is bad training for intercourse so, it is thought, rapid early intercourse can establish a pattern of premature ejaculation. This can occur when there is a fear of interruption by parents, or others – sex in the back of a car is a common example. Many a young man's early sexual experiences are furtive and hasty and he soon becomes hooked on very quick ejaculation times. This can work very well for him at a practical level, but often produces problems as he gets older. Prostitutes sometimes tell clients to hurry up, or even take steps to hurry them up, and if a young man's first experiences of intercourse are with them, then it's easy to see that this could encourage premature ejaculation.

As always, there are other underlying factors. The relationship itself may be in difficulties. A woman who is unwilling or disinterested in intercourse, either generally or with that particular man, may show her displeasure by asking him if he is going to come soon. On the other side of the coin, a man who has difficulty showing anger or hostility may do so by ejaculating prematurely. Similarly, he may try to control her by prematurely ejaculating when he feels unable to control her in any other way – or fears she may control him. This sometimes come about if his mother was dominating and he wanted to escape. Some men have difficulty in expressing anger or resentment directly – they are passive but nevertheless aggressive – and some perform better with a sexually determined partner who will do most of the work.

Examples of some of the causes of premature ejaculation

Physical (All rare)

- Infections of the genital organs, e.g. prostatitis, urethritis (disputed)
- Diseases of the nervous system, e.g. multiple sclerosis
- Injuries to the spinal column
- Painful intercourse e.g. due to painful penile conditions

Psychodynamic

- Fear of women; of their genitals; or of intercourse with them
- Fear of being controlled by a woman
- Misperceptions about the sexuality of women (that they are sexless)
- Misperceptions about the act of intercourse (= assault)

Psychological

- Anxiety about intercourse or sex generally
- Ignoring early body sensations that tell him the onset of ejaculation is near

Behavioural

- Earlier premature ejaculation i.e. he now has secondary anxiety

- Fear or expectation of premature ejaculation – i.e. he now has performance anxiety
- Inability to learn to control ejaculation
- Poor masturbation i.e. poor training (comes too quickly)
- Hasty early intercourse experiences

Biological

- Are all men naturally premature ejaculators in interests of safety and reproduction?
- Any anxiety from whatever cause (i.e. feeling unsafe)
- Not having ejaculated for some time and therefore feeling 'trigger-happy'.

Relationship

- Bad feelings about partner (usually unconscious) leading to a desire to punish her.
- A desire to exert control over a partner – control which can not be obtained in any other way.
- A desire to express rage or resentment towards a partner which can not be expressed in any other way.

Situational

- Fear of the sexual act to be undertaken e.g. extra-marital sex, cunnilingus etc.
- Woman increases self-consciousness of (inhibited) man.
- Anxiety about a new experience (e.g. first interourse).

What can we do about it?

If a physical cause is considered to be at all possible, medical advice should be sought.

A committed couple who want to make their relationship work at all levels and who don't want simply to blame each other or score off each other, should be able to focus attention on the right area. If the man feels that the woman in any way contributes to the problem he should say so. If he has negative feelings about her or wants to punish her or fears control by her these should be discussed and he should, with her understanding and agreement, find more open ways of expressing any anger with or fear of her. Where the problem is too infrequent intercourse, the cure is obvious and even if the woman is unable to cope with the frequency he wants she can, at least, help to fulfil his sexual needs and masturbate him instead.

As with impotence, open discussions about her sexuality and displays of it may help reduce his anxieties and misperceptions about female sexuality in general. This will usually work wonders. If she has any difficulties having orgasms and it is this that has led to his desire to avoid intercourse by prematurely ejaculating then this too needs to be taken into account. For example, if she can have orgasms during oral sex it makes sense for the man to do this during foreplay.

If the man comes too soon during masturbation he can, admittedly with some effort, learn to control himself better by stopping stimulation of his penis as he experiences the sensations warning him that orgasm and ejaculation will start if he doesn't. In this way he can learn to identify the warning sensations better. Just like impotent men, premature ejaculators often avoid penetration in their masturbation fantasies. Again, with some effort this can be remedied, perhaps by watching films of 'normal' intercourse. Unfortunately some men are made to feel even more inadequate by watching this kind of material but if they can become highly aroused and then incorporate it into their masturbation or intercourse fantasies the barrier can often be broken. If introducing a fantasy involving penetration produces immediate ejaculation – as it does in some men – the fantasy can be introduced after masturbation has lasted some reasonable length of time, say 5–10 minutes. Afterwards the man can try to introduce the fantasy increasingly early during masturbation. Some impotent men and premature ejaculators consciously fantasize about their own partner during masturbation, possibly to hold out of their consciousness some other female figure such as a mother or even a sister. Using other women in their fantasies, especially with the 'permission' of their own partner, seems to help at least some men. It can then become easier to fantasize about 'normal' intercourse.

One coping technique devised by some young couples is for the man to ejaculate once, in intercourse or by masturbation, and then to have more leisurely intercourse. With the true premature ejaculator this doesn't work but it is effective for the 'trigger happy' younger man.

Although some sex-books advise against it we have found that a number of men can solve the problem by using certain simple techniques. For example, using a sheath during intercourse can, over a few weeks, solve the problem for some men. The use of weak anaesthetic creams or ointments on the tip of the penis helps other men to succeed just by reducing the exciting sensations a little. Contracting the anus tightly at the end of each thrust helps others gain control as does deep penetration with only small movements of the penis in yet others. Due to 'tenting' of the vault of the vagina during a woman's sexual arousal the stimulation of the tip of the penis is actually reduced.

Yoga methods can also be used. In these, intercourse is undertaken in 'slow-motion' stages. For example, the penis is allowed to rest against the vulva for a period of time and then, in the next stage, just the tip is inserted. The penis is then inserted fully into the vagina in three or four more further stages. After each stage the man stops all movement and should focus his concentration on something like his heartbeat until all sensation has subsided. Then the next stage is undertaken. Intercourse then continues in this stop-start fashion. Because of its 'teasing' quality many women find this method very exciting for them but they should resist showing it, because having an obvious orgasm will very often produce one in her man.

Methods such as these are better than the man trying psychologically to ignore what is happening by, for example, reciting the alphabet backwards to himself. To be fair, some men benefit and gain confidence in ejaculatory control even from this, but it is not recommended by professional therapists because it distracts the man from recognising the preliminary feelings of orgasm which is how he eventually learns control.

A few men find it easier to learn to control a tendency towards premature ejaculation by using artificial vaginas or a so-called penis-enlarger as training aids.

Such aids are used as an intermediate step towards learning control with the penis contained in his partner's vagina. They are simply useful devices in the step-by-step progress towards normal ejaculatory control. Men who can't bear handling their penis and those who use poor methods of masturbation, (such as pushing the erect penis between their thighs), can benefit from these aids as can those who have a tendency to be over-awed by women. As well as learning control such men often need to use fantasies of 'normal' intercourse in an attempt to reduce their fears and increase their eagerness for it. Using such fantasies of real penis-in-vagina sex also prevents the sex aid from becoming a substitute for real intercourse.

Some men with a tendency towards premature ejaculation, or indeed impotence, find that they can function normally after having a little alcohol. It may be that the alcohol reduces their anxiety directly or perhaps indirectly by providing an 'excuse' should they subsequently fail.

It's also worth considering the psychological controls which are helpful. It is possible for a man to adjust or set his mind not to have an orgasm or ejaculate. He can simply decide not to, and then it is easy for him not to do so. Concentrating on the 'comforting' feelings of genital stimulation rather than the intense 'excitement' ones usually produces success. In self-masturbation, if he can learn to remain sub-orgasmic for as long as he wants, then in intercourse he can find it easy not to ejaculate at all. Of course, he should warn his partner that he doesn't intend to come but will enjoy her having as much satisfaction as possible. He then enjoys the pleasurable feelings in his penis but is nowhere near an orgasm at any point. In

this state, he can concentrate on adding to the pleasure of his partner by using his hands and mouth during intercourse. This is easiest to do in the left lateral position if he is right handed, in which he can easily stimulate his partner's face, ears, neck, arms, breasts, abdomen, thighs, bottom, anus and clitoris.

Concentrating on her helps his own control and by following this advice he can have intercourse many times a day if he wants to but he may have an orgasm and ejaculate on only the last occasion. This technique of what might be called 'non-come-intercourse' is easy to learn, and has many uses including coping with very differing desire levels – which can be very helpful for older couples – and helping a woman to learn to have orgasms in intercourse – which can be very helpful for younger couples.

Men who fear a loss of vitality or get tired if they have an orgasm early in the day can also use it if their partner prefers intercourse in the morning. Men who use this technique claim it adds to their sense

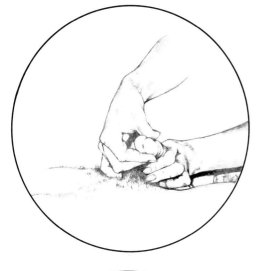

The man is erect and indicating to his partner that orgasm is near. This is her cue to stop stimulating him and to apply the squeeze technique (above). His erection has now subsided (below) and stimulation can safely be re-started

woman and man together are those which were first described by Masters & Johnson. They are probably best preceded by the stages of general 'exercises' as described on page 201 before going on to the special techniques devised to deal with the premature ejaculation itself. The general 'exercises' will hopefully help to restore a state of mind between the partners which takes them back to the trust and love of childhood. It also helps with the elimination of shame about sex, at least between themselves and enables them to be much more open to each other's needs.

The specific techniques advised are either the 'stop-go' game or the 'squeeze' game. Both are designed to make the man more aware of the feelings which precede orgasm and ejaculation, so that he can better identify and control them. In both, the man is placed in a position in which his partner can handle his penis without her arm being uncomfortable. One suggested position is shown overleaf. There are, of course, many others.

The aim is to make the game pleasurable and informative for both partners, so comfort is important. The woman will probably enjoy seeing the responses of the penis, the scrotum and the testes, the emergence of pre-ejaculatory secretion and the changes in colour of the glans penis, depending on the stage of arousal

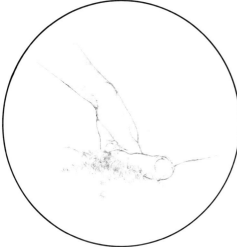

of energy and alertness during the day. In its most refined form a man can learn to control ejaculation for as long as his partner wants. A genuine desire to please the partner and an unfettered enthusiasm for intercourse with her are, of course, a great help and both become increasingly possible as his anxiety falls.

Sex games for premature ejaculators

The techniques that can be used by the

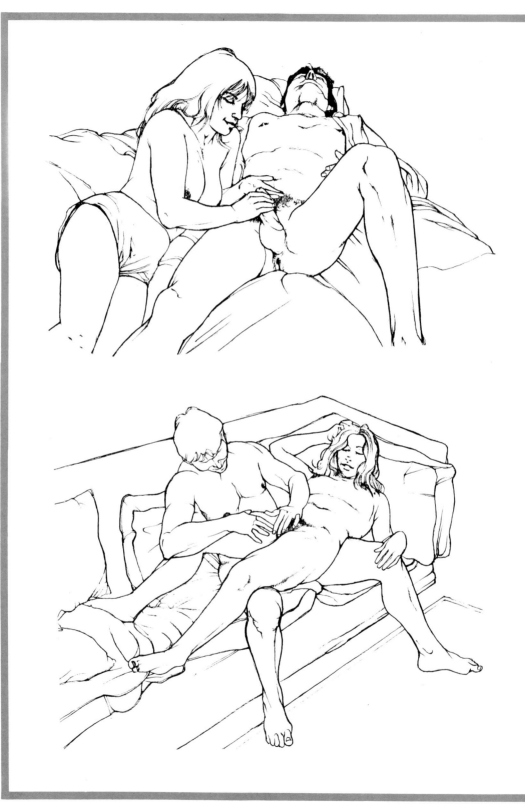

Mutual Masturbation

An essential part of learning about one's partner is learning how best to masturbate him or her. This can't be learned telepathically and has to be practised under the personal guidance and instruction of the expert . . . the person him or herself. As we see on page 203, knowing in every detail how your partner masturbates is a crucial building block in a happy and successful sex life. It is like learning to speak before you can learn how to converse. Here are the basic rules about mutual masturbation:

Get the position right

The reason that some couples find masturbating each other a drag is that they don't get into the right position. You must be comfortable. The diagrams show how best to do this.

If you are shy then use the non-threatening position shown on page 108. In this the person being masturbated faces away from the one who is doing it to them.

When adopting any position for this exercise get your partner's genitals as near yours as possible. This makes the whole thing really easy . . . at least from a physical standpoint.

Get the mood right

A warm room with no chance of interruption is essential. Other things such as a little alcohol, music, sexy reading matter or videos are optional extras.

Have a bath together if you like that sort of thing and have a cuddle first.

Keep the lights on

Because this is a learning situation don't switch off all the lights or you'll miss half of what's happening. Watching your partner can be very exciting. Many women say that one of their greatest turn-ons is watching a man climax.

Use plenty of lubrication

Whether the man is caressing her clitoris or she his penis be sure to use lots of wetness. The best and safest is undoubtedly saliva . . . and it's always available. Alternatives are KY jelly or baby oil but these make things very sticky which some people don't like. A man can be masturbated using talcum powder but this shouldn't be used for a woman because it can get inside her vagina and cause problems.

At no time should the penis or clitoris be dry or the whole thing will end in discomfort or disaster.

Talk about it

Although almost all men masturbate in much the same way, women show many differences, and even the same woman may well change her method of stimulation after she has become aroused. This means that the teacher has to tell the pupil exactly what he or she wants and more importantly what is NOT wanted. After a while actual talk isn't really necessary and communication goes on with hand movements, grunts and moans.

Be aware of special needs

When learning, bear in mind that your partner may like things done which don't only involve their genitals. Many women, for example, caress their breasts or nipples while masturbating and a man may want his anus stimulated or his scrotum or testes held or squeezed. Simply concentrating on the penis or clitoris might not be enough.

What to do

Whatever position you adopt settle down to doing the best possible job you can of masturbating your partner. Go for the best erection and orgasm you can produce. This first entails learning about how he or she masturbates. This can only really be achieved by watching several whole masturbation sequences from start to finish. You should be able to describe accurately all the following:

1 How your partner positions his or her body

2 What he or she does with the hands or fingers

3 How the penis or clitoris is stimulated at each stage of the arousal process.

4 What sort of pressure is used

5   How long the strokes are

6   Whether stimulation is continuous or intermittent

7   Whether the anus or vagina is stimulated too

8   Roughly how long the whole thing takes

9   The visible changes in the rest of his or her body. For example, many women get a measles-like rash as their orgasm gets close and their breasts swell

10 What other areas of the body are stimulated

11 What exactly happens during orgasm itself. How far the man ejaculates; how many spurts; how long he keeps it up the movement of his hand; what he does at the end of ejaculation and so on. A man should also see how and when his woman restimulates herself if she does so.

Only when you know the answers to all these points can you really be said to be an expert on your partner's masturbation and orgasms. Then you can start to reproduce what he or she best enjoys. Many women say that they get their best orgasms when the man does exactly the same things they do and the same is less frequently so for men. Once you find what your partner best likes stick to it on most occasions because when it comes to masturbation predictability has many virtues. Save experimentation for other forms of foreplay and intercourse.

It's important to be able to masturbate one's partner effectively so that one can relieve the sexual tension of the other at times when intercourse isn't possible for some reason. This mutual satisfaction is a duty of caring lovers especially at times when intercourse can't take place.

and the responses of the man to her. When the games reach the stage where he ejaculates, she will hopefully get pleasure from seeing the contractions of his perineal muscles, the ejaculation itself and his facial and body contortions. Her interest, and arousal, with its implied acceptance of his sexual pleasures, will help the man to relax, to become uninhibited and to respond freely. The woman should look for signs of embarrassment or undue muscle tension and encourage him to relax. When ejaculation *is* allowed she should note whether it seems full, free and sparkling or a restrained, inhibited, feeble leakage of a small quantity of semen. Open admiration of his penis may help if he has any residual fears of genital inferiority to other men, which are common.

In the stop-go game, the woman caresses the penis whilst encouraging the man to focus his attention on his sensations. When he is aroused and feels the earliest sensations of impending orgasm he signals her to stop. The erection may subside a little and after a while, when his arousal has subsided, she restarts the stimulation. This cycle is repeated three or more times in each session.

In the squeeze game the technique is the same except that the penis is also squeezed when the woman ceases stimulation. She places her thumb on the fraenum and the index and middle fingers on the opposite side of the penis, respectively on and just below the corona, as shown on page 105. A firm squeeze is applied for 10–15 seconds. This diminishes arousal sharply and the man almost always loses his erection at least partly. Eventually, the training can be made more realistic by lubricating the penis with KY jelly or baby oil before stimulation.

The games are then continued over several sessions, perhaps over two to six weeks, until the man feels confident that he is fully aware of all his sensations of arousal and can easily detect the feelings that tell him that orgasm and ejaculation are setting in. The aim is to learn to control his progress towards them and to feel confident that he finally comes when *he* wants to rather than being over-taken by his orgasm. When he does feel confident the games can go as far as letting him ejaculate. Eventually, the couple should be able to set a time, such as, say, 10 minutes, in which he will not have an orgasm and when he can be masturbated continuously, without stopping or squeezing, and control himself for this length of time. Confidence should now rise in both partners. If the woman has any tendency to become bored or impatient she can, perhaps, encourage herself by reflecting that she is training him to become a perfect lover for her. Each session can be preceded or followed by his stimulation of her by hand, or mouth if preferred. As explained earlier, the uninhibited communication of her needs, pleasures and responses is helpful to the treatment of the man and this stage also will allow him to overcome any aversion towards female genitals in general that he may have acquired in growing up. In other words, it is very helpful if simultaneously with the man learning to control his own sensations through the stop-go or squeeze games, he is also learning from the woman how *exactly* to please her.

Once all this is achieved the vagina is brought into the proceedings but it must be well lubricated. When both are aroused the woman straddles the man in the woman-on-top position and puts his penis into her vagina a little at a time to start with. If he experiences a sharp increase in arousal she will have to get off and squeeze his penis as described above. The idea is to get the man used to having his penis in her vagina, without moving, and without losing control of his sensations. This part of the training should be repeated several times over a number of sessions until he is confident about having his penis happily in her vagina. All this is repeated in the following sessions with the woman taking control of any movement and only handing over this control when they *both* think he can cope. The man can then begin to thrust in a careful and controlled way, all the time keeping his arousal in check. If a loss of control seems imminent then either the thrusting must cease until the sensation goes away or the penis may have to be removed from the vagina and be squeezed by the woman.

Eventually, thrusting can become more free and intercourse allowed to proceed to orgasm and ejaculation. By now these processes should be under the total control of the man and he can begin to focus on pleasing his lover more. The man will now be well on the way to learning how to have intercourse, as opposed to copulating, and, more importantly, during the process the relationship will have eliminated any bad underlying feelings.

What can anyone else do?

Where the condition is the result of deep relationship problems arising in childhood, psychotherapy may be needed. If the problem is the result of a disturbance in the present relationship, which may be the case if the premature ejaculation is of recent onset, then therapy directed more at the relationship than the penis may be the way to a cure. If the problem is based on anxiety about women in general, psychosexual therapy may be required if the couple cannot recognize and resolve the problem themselves. A sign that causes such as these are at the heart of the trouble is that the couple have tried the penile methods but they have failed. Men with general fears about women; who have never had an enduring relationship, and who have always ejaculated prematurely or been impotent may need both psychosexual therapy and social skills training.

Drug therapy can sometimes work. Some anti-depressant drugs, especially Anafranil (chlormipramine), even in quite small doses, can make it difficult for a man (or a woman) to reach orgasm. In this way men can learn control and one case, now followed up for seven years, has been totally successful following one course of the drug over six weeks. Admittedly, other techniques were used too but these had all apparently failed until Anafranil was added. Such drugs can only be obtained on a prescription. Anti-anxiety drugs, also obtainable on prescription, can be effective in helping some men with premature ejaculation but in far fewer than would be predicted theoretically if all men with this problem had a simple anxiety problem.

As with impotence, surrogate partners have been used in treatment. The idea is that a specially trained and accepting woman may be more able than the man's partner to help him overcome the problem. Success has been claimed, but the technique has not been fully evaluated. It is known that it can be dangerous to a basically good relationship.

Premature ejaculation is one condition above all others where the couple together have most to gain by solving the problem. Almost inevitably, the relationship is vastly improved as a result and in some cases they become near-ideal lovers in every sense of the word.

Retarded and painful ejaculation

What is it?

It may seem strange but some men experience ejaculation, or rather ejaculation in the vagina, as a dreaded and even painful experience. Most such men simply find it difficult or impossible to reach orgasm and ejaculation in intercourse. In men who feel pain it is sometimes experienced as an acute headache or pain in the groin but more usually it is felt in the penis. It may be described as a sensation of blockage or even of the penis being held in a vice-like grip. A few men also say that something is wrong with their semen. The pain may make it difficult for the man to reach orgasm and ejaculate. It may persist for hours or even a day or two after the event and no physical cause is ever found to account for the problem. The situation is different from those cases in which the man has a sense of burning, soreness on ejaculation, or urination, due to the presence of an infection of the urethra (urethritis) or elsewhere in the genitals.

Various drugs of the anti-depressant and anti-high blood pressure type can lead to retarded orgasm and ejaculation. Alcohol can have the same effect. Injuries to the spine and operations related to it can make orgasm and ejaculation difficult or impossible but even such men sometimes respond to psychotherapy and can func-

tion, if only weakly and rarely. Hormonal abnormalities can result in disturbances of orgasm and ejaculation. For example, a shortage of testosterone or an excess of oestrogen can have these effects.

As already mentioned, some men find it difficult to ejaculate inside or even in the presence of a woman. These men may also complain of disturbed sensations in their penis. It is not an excess of feeling, as reported by the painful ejaculators, but a lack of it. They may claim that they lose all sensation in their penis, or just in the glans, or alternatively, they may say the vagina is insufficiently tight or excessively slippery. This latter complaint, if made to the partner, can have a bad effect on her. The thought that she might be the source of his problem adds further difficulties to the relationship. Sometimes the complaint is not so much about penile feelings as about the loss of a sense of excitement and arousal.

Both excessive feeling and the loss of feeling can be explained on the basis of an unconscious desire to avoid not so much sex as the final fulfilment of the act. It is a special and limited form of sex avoidance. During treatment some cases of retarded ejaculation turn into premature ejaculators and some premature ejaculators turn into retarded ones. In the first instance, the treatment has made the man worse since he now wants to avoid the vagina, not just ejaculating inside it.

An inability to ejaculate in the vagina can be experienced by some men early in their heterosexual careers, sometimes after an initial bout of premature ejaculation. Men who have never ejaculated in the vagina are not at all rare. Retarded ejaculation can also occur in self – and, more especially, in mutual masturbation.

The condition may be variable and can be present on some occasions, or with some women, and not with others. On occasions the woman notices a sudden increase in tension in the man. This can sometimes correspond with the onset of a distasteful fantasy he is having. Up to this point, at which anxiety increases, the man may say subsequently that he was fearing that he would ejaculate prematurely. The over-excited feelings in his penis give way to a reduction of sensation or a total loss of sensation.

What happens or doesn't?

Men with a tendency towards painful or retarded ejaculation often have a history of associated difficulties such as occasional failure or difficulty in erection, or premature ejaculation or loss of erection in the vagina. Mild degrees of the condition may never come to anyone's notice, except incidentally, because the man learns to compensate for the loss of sensation or arousal as they occur by producing a fantasy of a type that excites him and makes up for it. He may also change his or the woman's position or reduce the degree of penetration to enjoy more sensation from his glans penis being at the vaginal entrance. Alternatively he might ask the woman to add to his sensation by stroking his scrotum, squeezing his testes, stimulating his anus or inserting a finger into it. The woman, by closing her legs together, with his on either side, helps in some cases. Others are encouraged by their partner using obscene language.

In some cases though, no matter what is done, the man can't bring himself to orgasm and ejaculation by any means. Eventually he has to withdraw and may either masturbate himself or get the woman to do it for him. If he is with an unfamiliar partner, he may produce the excuse that he is using the withdrawal method of contraception or that he likes to watch himself come. Some men can't experience an orgasm with a woman watching, or even if she is in the same room.

What causes it?

The causes can be very hard to disentangle. A man with a slight tendency towards retarded ejaculation, who has learned how to offset the loss of sensation or arousal himself, can be pushed into full retarded ejaculation by things such as sexual difficulties with women; a fear of pregnancy or after the birth of a baby. In the last case the man claims his wife's vagina has been too stretched to stimulate him sufficiently. Because of the way the vagina is constructed, this is an unlikely explanation, and the real cause is that his erstwhile lover has now turned into a mother, which may activate old Oedipal conflicts (see page 276).

The man's psychosexual history may reveal serious inhibitions over sex generally, or there may be a history of specific 'injuries' connected with orgasm or ejaculation. For example, he may have been caught masturbating at the moment of orgasm by his mother, or have been embarrassed or punished for wet dreams. In some instances the man has a history of having caused an unwanted pregnancy. In other cases the man's whole attitude towards women and his relationships with them are profoundly disturbed.

Some such men have a history of having visited prostitutes, yet they have not been able to ejaculate no matter what the woman has done to help them in the way of masturbation, oral sex or intercourse. The masturbation fantasies of other such men reveal an interest in deviant acts or homosexuality and the man is clearly 'aiming-off' from full intercourse, although he may seem to be enthusiastic about it.

Other sufferers from the condition are found unconsciously to view semen as an excretion and to put it in the vagina as a kind of desecration of the woman. Unlike the borderline deviant, such men are even less able to ejaculate in a woman's mouth and indeed find fellatio repugnant.

Sometimes the man is found to use a poor method of masturbation; he pushes his penis between his crossed thighs and rocks his body. Such men complain that a vagina is too unstimulating to bring them to orgasm and ejaculation. In a similar way, some men squeeze their penis in an abnormally tight grip in self-masturbation. Masturbation retraining, and the elimination of any deeper trouble is needed. Such men often seek anal intercourse in the hope that the grip around their penis will be tighter.

In mild cases where the man can cope with the problem himself the woman may be unaware of it, although realizing that something is not quite right. However, he may simply appear both to her and himself to be particularly capable of lasting during intercourse and the 'difficulty' is seen as a virtue. Younger women sometimes think that they are the culprit, and have stretched the vagina too much in masturbation – a groundless fear.

A woman who has had a baby may think it is due to her 'flabby' vagina and conclude that the situation is hopeless. Others may feel they have lost their attractiveness or that the man has another woman with whom he has been having intercourse and therefore cannot reach orgasm with her because he doesn't need one. Obviously, if the real basis of the man's problem is a fear of women, fear of sex or a fear of desecrating or impregnating them, then such reactions are likely to push him into full sex-avoidance.

Examples of some of the causes of painful or retarded ejaculation

Physical (all rare)

● Spinal injuries

● Operations affecting the pelvic nervous system

Psychodynamic

● Partner perceived unconsciously as mother

● Semen viewed as excretion

● Fear of experiencing orgasm/ejaculation inside or even with a woman

● Fear of exhibiting full sexual response to another person

Psychological

● Fear of losing self-control

● Fear of punishment for loss of control

● Belief that sex is for reproduction

● Fear of inducing pregnancy

Behavioural

● Poor methods of masturbation

● Secondary anxiety

Looking carefully at a man's sexual organs can really help a woman understand the mechanics of arousal. His response to her touch and interest are a delight to them both

Biological

- Recent orgasm/ejaculation

- Increasing age – most men become somewhat slower

- Some drugs e.g. anti-depressants etc.

- Consumption of alcohol

- Shortage of testosterone/excess of oestrogen

Relationship

- Woman hostile or suspicious

- Woman insufficiently stimulating (along with other factors)

Situational

- Vagina too large or too wet(?)

- Woman has difficulty e.g. excessive concern about avoiding pregnancy

What can we do about it?

From the descriptions already given, and the causes discussed, a couple may well be able to see the best course to follow.

For example, if the man has difficulty in ejaculating in the presence of a woman, or is abnormally shy about being seen whilst having an orgasm, or regards semen as excretion then the woman will have to reassure and encourage him, including the revelation of more details about her own sexuality. Encouraging him to masturbate in front of her and showing him that she doesn't think of his semen as dirt are obvious first steps. At first the woman may have to be a good distance away from him and not watching too obviously if he is to succeed. On the next occasion she can be nearer and finally close to him and stroking him whilst he masturbates. In undertaking all this the woman will be aware that she is undoing harm done to the man in childhood whether he can recollect such events or not.

The next step is to get him to relax and accept being masturbated by her and to allow her to share his pleasures in orgasm and ejaculation. If there is any difficulty they may have to use a vibrator on his penis to help bring on an orgasm and ejaculation. Progress towards these aims should be preceeded by temporarily stopping intercourse and working through the general exercises listed on page 201.

When the man has become accustomed to being masturbated to orgasm by the woman, one technique is for her suddenly and without prior warning, to straddle him when he is well advanced towards orgasm, putting his penis quickly into her vagina and moving so rapidly that he ejaculates. Another technique is for the man, once he has learned to ejaculate reliably, to ejaculate a number of times on the woman, especially her vulva, before he attempts intercourse. Another way, is for the couple to plan intercourse, and then to have it in the position he finds most exciting, and for the woman to add as much extra stimulation as possible in the forms which most excite him. Testicular and anal stimulation may be particularly helpful. French prostitutes are said to place a finger inside the anus of any client who has this problem.

The man can, of course, help himself by correcting any faults in his masturbation and by using fantasies of successful ejaculation within the vagina.

What can anyone else do?

Psychotherapy may be required for the deeper disorders of psychosexuality or the personality. Men who don't have a relationship, or who are incapable of forming an enduring relationship with a woman need to start with correcting these problems rather than the penile symptoms. This can be difficult because in some cases the man believes it is his penis which is at fault. On clinical examination his penis is found to be perfectly normal but he may nonetheless assert that it is defective in some way. For example, he may complain that it doesn't fully erect (even though his partner – if any – says it is normal) or he may claim it is bent and so on.

Women who avoid sex

Sexual avoidance in women is often harder to detect than in men, unless there is a medical reason which genuinely causes pain or discomfort, but the woman is too shy or embarrassed to say so.

The most obvious cases openly avoid men or avoid any sexual enticement to their partner if they are in a relationship. In the latter case the relationship, at least at the intimate level, is likely to have collapsed or, because of difficulties in herself or her partner, the woman is incapable of satisfaction and therefore wants to avoid the frustration of arousal by intercourse.

Women, after all, can have intercourse, but be psychologically uninvolved. A woman can act as if she were responsive when she is not and may even fake orgasms. Due, no doubt, to the way they are brought up some women appear to struggle against feeling any arousal and may, for example, be working out their shopping-list so as to avoid a loss of control. Others may ask their man to talk to them for the same, unconscious purpose.

Some behave like this only if the light is on and they are being watched by their man but can afford to let go and respond in the dark or if their face is not visible to the man, for example in the spoons or other rear-entry positions.

Others respond physiologically but not psychologically, and see themselves as being unaffected by sex, in spite of the fact they display all the signs of intense sexual arousal. This misperception of themselves is important, and if they are made aware of their responsiveness, they may even lose their sex drive altogether – at least for a time. As is the case in many sexual problems and difficulties in women, it is as if unconsciously they are behaving like a child being observed by its mother. In some women this thought is a conscious one. Once she is made consciously aware of her true responsiveness, the self-deception no longer works.

Another form of sex avoidance is being unable to have an orgasm. This is discussed later. Some women do have an orgasm but refuse to admit it, even to themselves. In others, the sudden loss of the ability to experience orgams is the first sign that, as far as she is concerned, the relationship is in trouble. Painful spasms of the vaginal muscles, (vaginismus) may prevent intercourse or deter her partner. Painful conditions of the genitals may lead to pain on intercourse, which can result in vaginismus, but in many cases no serious physical cause can be found – at least nothing that could be responsible for such severe symptoms. Vaginismus by definition is an unconscious tensing of the vaginal muscles but women who have painful vaginal conditions may also more or less *consciously* tense them up against the anticipated pain.

Expressions of a lack of enthusiasm either by words or behaviour may also have a deterrent effect but in some cases they are really being said to the woman's own super-ego (see page 283) rather than to the man. This is usually unconscious, but many women feel they ought to behave in this way when having intercourse with a man to prevent him regarding her 'an easy lay'.

Comparatively few women in a good relationship refuse outright to have intercourse, especially in younger couples, unless there is some obvious reason such as illness or genuine tiredness. The frequency with which jokes are made about wives' 'headaches' seems to be very misleading, judged from replies to direct questions put to thousands of couples over years of clinical experience. In general, women seem willing to oblige on most occasions whether they have much desire or not. Biologically such a situation would be likely to maximize reproduction or, at least, the potential for it.

Two further facets of sex avoidance in women are sublimation and deviance. The first is to do with the possibility of the sex-drive being diverted from genital activities to those which may not even appear to be sexual, such as, for example, writing, painting, music and so on. Some women certainly do seem able to suppress all their genital needs for long periods of time and to become immersed in other activities but whether they are masturbating or not is very difficult to say. Conventional wisdom has it that the total suppression of genital drives in women leads to emotional upsets.

Deviance, as said earlier, is thought of as a virtual male monopoly but this may be because it is more obvious in men because of its effect on their ability to

GET A MOVE ON. I WANT TO GET BACK IN TIME FOR CORONATION STREET

function. For example, if a man can only erect and ejaculate in a deviant situation, then his difficulty is obvious, at least to his partner and himself. Even if he can perform in intercourse he is likely to do so ineffiiciently and without much pleasure.

For pure mechanical reasons a woman could still function in intercourse and totally conceal her deviant needs, perhaps indulging them only in fantasy; she might say that she doesn't much want intercourse, or that she gets little pleasure from it. Such comments are common in women. In theory, at least, the situation could be parallel to that in men where sexual inefficiency and inhibitions merge with deviance and sex avoidance. The difference is that in women the main way that such disorders show is when it comes to pleasure and not performance. Even if a woman were aware of her deviant needs, they would not necessarily impair her ability to copulate, although intercourse, the way we define it (see page 200), would be beyond her. She might get more from masturbation to a deviant fantasy, or seek

a partner who might indulge her need whilst believing it was his idea. This is difficult to judge because women, in the main, will do almost anything their man suggests if the relationship is a good one.

Perhaps women are innately capable of greater sexual adjustment than are men, although against this it must be said that clinical evidence shows that for the vast majority, the only satisfactory conclusion to any heterosexual genital activity is seen as penis-in-vagina sex. If this is so, such a strong drive would tend to push down any sexual deviation in women, which then comes out in foreplay rather than the avoidance of intercourse. If so, then by the definition used throughout this book, such a woman is not a sexual deviant.

Of course, it could be said that it is not a basic biological desire for intercourse in women, but a cultural requirement which insists that intercourse is the only valid form of sex because it results in reproduction. Because women can respond sexually to so many different stimuli and because they are penetrated (they are passive rather than active) in intercourse, it is very difficult to arrive at any firm conclusion on this point.

Another difficulty is emotional complications. A woman may be sexually inefficient or even avoid sex with one man but respond wholeheartedly and eagerly to another, whereas the majority of men with sex problems experience them with most or all of their other partners, later if not sooner.

If we remember that this can only be a generalization, a fair conclusion suggests that the actual expression of a woman's sexuality is influenced by her upbringing, and is also powerfully affected by the sexual style of her partner. If he is free and open she will eventually tend to follow suit; if he is shy, avoids sex, is inhibited or even deviant, then she'll also tend to behave similarly. Just as women are more prepared to make adjustments to their personality in a relationship, so too are they prepared to adjust their sexuality. Men tend to get the sexual partner they deserve and if, in a good relationship, the woman appears to be sexually at fault the man should ask himself if he himself could be the cause.

Difficulties with desire and response

What is it?

In the past, women who had any kind of difficulty to do with orgasms were often labelled frigid. This term, except as a form of abuse, has now passed out of use because many women who have orgasm difficulties are still sexually responsive and lubricate easily. However, the word frigid implied an absence (or rejection) of sexual interest, desire, pleasure and response, and it is used in this way here as a convenience. Our culture, and the way we bring up young girls must take a good deal of the blame for disorders of desire and response in women. Unconsciously, negative feelings towards sex still persist, and do untold harm. They are passed on from the unconscious minds of mothers to the unconscious minds of their daughters. Virtually every woman is influenced by them to some extent, although they may well not be apparent to their conscious mind. The most severely affected women are those with desire and/or orgasm difficulties.

Within this basic framework, several different patterns emerge. Some women say that they never experience any sexual thoughts, wishes, desires or activities other than to submit to intercourse, from which they get little or no pleasure, and that they have always been the same. These are called primary cases. Others say they were different in the past, but started to feel this way as a result of stress or tension, such as discovering that their husband was involved in an affair. Such cases are called secondary. She may also feel trapped into staying with him, perhaps because of the children, but cannot bring herself to seek sexual gratification elsewhere, yet cannot forgive her husband for having wandered. She simply closes down on her sexuality, on sex thoughts or masturbation, afraid that the arousal of desire in herself or her husband would make her life intolerable.

Such women have clearly been deeply influenced by conventional attitudes towards a woman's roles and it is difficult to find the flexibility to repair any damage.

However, not all such women turn out

to be entirely frigid. Some are found to function normally, yet feel they have to appear 'nice' and sexless to others. This is often true of the young woman who is unwantedly pregnant; she is reproaching herself for her behaviour, and wishes to avoid similar reproaches from others.

Some women consciously believe they are sexless, but are in fact over-compensating against their sexuality because they were brought up to believe that overt signs of sexual desire are bad. These women deal with their drives in highly obscure ways, which are almost impossible to recognize as being sexual. For example, they may masturbate in ways that don't involve their hands. A married nurse used heel pressure, always sitting down with a foot under her vulva, especially when conversing with men. She had orgasms, but didn't consciously 'accept' or recognize them. Because women don't erect visibly and ejaculate, such self-deception is easy. This condition is amenable to therapy, but the therapist needs sympathy and skill to discover the truth.

A variant of secondary frigidity is in women who say they have never wanted intercourse, but nonetheless who have one or more orgasms when they do have it. When her natural desires break through or when she has intercourse, perhaps to keep the peace, she is normally responsive. Such women often function best when their cooperation is not invited, at least verbally; then they can feel that they are compelled to have sex by their partner.

Other inhibited women, and men, also function in a somewhat similar way. They may struggle against their sexual desires for days or weeks but finally when their desires exceed their level of inhibition, they function normally and even go over

the top. Their desire then subsides again for a few days or weeks. This 'clustering' of sexual activity with abstinence in between is highly characteristic of those men and women who are sexually inhibited.

Yet other women, especially younger ones, are normal in their sexual interest and desire, of which they are fully conscious, and can have intercourse, but their response is impaired. In the most severe form, the woman cannot even become aroused. No matter what she or her partner does she doesn't engorge and lubricate. Such women are usually fairly efficient at self-masturbation. In these cases the unconscious prohibition is on intercourse and they are exactly comparable with impotent men. This is much less common than impotence, indeed such cases are rare, but it can happen, if only temporarily, to young women at the outset of their heterosexual careers, or following some shock connected with intercourse, such as being caught having sex by their mother.

Some women are confused about their need for physical contact, comfort and closeness and their needs for intercourse. Many couples fall into the trap in which messages or direct invitations for physical closeness are misinterpreted as invitations to have sex. Many a woman says that she often wants cuddling but always seems to have to 'pay for it' by having to have sex. Either partner has to be able to refuse sex and not feel that they stand to lose or even threaten their love bond.

The other and much commoner form of inhibited response is seen in those women

This woman, admiring herself in front of the mirror, is learning to overcome her inhibitions from childhood

who feel sexy and are capable of arousal but who don't have orgasms. Some women can have an orgasm in particular circumstances but not in others; other women say they are not sure whether they have them or not. Although we defined the word 'frigidity' to mean a lack of interest and general unresponsiveness, in a strictly technical sense it means the inability to have an orgasm during intercourse. Today this condition is called anorgasmia or orgasmic dysfunction. The latter term is probably better because *an*orgasmia means 'no orgasm' whereas 'orgasmic dysfunction' simply says that something to do with orgasms has gone wrong.

A third of all women say they have been able to have orgasms from early childhood. Often they have been obtained in a whole variety of ways in addition to obvious masturbation. A list of such circumstances includes sliding on bannisters; rocking on the arms of chairs; washing the vulva; spraying it with water; exposing it to jets of air; rope-climbing; cycle-riding; horse-riding; tight jeans; movement on buses, trains or 'rides' in fair-grounds; being kissed or touched by a boy; hearing a man's voice; sitting next to a man on a bus; being shouted at; being stood over by a man; being late; listening to music or poetry; dancing; fantasy; ears being nibbled; holding back urine; dreaming, and many more.

However, even women who are as responsive as this may take time to learn how to have orgasms in intercourse. Presumably self-consciousness, anxiety and a lingering sense of doing wrong prevent them relaxing sufficiently to enjoy an orgasm, or a full orgasm.

Some women have orgasms easily in their early experiences of intercourse and then lose the ability to do so. The explanation here is probably that for them the intense excitement of their first few experiences is enough to overcome the negative forces such as anxiety and guilt which tend to oppose orgasm. So for them at the time the forces leading to full satisfaction and orgasm are greater than the forces opposing them. After a time, the phase of intense excitement subsides and the opposition forces gain the upper hand.

Other women say they first experienced an orgasm from masturbation around the age of eight or nine, while others are uncertain or unsure of whether or not they have ever experienced one. Questions about how to tell whether or not they've had an orgasm are commonly asked by late adolescent and young adult women – and by their mothers and grandmothers! Many of these women can masturbate; they don't seem to take an unduly long time; and they appear to be satisfied with a feeling of well-being afterwards; yet they have little or no awareness of having had an orgasm. Their chief conscious prohibition is against *enjoying* their orgasm. A trick is being played on their conscience; masturbation is allowed to occur provided it doesn't lead to great pleasure. This allows masturbation to be denied, at least to the woman herself. For example, females are allowed to wash their vulvas which can be utilised as a 'cover' for masturbation which can then be denied. The lie is not a conscious one – it is an unconscious trick. This helps explain why so many women claim with all honesty not to masturbate. If this all sounds tortuous, it just shows how difficult is the situation in which our culture places women when it comes to their sexuality.

Sometimes those who 'deny' their

orgasms during masturbation can consciously 'accept' them in intercourse, if only because intercourse is 'allowed' if you love and/or are married to the man – whereas masturbation is always forbidden. However, they may have difficulty before being able to climax during intercourse.

Other women who 'deny' their masturbation orgasms also 'deny' them in intercourse. The group of women who learn to masturbate, possibly at a very early age, using poor methods designed to avoid detection and reproach, often have later difficulties in achieving orgasm in intercourse, even though desire and arousal are normal, simply because of their poor training. In many cases the woman herself attributes her disability to some specific sexual event in her childhood, such as being caught and smacked for indulging in sex games, but probably the event was only the most memorable that occurred in a background of general sexual suppression.

When does it happen?

Orgasm difficulties are very common in young women in the early stages of their sexual experience. Some women, of course, persist in this stage and never learn.

Even in women who have orgasms in intercourse, occasional failures in desire, arousal and/or orgasm are commonplace because of distraction, disinclination, pregnancy or illness. Circumstances too may produce failure, for example, fear of detection. Having said this, some women say that they experience their most intense orgasms when there is an element of risk (of pregnancy, discovery or whatever).

Similarly, things to do with a woman's partner may lead to failure. For example, a woman may be unable to respond if her partner is smelly or drunk but, again, some women find it better under such circumstances. Inadequate foreplay or a sexual problem in the man may also lead to her failure to reach an orgasm but some women learn to cope with such circumstances and can have orgasms in spite of all such diffiiculties.

Women who habitually masturbate in unusual positions may also be unable to have an orgasm during sex unless intercourse occurs in that position.

What happens or doesn't

Some women fail to become aroused during foreplay, but others become aroused and lose lubrication as the time for penetration approaches or after it has occurred. These are exactly similar to the various forms of impotence in men – vaginal lubrication is for a woman what an erection is to a man.

Where desire and arousal are intact but orgasm is the difficulty some, perhaps many, women can reach orgasm in heterosexual situations if special conditions are just right. For example, some can have orgasms if their partner masturbates them or carries out oral sex on them but in no other way. Some women say that in the female superior position they can angle the vagina in such a way that can stimulate the clitoris or the front wall of the vagina but another possibility is that they still have unconscious fantasies of having a penis and when they are on top and have control over thrusting their fantasy is satisfied and they have an orgasm. Many others, need simultaneous stimulation of the clitoris in order to reach satisfaction during intercourse and the left (or right) lateral position is a good one for this purpose.

Other women can reach orgasm if some special additional sensation is added, such as anal stimulation, or obscene language. Yet others say they have to have a fantasy, often of someone other than the partner with whom they are having sex or of a sexual scene such as an orgy, if they are to reach orgasm.

In most of these cases the explanation is that due to the inhibitions imposed during childhood and which impair sexuality, albeit unconsciously, extra stimulation of one form or another is required for success. Sufficient trust in the partner is also necessary for most women so that they can relax and be unselfconscious.

It should also be noted that often, the ease with which a woman has orgasms has nothing to do with what the man does – or even *who* he is. Some women have their best orgasms with strangers and a few 'use' the man sexually – perhaps in a woman-on-top position to achieve their personal ends. Here is a scale of orgasmic failure (or success). It gives an overall view of the problem, and shows what can be achieved either with self-help or professional help.

Summary of orgasmic failure or success

◆   The woman has never (consciously) had an orgasm – she may in fact appear to be very aroused and her man thinks she has had an orgasm but the woman herself doesn't think so, even though she might feel pleasantly satisfied after her 'non orgasm'. (See page 127 for what do to)

◆   The woman may have had one or two orgasms ever but doesn't do so regularly

◆   The woman has orgasms during self-masturbation only

◆   The woman has orgasms after arousing foreplay and her man can masturbate her well

◆   The woman has orgasms with a vibrator but in no other way

◆   The woman comes only with oral sex

◆   The woman has easy orgasms in front of her man but never with his penis in her vagina

◆   The woman has orgasms with a penis in her vagina but needs extra stimulation (to the clitoris usually)

◆   The woman has orgasms with a penis in her vagina but needs no other stimulation (except during foreplay)

Many couples find that early on in their relationship the woman masturbates easily and greatly enjoys her orgasms but only in private or with the light off. Slowly she becomes less inhibited and by her 30s may be quite happy to have her partner masturbate her in broad daylight and to have oral sex with the lights on. As the woman's inhibitions are shed she becomes orgasmic in increasing numbers of situations and eventually will climax almost every time her partner caresses her in the way she likes. By this stage the woman is usually quite at ease masturbating in front of her man and it is but a short step from this to masturbating herself or him masturbating her during intercourse. Some love-making positions favour this more than others – especially when it comes to the woman masturbating herself.

As long as a woman sees masturbation as something 'private' and by implication 'dirty' that she does only to herself the couple may never progress to penis-in-vagina orgasms – if that is what either wants – and many women do because they get their most satisfying orgasms from intercourse. From the man's point of view this can be exceptionally exciting not only because the genital feelings are so good as his partner's pelvic muscles contract around his penis but emotionally too as she is obviously enjoying herself with his penis inside her. None of this necessarily means that the couple should aim for or have simultaneous orgasms which are probably more trouble than they are worth for most people.

As experienced by the woman, a failure to have an orgasm may result in very little distress to her. Many say they are satisfied if the man enjoys it and that they are not bothered about themselves. Some couples solve the problem by masturbating the woman before or after intercourse and this may explain the apparent lack of concern. In other cases the woman probably is having an orgasm, although perhaps a weak one, but is 'denying' it as we described earlier. Yet other women experience the lack as a reflection on their femaleness and say it damages their image of themselves as a woman.

Other women complain they nearly reach orgasm but always just fail. Some describe it as being able to see something through a barred window but not quite being able to reach it. Others complain of their legs twitching. In these women it seems that as they begin to approach orgasm, vigilance increases and muscles contract. When the move towards orgasm has been suppressed the vigilance relaxes only to be repeated as orgasm is neared again. Some such women have a history of being caught and punished for masturbating when young.

Yet other women only become concerned if their man becomes concerned and then out of fear that he might test himself on another woman they can become desperate. In this state such women are even less likely to reach orgasm.

What causes it?

As already described, cultural attitudes; our requirement for ladies to be 'nice' and frigid; unpleasant sexual experiences; poor masturbation and being conditioned out of orgasmic abilities are the chief causes of failures of desire, arousal and response.

Secondary orgasmic dysfunction can arise if a relationship has deteriorated emotionally or if the woman is in the process of de-loving her partner to justify extramarital sexual activity. Secondary anorgasmia is probably most commonly caused by this. Other causes include depression, anti-depressant drugs, fear of pregnancy, recent pregnancy, lesbian preoccupations and, possibly, certain diseases.

In some women the cause seems to be due to, or aggravated by, early childhood relationships. An obvious possibility is a severely unresolved Oedipus complex in which all penises are unconsciously thought of as a prohibited penis such as that of a father or brother. Clinical experience suggests that such cases do occur although the presence of Oedipal residues seems to disrupt female sexuality to a much lesser extent than that of the male. Possibly they disturb the capacity to love another man completely to a greater extent than they disturb sexual functioning.

In yet other cases, the woman seems, especially after she has become a mother herself, to identify with her own mother whom she regards as sexless. If the belief that sex is for babies is deeply rooted, orgasm problems can arise after starting oral contraception, after sterilization or at the menopause. Other women, probably as a result of being criticized a lot as little girls, are unable to relax sufficiently with any other person, including the man they love, and so can't have orgasms. As with some men, some women can't have an orgasm even by self-masturbation if the man is watching or even if he is present.

Examples of Some of the Causes of Disorders of Desire & Response

Physical

- Any illness
- Diabetes
- Some disorders of the nervous system
- Anorexia nervosa

Psychodynamic

- Partner unconsciously perceived as father
- Incomplete acceptance of female role (e.g. fantasies of having a penis)
- Identification with mother (perceived as sexless)

Psychological

- No risk of pregnancy
- Risk of pregnancy

- Depression
- Death of a parent or close relative or friend
- Inability to relax
- Feeling of having been mutilated say after a hysterectomy or mastectomy
- Self-consciousness – fear of criticism
- Fear of loss of control
- Fear of pain
- Latent lesbian thoughts

Behavioural

- Conditioning out of sexuality in childhood
- Adverse sexual experiences in childhood
- Poor methods of masturbation

Biological

- Some drugs e.g. anti-depressants
- Hormonal deficiences
- A high clitoris (?) see page 132 for further discussion

Relationship

- Deterioration in emotional relationship (falling out of love)

Situational

- Poor foreplay
- Partner puts her off for some reason
- Fear of discovery/being overheard
- During an extramarital affair

A group of causes not so far considered are those involving abnormalities of sensation. Some women, like some men, complain of a lack of sensation and others complain of disabling painful sensations. Although some cases of both conditions are due to physical causes others are not. They are all considered later under 'Disorders of feeling'.

What can we do about it?

If a physical cause is suspected a doctor should be consulted but it is only rarely that a convincing physical reason is found. True depression always requires medical advice; it is a genuine illness.

It is less common for women to involve physical explanations for their sexual difficulties than it is for men but some go for a medical examination to be reassured that they are physically healthy. If the difficulties appear to spring from contraception, medical advice may be required. Oral contraception itself probably doesn't lead to depression or to a loss of sex drive but associated psychological reactions may do so. Some women can function more efficiently if there is some risk of pregnancy and may, for example, be happier with an IUD or diaphragm than with the pill because they are less efficient contraceptives.

Turning to the culturally-inspired psychological causes of sexual inefficiency, or frigidity, in women, the first step is for the woman herself to want to improve, not to please her partner so much as to please herself. Almost any woman can succeed if she is given help and is sufficiently determined. Although the underlying inhibitions and attitudes have been given to her by others they nevertheless lie within *her* and can only be overcome by her own efforts – albeit with help from her partner, a professional or both.

The first step along the journey is for her to recognize that she is under-developed psychosexually and that her sexuality is something she possesses herself and is not something that is done to her. If she isn't able to do so she needs at least to accept the sexual aspects of her body and mind. To achieve the former she could, for example, carry out stripper exercises in front of a long mirror pretending it is a male audience. Instead of being revolted at the sight of her body she should try to pose and move erotically, stroking and admiring herself rather than giving way to feelings that she is being dirty or bad. She could finish the exercises by opening her legs and vulva, stimulating it and watching the swelling and change of colour as it congests with arousal. Some women who think they are unarousable or aroused only with difficulty have never watched this response of their vulva to stimulation and are often surprised at how quick and vigorous it is. If she does not normally stimulate her vulva by hand to masturbate she should practise doing so, and hopefully learn to achieve an orgasm in this way. If she can masturbate 'normally' but takes much longer than a few minutes to reach orgasm she could practise frequently with as much excitement as possible, so as to improve her performance.

Some women are vastly encouraged in all this if they can discuss it with a trusted woman friend, or if they read some books devoted to female masturbation, or look at magazines or videos showing women touching their vulvas. This helps to overcome the tendency to believe uncons-

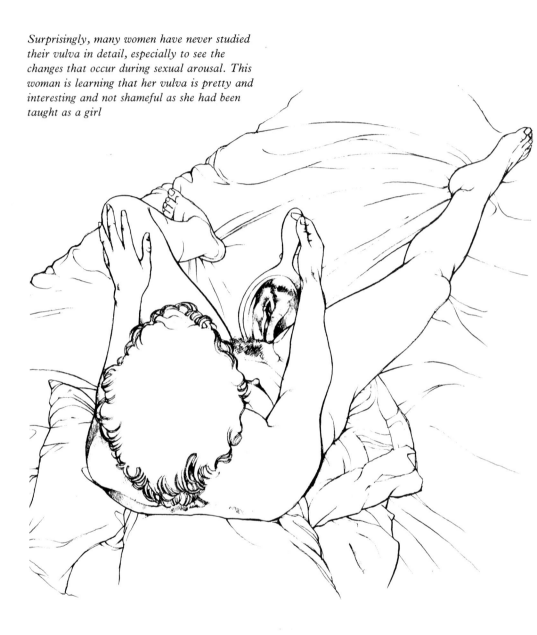

Surprisingly, many women have never studied their vulva in detail, especially to see the changes that occur during sexual arousal. This woman is learning that her vulva is pretty and interesting and not shameful as she had been taught as a girl

ciously that she is the only woman who wants to touch herself genitally. In some areas of the country there are pre-orgasmic groups. They are called *pre*-orgasmic because women who have not yet had an orgasm and who are therefore pre-orgas-

mic, can join other women to exchange experiences, receive practical advice, report progress and generally encourage each other.

Some women have been made to feel so bad about touching themselves that it makes them so tense that they can't have an orgasm. Such women can often succeed using a vibrator. Most are designed to be applied to the vulva or to be inserted into the vagina (see page 221 for more details). Some, which are sold for body massage, can only be applied to the vulva (as opposed to being put into the vagina) but they run from the mains and the strength of the vibration can be adjusted. Provided that they want to succeed, most women can have an orgasm using a vibrator. In a woman who has not had orgasms, or at least not consciously, earlier, the quality of the resultant orgasm usually improves rapidly and the time to orgasm becomes shorter. After a time, as they become more skilful, most women discover they can get more precise stimulation using their fingers and so tend to use the vibrator less. Addiction to a vibrator is rare but it is a good learning device.

All this is only half the story, because many women with these disorders of desire, arousal or orgasm are unable to fantasize about sex. Like some men, but more commonly than them, some women can fantasize about a sexual scene but are only observers and never participants. They are a kind of psychic peeping Tom. Yet other inhibited women can conjure up sexual fantasies but their true content is disguised as symbols. As in men, other women who have difficulties, find that they may lose their arousal in masturbation when using certain fantasies or, more commonly, that they can't have an orgasm, within a reasonable time. Alternatively, they may switch their fantasy to something else just prior to orgasm.

Some women have to try very hard if they are to overcome difficulties in fantasy. Some find books useful to provide material and others use letters from men such as are published in the letters columns of some men's magazines. Reading this kind of material in a warm bath, perhaps even after a little alcohol, helps set the scene for some women.

Although all this could be discussed with the partner from the outset, it is best for him not to be directly involved until the woman has started to make progress on her own. Some men become hostile over their women masturbating themselves, especially if they use a vibrator, seeing it all as an oblique criticism of their masculine capacity to satisfy the woman. It's much more sensible to try to think of it as belated self-training. Also, of course, such a man could reflect that masturbation in men and women is somewhat different in that whereas men can either have sex or masturbate, but not both, women can happily have either or both as often as they wish at least until soreness and tiredness overtakes them. In fact he should aim to be very encouraging to his partner and help her in every way by, for example, getting erotic literature for her and a vibrator if she's too shy to buy one.

Once the woman feels more confident about her own sexuality, and feels she can cope with the presence of her partner, he can then become involved and help her. She should try to enjoy 'showing-off' and to notice and enjoy her partner's signs of arousal in response to her display. He can help, at first, by stroking her and with words of reassurance and encouragement whilst she masturbates. Eventually the aim is to learn to masturbate her as well as she can herself. Some couples may prefer to work slowly towards this end by going through the stages listed on page 201 before starting on genital stimulation. Some women find it easier to respond to masturbation by their partner using the non-threatening position recommended by Masters and Johnson (see page 108).

In general, the mind exerts a greater power in women than in men, whether to enhance or impair their sexuality. Inhibitions leave some women psychologically castrated whilst others, with freer attitudes, can reach orgasm easily, often by a variety of means including the use of fantasy alone. If a woman can deal with the inner restrictions on the expression of her sexuality she can have orgasms by masturbation. Again, provided things are favourable and the woman has an acceptable partner, virtually all such women can learn to transfer their capacity for orgasm from masturbation to intercourse via being masturbated to orgasm by their partner.

Once this has been achieved then using positions such as the left lateral allows either the woman or the man to continue to masturbate her, by hand or with a vibrator, whilst intercourse is in progress. Of course, the foreplay which precedes intercourse should be as effective as possible in arousing the woman and should be based on learning about her specific needs and pleasures. For example, if the woman gets little pleasure from the stimulation of her breasts, or is even put off by it as some women are, then she should say so in order that time is not wasted on them.

Some women are nervous about telling their man exactly how and where they like to be stimulated because they fear their man will interpret it as an adverse criticism of his techniques. Both attitudes are pointless and detrimental to the establishment of intercourse. Similarly, the exchange of fantasy material between the two will probably have opened up the most

arousing and exciting ways in which to arrange it and the man should have found it possible to gauge what mixture of love, romance, domination and directness will help his partner most.

During intercourse the woman can add to her own sensations, and so help her own progress to orgasm. She can do this by making rotary movements with her pelvis which have the effect of sweeping the penis round the walls of the vagina. Because the vagina is sensitive to movement within it this is a good way of increasing stimulation. Rotary movements of the pelvis can lead to considerable excitement, or even orgasm, in some women. Women who masturbate by muscular movement methods often don't touch their vulva and yet can reach a climax by movements such as these. Furthermore the woman can learn to control her pelvic muscles and contract them on the inward thrust of the penis. These exercises are discussed in more detail on page 36.

In effect, self-help treatment consists of the woman going through normal psychosexual and heterosexual development. Women who have little or no sexual desire can be seen from a psychosexual viewpoint as being young girls who are still under the control of their mother, or their conscience, and who are fearful of punishment, such as the loss of love, unless they behave sexlessly. The task of the man is to help liberate his woman from this control. The difficulty is that many such women say they can't accept advice and help from their partner because it is not disinterested – he simply wants her for intercourse and is therefore really thinking of himself and not her. However, if the man takes a real interest in her sexuality and her progress, and applies his knowledge and intelligence to her problems rapid progress becomes possible. Dramatic changes are often seen in such couples. As every woman is different the ways in which help is given has to be personalized. The foregoing account is only of the most general kind. If a woman can not make progress with the help of her partner the services of a sex therapist may be required to direct both their efforts.

What can anyone else do?

Some women are tempted to try other partners, either on their own or in the form of group sex but experience shows that this is not necessarily helpful in the long term. Other women, unless they really settle down to making themselves better with the help of their partner, pass from relationship to relationship, enjoying sex initially but finding themselves unable to sustain it and then moving on again because the real problem has never been dealt with. The disturbance is within their personality or their ability to love, and psychosexual therapy may be necessary.

Disorders of feeling

What is it?

Some women complain of a lack of genital sensation during intercourse whilst others complain that the sensations are painful. Pain on intercourse is called dyspareunia and, of course, may be due to damage, infection or other disorders of the genitals. In some women the pain continues to be experienced after any underlying condition, such as inflammation of the vulva, has cleared up and in others no physical cause for the pain is ever found.

Most, but not quite all, women are put off sex by dyspareunia, and women who experience no pleasurable sensations from their genitals find it difficult to have an orgasm. If intercourse is painful, as a result perhaps of inflammation, in some women the muscles surrounding the entrance to the vagina go into painful spasm called vaginismus. This is really a cramp of the vaginal muscles which makes penetration difficult or impossible.

Vaginismus can, however, arise in women with no physical cause to account for it. Mild degrees of it are not uncommon in early attempts at intercourse and are probably due to doubt, apprehension and fear of pain. Of course, if a girl's hymen has not been stretched or broken earlier and especially if it is somewhat thick, then there may indeed be a reason for the pain but this isn't common. Although it adds to the difficulties, especially of an inexperienced man, this form of vaginismus usually subsides. However, in some women the vaginismus and her general reactions to attempted penetration are so strong that intercourse is impossible. This situation can persist, and there are virgin wives of twenty or even thirty years standing.

Mild or transient attacks of vaginismus can occur secondarily in women who have previously had trouble-free intercourse. In some, especially the unmarried, an initial slight spasm may occur but this soon passes at the start of intercourse. A bout of mild vaginismus can also arise in women who have become emotionally upset in a relationship, but this is more likely to result in initial pain on penetration, in spite of adequate lubrication, rather than as a response which is so painful that it makes intercourse impossible.

Overcoming vaginismus by learning about the vagina and inserting fingers. As well as increasing her confidence she stretches the hole in her hymen to make progress to intercourse easier

Women who report a lack of genital sensation in intercourse may be found to have some cause such as weak vaginal muscles – sometimes the result of damage during childbirth. However, the cause can also be psychological. An old suggestion was that their lack of excitement was caused by the clitoris being placed too high above the vaginal entrance to receive stimulation or that the foreskin of the clitoris was too tight or large thereby shrouding the sensitive tip from stimulation. Neither explanation is now thought to be very plausible and a more recent view suggests that the clitoris is stimulated, not directly by the penis, but by the rhythmical tugging on the inner lips during the in-and-out motion of the penis during intercourse. The movement of the inner lips is transmitted to the clitoris very easily because they are joined to the skin around the clitoris where they meet at the top of the vulva. It has also been suggested that the principle source of pleasure a woman gets in intercourse comes from the movement between the tip of the clitoris and its foreskin. This could be why so many women during masturbation stimulate the area immediately around the clitoris rather than the clitoris itself.

Serious degrees of vaginismus are not very common and neither are complaints of genital insensitivity, but both conditions could be explained in terms of an unconscious desire to avoid intercourse. Vaginismus, in its full form, prevents intercourse by unconscious and involuntary psychological forces causing the vaginal muscles to contract. The unconscious prohibition is on intercouse but not on desire or arousal. Many such women thoroughly enjoy being masturbated and having oral sex carried out on them. Women without feeling actually undertake intercourse, or copulation, but, in a sense, deny they are doing it by suppressing all genital sensation, and even orgasms.

When does it happen?

Vaginismus starts when intercourse is imminent and often before the penis, or any other object such as fingers, a vibrator or a tampon, have even touched the entrance to the vagina.

Vaginismus can be primary in that it is present from the very first sexual encounter, or secondary. Secondary vaginismus can result from painful conditions of the genitals but even so it is possible that the women in whom it occurs have an unconscious proneness towards it already. The painful condition provides an 'excuse' to produce vaginismus and this may well explain those individuals who continue with the vaginismus long after the original painful condition has healed. Unfortunately, many doctors cannot see the reality for what it is and continue to reinforce the woman's view that she has something wrong with her physically.

What happens or doesn't?

In fully-fledged vaginismus the woman will begin to close her legs as the penis or other penetrating object begins to approach her vulva. The pain and spasms start to intensify as the vaginal entrance is touched. At this point, and certainly if any degree of penetration occurs, the woman often writhes around, screams and arches her back. The reaction is often like that of a small child exposed to pain or the fear of it. Psychosexually the woman *is* a child in respect of her vagina.

What causes it?

Women with a serious degree of vaginismus almost always have a history of avoiding their vagina. Unlike other adolescents and women they have not explored it, have never inserted a tampon, have never used it in masturbation, have never allowed a man to put his fingers into it and so on.

Their hymen is usually intact and their sexual fantasies have never progressed as far as penetration. Psychologically the woman doesn't have a vagina or, put another way, her body image, or the picture of her body she has in her mind, does not include a vagina – or, at least, not a realistic vagina. Her vagina is not on her sexual agenda and therefore neither is intercourse. To her, anything pressing between her legs is seen as pressing on an intact body surface with no hole in it and is therefore painful. Some even describe the penis as 'knife-like'.

Some of the women afflicted with this condition give a history of painful genital experiences in childhood or adolescence, but most women with such experiences do not later develop vaginismus. Others believe their vagina is a minute passage which could not possibly accommodate a penis. When asked to draw a life-sized vagina, it comes out as less than one inch long and very narrow. Some have a deep fear of men, sex and the penis but others are very friendly indeed towards all three, provided penetration is not attempted.

A virgin suffering from vaginismus can be loving, especially if the relationship has been going for years. In these cases we become suspicious of a deep and unconscious level of collusion between the partners. The woman frustrates the man because he unconsciously wants to be frustrated; the two are well matched! Nevertheless the man may have bouts of anger and aggression and threaten to find another woman but he rarely actually tries. Unlike many other problem relationships, the woman with vaginismus seldom seems to contemplate trying herself out with another man.

Vaginismus then seems to arise in two forms. In the first, the woman, usually young and inexperienced goes for treatment early on, and these cases are usually easily cured. In the other, the couple have been together for years and usually only ask for treatment when they want a baby – or even later in life for some other reason. Such cases, contrary to what is claimed in most sex books, are usually not easy to cure and failure is common.

It is difficult to escape the conclusion that both vaginismus and a lack of genital sensations fit into a spectrum of female sexual disorders in just the same way as male sexual problems can be seen as a spectrum. The spectrum is not so clearcut in women because they can have intercourse under psychological circumstances which would disable a man and prevent him from performing. One end of the spectrum shows in women who avoid men, and who are latent or declared lesbians (although most lesbians have had some experience of heterosexual intercourse, unlike most homosexual men). Next, are those women who are apparently willing but who lack desire and those who have difficulty in arousal. Closely related to these are women with vaginismus who want but cannot accept intercourse and women who have intercourse but with no sensation. These last can be thought of as extreme examples of those women who have sensations but cannot reach orgasm.

The causes of the disorders of sensation are the same as those causing disorders of desire, arousal and orgasm. Why one woman should, for example, have vaginismus and another fail to reach orgasm is not known but obviously a woman who unconsciously perceives a penis as being a desired but prohibited paternal one might be more likely to have vaginismus whereas another who was smacked for masturbating as a child might be more likely to have difficulties with orgasm. Again, a woman who cannot fully accept her female role may be more likely to develop vaginismus whereas one who has a fear of men, perhaps because of an awful father, may be more likely to become a lesbian. Probably, things such as the actual nature of adverse experiences, their intensitity, the personality of the woman and her position in the family also affect the final outcome.

What can we do about it?

If vaginismus is secondary perhaps as a result of a painful genital condition then medical assistance must be sought. If loss of sensation is secondary, for example, after childbirth then a gynaecological examination and perhaps even treatment will be necessary.

If vaginismus is the problem, and especially if it has been allowed to persist for some time, then an assessment of the situation is required in the light of what is said here. If the man's cooperation is being used unconsciously to maintain the situation then recognizing this and both partners altering their attitudes is the only possible way forward. Changes in the man are as necessary as changes in the woman. Many partners of women with vaginismus of the long-established type will not accept this viewpoint and this is the reason why treatment of long-established cases of non-consummation so often fails.

With cooperation and insightful discussion between the couple it may be possible for them to come to intelligent and sensible conclusions about the deep underlying causes for the woman's avoidance of penetration. For example, the woman's experiences of sex as a child; her relationship with her mother and father; her hearing or seeing her parents having intercourse; her early fantasies about how children are born; her first factual information about intercourse and her reactions to it, especially about any mention of pain and bleeding; her sexual fantasies; how she masturbates and so on may all provide clues. Sometimes such memories are not available to conscious recall but nevertheless their existence can often be deduced from other evidence.

In all sexual problems in both men and women, a sympathetic and interested partner using their knowledge of the other and using their intelligence can elicit, listen to and attempt to evaluate evidence of this kind. In the case of long-established vaginismus both partners need to help each other in this way.

The next step is for them both to try to establish normal psychosexual development in the woman. Most girls begin to incorporate the vagina into both fantasy and masturbation in mid-adolescence. The woman with vaginismus has failed to do so because of the sort of influences which affected her in earlier life. Such a woman must try to fantasize scenes of penetration, trying to see it as exciting rather than frightening, during masturbation and then try to insert one and then

two fingers into her vagina intermittently during masturbation. The fingers should be rotated within the vagina rather than being thrust in and out. Women with vaginismus experience thrusting movements within the vagina not as arousing but as frightening and it is this thought that brings on the muscle spasms.

Education helps here. Looking at her vulva and the entrance to the vagina in a mirror is a good start. Realizing the actual dimensions of the vagina, as shown on page 29, helps as does the thought that the vagina is so constructed as to allow the passage of a baby's head. Seeing so-called 'pornographic' films in which actual penetration and thrusting are visible is an enormous help to some women. Thinking of the pleasures of penetration, of the pleasure the vagina gives the penis and about their partner reaching orgasm and ejaculating within the vagina can all add an incentive to get better.

Some women can make quicker progress using dilators (special cylindrical tubes made of tough glass or other material) of increasing size to learn to accept penetration whereas others can manage best with their partner's fingers or a vibrator. Most vibrators have a tapered end which some women find useful. Whatever method is used eventually the woman must learn to insert her own fingers. When this has been achieved then intercourse, attempts at which should have been abandoned at the outset, can be resumed with the woman in the 'on-top' position so she has total control over the depth of penetration. Some women at this stage find the doggy position best.

If the woman prefers to learn to accept penetration with the help of her partner's fingers initially he has the opportunity to teach her voluntary control over her vaginal muscles. The spasm of vaginismus, is of course, involuntary, but learning voluntary control of the pelvic muscles helps to beat this tendency for spasm. (See page 36 for a description of pelvic muscle exercises.) After sufficient foreplay to get her to lubricate, and using KY jelly as well if necessary, he has to persuade her to open her legs wide and approach her so carefully and gently that any tendency to close her thighs is overcome. After separating the inner lips, he very gently begins to introduce the tip of his index finger. As the muscle goes into spasm, which he can feel, he stops moving his finger until she relaxes. The women then contracts her vaginal muscles voluntarily as hard as she can and, after a while, relaxes them. As she relaxes, the tip of the man's finger can be advanced again. The tip of the finger is then rotated round the vaginal entrance very gently at first, and then more firmly. By a combination of repeatedly advancing the finger, stopping, getting the woman to contract her vaginal muscles and relaxing them and rotating the finger the aim is to overcome the fear and encourage the woman to discover the pleasure of stimulation of her vaginal opening. Once this is achieved there can be rapid progress.

Where, as a result of many previous failed attempts at intercourse, a bad scene has been established, the woman's vaginismus may have become a conditioned response to any attempt at penetration. In this case desensitization techniques can be used. Further attempts at penetration are abandoned and instead the woman relaxes, perhaps using self-hypnosis and fantasizes in stages. At first she concentrates perhaps, on a fantasy of lying naked in the normal female intercourse position with her legs wide apart and her partner being nearby but clothed. When this fantasy is acceptable and causes no alarm the next stage may be to fantazize him being there naked. After this the next fantasy may be of him erect, followed by fantasies of him approaching her leading on finally to fantasies of penetration. Each stage of this should be done while having an orgasm by self-masturbation as this reinforces the pleasure of the fantasy. Then the woman starts on the penetration exercises outlined above.

What can anyone else do?

A doctor can prescribe tablets to relieve anxiety and help with relaxation. A gynaecologist may advise an examination under an anaesthetic. After being anaesthetized the vagina is fully explored and the findings reported to the woman when she comes round. If not carefully reported, an examination often puts the partner, who may actually be the culprit, in the 'right' by saying that since her vagina will accommodate the gynaecologist's whole hand, she is obviously totally to blame for the problem.

If the couple cannot produce the calmness, determination and firmness necessary for success, a sex therapist may be required. A behaviourist or suitably trained hypnotherapist can help if the woman has become terrified of penetration and is unable to practise desensitization. A psychosexual therapist or analytically orientated therapist is required if none of this works and the original cause is deeply embedded.

A stage in the treatment of a woman with vaginismus. Her fantasy is now of being naked close to a man

Oral Sex

Some general tips for both sexes

Using the mouth on your lover's body is a normal part of natural love-making. Most couples enjoy kissing but many never go beyond that. Here are some nice things to do all over the body:

◆ Run your lips over various parts of your lover's body to find where it feels best

◆ Do the same thing with your lips slightly apart and run your tongue into various knooks and crannies. Be careful not to tickle. The boundary between tickling and pleasure can be very fine

◆ Actually lick your partner's skin . . . not just breasts and other obvious erogenous areas. Try places you've never tried before

◆ Apply gentle suction to your partner's ear lobes; finger tips; toes; nipples and so on. This can follow on to nibbles and bites but be careful not to hurt

◆. Blow gently into various places (not the vagina) and see what feels good

When it comes to oro-genital contact a few general things are worth remembering:

◆ Never bite the sex organs however playfully . . . in the heat of the moment it's very easy to get carried away and hurt

◆ Always be scrupulously clean. Wash your genitals every day and especially just before you are going to make love. It's fun to bathe together and you can make washing each other a part of foreplay

◆ Agree rules beforehand, especially when it comes to whether the woman is going to 'deep throat' her partner and whether or not she's going to swallow the semen. A sudden thrust of a penis deep inside a woman's throat is not only bad sexual etiquette but can be very dangerous

◆ Never blow down the genitals . . . it can actually kill a woman by forcing air into her uterus

◆ Don't indulge in oral sex if you have cold sores

How to do it

Man to woman (Cunnilingus)

● The considerate woman who likes this will always keep her pubic hair neatly trimmed so that it's nice for her man

● Get into a comfortable position in which both of you are quite relaxed

● Make sure that the man's head isn't angled awkwardly so that he gets a neck-ache

● Perhaps put a pillow under the woman's bottom to raise her vulva and make genital contact easier for the man

● Spend plenty of time caressing her before you start on the vulval area

● Start by nuzzling into the vulva and then start to kiss the hair and all around the edge of the hair area

● Then kiss the large lips and run your tongue along the length of the large lips

● Suck the small lips gently

● Lick the area around the vagina and the area immediately beneath it

● Poke your tongue into her vagina and push it in and out

● Kiss and lick all around the clitoris taking care to go gently on the tip itself as this can be exquisitely sensitive for many women

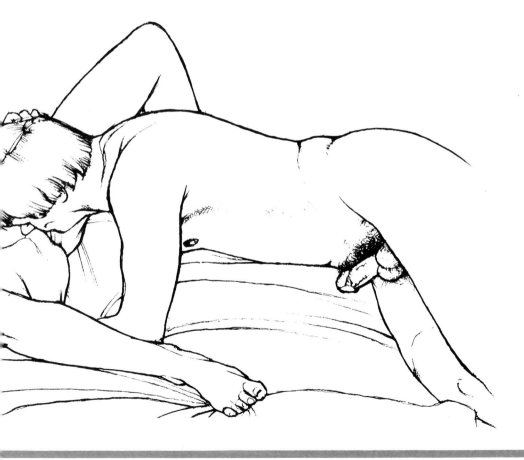

● As she gets more aroused put a couple of fingers into the vagina but keep on caressing her clitoris with your tongue (a few women prefer a vibrator to fingers)

● Stop from time to time to tease her and then re-start

● Always use plenty of saliva to lubricate the area otherwise things can get sore

● Be guided by the woman herself as to what she wants done and do it

Woman to man (Fellatio)

◆ The thoughtful man always keeps his penis scrupulously clean especially under the foreskin if his partner enjoys oral sex

◆ Agree whether the sex play is to end in oral intercourse or is being used as a form of foreplay (most couples will know about this without having to ask)

◆ When approaching the penis be careful not to bend it too far down towards the legs as this can be painful

◆ Stroke or lightly scratch the scrotum – perhaps stretching it a little to do so. Do not hurt the testes in the process unless the man likes this in which case they can be gently pulled downwards and squeezed

◆ Get into a comfortable position in which you won't get tired easily

◆ Keep your teeth well out of the way all the time

◆ Run your tongue up and down the shaft of the penis

◆ With the penis tip in your mouth continually circle it with your tongue clockwise and then anti-clockwise ensuring that the tongue is in contact with the penis head all the time

◆ Expand this last measure to include sliding the penis head in and out at the same time

◆ Hold and stimulate the scrotum and testes if he likes that

◆ Never have your hands idle . . . ensure that they are giving him pleasure somewhere all the time

◆ Swallow semen if you want to, it's perfectly harmless to do so but if you don't, spit it out into a paper hanky discretely

◆ Take the penis into the palm of your hand and moisten the head with saliva

◆ Put the head of the penis into your mouth and insert it as deeply as you feel comfortable with

◆ Move your mouth up and down so that the penis moves in and out of your mouth using some suction

◆ Take the penis out of the mouth and lick the top as if it were an ice cream

◆ Stimulate the tip of the penis with the tip of your tongue

◆ Gently flick the vertical ridge of tissue that runs from the horizontal rim on the underside of the penis

Is how a couple hold hands an indicator of their emotional and sexual relationship? It can be. The woman above is allowing her hand to be held as if it were a favour to her man. She is saying 'I might'. Below: They are truly holding hands, clasping each other gently as equal partners. She is saying 'I will'.

EMOTIONS & HOW TO DEAL WITH THEM

Sex is a very emotional and emotive subject. Most people have opinions about it and many people have very strongly held views which bring them into conflict with either themselves or others throughout their lives.

Sex also produces very powerful *feelings* in ourselves and others, the effects of which can be good or bad. Because we are brought up in a basically sex-negative culture we tend to start off our permanent relationship in life with plenty of negative feelings: guilt, fears, myths, shames, jealousies and so on. Certainly the initial romantic glow is a positive emotion but for most couples this is relatively short-lived and the reality of the other emotions gradually takes over.

To many, and especially to women, the word 'emotion' when linked with sex usually conjures up ideas of romance and love but this isn't necessarily so for most people for most of their lives. The biological urge to have intercourse has little or nothing to do with romance though we have conditioned ourselves into believing it has. For countless millions of people, both throughout history and around the world today, marriage is a cultural bond that has more to do with kinship, property, power and procreation than romance. The concept of romance being linked to or being necessary for marriage is very recent in human terms, dating back to 17th century Arabic culture.

Most people see sex as a natural part of the man-woman relationship that ensures the continuance of the human race. It is a recent and to a great extent artificial prerequisite that those who marry should feel romantically attached or 'in love' and it is arguable that it has done a lot of harm. Nevertheless, romantic love is now seen by most people as essential and a sign that the relationship is 'real' and flourishing. Happy individuals of both sexes often say that romantic love is more important to them than is sexual love. This can all too easily run the risk of drowning the other requirement for a really good relationship, namely, that the couple be true friends. Anyone can act romantically but only selfless and loyal friendship will stand the test of time. Perhaps romance is best thought of as an emotional dressing-up game. This makes it a valued asset rather than potentially dangerous, and more likely to remain a part of even a very long standing marriage.

Perhaps the greatest harm is that girls in our culture are brought up to think feelings of sexual arousal are unacceptable and have to find some kind of justification for indulgence so that they and, hopefully, society will sanction their behaviour. They thus exaggerate their feelings of love in order to accept the genital component of the relationship. 'They're so in love' seems to be a catch-all phrase that excuses the most inappropriate and ridiculous behaviour in two young people who simply want sex and a feeling of closeness and friendship. Our culture forces youngsters to protest their love when often none is present. This in itself debases the whole notion of love.

How much more valuable and sensible the whole thing would be if we could just accept that the young want to learn about being in love and enjoying sex just like everybody else. It would also help if we discouraged them from making emotional excuses for what are, after all, perfectly naturally biological urges.

Of course sex is a very powerful area of our lives and emotions run high. As a result the potential for emotional damage is great at any age but especially in the young who may not yet be emotionally mature or able to cope with the surges of feelings that are involved. Some adults too never really learn to handle sexual emotions and never come to terms with them.

Children and parents

But sex and emotion are linked from the very earliest days in the cradle – they don't just come together in our teens. Because our culture finds the subject embarrassing and even shameful, parents start to react emotionally to their child's sexuality from the very first few weeks of their lives. Not surprisingly their children soon pick up these unconscious and unspoken emotions and build them into their behaviour. Very few parents are totally at ease with their 2 year old child playing with his or her genitals and most, even today, still

make some kind of negative response or even smack their child for such sexual interest.

As children grow, games of doctors and nurses, mummies and daddies, hospitals and so on all give them a chance to explore each other's bodies but by this stage they have already been made to feel guilty about their bodies and they're only 2 or 3 years old! Nudity is taboo in many households, lavatory doors are kept locked, genitals and sex are never mentioned, sex questions are answered guiltily, hastily, falsely or not at all and so on.

All of this makes children very puzzled because it appears to them that sex and everything to do with it has definite emotional overtones. Sex, they can sense, is something about which Mummy and Daddy have intense *feelings* which they don't have when discussing the greenhouse, for example.

So it is that girls especially, modify their behaviour so as to cause the minimum of emotional hassle both for themselves and their parents.

A vital part of this story of early emotions is the implicit sexlessness of parents and especially mothers. Most girls, if asked, say that their mothers don't have sex and certainly don't masturbate. Some parents are never demonstrative or affectionate in front of their children and mothers can seldom discuss sex with their children in a personal way. Even if the children know about the 'facts of life' they tend to assume that their parents did such things just to have them and certainly wouldn't be doing them now just for pleasure.

Growing up

Too often, a fear of the opposite sex, no

matter how unconscious, can be learned early in life from indifferent or hostile parents or brothers and sisters of the opposite sex. Quite often a dominant, critical and punitive mother who wants (unconsciously) to take revenge on the male sex generally for distress suffered at the hands of men brings up a son in such a way that he is afraid of women. His male self-esteem may be weak but he may later over-compensate by being a bully, especially of women who depend on him and criticize him. The woman may even have been attracted to him in the first place by his apparent 'masculinity' without realizing that it was really a disguise for his weak male ego. Unfortunately, by the time she finds out the truth the marriage is often on the rocks. Such a man dare not give in to a woman because in doing so he sees himself returning to his childhood and being submissive to his mother. Such men often batter their wives.

But not every inadequate man need end up battering his wife. Many do very well if their wives understand the situation. A helpful wife will boost her husband's confidence and build him up at every opportunity, so undoing the damage his mother did. Within the intimacy of a good relationship a man can be freed of his previous disability with the understanding and loving care of his wife. Often, such men intuitively seem to seek out a partner who will do this for them or, at least, be a kind mother.

From this rather dramatic (but not uncommon) example we can draw a general principle which seems to hold good for marriage in general; that is that a couple should do everything they can to boost each other's ego (self-esteem) and never do anything that attacks the other's per-

sonality. Marriages are made between personalities and if they are attacked there may be nothing left. This works both ways, of course, with the wife constantly building up her husband and vice versa. It involves a gracious acceptance that one partner is better at some things and the other better at others. Each therefore feels strong and secure in certain areas of the marriage and can 'afford' to be weak in others.

Negative emotions and rows

We mentioned rows earlier as an example of a hidden sexual problem. A woman might say that her husband refuses to row with her, she cannot clear the air and so becomes frustatingly bottled-up. There are certainly many men who dislike rows with a woman – possibly because women, thanks to their superior verbal skills, so often win. Additionally or alternatively, a cross woman may re-activate childhood fears of an angry mother and so make him feel small. As a consequence he may side-step and denounce the woman's problem as being silly.

In such rows the woman, because she feels hurt or neglected, may say more wounding things than she really feels simply to provoke a serious response from her husband. Such over-dramatizing of the argument wouldn't be necessary if men were more sensitive to their wives' needs and feelings at an earlier stage and in a good marriage things should never get this far – but they often do.

Sometimes behaviour like this is produced by premenstrual tension. A wise husband keeps a note on the family calendar of his wife's premenstrual days and makes and extra effort to be caring and supersensitive at this time. Premenstrual symptoms can now often be treated, so it is worth seeking medical help.

Many men sulk, mooch around the house or go out to escape when a row is in the air. This does nothing to help the situation because the woman still feels scorned, overlooked, unloved, treated as worthless or whatever sparked off the row in the first place. She needs loving care and understanding but her husband, by behaving like a small boy, cannot provide it. The underlying problem is not resolved and emotional tension results. The next time a problem arises the couple, already on a plateau of tension, spark each other off more readily and open hostility may then become the norm.

This is exactly why rows are so troublesome in so many relationships. Both partners have regressed to childhood . . . the woman sees something wrong she wants put right for her and the man sees an unfair and hostile mother. Neither can help the other and the whole situation deteriorates. In those cases where the man starts the row, often as a result of sexual resentment against the woman which he doesn't bring into the open, it is the injustice of his initial attack on her which makes her feel scorned or even rejected. It is this injustice that she wants righting that leads her to fight back. Just as with rowing children, it's often essential to have an adult to come into the picture to settle things. This means that if the row is to be settled one partner must become an adult again. At this point the views of the other can be considered dispassionately and thereby acknowledged. Loving behaviour and soothing words may then calm the partner, as will promises of justice and recompense. It's at this stage that other adult behaviour, such

as intercourse, can help smooth things over. True friends can row easily but soon make up again. For some rules on how to keep your communications working at the adult level, see page 183.

Positive emotions and sex

The ability to behave normally and naturally in the presence of a sexual partner and to be able to value the opposite sex are signs of full emotional maturity, yet when judged this way few people are fully mature in our society. Many adults harbour child-like notions of the opposite sex, and others treat their partner as a child never allowing their sexual adult roles to dominate the proceedings. But what do we mean by maturity in this context?

A mature person is one who is reasonably independent, but not excessively so; is capable of giving and receiving emotionally as well as in other ways; is free from undue agression; is a productive member of society; is largely free from childhood feelings of inadequacy, self-centredness and inferiority; can tolerate frustration for a reasonable period of time; is flexible and adaptable; and is capable of dealing with individuals as individuals and not as belonging to a stereotype.

There are also sexual aspects of maturity. These include such things as relative freedom from oedipal influences, freedom from undue anxiety about sex, acceptance of one's own sex role and its pleasures and the acceptance of the genitals, role and sexuality of the opposite sex.

The translation of an interest in the genitals of the opposite sex from a pornographic one to an intelligent one is a

Scene from 'Last Tango in Paris': the total acceptance of each other is fundamental to good loving

real sign of sexual maturity. Not long ago the idea of topless bathing and scantily clad women being judged in bathing costumes was as outrageous as the suggestion of a 'pretty vulva' or 'sexiest penis' contest would be today but both show a perfectly innocent and natural interest in and acceptance of sexual anatomy.

Shedding all one's cultural inhibitions about sex when alone with one's partner is a vital part of being sexually mature. This is the foundation for positive emotions about sex which can be shared with another human being. It naturally leads to a situation in which nothing one does or thinks of doing with one's partner should be considered 'rude' or unacceptable in itself.

An example of this is the sharing of erotic fantasies within a relationship. See page 245.

Having and showing a delight in each other's sexuality is also a sign of sexual maturity. Most women are delighted by the effect that their bodies have on their men and most complain that their men are too unadventurous. On the other side of the coin are the women who feel their man must have gone off them because they have been together for so long that he has seen it all many times before. Clinical experience suggests that this is often not true. Men married 30 years or more say that their wives' bodies still excite them as much as they ever did, wrinkles and all, so whatever women think, *their* man usually still finds them a source of sexual delight as the years go by. The value of her body *to him* is thus undiminished with the passing years. Men often tease women about their bodies in an adolescent way but this is silly and gives them the wrong impression.

Another dimension of sexual maturity is an ability to use sex for it's own pleasures and not to serve some other purpose. A simple example is people who masturbate when faced with a problem instead of trying to solve it. Women and adolescent girls can misuse sex to gain attention and, perhaps, love rather than for sexual pleasure. A man with a weak ego who feels he has been *bested* in some respect important to him by other men may have to have a woman urgently to restore his self-esteem. All this is a misuse of sex.

Coming to terms with other members of the opposite sex is also a vital part of being sexually mature. In our culture the aim is to be monogamous (have one partner) for life yet other members of the opposite sex still exist and won't go away.

It's easy to see that a sexually mature person will spend a lot less time and energy being emotional about sex because the whole subject will be much less highly charged than is normally the case.

Such people accept their own sexuality, revel in it and in that of their partner; enjoy everything about their body and that of their partner and feel sufficiently mature and confident to reveal anything and everything about themselves to their partner yet still retain their own individuality. Such people weather life's sexual storms well; are not easily threatened with feelings of jealousy, guilt, inferiority or fear because their relationship is so strongly founded that it can cope with the reality of other people's sexuality in the world outside them.

But such maturity and positive attitudes to sex are, unfortunately, rare in our society. Negative attitudes are more common and result in the casualties of relationships that we see all around us. Thankfully, many of these negative attitudes and emotions can be changed as we shall now see.

Negative emotions and sex

As pointed out above negative emotions about sex are probably the commonest source of problems. The trouble is that most of our sexual attitudes and beliefs exist in our unconscious minds and aren't directly accessible to us. They emerge as thoughts that impair action and pleasure. An example is an uneasy feeling that masturbation might injure your health. The problem in sexual matters isn't *doing* but *enjoying*. Even seemingly inhibited people who will *do* anything often have a shallow sexuality. What they do not do is to get much pleasure from their pursuits. Their block on receiving pleasure comes mainly from negative cultural attitudes and notions about sex which produce harmful barriers to sexual fulfilment of which he or she is unaware at the conscious level.

But wherever they come from our fears, guilts and sexual myths are not necessarily permanent – they can be changed and this gives hope for the future in any individual or couple's life. Detecting and changing negative emotions about sex is never easy though because the barriers have been built into our personalities over the first 20 years of our lives and untying these old knots is very difficult.

A practical and effective way of un-learning harmful thoughts that reduce your pleasure is called *thought stopping*. Put simply it works by uncoupling a negative thought from your thought pro-cesses and substituting instead a positive, enjoyable one. Why it works is not under-stood but it's probably because our brains can only cope with one emotion at a time and because one emotion can flood out another. It is well known that a fairly serious injury sustained during a sport can go unnoticed during the game only to be complained of when the final whistle blows. So it is with emotions. Love crowds out hate. Laughter inhibits sadness and sexually pleasant feelings can crowd out guilt and fear.

So what do you do? The moment a negative thought comes into your head that makes you feel anxious, fearful or guilty about anything sexual ('What would my mother say?' 'This feels so good it must be wrong' 'I really shouldn't be doing this at all') shout 'STOP' loudly and crash your hand down on something. Quickly replace the thought with another one that pleases and excites you.

Obviously you'll need to get ready a shortlist of thoughts that are good replace-ments and after a very few private practice runs you can leave out the shouting and the hand banging and simply 'shout' stop inwardly to yourself. Like all behaviour modification it takes practice and is a form of conditioning. Your list of lovely thoughts can be anything at all and need have nothing whatsoever to do with sex. Whatever you choose the thoughts will, by definition, be extremely good for *you*. They might be a walk in your rose garden; having your first novel published; flying a micro-lite aircraft; winning at Wimble-don; in short, anything that would make you blissfully happy.

Practice thought stopping 8 or 10 times a day and do it whenever any negative thought enters your mind. Gradually over a week or two many of your negative thoughts will occur less frequently and you'll be quite capable of flooding them out when they do occur. This is especially true if you have explored the *reasons* you have such negative thoughts, especially with the help of a trained professional or an intelligently interested partner.

But thought stopping may not be enough on its own because so often nega-tive emotions about sex are tied to a person, often one's parents or other au-thority figures. A useful technique in such cases is called *silent ridicule*. What you do is to conjure up a mental picture of the person doing something quite ridiculous so that he or she no longer appears to be on a pedestal to you. People use the most amazing mental techniques in this game and often have their ridiculed figure dressed in outrageous clothes (for exam-ple, a Walt Disney character outfit) while being humiliated in some way. Coupled with this you can try to imagine very weird

conversations with the person – dialogues which put them down – not unkindly but firmly. For those who bring their mothers (or less commonly their fathers) to the marriage bed this kind of mental game can greatly help in combatting negative influences on the situation. The success of these two techniques depends on being able to call up the ridiculing scene or conversation whenever the authoritative figure comes unwanted into your mind and spoils your pleasure.

Of all the sexually negative emotions guilt, anxiety, feelings of inferiority and jealousy are the most important and the commonest so let's look at each in turn.

Guilt about sex

There are few pleasures in life over which people feel more guilty than sex. The capacity to experience guilt appears to be an inborn characteristic which is said to be peculiarly human. The sense of guilt is even there sometimes *before* the offence – committing the offence simply provides something for the guilt to latch on to!

Our first experience of guilt is probably in the early stages when as a baby we first become aware of our own hostile feelings. These feelings together with parental injunctions in childhood help decide what sorts of things can produce a sense of guilt later in life. It is really a form of aggression turned against one's self.

Defined simply guilt is a feeling that you shouldn't be doing something, or that having done it you deserve punishment. There is usually at least some element of pleasure or gratification in the action that is producing the guilt. Of all the negative

A man anxious about sex, ignored by his partner . . . Is it surprising that he retreates to the television and food?

sexual emotions guilt is by far the commonest and to many it feels a real and almost essential part of them. Some people say that their guilt actually seems to be protective, both to themselves and to society. 'After all, if I didn't feel any guilt about sex I'd be dashing around having sex with everyone I fancied'. Such people argue that sexual guilt must be natural in some way – Nature's way of restraining us from behaving like sex maniacs. However, not all cultures instill guilt about sex.

The real problem with guilt is that it can harm a sexual relationship for no beneficial reason. It is just a continuation of childhood prohibitions which can only be broken at the expense of feeling guilty. For example, guilt places a plate glass barrier between some people and their feelings. They worry because they do quite normal things such as masturbate or have sexy dreams and fantasies. They feel bad and so cannot do the things they want to do.

Really exciting and relaxing sex involves an ability to lose oneself entirely in what's going on, to be natural and to be free of adverse influences. The couple with a good relationship can and does run their

life like this and guilt doesn't get much of a look in. Nothing they do together makes them feel bad or guilty and they feel free to ask anything of their partner.

All of this might sound like a fairy tale to some readers but if it does they should read on; sex without passion, sex without love, sex without abandon becomes more like copulation which is, to put it crudely —scarcely one up on what animals do. We could and should do better.

Masturbation

Masturbation is probably the commonest source of sexual guilt and few people come to adult life *not* feeling guilty about it – at least to some extent. Such guilt can produce a 'real' sex problem – such as premature ejaculation (see also page 98).

But nobody 'knows' that masturbation is 'wrong' the day they are born. Given that this is so, guilt can be unlearned by reversing some of the processes that caused it.

The first stage used in helping people to unlearn guilt is to put the cultural attitudes of our society into perspective in the light of what the rest of humanity does. Some people imagine that our western ideas about sexuality are universally held to be true and are surprised that other human cultures think so differently on the subject. This often makes them ask themselves questions about *why* they should feel guilty about something that other cultures take as normal. Just knowing that there is no pre-set collection of rules about sex that governs mankind in some inexplicable way defuses the situation greatly and

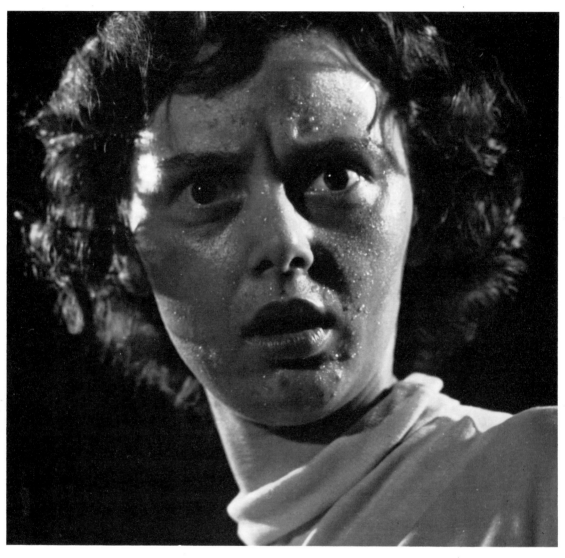

10 on the guilt and anxiety scale

allows the second stage of guilt unlearning to proceed.

Perhaps the most important thing to bear in mind about unlearning sexual guilt is that you don't have to become someone else or take on a new way of life in order to do it. You neither have to become promiscuous nor chaste to lose your feelings

of sexual guilt. You still remain yourself. Obviously it helps enormously to talk over your guilt with a trained professional but here's a good exercise to do either alone or as well as this. It is called *graduated calming* and reduces negative feelings in small steps.

Graduated calming (desensitization) is a type of behaviour therapy that, like thought stopping, can help unlearn sexual guilt. It is based on the common sense principle that negative feelings such as guilt and fear cancel out positive feelings such as love and relaxation. It's also more difficult to feel guilty if you are very relaxed or very sexual.

Here's how to do it. Start by re-learning or practising your thought stopping. Then, starting with a pleasant state of mind – being relaxed or erotically aroused – bring to mind a scene that makes you feel guilty. Then switch out of that back to your pleasant state. The next stage is to break down your guilty thoughts or action into a series of small steps so that you can learn to cope with the guilty scene little by little.

When it comes to sexual guilt it is useful to work out a scale of guilt for yourself so that you become aware of the physical and emotional sensations that you associate with guilt-provoking thoughts and actions. Only by doing this will you be sure

---

0   *Total relaxation. No guilt*

1–2 *Mild guilt, Not very noticeable*

3–5 *Moderate guilt. Definite feelings of being uneasy. Beginnings of tension headache; 'butterfly' feelings in the stomach. Muscle tension*

6–7 *High level of guilt. Heart pounding. Head or stomach aches. Real distress and discomfort*

8–9 *Intense, severe guilt, approaching panic. Something you want to avoid at all costs*

10 *Panic. Emotional chaos. The worst guilt you can imagine*

---

you are losing your guilt.

Dr Debora Phillips, a renowned psychosexual practitioner in the US, uses the table below, as a basis for guiding her patients in their guilt assessment.

Once you can recognize the effects guilt is having on you you'll be able to stop once things get unpleasant and go back a stage (see below) until you feel at ease with yourself.

The next thing to do is to make out a list of things on a guilt scale that apply to your particular problem. Remember that by 'your' problem we mean a problem that either of you has. After all, if your partner has a sex problem, it is is yours too.

Let's take oral sex as an example. Although there are many reasons for a woman disliking the idea of fellating a man such as, for example, thinking of semen as excretion or feeling guilty about doing anything so intimate to an organ they have been brought up to think of as not being of interest to a 'nice' lady. This can be a fraught issue in either sex but let's look at the woman for a moment. Many a woman knows that her partner would like her to perform oral sex on him and she'd like to be able to do it both for her sake and his but just *can't* bring herself to because it makes her feel revolted and guilty. She knows that this is the sort of thing whores do and whilst she'd like to do it to please her man she certainly isn't going to 'behave like a tart'. Let's look at a list of guilt-provoking thoughts that such a woman might draw up for herself.

1   Touching my own vagina and my husband's semen

2   Feeling dirty if semen leaks out after sex onto my thighs or onto the bed

3 Semen on my abdomen making me feel dirty

4 Kissing my husband's penis in the dark

5 Taking the head of his penis in my mouth

6 Running my tongue up and down his penis

7 Kissing his scrotum

8 Taking his whole penis in my mouth and moving it in and out

9 Doing all the above in the light so that he can see me doing it

10 My mother knowing I was doing this.

Let's see how this list of increasingly guilt-producing things can be overcome little by little, stage by stage so that this woman can eventually feel fairly happy about oral sex. The basis of this desensitization is that although the end points (9 and 10) are extremely guilt-producing Point 1 isn't too daunting and is a starting point with which it is possible to cope.

First get some hand or baby lotion and after a nice warm bath spread some over your thighs and tummy. Concentrate on the slippery feeling and massage it into your skin. Smell and enjoy the pleasant feelings and odour. Think of something sexy or read an erotic book. Build up your level of sexual arousal so that guilty feelings don't arise and use your thought-stopping whenever you need to. Sex involves both partners producing fluids when they are excited. Both have characteristic, but not at all unpleasant smells. Once you are totally happy with this

sensation, masturbate if you want to dipping your fingers into your vagina and smelling your natural secretions. Once you can do this with ease you are ready for the next step.

When you next make love and are really turned on allow your partner's semen to leak out of your vagina a little and massage this into the skin at the top of your thighs just as you did with the cream. When you are happy with this stage go onto the next.

Get each other really aroused and then when your partner is about to ejaculate ask him to (or just push him into position so that he can) come over your tummy. Either let him or you yourself massage the semen into your skin. You can wipe it off with a tissue once you've done it for a while.

If any of this makes you feel guilty or revolted stop it and go back to a stage until you feel completely relaxed and have none of the signs of guilt that you listed in your guilt symptoms list. This might take several weeks.

Continue down the list item by item until under very strong sexual arousal you can go right to item 9 without feeling bad. By this stage No 10 won't bother you any more because you'll be so enjoying 1–9 you couldn't care less what your mother would think. The day you stop wondering what your mother would think is the end of your problem.

The secret of success is to break down your main guilt-producing activity into 10 small items, each of which can easily be handled at one or two learning sessions. When constructing your list it's easy to start off and easy to put in 1 and 10, so do these first and fill in the others so that each one is just a little bit more guilt-provoking.

When it comes to putting the list into

practice, as soon as you feel at all bad, go back a stage and increase your comfort or level of erotic sensations and try again, perhaps another day. Your good feelings will flood out the 'dirty' ones and you'll slowly but surely go up the scale. Never try to do more than one item per session or you could lay a trap for yourself by being too ambitious and fail miserably in your own eyes. Only when you are totally at ease with any one stage and feel that it is a natural part of your life should you go on to the next. The only rule is that pleasure beats guilt at the end of each session.

Some men also have problems in performing oral sex on a woman. They should follow exactly the same technique. Of course we are not implying that oral sex is obligatory. Some people don't find it very exciting.

Anxiety and how to deal with it

This, like guilt, if present to any serious degree reduces sexual pleasure and reduces intercouse to mediocre copulation. But whereas guilt makes you feel bad (immoral, sinful, worthless, rude, like a whore, deserving punishment, and so on) anxiety produces more *physical* symptoms. Anxiety makes itself felt as a pounding heartbeat, muscle tension, panic, excessive sweating, a desire to urinate, a headache, an inability to lose oneself in the situation (extreme awareness of what's going on), jumpiness (an inability to relax) feelings of bursting and of nearly going mad, poor sexual arousal and several other symptoms which are specific to individuals and of which you'll probably be only too aware. Many sexually anxious women come out in rashes usually over the upper

chest, throat and face, for example. All of this makes sex a pretty joyless experience; the person feels numb, tense, experiences few sensations, remains silent and may even fake an orgasm to please her partner. Men can have parallel problems too.

Just as with guilts and fears anxieties too can be unlearned.

Perhaps the first to be unlearned are the stereotypes of the way men and women 'ought' to behave. Men are supposed to be always available and ready for action, ('show them a square inch of naked flesh and they're away') and women are supposed to be virginal and demure and lie back and enjoy it (or not!). Today, as people become more sexually honest, a lot of men are saying that they don't feel at all macho a lot of the time yet are anxious about it in case their woman thinks them odd or even homosexual. Women too are more likely to express their sexual desires but this in turn often makes them anxious in case their man thinks they're loose or vastly experienced. Cultural stereotypes and attitudes thus produce anxieties right from the start of a new relationship.

Many people are anxious about, or have some of the misunderstandings about sex discussed on pages 175 to 183. Factual anxieties are easily overcome with the help of a good book or a few words with a sexual counsellor or a doctor but other anxieties resulting from psychosexual imbalances or immaturity are much more difficult to unlearn and before they can be unlearned they have to be understood.

Some common fears and anxieties

1 *The fear of letting go* – of being totally open and vulnerable. This holding

back is probably the greatest enemy of enjoyable sex there is. Linked with this is

2 **_The fear that one might laugh_**, cry, shout, make a noise, look silly or un-attractive during an orgasm or even during foreplay. This leads many people to curtail their enjoyment of their orgasms in the interests of their dignity and appearance in front of their partner. Women can be encouraged to act (like an actress) how they imagine an abandoned woman would behave. After a few acting sessions with her partner many such women actually start to behave like this naturally much to the delight of their partner. There are few bigger turn-offs to a sex partner than making love with someone who appears unresponsive or critical. On the other hand for many people there are few greater turn-ons than a partner who moans, crys, sighs, expresses delight in all kinds of ways, squirms, wriggles or laughs, to name but a few. Men can be as inhibited as women about showing their animal selves.

3 **_The fear that undressed you'll look horrible_** have a fat tummy, show off your appendix scar, or appear disappointing to your lover. This works both ways round. Men commonly fear they have a poor physique or aren't hairy. Women usually worry about excessive body hair and small and flagging breasts.

If you are overweight then go on a diet. If you are flabby, take exercise regularly rather than retreating from your partner because you feel unacceptable. Lovers rarely scrutinize each other minutely and even quite major 'problems' such as birthmarks are overlooked during sexual excitement.

4 **_Genital fears_** are very common. 'My vagina will be too flabby after the baby'. 'My vulva is smelly and not much to look

at'. 'A woman's vagina can trap you'. 'My penis will be too small', 'I might not erect' and so on. The list is endless. Many of these fears have a factual or anatomical misunderstanding at their root as we have seen and pure factual information usually dispels them quickly. Having said this though pure factual knowledge is often *not* the total answer and the individual goes on having trouble until they *understand* the underlying problem – often psychosexual in nature.

5 **_Fear that you'll disappoint your partner_** This can occur either in the early days of a sexual relationship, when each is trying, at least to some extent, to impress the other, or in a long-term relationship when one may fear that he or she is not good enough, exciting enough, inventive enough or whatever. The answer to this one is to discuss with your partner what he or she most enjoys and by talk and trial and error to keep continually exploring and growing so that you have no fears at all about being a disappointment. Just a note of caution here though, not every sexual encounter, even between experienced couples goes off like a firework display every time. Most couples probably have super sex only once or twice in every 10 times they make love. The rest are passable encounters that they enjoy well enough. If you aim for the stars every time you're bound to be disappointed some of the time because it's relatively uncommon for both partners to feel especially relaxed, free from worries and tensions, not tired physically and so on. If sex is a disappointment for yourself or your partner more than half the time perhaps you should seek professional help but this is only a rough rule and some people aren't prepared to put up even with this much disappointment. Living as

we do in a society in which sex is ideally linked to love, many people fear that sexual disappointment will lead to (or be the product of) a loss of love. For such people even a single disappointing sexual encounter can be threatening to their love bond on the basis that 'Any woman who really loved me would have done X or not done Y'. Clearly linked to this are:

6 ***Performance (or lack of performance) fears*** These can be of a general or a specific nature. 'Will I last long enough?' 'Will I have an orgasm with his penis inside me?' 'Will I be as good as his/her other lovers?' 'Will he be upset if I rub my clitoris?' 'Will I know what to do to turn her on?' These are just a few examples of commonly experienced performance fears.

Many of these are unnecessary and unfounded and can be overcome with loving behaviour and encouragement. Experience together helps but more serious performance difficulties may need professional help to sort out.

7 ***Fears about acting out fantasies*** 'Will I look silly?' 'Will he think I'm a pervert?' 'Who'd want to make love to me dressed like this?' 'Will she leave me or stop loving me if I tell her what I really want to do?' We look at sharing fantasies on page 245.

8 ***Masturbation fears*** 'Surely he expects to be screwing me not masturbating me?' 'Will he expect me to stimulate him as I'm having a period?' 'Won't all this masturbation put him off making love?' 'Won't I get hooked on masturbation and not want sex at all?' None of these should be any problem in reality because men usually enjoy being masturbated and can be just as happy being relieved in this way as by having intercourse (at least in the short term) and women who masturbate a lot (or whose partners masturbate them) tend to have high intercourse rates.

9 ***What shall I say?*** Protestations of love (or lust) are all very well for those who like it but they aren't necessary. Some couples enjoy using crude language and even the most refined lady when sexually aroused may ask her man to 'fuck my cunt, you sexy bastard' or words to that effect. This is a great turn on for most men because it shows that she has reached a stage in her arousal that enables her to behave in an uninhibited, earthy way. No woman who is anxious about what her mother might think would ever say such a thing but she wouldn't be nearly as good in bed in other ways either.

If it gives a man a harder erection and enables him to penetrate his wife more deeply and enjoyably this surely must be in the interests of the couple's sex life. However, the need for talk can be a sign of inhibition, as already mentioned, and, if rational, can give offence to the partner who feels the talker is not as immersed in the pleasure as they should be if they were really enjoying it. Most people, if they utter any sound at all, make baby-like noises of pleasure.

10 ***Fear of the unknown and unfamiliar*** Most couples today are probably more sexually adventurous than were their grandparents but this brings not only pleasures but pains. The main negative emotion is fear or anxiety that what the individual wants to do (or is asked to do) might be dangerous, 'unnatural', painful, illegal, addictive (I might get so hooked on it that normal sex will never be the same again'), socially unacceptable ('what would people think if they knew I did *this*?'), noisy ('will the children hear?') etc.

This is a good anxiety to end with

because it highlights the real problem behind all sexual anxieties – the fact that the anxiety-producing situation or request from one's partner so reduces the quality of one's enjoyment that the whole love-making episode becomes unpleasurable as a result. The answer for sure is not to stop experimenting, talking while making love, expressing your emotions or whatever, but to unlearn your anxieties so that your love-making becomes free from anxiety. If any of the things we've mentioned make you anxious then it'll spoil sex for you at least to some extent and possibly even entirely.

But overcoming anxiety and fear needs motivation – you have to want to overcome it. Some people are so inhibited sexually that they lean on their fears as a justification for having sex rarely and with little pleasure. *Pleasure* makes these people anxious because they have been reared to think they are sinful or naughty for experiencing pleasure. Such complicated cases need careful professional treatment.

Let's assume though that you are one of the more usual group of those with a sexual anxiety and that you want to be rid of it because it spoils your pleasure or that of your partner. Here's what to do. The first, and most basic principle is:

If a thing makes you too anxious – stop doing it

This is the most important step because as long as you continue to make yourself anxious you'll dig yourself deeper into the pit you're already in. This applies particularly to performance anxieties which almost never improve unless you stop what you are doing and unlearn them systematically. Very often simply giving yourself permission *not* to do something, makes it all the easier to do it – strange though this may seem.

Gradually unlearn the anxiety-producing situation

This involves a step-by-step desensitization to the anxiety-producing thing just as we suggested for reducing guilt and it works in the same way. One big jump might well be impossible even to contemplate let alone achieve but several tiny steps can be worked on and the problem overcome over several weeks or months.

The first step is to relax and to remove all anxiety-producing situations surrounding your problem. Pleasure and relaxation reduce anxiety and even prevent it, so the secret of success is to be able to relax, to be sensual with your partner and to be able to fantasize about positive, helpful things so that whenever your step-by-step approach to your anxiety-producing behaviour produces symptoms you can let it go and fall back into your relaxed, sexually aroused state and leave it there until next time. Unfortunately, anxiety is such a powerful emotion and such a killer to pleasure that you'll need a lot more pleasure than you think in order to overcome even a small amount of anxiety. This might mean that you'll have to build up your pleasure-receiving abilities with your partner so that you really *can* enjoy yourself and relax. There are several ways of doing this that are discussed throughout the book.

Here is a 10 point scale of signs and symptoms you might experience:

0   *Completely relaxed. Not an anxious thought around*

1–2 *Slight anxiety. Not enough to worry about. Sweating a little. Wondering if you have to go through with it*

3–5 *Moderate anxiety. Feel uneasy. Moderate tension. Butterflies in the tummy*

6–7 *High level of anxiety. Heart pounding. Profuse sweating. Body shaking. Restless. Pains in head or stomach. Feel really distressed*

8–9 *Horrible anxiety. Want to run away*

10   *Total panic. The worst anxiety you can possibly imagine*

Now let's see how a man's anxiety over, say, being seen with no clothes on (making love with the lights on) can be overcome.

First get sexually aroused to a very high level. Read an erotic book, watch erotic videos or do things with your partner that turn you on but don't involve nudity. Then follow this gradual approach to being nude remembering to stop when any stage becomes too anxiety-producing and never do any of the items on the list above the one you are happy with. Completely ban all higher items on the list until you can confidently cope with the lower ones without any suggestion of anxiety.

This problem might seem odd for most men who are after all exhibitionists about their genitals, but because they were made ashamed of, or even punished, for showing their genitals in childhood it is an enormous problem for some men.

Here is a list that could be of help to such a man:

1   Lie on the bed clothed alongside your partner reading a sexy book or a girlie magazine showing a man naked with a woman

2   Lie in bed naked under the bedclothes with your partner with the lights off

3   Lie in bed naked under the bedclothes with your partner with the lights on

4   Lie in bed naked with your partner, no covers with lights off

5   Lie in bed naked with your partner, no covers with lights on

6   Undress in front of your partner with the lights on

7   Walk around naked in front of your partner

8   Encourage your partner to comment on your naked body

9   Ask your partner to take photographs of you naked

10   When all this has been achieved repeat the whole list but this time when you have an erection.

You'll probably find as you climb the list and are easily able to achieve more without feeling anxious that your masturbation or intercourse fantasies change too. Let your mind jump ahead on the scale and even encourage it to do so during masturbation but don't actually *do* the thing unless you've slowly and gradually worked up to it. One sexy dream about being seen naked and erect by a woman doesn't mean your fear of nudity is over – it almost certainly isn't but your unconscious mind is beginning to be freed and it won't be long before your conscious mind follows suit.

Take one sexual anxiety at a time and with the help of your partner overcome it in the way suggested. Soon, over a period of time, you'll have demolished most of your anxieties and will be able to enjoy sex better and give your partner more pleasure. If you come across a situation that produces so much anxiety that you can't even start on it, perhaps it would be sensible to seek professional help if it's bothering you or your partner that much.

There must be a point at any stage within a sexual relationship when one partner can say 'no' without loss of face, without feeling bad and without having to apologize.

We all have our 'final position' on any subject and are entitled to do so. The problem comes when the refused partner becomes so upset by the refusal that he or she starts to condemn the refuser as unloving or sexless and starts to look elsewhere for satisfaction of his or her needs. This need never happen in a caring relationship in which there's a genuine will to make each other happy. One solution is to look for ways around the problem in a practical sense.

Usually the answer is not to look at the refuser but at the refused. He or she often has a basic problem deep down in his or own psychosexual development that makes such a need seem very important. Clearing this ground and giving the person insights into the reasons for the needs can often reduce the value the person puts on the particular practice and takes the pressure off the situation to everyone's advantage. Of course, all of these things occur along a scale and no one would be at all harsh on a person who draws the line at anal sex for example.

Where any one couple draws the line varies enormously of course, and if they can't agree on where it should be drawn, the refused will often either give up sex, seek answers outside the relationship or the relationship will break up so allowing the couple to find others who are more suited to their needs and anxiety levels. We all try to function within the levels of what makes us anxious whatever we're doing, in our jobs, our choice of friends and so on. A couple who get married without having discussed and worked through their real sexualities together run the very considerable risk of discovering later that each has very different levels of sexual anxiety or that anxiety can be produced in one by things that the other very much wants.

The vast majority of these desires can be overcome, or accommodated in some other ways, perhaps with professional help, but sometimes the couple realize when undergoing sexual counselling or therapy that the gulf between them is so wide that there is in reality little hope. This sort of dilemma is one of the most important reasons for making courtship a time of totally honest and full declaration of one's sexual appetites, needs, desires and fantasies. Courtship is no time to fake

Alienating activity can destroy so much in a relationship that even the first step towards intercourse can leave either or both partners in despair, perhaps not knowing how to explain how they feel

How to Strip

There is one golden rule when it comes to men stripping: **Remove your socks early on in the procedings.**
Here's what to do:

● Prepare the background as outlined on page 340 for women (but skip the make-up!)

Strip tease for men

Men find stripping more difficult than do women. This is partly because women are more naturally exhibitionist and partly because men's clothes are less obviously sexy to look at so they look less sexy being removed. Having said this though some men can be really sexy when stripping.

● Start by removing your tie slowly and sexily. This can then be draped around your woman's neck or anywhere else you decide.

● Next undo your shirt buttons slowly from the top to expose your chest. Reveal one nipple at a time in a teasing way and then re-cover it.

● Remove your shirt but NOT over your head. Undo all the buttons and let it fall to the ground around you.

● Loosen your trousers at the waist and then remove your socks. If you leave taking off your socks until any later then this you'll end up looking like a Brian Rix farce and just as ridiculous.

● Undo your trousers and edge them down slowly to reveal your bottom turned to your woman. Dance about and prance around sexily.

● Dance around some more sticking your pelvis out and rotating it to the music.

● Put your hand inside pants and appear to stimulate your penis.

● Turn your back to your woman and slowly tease down your pants one side at a time to reveal one buttock at a time. Slowly pull the pants down and throw them over to the woman.

● Gyrate around to the music flicking your penis upwards and outwards towards her sometimes quite close to her but don't let her touch you.

● If you are any good she should have stopped doing the crossword by now!

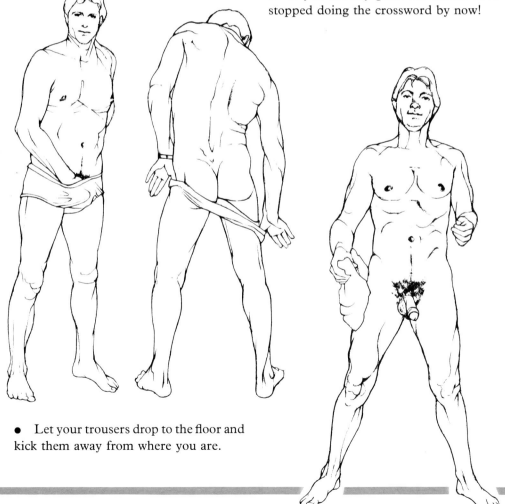

● Let your trousers drop to the floor and kick them away from where you are.

orgasms, to pretend to enjoy things and to fool one's partner – it's far too serious a stage in the man-woman relationship. This is the time to find out whether what seems perfectly reasonable to you makes your partner crippled with anxiety. It's also a good time to start harmonisation because there's usually a lot of goodwill and romance around which helps both parties do what the other wants. One of the greatest difficulties with such problems later in marriage is that a lot of this fund of goodwill has gone so making adaptation more difficult or even impossible especially if the couple are no longer communicating.

On the other hand, a couple who know that they are compatible can grow together over the years and reduce one another's anxieties as they become used to each other emotionally and physically. The problems then arise if one grows faster in coping with sexual anxiety barriers than the other and an imbalance results. As we have seen, the majority of such imbalances can usually be easily treated by the couple themselves or by a professional.

Feelings of inferiority

A capacity to feel inferior is probably inborn. Children inevitably feel inferior to adults and even to children a year or two older than themselves. It is easy to see that such feelings are important because they protect an individual who is inferior in some respect from challenging a superior one and thereby risking the chance of being harmed. Overcoming feelings of inferiority and acquiring competence is a part of growing up.

Perhaps as a result of an actual inferiority, harsh parental criticism or teasing from other children or a combination of all of these, feelings of inferiority may be carried forward into adulthood in an exaggerated form. Men with unresolved problems from early childhood also often seem to have a marked sense of general inferiority to other men. Individuals who as children felt, rightly or wrongly, that they lost parental love to a brother or sister may also grow up to feel inferior.

Such feelings can easily influence personality development. For example, late-developing boys have, during early adolescence, a little boy's penis whilst other boys of the same age will have a near adult one. This is a homosexual stage in boys during which they usually show and compare penises, pubic hair and so on. The late developer often feels inferior and disadvantaged and this can affect his personality characteristics for life.

In the same way a woman who feels, for example, that her breasts are unattractive, may become preoccupied with their inadequacy and minimize her contacts with both sexes because she feels so inferior. The suspicion, of course, is that such a woman is using her breasts as a focal point to express feelings of inferiority about herself generally. Such feelings may have been present before her breasts even developed.

About a third of men worry that their penis is too small. Because there isn't much difference between the vast majority of penises, at least when they are erect, the fear is groundless but it may be saying something about their concern about their male sex duties and role. Such a feeling of inferiority may tend to inhibit any opportunities they have to have normal sexual adventures.

Feelings of inferiority are closely akin to depressive feelings of being worthless and to feelings of guilt. For example, a man who feels guilty about masturbating may also feel inferior because he has done so. Such feelings are not at all uncommon, especially in less well educated men who have been brought up to believe that a real man can always attract a woman for sex and so has no need to masturbate. In effect this means that if he masturbates he is not a real man but an inferior one.

A sense of inferiority can also be caused by a bad experience. For example, a man who experiences impotence and is criticized by the woman may start to feel inferior as a man, especially if she compares his performance adversely to that of her previous lovers. His sexual morale may sink so low, as his male ego is punctured, that it never recovers. A few women seem to go in for this kind of behaviour to get revenge on the male sex in general. One such woman, for example, would lead young men on until their erect penis was revealed and then view it with lofty disdain and refuse to have intercourse with such an 'inferior specimen'. Another would concentrate on seducing married men and when intercourse was over would ask how his wife could put up with such a sorry performance.

In these ways feelings of inferiority can come about in people who have no basis in fact for such feelings. Conversely, some people who have adequate physical reasons to feel inferior refuse to do so. For example, a man with a 4″ erect penis adopted the view that it was 1″ longer than the vagina and was therefore totally adequate. He openly mentioned his deficiency to potential partners but said it made no difference because he was a de-luxe performer in intercourse. Women found his open, happy and self-assured outlook highly attractive and he was never short of willing female attention.

Other people over-compensate for some real or imagined source of inferiority. For example, some men after having had a vasectomy unconsciously view the operation as a form of castration (which it is not). They then over-compensate for the resultant feelings of inferiority this produces by chasing every woman in sight.

Without much real evidence to support

the contention it is often said that women feel inferior to men. The whole area is a battle-ground but, on the assumption it is true, various explanations are put forward to account for the situation. These include, for example, hormonal explanations to the effect that higher levels of testosterone in the male make him self-assertive where-as female hormones make her submissive. Others believe it is attributable to the different ways parents bring up boys compared with girls. Others think that such skills as males possess are more valued by society than those which females possess. Another suggested reason is that girls are taught to bare themselves and crouch down to urinate which makes them feel inferior to boys who are taught to urinate standing up. In Ancient Egypt it was the opposite, females standing to urinate and males crouching. Women and men were probably more truly equal in that society. In a similar way, another school of thought asserts that girls feel inferior to boys because of their smaller phallus (clitoris).

The real truth is that women are superior to men in some respects and inferior in others. The concept of inferiority and superiority when viewed in this way is a pointless one.

It is hard to escape the conclusion that the sexes complement each other in every way and are intended to work in loving and appreciative cooperation with no conflict. This battle between the sexes is one battle that need not be fought.

Jealousy and how to deal with it

Of all the negative sexual emotions jealousy is the most dangerous because it can be lethal. People do the most extreme things

out of jealousy and it is a common cause for murder.

The capacity to experience jealousy is inborn and does not have to be learned. It is derived from the erotic instincts and is to do with love. It is a form of anxiety experienced when a person fears that his or her love object may also love a third person, perhaps more than them.

The first experiences of intense jealousy arise in the triangular oedipal situation in which the child is jealous of the access the same-sex parent has to the opposite one. Children may also feel jealous of the relationship a sibling has with the parents, especially if they feel insecure. The arrival of a baby, for example, may cause an older child to have temper tantrums. The older child will also regress behaviourally to an earlier stage so as to compete for the attention that the baby is getting. The jealous child may also show hostility to its rival and this is usually condemned by the parents. This accounts for the tendency to feel ashamed in admitting to such feelings later in life.

Jealousy is a part of the human condition and is inseparable from love. A father may be jealous of the special love his wife shows to their children and a mother may be jealous of a good relationship springing up between the children and the father. A mother may also be unconsciously jealous of the sexual attractiveness of her adolescent daughter and this can be an important component of the conflicts which can arise at this stage.

An excessively jealous child will grow into an excessively jealous adult and some men and women are unreasonable in their suspicions that their partner may be involved elsewhere. Generally it is said that girls and women are more susceptible to jealousy than are boys and men. However, an excessively jealous individual can turn into a pathologically jealous one and in such cases a man is more dangerous than a woman, if only because of his greater strength. Such people often entertain the most bizarre delusions and need psychiatric treatment.

Jealousy needs to be distinguished from envy. Jealousy is a triangular situation – even if the third party is imaginary – whereas envy is to do with two people. A girl may envy her sister's better looks or a boy his brother's prowess at football or in chatting-up girls. Similarly, women can envy the sexual freedoms granted to men. Men can also envy women their ability to bear children, their greater sexual capaci-

ties and their lot in life generally which many men suppose to be easier than that of theirs. Adolescent boys can also envy girls because the boy has to ask the girl – and thereby risk rejection – rather than the other way round.

It is impossible to think of love without jealousy – a wholly negative emotional state in which the sufferer becomes anxious, suspicious and angry in response to real or imagined threats to the love-bond between him or her and another. A certain degree of sexual jealousy is probably normal and it has been extensively studied and copiously represented in literature over the centuries. Such normal jealousy probably plays a part in holding couples (and their families) together and probably stops errant partners from indulging their sexual whims more than they otherwise would. Men particularly are often annoyed at the sharpness and cleverness of their women in detecting at an early stage their developing involvement with another woman. This may be the result of the greater tendency of women to be jealous and thus suspicious, but whatever the cause, it is a powerful deterrent.

Jealousy is a strange emotion because it has a large component of self-pity and selfishness to it. In jealousy there is often more self-love than love. Any situation that makes one of the partners feel at a disadvantage in the struggle to obtain or keep a mate predisposes the handicapped person to sexual jealousy. Impotence on the part of the husband or frigidity on the part of the wife or a marked disparity between the sexual appetites of the couple are often predisposing factors.

There are perfectly well-recognized psychological and medical causes for sexual jealousy too. For example, mental

Part Two

subnormality and certain sorts of brain damage are known to cause it. Drunkenness makes people jealous as do cocaine and the amphetamines. During pregnancy, in the post-natal period and around the menopause women often feel more jealous even when there is no reason for them to do so. This could be hormonal in origin but is more likely to come about because at these times women feel disadvantaged in comparison with other women.

Often jealousy is a sign of inferiority, a feeling of threat because of the possible loss of love. This often means the person has little or no self-confidence and as a result sees every man, or woman, friend or hobby as a threat to the relationship. Such people have often had poor experiences of loving in their childhood and are extremely sensitive to any signs (real or imagined) of love withdrawal. Anything that takes their partner away from them is seen as a threat to their love bond. At the extreme end of the spectrum some such people panic if their partner is simply late home from work or shopping.

In a monogonous society such as ours in which we try to make a serious one-to-one commitment to another individual, the thought of losing that person to someone else is often too much to bear, especially for a middle-aged woman who, perhaps understandably, feels unable to compete in youth and looks. A woman in her middle years is in reality likely to have difficulty finding a new partner.

When it comes to dealing with jealousy in practical terms the trouble is that the truly jealous person sees problems where they don't exist and so ruins an often perfectly good relationship. If every time the train runs late she imagines her husband is seducing a girl at work then she won't be warm and welcoming when he comes home and may even withdraw from sexual activity, at least in part. This understandably upsets her husband who then *might* seduce the girl at work in desperation. Many women, especially those with a low self-esteem, believing that all men are basically sex-mad and that most women are more attractive than her, can't or won't believe that the relationship between the husband and the other woman amounts to nothing. Such jealousy then feeds on itself, sometimes in a self-fulfilling way.

Very jealous men are usually found unconsciously to view their partner as if they were their mother. Often their childhood relationship with their mother was deeply insecure. Such a man seeks to control all the movements of his woman and frequently checks on her whereabouts. He becomes almost deranged when she speaks to another man and accuses her of being a whore and worse.

How we handle jealousy depends on many things including our own personality; the way we were brought up; whether the other man/woman is imagined or real; on the quality and nature of our relationship and so on.

Even jealousy caused by a proven infidelity *can* be coped with in a good relationship and should be used as an opportunity for a total overhaul of the marriage and a re-appraisal of what caused the person to wander.

Most extramarital dalliances and affairs are probably superficial, sexual adventures but because of the powerful feelings jealousy produces are often escalated into major marriage-breaking dramas quite unnecessarily. More marriages have probably been ruined on these grounds than on any other yet usually such dramatic action is ultimately the wrong answer unless, of course, the relationship was so poor that the slightest knock killed it off.

'Justified' jealousy simply has to be lived through. So how can jealousy be overcome? The woman whose husband goes off with another woman and sets up home with her is bound to feel jealous and this is perfectly normal. In time she'll get over it, though it can take years, but like grieving the loss of anyone it's a slow business and a painful one. Professional help can be invaluable especially as one's self-esteem hits rock bottom at such a time and suicidal ideas are not at all uncommon.

How to cope with jealousy

This method, unlike the others we've discussed involves thinking only not doing.

Draw up a list, as we've done for anxiety and guilt, of increasingly jealousy-producing things.

Such a list might run as follows:
1 My wife surrounded by attractive men when out shopping
2 My wife dancing with another man at a party where we are both present
3 My wife going out with her woman-friend to a dance
4 My wife being brought home in the car of a man she meets at the dance
5 My wife kissing the man good-bye before she gets out of the car

Now get yourself into a relaxed state, and make sure that your anxiety level is zero. Think of something lovely (non-sexual or

sexual) or get yourself sexually aroused by reading something erotic. Once you are perfectly relaxed imagine the scene lowest on your list for a few seconds and then go back to your baseline of relaxed thoughts or fantasies. You could devise simple physical things to get you back to zero such as counting the rings on the curtain pole or the patterns on the wallpaper. Once you are safely back to zero on your scale of anxiety go back to your jealousy-producing thought at the bottom of the list and keep doing this jumping between thoughts until you are totally happy with the scene you have in your mind.

Slowly work up the scale until you can, perhaps over some weeks, cope with any of the thoughts without anxiety or panic. The results can be very powerful. The next time you go to a party and your wife chats up another man you won't despair or take it out on her afterwards but will relax and enjoy yourself instead of imagining how and where she will be flirting with the man. This will so defuse your jealousy that you'll become much better at coping with her and if she's turned on by other men she meets (which she will be if she's normal) she can use her fantasies of them to improve the ardour of her lovemaking with you.

Sex as a battleground

It's easy to see that with all the anxieties, guilts and jealousies we bring to marriage that sex could all too easily become a battle ground. We are all inhibited at least to some degree; anxious about something; have been made to be guilty about lots of things and feel jealous (though not necessarily sexually) of someone. Add to this the fact that many men are vulnerable when it

comes to criticism of their sexual performance and women when it comes to their appearance and sexiness and it's all too apparent that sex is a ripe area for fights. Only the strong can afford to be gentle and most people feel pretty weak on many sexual matters, especially their sexual emotions.

Sex is, contrary to many people's beliefs, not the most important cause of battles within marriage. Money, how to bring up children and lack of emotional warmth almost always come higher on the lists of causes of rows in marriage. Some of course are just excuses for what is really a sexual row deep down. But having said this dissatisfaction in these other three areas all too frequently spills over into the sexual arena and miserable people tend to go off sex. Unfortunately, too many people carry over arguments in one of these areas into sex – so a person with money problems may well go off sex or pick fights over sex because they are genuinely worried about financial problems and are really stressed as a result or because they (perhaps unconsciously) think badly of a partner who could put them in such a position.

Sex is often used as a weapon to punish an unsatisfying or unsatisfactory partner for actual or supposed weakness, failings and let-downs. Many women see their sexual 'favours' as sweets that they bestow mother-like on their 'little boy' when he is good – that is when he does what she wants. They then withhold sex or have mechanical sex when he doesn't come up to expectations – as a form of punishment.

The inhibited man, and there are many of them, accuses his normally-sexed wife of being a nymphomaniac and the reverse can happen too. We all have 'ideals' against which we judge our partners (and others of the opposite sex) and when they don't behave according to our stereotype

One answer to overwhelming anxiety is to escape into loneliness. Many inhibited and anxious people end up feeling that anything is better than risking failure

we become angry, depressed, or frankly war-like. 'If you were a real man . . .' is the sort of damaging and hurtful remark that slips out in these kinds of arguments. Women occasionally castigate men for their performance (or lack of it) and men attack women for their appearance or lack of sex interest and passion. Many of these battles arise from factual misunderstandings and myths, some of which are outlined on pages 175–183.

Following on from these misunderstandings are the commonly heard complaints that men and women are so different. As Professor Higgins in My Fair Lady put it . . . 'Why can't a woman be more like a man?' Many people think that the sexes should feel and think alike, especially about sex but they don't and that's part of the delight of the differences between the sexes. Men are, and probably always will be, the sexual doers and women the more passive receivers (after all, a woman can just lie back and accept a penis but a man has to make it happen).

It is the similarity of personality in a well-matched relationship which makes full communication possible and the differences between the sexes that gives something of abiding and exciting interest

to communicate. Similarity and difference are, paradoxically, the basis of heterosexual love.

Unfortunately, sexual battles have repercussions elsewhere. A woman feeling unfairly criticized may become sloppy at home and at work; even neglecting child care and parenting; her husband may be increasingly left out of her life; they proliferate 'no-go' areas (see page 183) and all too easily lose any joy there might have been in the relationship. *He* may then retreat to drink, work and the company of other men and *she* to tranquillizers and other women and the scene is set for possible divorce.

So for most women the emotional relationship has to seem to be right (or very nearly right) for her to be practically interested in sex. As women are so much more emotion-centred than are men, and are more emotionally sensitive to what's happening within a relationship, it is they who are the barometer of sex in a relationship. Often a man is insensitive to her emotions and pushes on with his demands for sex when she isn't ready. It's because women are so different in this way (not less sex-centred but more easily put off sex when the emotions aren't right otherwise they feel like a whore) that many men often give up in despair.

Such a man, and there are millions of them, says that women are so fickle, their sexual desires and moods so unpredictable, their demands so unreasonable and their sexual responses so unreliable that he despairs of ever being able to see what makes them tick.

Women, on the other hand, frequently say that men can't be trusted emotionally and that they're much more vulnerable to other women than women are to other men. In practice this possibly turns out to be true. Men fall in love much more easily than do women according to research in the US and do so many more times than do women. This lack of emotional trust seems relatively unimportant to many men who see the emotional side of a relationship very differently. They are, they argue, good husbands, fathers, providers and so on, so what more could the woman want! As judged by women's interest magazines women are more geared to stable nest-making and an emotionally unpredictable nest makes the job of childrearing extremely precarious and even impossible. Just bear in mind that about 55% of all the children of divorced parents end up in the care of a local authority at some time, so obviously the average woman's fears about being able to cope alone with rearing a family are well founded.

As seen in this section, sex is a highly emotional business and the sex and love lives of many couples are spoiled quite unnecessarily because either or both are emoting when they should be thinking and being rational.

To many couples being emotional and letting their bad feelings rule the relationship is all too easy. They say things like 'It's just the way I am, I can't help how I feel' as if that excused everything. Unfortunately, it doesn't if only because a man-woman partnership involves the intimate feelings and emotions of someone else who may not be able to live with such a take-it-or-leave-it philosophy of life. Giving way to emotions is relatively easy – it's fighting them that takes the effort. Hopefully, after reading this chapter you'll be better able to do this.

Sexual misunderstandings and how to overcome them

Good and bad communication

Ideally, good communication between a couple would leave no room for misunderstandings. Unfortunately, this ideal doesn't exist for most couples for two main reasons. First, communication is a highly complex business that involves far more than just words. This means that whilst we are apparently conveying the truth about something we can in fact unconsciously be trying to conceal it. It also means that however hard we try our unconscious wishes largely determine what we actually communicate to our partner . . . or indeed to anyone else. So someone can betray his or her real feelings or personality by a glance away from the other person or by a shift in the way they hold their body, both of which actually say more than the words they are consciously using. In this way we communicate things of which we are almost totally unaware, especially to our children.

Second, as we grow up we acquire all kinds of attitudes, feelings, expectations, wishes, hopes, fantasies and much much more which all go to form our personalities. We then bring this jig-saw to our marriage partnership where many of these earlier lessons are reactivated within the new man-woman relationship. Once the initial bloom wears off the relationship facets of the personality that were ignored or papered over for a quiet life begin to emerge and the resulting disharmonies have to be dealt with. It is now more than ever that a couple need to communicate but if sex is involved they often find it very difficult.

Personal sexual experiences are seen by many couples as too 'private' to discuss even between themselves. So is it any surprise that with so little practice and seeing the whole subject area as taboo ("'nice' people don't talk about their sexual feelings and practices, do they?") many couples go for years or even a whole married lifetime without really sharing their sexual thoughts, fears, guilts, worries needs and joys with their partner.

There are other problems too with the words we want to use when talking about sex. Few of the words there are come easily to most people – they either sound too medical and technical or too crude and either can get in the way of real communication. So it is that even a couple who are really trying hard can come to grief simply with the language. 'Making love' to one partner could mean 'fucking' or 'screwing' to the other and both might in fact be copulating. It might seem like the counsel of perfection but couples almost have to define the terms they use *before* any discussion so that at least they are talking the same language.

Communication between two human beings is an extremely complex business and involves far more than talking. Body language is a vital part of communication between people and especially lovers. Touching and other physical contacts are powerful ways of communicating too. The way we dress says a lot about our sexuality (and personality) as does our choice of music, cars, hobbies and so on. Some couples become very good at almost wordless communication, especially after several years together. They often know what each other is about to say, for example. Pheromones, well proven to be important chemical messengers in the animal world are now being recognized as being of importance in human communication and it's quite possible that these act as a primitive but sophisticated chemical communication system between men and women.

Good communication between a couple goes on all the time – they communicate at every level of the mind and body and often don't need to speak at all. The right glance at the right time, the tiniest touch, or simply not saying anything in a particular situation can all speak volumes to the other. Such a couple almost never need to communicate formally on sexual matters because they are permanently in touch with each other's feelings and emotions and intellectual dissertations about who wants or needs what are rarely needed. A couple who communicate like this will know when either or both are ready for sex and when they are not and because of their understanding and sensitivity to each other's needs little discussion is required to provoke or to avoid sexual activity.

Unfortunately, many, if not most, couples are some way off this kind of ongoing communication. They see communication as purely a talking business and because they are ill at ease and tense on the subject of sex find talking about it very difficult. They don't realize that a little smile or a certain touch is worth a thousand words or that a cuddle at the right moment could avoid a lengthy argument. Men are, perhaps, particularly at fault here.

Most couples start off their courtship days with a fund of goodwill yet over the years this dwindles for most. Why should this be?

First, there are the simple problems that arise from living with any other person.

Adjusting to another human being, his or her idiosyncrasies and personality, takes forebearance, an ability and willingness to be flexible and a willingness to see one's partner as a unique individual and not as a stereotyped 'man' or 'woman'. This can be difficult unless there is a fair amount of goodwill. Very often this goodwill is based on the sexual relationship which can, and often does, glue the couple together when living together becomes difficult for whatever reason. For many the fund of goodwill withers away and cracks appear which are too wide to be filled by the remaining sexual relationship. The whole relationship then begins to crumble. There are ways of preventing all this as we shall see.

Second, and much more important, are the misunderstandings that creep into the relationship – misunderstandings that need not be there, that are often erroneous or misleading and injure the relationship because they are never really discussed.

Let's look at some of the commonest of these misunderstandings now.

Some common misunderstandings affecting sex

First of all and most crucial to the whole subject is the cultural belief that men are basically sex-mad and want to have intercourse with anything in a skirt and that women are basically 'nice' and would run a mile if they saw an erect penis. Almost all the important sexual misunderstandings are variations of this sad and dangerous stereotype.

Neither is, of course, true and to behave as if they were creates countless arguments and misunderstandings that ruin perfectly good relationships.

1 *Men are natural sexual aggressors and should make the first move* Many women feel that because they are so 'nice' (i.e. sexless) they should never make sexual advances, even to their husbands, and most are brought up to feel that sex is something that is done *to* them. In reality sharing responsibility for initiating lovemaking or indeed any other sexual activity is a liberating and exciting part of a sexual relationship, provided the man isn't too passive and the woman too inhibited. Every woman likes to feel wanted (for herself and not just for sex) and especially so in a one-to-one relationship that has been going on for several years. No man wants to feel taken for granted, especially when there are sexual opportunities elsewhere to which he has turned a blind eye in favour of his one-to-one relationship. By initiating sexual encounters, at least some of the time, a woman shows her husband that she *really* wants him and isn't just going along with his demands to please him or because she loves him (which is what many men think). A sexually over-assertive woman, on the other hand, can be a turn-off for a conventionally brought up, somewhat inhibited man who unconsciously sees women as sexless, as his mother gave the impression she was.

2 *Women are basically sexless and 'nice' and only have sex to show they love their* **man** This is a very widely-held view which is hardly surprising the way we bring children up in our society but it has no biological basis in fact. On the contrary, research has found that women are the superior sex when it comes to sexual matters. They are ready and willing for sex throughout their menstrual cycle (unlike the vast majority of female animals which come into heat only a few times a year). They are more erotically sensitive over a larger proportion of their bodies than are men; they have the capacity to enjoy frequent orgasms which do not exhaust them and neither do women, unlike men, release reproductive cells at orgasm; they experience sensual and even sexual pleasure from several body functions including breastfeeding, urinating and contracting their pelvic muscles (some women have orgasms by doing these things); they can enjoy repeated intercourse time after time until vaginal soreness limits activity and they are probably more psychically sexual than men too. (They are certainly more emotionally in touch than are men.)

In other words, research over the last decades has confirmed what some clinicians have known for centuries – that women are more occupied with sex in all its forms than are men and are kitted out to make the most of their sexuality.

Certainly it is true that in our culture men tend to make the final approach in sexual situations but women almost always control the run-up to this stage right from the very first meeting – biologically they are the seducers.

The notion of the sexless woman is now so thoroughly debunked that to hold onto the idea in spite of the evidence is to live in the land of the horse-drawn carriage. Of course many people *do* still believe this myth unconsciously and many women still act out the part of the nice, sexless creatures they imagine they ought to be. They can, of course, placate their consciences and appear to be unwilling or even to refuse and are then 'forced' to have sex. This is a very common sex fantasy in women. Clinical work, however, shows that even the 'nicest' (that is, the most culturally inhibited) wife can become an eager partner with her husband within a very few treatment sessions.

3 *A woman who won't behave sexually the way I want, doesn't love me* Because love and sex are so intimately bound up in our society and in our psychosexual devel-

opment and as most young women give as their main criterion for making love with a man that they love him, the subject of love and sex are inextricably intertwined from day one of a sexual relationship. As we pointed out earlier women often exaggerate their loving feelings (to themselves) so as to justify their need for sex and men tend to exaggerate their emotional feelings to the woman so as to convice her that she should have sex with them. This behaviour, sanctioned by centuries of cultural conditioning, then fools the man into thinking that the woman is having sex because of the love she feels and not because (as may well be the case for *him*) she simply wants sex with him. Once they have been married for some time and sexual disagreements or differences occur he immediately and understandably interprets them as a sign of her not loving him because he has learned from experience that a woman will do anything for the man she loves. In this way quite harmless and small sexual problems are seen as a sign of love withdrawal and the husband is deeply hurt, especially in our monogamous society in which he has no socially sanctioned sexual alternative.

If only couples could be honest with each other from the start, honest enough to disclose that they have separate but interlinked needs – all would be well. Then love would continue as the background emotion within a marriage and either or both would initiate sexual activity whenever they wanted to and would feel free to refuse whenever they didn't. One can't throw the whole love bond in a relationship into the ring every time one doesn't feel like having sex or a particular sexual pursuit, yet this is exactly what happens in millions of bedrooms year in and year out.

4 ***Sex is dirty, sinful and unpleasant*** We look at this on page 299.

5 ***Nice women don't seduce men*** Yes they do, and always have done since Eve met Adam.

6 ***Ladies don't move*** This may be true but it takes a woman to have pleasurable intercourse and 'ladies' miss a lot of the fun. This myth comes back once more to the basic belief that a man should do things *to* a woman and that the woman herself has no innate sexuality of her own. This means that women are supposed to rely totally on men for their sexual satisfaction. Lots of women believe this should be so if they are to remain 'nice' and it is a common reason why women are so ashamed of masturbating after marriage.

In any loving relationship the couple are trying to please each other in the best possible way as they make love. If this means the woman moving during intercourse, either for her own pleasure or that of her partner, who is to say she should not? The sexually at ease woman 'uses' her partner's penis to stimulate her just the way she wants so as to produce the best possible sensations for her. Needless to say this intensely excites the average man which is not a bad side effect.

Some women simply can't move during sex because their man is lying on them so heavily. This is a basic matter of sex manners – the man should take his weight on his elbows and knees and so allow the woman to move if she wants to.

7 ***Men know what to do without being told*** This is an especially harmful myth because it is painfully untrue and ruins marriages. If anything, men have more to

learn about sex. There is a greater learned component to male sexuality than to female and also women are very much more varied in their sexual responses which means men have more to learn about any one woman and her sexuality.

Even a very widely experienced man will not necessarily know what any one particular woman most enjoys. Certainly his experience with other women will give him a head start knowing what to try but many women, in the hands of such a lover get annoyed or frustrated because he won't do exactly what *they'd* most like. Yet they often won't say what this is or show him. They complain but won't help him learn by giving him adequate cues. If only women could be helped to believe that there are hundreds or thousands of men around the world who would, given the right encouragement, be right for them sexually they would be saved endless heartache and searching for the one and only knight in shining armour who somehow 'knows' what to do.

'It takes two to tango' as the saying goes, and no man can be expected to know by intuition what will be best for any one woman. Certainly there are a few basic principles that apply but women (more than men) are infinitely variable in their sexual likes and dislikes – many of which remain undisclosed throughout even very loving and otherwise happy marriages. Here is a subject that must be shared and communicated in every possible way if the marriage is to survive and flourish. But once again it comes back to the very first point we made. If the woman sees herself as being too 'nice' to ask for what she wants and then berates her husband on the grounds that 'if he wasn't useless he'd *know* what to do' she has only herself to blame when things go wrong.

Although men are supposed to have all the answers, in fact they have more to learn. By interacting with the opposite sex they can overcome their fears

In a perfect world couples would share all of this kind of information during courtship so that they could see whether or not they were going to be able to satisfy each other in the way each wanted. If this kind of sharing can be established during courtship when emotions and the fund of goodwill is at its greatest, there's a chance that the habit will die hard and be a valued part of their marriage for years to come.

A shy or bashful woman doesn't need to sit her man down and give him a Nobel prize-winning lecture on the subject of what she wants – she can clearly guide him without saying anything at all over several weeks or months of lovemaking. By being obviously pleased and praising him when his behaviour is most enjoyable to her and not responding in this way to everything else he'll quickly learn and there will have been no great heart-to-heart discussions on this difficult area. All of this pre-supposes that the ability and willingness of both partners to do whatever most pleases the other is seen as vitally important in any serious relationship. Unfortunately, in our culture 'nice' women might not be able to say what they want because by definition 'nice' girls don't want anything sexual.

8 *If a woman doesn't have an orgasm she'll be dissatisfied* Although most women enjoy having an orgasm (or several) before, during or after intercourse, this is by no means essential and many women enjoy sex for a lifetime without ever having an orgasm with their partner's penis in the vagina. For a man, the endless holding back waiting for his woman to have a vaginally-induced orgasm can be very destructive to his enjoyment and to the relationship and eventually breeds resentment. Many women, seeing this, fake orgasms to please their man and then when he has fallen asleep may masturbate to release their sexual tension.

None of this is necessary and most of it is potentially harmful. The answer is simple. If the woman wants an orgasm and doesn't easily get one from a penis-in-vagina stimulation alone, she should either caress her clitoris herself during lovemaking or get her man to do so. She can then have an orgasm with his penis inside her. Some couples find that an orgasm before intercourse is best and other women like sex first and then to be masturbated or to masturbate themselves. Few women come off simply from the stimulation of penis-in-vagina sex alone.

The end result of good sex should be that both feel relaxed and sexually relieved but how this is achieved is up to the couple. Some women need to have a clitorally-induced orgasm after the penis-in-vagina one during sex in order to feel really relieved of their sexual tensions. They are often secretive about it for fear of offending their man and a thoughtful man will either masturbate his woman after sex or be happy to have her do it while they cuddle each other and go to sleep.

9 *Simultaneous orgasms are best* This is another harmful myth because lots of couples strive for an impossible dream and feel a failure as a result. Certainly coming off together can be superb but for many the effort of concentration (the woman accelerating and the man holding back) can be so great that the whole performance becomes too arduous. Anything like this that intrudes on a couple's unselfconscious sexual enjoyment of each other is in fact inhibiting not, as many people imagine, a sign of how liberated they are. Far too many people are spectators at their own intercourse experiences (they are too self-aware) and then wonder why they can't truly enjoy sex. The answer is that they usually have some underlying inhibition or fear of sex which shows in their masturbation fantasies. On the other hand, simultaneous orgasms can happen even without trying. One partner, realizing the other is building up to an orgasm can trigger off their own.

10   ***Men are always ready for sex***   This common myth goes hand in hand with the 'Men know what to do' myth. Many women believe that you only have to show a man a square inch of naked flesh and he'll erect and be ready for anything. Alas, the truth is rather different for any man much over 25. Men need exciting just as women do and as they get older they need more arousing behaviour to turn them on than most women realize. The follow-up myth that goes with this one is 'If he really fancied/loved/wanted me he'd get an erection double quick'. It is true that the most flattering thing a man can do for a woman biologically is to erect for her but any failure to erect isn't necessarily a criticism of her. The real reasons may date back into his childhood, long before he knew her.

All but young men, some of whom can indeed get erections many times a day at the drop of a hat, need time and the right mood if they are to get a good erection. Don't forget that a woman needs only to be willing and not necessarily aroused at all in order to receive a man's penis but a man needs a nearly full erection if he's even to get started. Coupled with this it should also be remembered that a man can feel very loving and even sexy yet not have an erection. Some women find this difficult to believe yet know very well how they sometimes want to be made love to yet are not fully aroused sexually.

11   ***Once you start making love you have to go on until one or both have an orgasm***   Many people believe that once they begin to cuddle and start foreplay they're committing themselves to a full-blown performance with orgasm for one or both as the only acceptable end-point. A couple who communicate well won't let this happen and each will have the maturity to tell the other that they only want to cuddle or to be masturbated or masturbate the other. It is usually unwise to perform under duress in bed because that's how resentment sets in. No one wants to feel used but this means being honest and having the kind of relationship in which 'no' or 'maybe' is just as acceptable as 'yes'. On the other hand of course, the reluctant partner can, perhaps, be coaxed into eager willingness and the process can be enjoyable.

Of course what isn't at all acceptable is to build up expectations in your partner that intercourse is about to take place and then to leave him or her high and dry. Nobody can stand much of this and it poisons a relationship very quickly.

12   ***Women get aroused as quickly as men***   Whilst it is true that any woman who can open her legs can receive an erect penis such a crude definition of intercourse is acceptable to few people today. Although women become aroused

as quickly as men most women hope for loving behaviour and foreplay of various kinds before being penetrated. Sex books and 'experts' have written widely about the 'necessity' or desirability of extensive foreplay. Foreplay, whilst enjoyable for most women and some men much of the time, is by no means essential on all occasions and 'quickie' sex can be just as enjoyable as that preceeded by prolonged foreplay.

13   *It's bad manners at best and unloving at worst to fall asleep after sex* When it comes to afterplay we are led to believe that a loving, mature couple will discuss Beethoven or other matters of great importance and that this is a sign of perfect sex. There is no reason to believe that this is so although it's true that a few couples will feel exceptionally close after sex and may want to discuss a particular problem or pleasure in their lives. Most though fall asleep, often in each other's arms or cuddling into each other as the culmination of a loving, relaxing and tension-relieving sexual experience. Provided each has had the orgasm they need and neither is left high and dry, what could be a better way to end such a pleasurable exchange of feelings? Most couples make love in the evening (studies have found that the peak time for intercourse is around 10.00 pm) so it's not at all unreasonable to make sex the prelude to a deep and relaxing sleep. It is much better than sleeping pills. If the woman wants to masturbate and is too shy to do so openly, the sooner her man goes off to sleep the better. Some women say that a lover who drops off to sleep has 'given his all' and that she feels pleased about this. For the couple that doesn't fall asleep the mood of the situation will dictate what they do after sex. This will depend on the circumstances and for some the tender moments after intercourse can be a perfect time to talk or cuddle.

14   *Sex is for babies – not pleasure* This is a compelling 'message' that is believed at least to some extent by all women unconsciously. To claim that sex is only for babies is of course nonsense. Even before the coming of effective contraception sex was not inextricably linked with babies because although human females are made to be sexually responsive all year round throughout their whole sexual life they can only conceive on a few days during each monthly cycle. Clearly such an animalistic view of sex is completely untenable even on biological grounds.

If sex were truly only for babies then women would have been designed to ovulate each time they had sex (like rabbits) but this is of course not the case. Sex was historically linked to producing babies to the extent that unprotected intercourse results in pregnancy if the intercourse takes place at the time of the month when the woman is ovulating. What modern contraception has done is to remove or reduce the chances of unwanted conception occuring during those few days each month.

We can't go into this vastly important subject in the depth it deserves but unconscious notions of what sex is *really* for run very deep in our culture and for millions of western women any sexual activity that frustrates the 'natural' function of intercourse (producing a baby) is unacceptable at least in part. This produces barriers to subjects as different as mutual masturbation, anal and oral sex and even foreplay.

At one (not uncommon) extreme is the woman who sees anything but penis-invagina sex as perverted.

15 *Nice girls/women don't masturbate*

Yes they do and depending on how you define 'nice' it can be argued that nice girls do it more than naughty ones. Statistics about the subject are difficult to come by because female masturbation is such a diffuse and variable commodity compared with men's. Women have orgasms from the widest range of activities, some of which aren't at all overtly sexual. A few women have orgasms and don't even realize it, so inhibited are they. Their bodies are reacting by having an orgasm but their brains shut off the information.

Clinically, over 90% of all women admit to masturbation and about 30% say that they can never remember a time since infancy when they didn't enjoy genital play. If by 'nice' one means 'religious' or 'strictly brought up' then such girls masturbate more than their 'naughty' sisters who go out with boys and have first intercourse at the normal age (about 18).

Masturbation is a natural and normal form of sexual expression in girls and women of all ages. 'Nice' girls feel guilty about it and may even deny that they do it but this is the only difference between them and their 'non-nice' sisters.

16 *If a man doesn't want sex he must have another woman*

This is clearly linked to misunderstanding No 1. Men aren't always ready for sex, as we saw in misunderstanding 10. On the contrary, many men today with the pressures of work or redundancy, don't function nearly as well or as often as they'd like. To suggest that any temporary malfunction is necessarily anything to do with him fulfilling his needs elsewhere is deeply hurtful and is usually, but not always, untrue. Most men who go off sex or can't maintain an erection have other reasons at the heart of their problem. Unfortunately, given the harmful linkage between sex and love to which we have already referred, too many women see any fall in sexual performance on the part of her man as a sign of the loss of her sex appeal and most women react very badly to this. For many the argument then continues: 'If he's not doing it to me he must be doing it to someone else'. Much more likely is that he is worried, anxious, overworked, drinking too much or one of many other things.

17 *Sex is physically bad for you because it depletes your energy*

Many businessmen and men who have to face some kind of ordeal in the next day or two (for example athletes) refrain from having sex in the mistaken belief that it will weaken them or make them less effective in some way. Historically it was taught by some priests and doctors that one ejaculation had the same debilitating effect on a man as losing a pint of blood but there is no evidence whatever that sex is in any way weakening physically or mentally unless done to excess. It could possibly be argued that building up a degree of sexual tension that is not discharged sexually gives a man a level of extra push that he could gainfully employ elsewhere.

Of course there are countless other specific sexual myths and misunderstandings about everything from female sexual anatomy to menstruation and conception but they would require an entire book to themselves to describe and discuss. Most of these are easily dispelled compared with those discussed above because they are based on incomplete or frankly inaccurate factual knowledge rather than inappropriate attitudes and misconceptions.

Many of these misunderstandings about sex can lead to problems with communicating about sex within a relationship though there are many other causes for failed communications and rows are common over money, the disciplining of the children and many other non-sexual areas of life. One major study found that of all the complaints about marriage 'lack of communication' came top of the list with 'constant arguments' second and 'unfulfilled emotional needs' third. Fourth came 'sexual dissatisfaction'. So it's clear that being unable to feel understood and being unable to understand oneself are major problems in marriage.

Some rules for good communication within a sexual relationship

1 *Keep 'no-go' areas to an absolute minimum*

A lot of marital hostility arises over what may be called 'no-go' areas within the relationship. Subjects as diverse as children's schooling, the woman's weight, his drinking friends, religion, oral sex and so on are out of bounds, skirted round or never actually discussed. One or both partners harbour strongly-held views yet can't get the other to discuss them or come to an agreement at all. Slowly these 'no-go' areas within the marriage grow in size and number until the couple are only relating in the most superficial way, skimming over the surface of life. As soon as any discussion starts to be valuable it hits a

'no-go' area and hostility or silence breaks out. Eventually such a couple end up saying little to each other and rowing when they do speak. The cure for this state of affairs is to have a minimum of 'no-go' areas in the first place.

Clearly no two people will agree on everything but a good friendship can withstand quite a lot of disagreement. After all, by definition there are usually no absolute answers to the problems being discussed and one person's views are worth about as much as another's. Many 'no-go' areas aren't really serious anyway but sitting down and thinking about them or listing them may show up quite a lot. For example, many men resist any attempt by their partner to discuss sex. As he is the performer he immediately jumps to the conclusion that he is being got at – however indirectly. This can be extremely frustrating for the woman.

All this is so easy to see and understand yet we still don't educate boys to be sufficiently sensitive to women's emotions. In fact the opposite is the case. Some boys grow up believing that women are totally different creatures, that they're basically illogical, incomprehensible, unreasonable and even slightly mad and then we wonder why they treat women so badly when they become men. Similarly, many of the more extreme voices of the women's movement that suggest that all heterosexuality is an exploitation of women by men and that women should stand up against their husbands come what may are also unhelpful because they engender misplaced hostility and even hatred. To 'castrate' a man psychologicaly is not the way to get the best out of him. The only hope for better man-woman relationships is to encourage people to understand each other better, and to benefit fully from their differences. The sensible path is, as always, somewhere between the two extremes. Of course, women aren't creatures from another planet that are unfathomable by men and likewise women don't need to be so angry that they antagonize even those men who are well disposed towards them. The French have a saying . . . 'to understand all is to forgive all'. It wouldn't be a bad motto to hang above every marriage bed.

2 Never forget that your partner is probably your best friend

When things go wrong in life we tend to take them out on those nearest and dearest to us and to some extent this is what a loving and caring relationship is about. It can withstand a certain number of knocks as each partner soothes the other and calms the troubled waters when necessary. However, such behaviour can be displaced anger or frustration with other people outside the relationship and the partner gets it in the neck instead of, for example, the boss at work who *can't* be screamed at. Unfortunately, there is a limit to what any one individual can take and repeated or constant emotional onslaughts on a spouse instead of the person or situation that's causing the underlying problem will sooner or later damage the relationship. We all have to let off steam sometimes but it shouldn't become a habit. The danger in these situations is that phrases like 'How would you understand, you're only a woman' and 'What sort of a man do you call yourself?' slip out but are deeply wounding and hard to forget.

Be open and honest certainly but bear in mind that even your best friend has limits of tolerance and can't be expected to take endless anger, blows, criticism, bad language, bad temper, overdrinking, extreme tiredness or other forms of stress-induced behaviour. Seek professional help if you find (or your partner complains) that he or she is having to bear too many of your burdens.

3 Prevent arguments from ending up as full-scale rows

It makes sense to discuss even emotionally difficult subjects within a good relationship but it sets the detonator for an explosion unless you control things pretty carefully. Try to argue constructively and single-mindedly. Unfortunately, even a sensible discussion often ends up spreading far and wide across all sorts of areas of concern and by the early hours of the morning every conceivable grievance is likely to have been dragged up. The endpoint is one storming out, sleeping in the spare room, going off out somewhere or someone getting violent.

Women especially need to feel able to get grievances off their chests but many men are so immature that they'll do anything rather than face the music and so retreat leaving the problem unsolved.

When having a discussion about an emotionally charged subject keep to that subject and closely related ones and avoid wild generalizations and upsetting statements that you'll regret the following morning. Try to listen at least as much as you speak and don't shout your partner down.

The time to discuss the offence that the partner has given is early on and before frequent repetition leads to fury. If even an apparently small and silly thing upsets your partner you have to take it seriously from the moment it is revealed.

4   *Don't make assumptions about your partner based on yourself*

We all make rather thoughtless assump-

tions about others. A simple example, already given earlier, is of the man who unconsciously assumes his wife's attitudes towards sex are the same as those of his mother. This can easily come about because mothers give such misleading impressions to their children when it comes to sexual matters. By the assumption that his wife is a 'nice lady' he deprives her of the need to be a real, flesh and blood woman. A similar example, is the man who

thoughtlessly believes that because he gets pleasure from his penis a woman must be masturbated using her vagina.

Women make the same sorts of mistake emotionally. A woman may say to herself in effect that 'I love him so I would do A, B or C for him but I wouldn't do X, Y or Z because X, Y and Z are unloving.' She then studies her man and concludes that because he is doing X, Y or Z and not A, B or C he doesn't love her. It is this sort of interpretation she places on his behaviour and what he says that leads her to feeling scorned and hence to start rows. As a result of her misinterpretation, based on her own definitions, she has made herself feel insecure and the man cannot win. A very common example is a woman wanting her man to tell her that he loves her. But he tells her something else which he feels sure she will interpret as being the same thing. So he says 'Of course I love you. Don't I do the things around the house, work my fingers to the bone for you and the family' and so on which, to him, are signs that he loves her. Perhaps because she sees these things as his duty and has never considered them as a way of showing his love she fails to receive the message he is putting across which is 'I love you'.

All of this just shows how vigilant and open we need to be if we are to stop making false and harmful assumptions about one another in our relationships. Sometimes these assumptions can be slowly righted as a by-product of a loving life together but on other occasions you'll need to sit down, possibly with a professional, and work

Even when doing their own thing a couple can be together enjoying each other's company

things out carefully step by step. It's often amazing just how difficult these assumptions can be to work out, so deeply entrenched are they.

5 *Never use threats to get your own way*

This is especially harmful because by threatening to walk out of your marriage if your partner does or says something that is annoying to you, you may find yourself in the situation of having your bluff called and then regretting it. As with all areas of marriage, disagreements should be aired and discussed in such a way as to take into account the other partner's views which may be very different from your own (see 4 above). You may be working on totally erroneous assumptions but have never realized you were. Even if your partner goes along with your argument (under threat) 'for a quiet life' he or she will hardly feel very good about it and the seeds of longterm marital disharmony will be sown.

6 *Never punish your partner*

Many couples, when they feel bad about something, (often something they haven't been able to talk through) punish each other both deliberately and unconsciously. On other occasions the punished one will retaliate and punish the other. In neither of these situations do they necessarily hit each other – the punishment is all mental, emotional and sexual. They give each other the cold shoulder in and out of bed; will say very little often for days on end; standards of housekeeping fall to a basic minimum; children are used as a weapon to get back at the 'offending' partner; and sex is rationed, turned off entirely or carried out grudgingly without emotion or pleasure.

Any such punishing behaviour has a very damaging effect on a relationship and makes talking and other forms of communication almost impossible. It draws up battle lines. Someone has to give in eventually if life is to get back to normal and this can be humiliating for the one who backs down. The whole episode often remains as a scar on the marital relationship.

If ever you feel yourself about to punish your partner stop yourself and get down to some or all of the communication training skills we discuss below. Most loving couples regret such warring episodes, so nip them in the bud early. A few, however, enjoy rowing because they get more out of sex in the making-up afterwards!

Improving your communication skills

There are several levels at which we communicate with our partners and we need to be aware of them all so that we can make a conscious effort to improve things.

The three areas that we can change in the way we communicate are:

1 The way we think about our partner (head)

2 The way we feel about our partner (heart)

3 The way we behave (hands)

1 *Thinking about your relationship* (head work)

What to do Spend some time alone and think things through on your own. Make a list of the things that are bothering you and see if you can work out a plan to improve your communication with your partner. The rest of this section should help. Start off by creating space in your life to discuss things between the two of you. Busy couples, and especially those with a family, often find it extremely difficult to put aside enough time to talk about anything, let alone their relationship. We know it'll sound silly to some but try making an appointment with each other and put it in your diaries or on the family calendar. Make it for a reasonable time of the day – not 10.00 in the evening when you are both tired. Make a simple agenda on a piece of paper and each take it in turns to raise a point for discussion.

Learn to communicate at the thinking level by practising one or more of the following games:

Go to bed, cuddle and perhaps massage each other (see page 194) and when you're relaxed get a piece of paper each and write the following words down the left hand side. Copulation, intercourse, masturbation, oral sex, orgasm, genitals, penis, vagina, clitoris, anus, testicles, breasts, nipples, menstruation, semen. Now you both, on your own, write against each of these what your private words are for every one of these sexual terms. Before you start, decide on a reward for who gets the most in the column. Once you've finished, swap your pieces of paper and take it in turns to read out what the other wrote. This is one way of breaking down the unspoken barriers that have arisen during your relationship and can spark off all kinds of discussions from which you can both learn. We all have our private language as loving couples, and also have unspoken ways of communicating loving intentions. But in many couples one or other has forgotten the language and can't communicate. When a husband says, for example, 'I'd love an early night tonight' he almost certainly doesn't mean he's going to bed at 9.30 to sleep. He really means 'I'd like to make love to you tonight'. The couple probably used to understand the language but have now got to the stage where they take the words literally yet can't actually bring themselves to say what they really want.

An extension of this word game can be played using other words (not necessarily of a sexual nature) about other important areas of life. Give yourselves prizes for getting right your partner's views on say, private education, obscene language, erotica, capital punishment, Mr. Jones' new car, simultaneous orgasms, or whatever you think matters to your spouse. Once again this is simply a device to get talking and to show each other just how you really do think about things that matter.

2 *Learning to feel about your relationship* (heart work)

With all the emphasis on genitality in modern life many couples lose sight of the possibilities there are for loving behaviour on a day to day basis. Many people start off their married lives being very close and romance abounds. As the years trickle by and children put stresses and strains on the marriage loving behaviour is often the first to suffer. This is a shame because unless one feels loved and loving, the physical side of sex may mean little and often slowly fades.

Loving behaviour involves feeling lovable, feeling loving, and allowing yourself to be loved in the ways that your partner wants to love you. All are equally important to a good loving relationship. The phrase 'making love' is a particularly useful one but has now become synonymous with having intercourse, which is a pity because couples can make love all day but having intercourse is a rather specific subfraction of the business of making love.

Making love has more to do with a couple's whole life style together, physical and emotional, a small part of which is intercourse. Couples who make love according to our definition do not copulate, they always have intercourse. So what do we mean by making love?

First of all it's a continuous, ongoing process that is ideally an important part of every couple's life. Obviously none of us can spend all day having intercourse and wouldn't want to, even if we were physically capable of it, but we *can* spend all our time together making love in the widest sense of the word. Everything we do together should show our love and affection for our partner – it shouldn't be something we switch on just when we want sex. A couple who live like this might not have intercourse very frequently but they are constantly tuned in to each other's physical and emotional wavelenghts and intuitively know when they want sex and when they don't. Such a couple have a mutual language, share their thoughts easily, and often know what each other is thinking about. As a result, they are so at ease that they can communicate about anything without a fear of misunderstanding.

Rediscovering love in a relationship needs working at yet many people feel that if it needs 'that much effort' it can't be right. Too many couples in trouble feel that everything should come right as if by magic and that to force the pace by artificial methods is to try too hard to save something that should perhaps have died. Obviously this kind of decision will sometimes have to be made but it is rarely necessary. Most partnerships reap the benefit of single-minded effort and hard work; in therapy couples tell how they make giant strides – far beyond what they had ever thought possible.

During courtship a couple build up a vast store of mutual pleasure and enjoyment. It's a time when they feel 'in love' and during which they have an exaggerated sense of how wonderful their partner is. They both want to be in each other's company to show appreciation of each other with gifts and feel excited even at the thought of seeing each other. They take great pains to learn what pleases each other and act accordingly. After several years together a lot of this magic goes but it needn't because you can re-kindle the fires of courtship and keep romance alive in your marriage. As it's difficult suddenly to start behaving in a way which has become unfamiliar over the years try starting things off by using an artificial but extremely valuable technique called the sensual holiday.

The sensual holiday

A sensual holiday is an hour, a day, a weekend or any length of time when you make a conscious decision to throw out your old routines and roles and start all

over again learning and teaching each other to be intimate. In short it's a planned return to courtship but with the benefit of maturity. Of course this idea isn't new. Couples have always taken weekends or short holidays away together to recharge their emotional batteries and to re-learn to communicate with each other. But a sensual holiday is more, it's a time when a couple devote themselves to *themselves* alone and develop sensitivities and intimacy. It's also a time for romantic behaviour and games.

A sensual holiday doesn't just happen it is planned for and eagerly looked forward to. It's fun to take turns in planning your sensual holiday so that each has a turn at deciding what will happen. This planning greatly enhances the anticipation and desire and involves drawing up a list of things to do in preparation. For example, you may buy your wife a pair of really beautiful panties, arrange for some flowers to be sent to your 'holiday' spot, arrange to see a sexy play or film together and so on. All of this can be quite difficult for the more shy partner so it's best for the more outgoing and adventurous one to plan the first holiday to get things moving. All of this helps each of you to think more imaginatively about the whole of your relationship.

As part of the preparation you could prepare some sexual tokens which your partner can redeem at any agreed time on your sensual holiday. You simply dream up the things you'd most like to do or have done to you and write them out on slips of

Even a walk in the country for an afternoon can be a sensual holiday

paper. You can give your lover these slips a day or two before your holiday so that he or she can get pleasure from the anticipation. In practical terms it also gives him or her the chance to prepare things.

Here are some ideas for your tokens (undoubtedly you'll be able to improve on this list according to your own needs and pleasures).

◆ A night in an (expensive) hotel

◆ Quickie sex in a public or semi-public place

◆ Champagne for breakfast

◆ Heavy petting in the back row of the cinema

◆ One sensual massage (see below)

◆ One evening of total submission to your wishes

◆ One evening at a hotel pretending to be a whore with your partner.

A US expert in this field has a patient who sends her tokens to her husband at work but you can work out your own method of delivery.

Of course your holiday need not only be sex and romance-centred it could, and probably should, also include other situations you enjoy indoors or out. Perhaps a whole day in bed would be your idea of bliss. A day going around picture gallery or climbing could be equally blissful if that's what turns you on.

But whatever you do or wherever you do it the idea is to get out of your rut of unromantic lovemaking. This means making a specific effort to change the time and place of when you make love. If you always make love in the bedroom try the garden, the living room floor, a hotel room, out of doors and so on. Next change what you do. Ask your partner to massage a certain part of your body; keep the lights on if you usually switch them off; make love with the woman dressed in her sexiest underwear; play sultan/sultana games in which the woman teases and seduces the man and so on. Teasing is an exciting part of a sensual holiday. Go for the unexpected and build up the sexual tension and romance by giving sexy cues and lists of exciting things. Many men like to think of a woman naked under her skirt when she's out somewhere. Whisper in his ear just as you are about to go into a restaurant or hotel that you are wearing your black suspenders or no panties and he'll be so aroused he won't be able to eat! It'll probably turn you on too!

Part of this teasing, and a very effective one, is to agree on a ban on intercourse for a fixed time period at the start of your sensual holiday. If you are going away for the weekend, for example, agree that you won't have sex until the second day. Everything else would be allowed but not sex. This builds up the excitement and anticipation and greatly adds to the experience when it happens. Not many couples given a good build-up to their sensual holiday can cope with much abstention but that doesn't matter. Breaking the ban is fun too! More seriously though a ban on intercourse means that you put more effort and thought into non-intercourse pleasures and delights and make lovemaking less the centre-piece. One of the most boring facets of long-term relationships is their predictability and the inevitability of the end or goal. By banning intercourse, if only for a day or two, you are forced to look for other ways of pleasing each other.

Obviously every couple will make up their own sensual holidays to answer their own particular needs and fantasies so what's been outlined here can only be a guide.

But once back from your sensual holiday you'll have to make time to spend together sharing and caring so that you can build on the goodwill and increase in romantic feelings you've created. It's not a bad idea to put an evening a week aside for yourselves – perhaps to discuss things that matter or even to build on your sensual holiday experiences and pleasures. All of this may seem somewhat strange and even artificial but no improvement in one's emotional and sexual life occurs without effort – so give it a try.

Getting yourself fit to love

Many couples have poor opinions of themselves and their bodies. Is it surprising then that when we get down to tough talking about their marriage problems, they complain that deep down they consider themselves unlovable and unattractive? How can they possibly hope to be able to make love all the time as we are suggesting?

There are lots of practical things one can do to improve one's own self-image. Ask yourself the following questions. Have you let yourself go looks-wise? If so, rethink your clothes and appearance with good advice if necessary. Have you put on too much weight so that your clothes look nothing on you? If so, go to a slimming club, see your doctor or buy a good book and get those pounds off. Is your job boring you to death? If so, it could be you rather than the job that is at fault. If not you could change your job. Many say that their unsatisfactory job makes them feel worthless. Once you get out of the rut you begin to have more self-esteem and this improves your lovemaking. Are your children or family getting you down? If so, see your doctor or another professional adviser and get things sorted out: don't let them drag you down. And so on. Go through your life, talk it over with your partner item by item and see how you can improve your self-image.

One of the killers of self-image for many people today is that they are so busy, especially if they have families. Being too busy can leave one feeling like a drudge, and can kill self-confidence and a lot of life's pleasures. Decide between you both how you're going to organize things practically so that you can take up an interest or hobby. Switch off the TV! Go to an evening class, start up a home business, do anything which *you* enjoy such as joining a drama group, taking up a unisex sport and so on. Do something that your partner has no specialist knowledge of and give yourself the confidence of doing something alone and independently. You'll find that this will provide a new interest for yourself and will give you new things to share with your partner. Of course, none of this means that you should start spending so much time apart from each other that the relationship suffers – but you don't have to – an evening or two a week will hardly drive you apart.

Once you've started to sort out your life and your physical appearance you'll feel so much better that you'll automatically feel more loving and lovable and, incidentally, you'll probably find that sex is better too.

But this isn't enough, in parallel with these changes start a programme of improving your physical lovability. You can do this on your own at first. If you are already a very loving, physical person, skip over the next part and go on to the next stage.

A simple self-discovery programme for men and women

Put aside an hour or so for yourself when you know you won't be disturbed. Run a hot bath. Stand completely naked in front of a full length mirror and get to know your body. Imagine that it is the first time you've seen yourself naked and look at yourself as you never have before. Don't gloss over things you don't like about your body. Try to see the good points too and remember that you are you and nobody else. Be honest about anything you could improve (a pot belly or fat thighs for example) and decide to do something positive about it. If you don't like what you see in the mirror, no matter how much your partner loves you, you'll continue to be disappointed until you come to terms with it or change it. You don't have to have a 'perfect' body to be highly attractive. You don't have to apologize for being you but if you're unhappy with the way you look, do something about it. If this proves impossible, instead of moaning or feeling inferior learn to adjust to and accept those things which can't be altered. Concentrate on your good points though and put your bad ones (especially if they can't be altered) into perspective. You aren't a clothes horse, a model from Vogue or a macho film star; you are yourself.

Look at your body and when you've explored every inch, get into the bath, soap yourself all over and start exploring your body physically. Go through the motions slowly and systematically, letting your hands run all over your body, sliding your fingers into all the hollows, folds and creases. Close your eyes if you want to and wallow in it. See how different the skin feels over different parts of your body and see what you'd most like done to each area to produce the nicest sensations. Keep the water hot and keep exploring until you're relaxed.

Get out of the bath and dry yourself gently, then lie on your bed in a warm room and try to think about your feelings about what you've done. Did it make you feel good, bad, guilty, silly? If so, why? And how do these feelings relate to the way you feel when you're with your partner? Did you think it a waste of time? If so, why? Don't you see yourself as important enough to spend time on or would you rather be watching TV? Think about the fact that many of us have become so unused to giving ourselves pleasure that we are almost incapable of really pleasing someone else or receiving pleasure from others. Compare how the feelings you've just had compare with other loving, sexual, sensations you've had with people in the past. How do your current feelings match up?

All of this should make you begin to question how you feel when you are with your partner in bed. Have things become slipshod, hasty or makeshift? If so, how about changing things now – today – so that your physical lovemaking doesn't slip away from you further.

Now you're relaxed you can repeat the whole bath routine but with body lotion. At the end, if you feel like it, masturbate and submerse yourself in the feelings.

Once you've done this a few times and your partner is equally practised, the time will have come to start doing exactly the same things together. Sensual massage is described below and you can now have a go at that. Get your partner to do what you find is sensual and exciting and to do it for long periods of time, talking and sharing your thoughts and feelings as you do so. Guide each other as to exactly what is *best*, not just pleasant, and learn over several sessions exactly how best to please each other. *Don't have intercourse for the first few sessions* and keep away from breasts and genitals. Keep the relationship on a loving, caring, affectionate plane. If you get really aroused, masturbate each other if you have to but better still get used to pleasing each other physically without *having* to have sex. When and only when you can both give each other lovely sensations that are an end in themselves, start having intercourse at the end if you want to. Many couples don't want to – they simply enjoy the stroking, cuddling and massaging as an end in itself. There is no goal to aim for in this sort of love-making and it can be as relaxing as intercourse and just as pleasurable. The most important lesson to come out of this is that physical intimacy and pleasuring doesn't necessarily mean 'I want sex'.

3   *Things to do* (hand work)

Along with the brainwork and romantic work you'll be doing goes the practical, physical things that will need working at if you want to improve your communication with your partner.

The sensual holiday. Just as individuals need space and a degree of privacy, so do couples . . . especially young ones. This can often only be achieved by getting away from family and friends to be totally alone

Sensual massage This is basically a type of massage performed first by one partner on the other and then the other way round. There is only one rule – the partner who is being massaged has to tell the other exactly what feels nice and what does not. The only goal is for the massager totally to devote him- or herself to pleasing the other, whatever it is that he or she asks for. Sensual massage is not genital, in fact we suggest that nipples, breasts and genitals are usually avoided initially. It also is not necessarily a prelude to intercourse, although sometimes intercourse will follow naturally. The very fact that the couple end up pleasing each other, yet do not feel they *have* to go on to intercourse can be a relief for both and it often eases the sexual situation greatly.

The massaging or pleasuring is usually done with both partners completely naked and baby oil or special, warmed massage oil can be used. Take the phone off the hook, put on some music you both enjoy, and put a sheet on the floor or massage each other on the bed. The key to really good sensual massage is that there must be constant feedback – at least for the first few times, until each knows exactly how to please the other. Even in the couple who massage each other several times a week, the needs or wishes of one partner may change, and the change should be picked up and acted upon by the one who is massaging. Be careful that you do not fall into the trap of one partner always being the 'giver' and the other the 'receiver'. The one who finds it more difficult to receive often needs help and loving care more than the other partner.

Sensual massage is a sharing event between two people not something that one partner does *to* the other – it is a two-way team effort. In this way it is very good training for intercourse. It is very pleasant just to cuddle together afterwards and go to sleep, although sometimes the massage will end with intercourse.

A couple doing this several times a week are making time for each other, caring about each other's responses, talking to each other more and, as a result, finding it harder to be angry, especially over little things. Their quality of life is improved greatly as a result and they find it easier to communicate physically and emotionally about sexual matters.

Now you're well on the way to being what you want, get started on your communication with your partner. Sensual massage is a very real and valuable form of communication and makes talking easier. In the early days at least you'll be talking a lot, telling each other exactly what you like and don't like. When you feel more at ease with yourself you'll find it easier to communicate on other things too.

Learning or re-learning to communicate should proceed along all of these lines roughly in parallel. It will take time in the early weeks or months and you'll need to do less of other things to make time for yourself and your partner. But this in itself often works wonders because most couples have simply got out of the habit of spending time with and caring for each other. Things have become sloppy, hasty and skimped both in and out of bed and as a result they communicate very badly. Just bear in mind the study mentioned earlier that found that failure of communication was the commonest cause of marital distress and you'll see why we have devoted so much space to the subject.

Intercourse – perfect communication

Perhaps the ultimate in communication between a man and a woman is sexual intercourse. Really good intercourse involves sharing and caring behaviour between two people who are tuned into each other's needs. An experienced couple don't talk about what each best enjoys — they have learned to read each other's responses both emotional and physical and have intercourse rather than copulate on almost every occasion. We summarize the difference between intercourse and copulation in the table on page 200.

As already said, readers of current sex books and articles in the glossy magazines could be forgiven for thinking that everyone (but them) was having a superb sex life. Alas, this is not so. Most people are dissatisfied with their sex lives, at least to some extent, as surveys have always shown and even so-called happily married couples often have sex problems that bother them – if not enough to make them seek outside help.

Because most people have the impression that everyone else is 'eating out at the Ritz' in sexual terms their humble fair at their 'transport café' seems poor in comparison. This is a shame because most couples are tolerably happy making love in a fairly restricted number of ways at a frequency they have come to accept, even though it may not be 'ideal'. The concept of ideal sex is a very harmful one and most sex books promote such harm rather than cure it.

Good sex is fairly easy to define. It is pleasurable for both partners on most occasions and leaves both feeling relaxed and happy. That's all that can be safely said. There are no absolutes in the sexual life; no ways of measuring pleasure, the happiness or joy of just cuddling each other, having a real friend and so on. A good sexual relationship will, however, be totally self-contained making it unnecessary and unlikely that either partner will need to look outside for emotional or sexual needs to be fulfilled.

These then are the basics of good intercourse and everything else is a frill. Most couples, however, live their sex lives in a kind of fantasy world peopled by sex-mad athletes who apparently dwarf their own humble efforts. This breeds a sense of inferiority in those who tend to feel inferior and resentment in those who feel they should be getting 'more of the gravy'. The fact that there is in fact very little gravy elsewhere is a very unfashionable truth.

FAILURE TO FIND SEXUAL FULFILMENT

Occasional failure to perform

Almost all of us have the occasional sexual failure from time to time but such failure need go no further and may be of little significance except on that single occasion. Alcohol, tiredness, worry, stress, health problems, emotional problems, off-putting things in the environment (such as a baby crying or the neighbours or in-laws across thin walls) personal hygiene problems and many many others can all, either together or singly, produce a one-off sexual failure.

The problems start only when such a failure is blown up in the individual's mind to be more important than it is so that it becomes an ongoing source of failure. The causes of such failures can be pretty obvious if you know what to look for and the list above is a good start.

Unfortunately many, if not most, of us tend to latch onto an occasional or even a single bad sexual experience and blow it up into something far larger than it deserves. 'She no longer loves me'; 'I must be unattractive to him'; 'Perhaps it's my age/ time of life'; and so on are the sorts of things that go through people's minds and

Scene from 'Casablanca': some people retreat to alcoholism when they fail to find sexual fulfilment. Others can never be sexually fulfilled because they have a drink problem

even get said. Such attitudes breed resentment, anger or just plain disappointment and arguments start out of bed on matters that are nothing whatever to do with sex. A man whose wife occasionally 'lets him down' sexually soon starts to find fault with her housekeeping, her appearance or her child care and open hostility can soon become the norm. This soon escalates into full-scale resentment and a vicious circle builds up so that the 'failing' partner becomes a failure because he or she is cast in that role by the other and finds it difficult to break out of it.

One of the commonest problems is that the failed partner becomes over-interpretative and begins to accuse the other (either in their mind or in fact) of all kinds of things. So it is that a man who occasionally can't maintain his erection is suspected of having sex elsewhere ('which is why he can't perform with me!') or a middle-aged woman who doesn't get aroused easily is 'going through the change of life and will be sexually useless from now on'.

Unless there are obvious reasons for the occasional failure, the best rule is to accept things at face value and not to over-interpret what you see. The chances are that you'll get the wrong end of the stick and make things worse. Sadly, many couples are on the look-out for more trouble

COPULATION	INTERCOURSE
'Fucking'	'Making love'
Possible with anyone	Personalized to one's partner
Self-centred	Partner-centred
Solely inter-genital activity	A form of inter-personal communication
No commitment necessary	Commitment essential
Involves genitals only	Involves genitals and whole personality
An end in itself	Part of a couple's life-style
Requires only limited cooperation	Requires full cooperation
Partner's preferences unimportant	Partner's needs crucial
Satisfaction of partner incidental	Partner satisfaction fundamental
Uninsightful and unimaginative	Requires insight and imagination
Tends to pall eventually	Improves with time
New partners may be sought	Value of partner increases
Tends to be stereotyped	Varied if necessary according to needs
Restricted horizons	Limitless horizons
Failure hard to cope with	Adapts to occasional failure
Emotions may be involved but not necessarily	Emotional involvement essential
Aims solely to relieve sexual tension	Communication is as important as tension relief
Self-revelation unnecessary	Based on self-revelation
A form of masturbation using partner's genitals	Based on knowledge of each other's secrets
All sexual relationships start here	Policy is one of continuous improvement
Many relationships remain here	Is based on uninhibited awareness of possibilities
Short-term gain	Life-time investment
Never involves intercourse	May involve copulation ('quickie') to please partner or self

Progressing from Copulation to Intercourse

This is only a suggested guide and is capable of endless variation and adaptation. Having said this, clinical experience with couples over many years shows that it works. The fundamental point is that there must be a basic willingness to change, to cooperate, to grow together and to abandon old restraints and inhibitions. The ideal is to have the freedom and curiosity of a child and the ardour of an adolescent. The essence of this plan is that it increases personal communication on sexual matters and so helps communication within the relationship generally.

	Action	*Hints & explanations*
1	Set the scene – make it relaxing and warm	Tension and fear of interruption are counter-productive
2	Both undress – completely naked if possible	Try neither to be too excited nor too inhibited. Try to feel free
3	Woman lies face down	The idea is now for the partners to explore the pleasures they can give each other's body excluding the genitals

4	Man explores woman's reactions to various types of stimulation of her neck, back, bottom, legs and feet	The aim is to discover which parts give her most pleasure and what form of stimulation (e.g. light stroking, gentle scratching, kissing and superficial massage) is nicest for her. Woman must tell and he must observe her reactions to pick up things she doesn't say
5	Using warm baby or massage oil the man massages the woman's rear surfaces	The aim of this stage is to promote relaxation and trust in an atmosphere of loving warmth (see page 194)
6	Woman repeats steps 3, 4, and 5 on the man	Ignore signs of sexual arousal. Woman may have to get weight over her shoulders to give sufficient pressure to please man in deep massage
7	Cuddle and discuss the experience. Sex is best avoided at this stage. Practice expressing love in other ways	The aim is to establish new patterns of communication; to break old habits (which is why sex is best avoided); to build up sexual tensions and to reduce inhibitions
8	If possible repeat steps 3, 4, 5, 6, and 7 several times over a number of days	Time, not necessarily a lot, needs to be set aside for each other – but anyway this should be the pattern of the new relationship
9	Repeat 8 but include brief and light stimulation of the breasts and genitals *in passing*	The idea here is to build up sexual tension further (which is of use in establishing new patterns later on) but not to reach orgasm (at least not together)
10	Woman inspects man's genitals at leisure and in complete detail, using both sight and touch	This must be thorough. Examples of questions she should be able to answer afterwards are: How is foreskin (if any) actually attached to penis? How far do hairs extend along the shaft? Are the testes equal in height and size?

11 Man inspects breasts and vulva in minute detail

Examples of questions he should be able to answer are: How is the female foreskin constructed? Where does the exit of the urethra (urinary passage) lie in relation to the entrance of the vagina? Does the vulva change in any way whilst being inspected? Steps 10 and 11 can be combined in the same session

12 Woman asks man to masturbate in his usual way in front of her and to ejaculate, perhaps after repeating steps 1 to 6 if required or if man is shy

Woman to notice exact position of his hand; the location of his fingers; the amount of pressure; the rate and extent of movement of hand, and type of movement; the changes in his scrotum and testes; his facial changes; the amount of pre-ejaculatory secretion; the size and force of the initial spurt of semen and the number, speed and force of further spurts. At what stage does the man stop stimulating himself?

13 The couple cuddle and discuss this experience and its effects on both of them

Deeper communication can now start by the woman asking about the frequency and location of his masturbation and its associated fantasies. This is a loving and trusting act and should not be undertaken until the woman feels capable of coping with the fact he is likely to fantasize about other women. She can ask how and when masturbation first started, with whom etc.

14 Man asks woman to masturbate in front of him

Man to note her body position; leg position; hand position; location of fingers and the rate, type, range and pressure of movement. Does the method she uses change during the act? Does she insert fingers into her vagina? What facial, breast, vulval, clitoral and skin changes occur? Does she stop stimulating herself periodically or stimulate some other area?

15 The couple cuddle and discuss the experience and its effects on both of them

The woman might want to discuss her shame and the man his disbelief that she does masturbate and his excitement about it. The origins and frequency of her masturbation should then be discussed and her fantasies explored. (Women who masturbate by non-genital means should show their method and those who deny masturbation should be asked to rub their vulva as if they were masturbating. (Steps 12 to 15 can be combined in the same session)

16	Man masturbates woman, perhaps after steps 1, 2, 3, 4, 5, and 9	The aim is for the man to learn to masturbate her as well as she can herself. She must be prepared to guide him, and lovingly correct him until he does exactly what she best enjoys
17	Woman masturbates man	The aim is for the woman to get the man to relax and enjoy himself the best he possibly can. He may have to give further instructions or demonstrations to achieve this
18	Steps 12 to 17 are repeated, and improved, over a few weeks, fairly frequently so as to avoid loss of momentum	During these sessions more fantasy material can be exchanged and books may be jointly read leading to further discussions. Sessions can start, perhaps with steps 4, 5 and 6 so as to build-up sexual tension. Experimentation and variations can now be introduced. Hopefully, the woman will learn to come more quickly (and repeatedly if she wishes) and the man to last longer if necessary
19	Step 18 is now elaborated so as to increase arousal and pleasure even further	The aim here is to use knowledge of the partners and their fantasies to increase anticipation by the use of eroticism. This can include one partner stripping sexually; the stripping of a partner; sexy underclothes; provocative displays; different locations; looking at sexy magazines together; films and videos; bathing together; romantic activities; in short anything which increases sexual excitement

ITS MY TURN FOR THE CROWN

20 When both are in agreement that they have negotiated steps 1–19 to each other's satisfaction – start intercourse. Don't go any further than step 19 unless you are both happy you have got the most out of steps 1–19. Hasty rushing on will lead straight back to copulation again

This step should be a natural extension of the previous activities rather than a red-letter day. As well as taking into account what has been learned about the sexuality of the other, each partner should work out how to add something extra based on his or her insights into the other. For example, this could take the form of a 'game' approach. Hopefully this will be a completely different and vastly more satisfying experience than previous copulation. For many women, positions will have to be used where step 16 can be incorporated into the act of intercourse

21 Elaboration of step 20

This step is highly personal, as is intercourse itself, and will vary from couple to couple allowing them to learn to adjust to moods, circumstances and change. The emphasis is not on genital gymnastics but upon the giving and receiving of further pleasure through exploration and communication

22 Exchanging control

The idea here is for each partner to take total control occasionally and lay down exactly how they want foreplay and intercourse itself to be carried out. The other adopts the role of sex-slave and does anything requested or ordered. This prevents stereo-typing and boredom and can reveal all kinds of exciting new positions and variations

23 Periodic re-assessment.

Progress should be continuous but the occasional devotion of total time to each other, as on a sensual holiday no matter how brief, should be used to keep intercourse under review and to renew its pleasures

after one failure and the cycle of failure-anxiety-failure sets in. Some people, because of their personality, convert any minor set-back into a major tragedy.

Intermittent failure

Some people have intermittent failures – they fail sexually every time a particular group of circumstances occurs in their lives. These are usually fairly clear-cut and can to some extent be avoided or if not, lived with in the knowledge that the problem arises under certain quite specific circumstances and not at other times. Obviously many of the reasons for occasional failure mentioned can be prevented to some extent if only one is aware that they are the cause of the failure.

But the couple that over-interprets the occasional failure are often having trouble

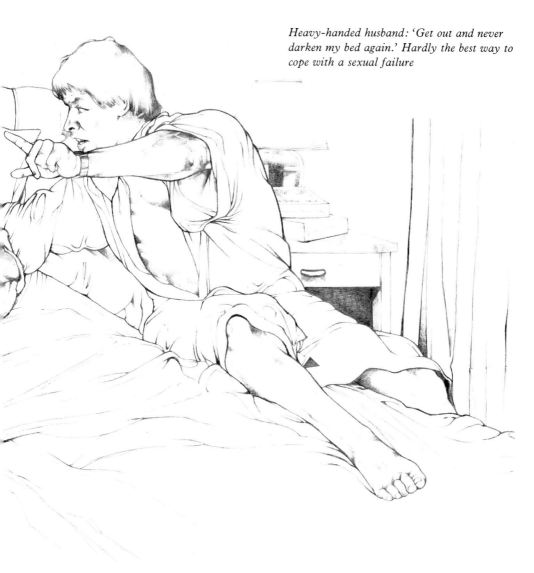

Heavy-handed husband: 'Get out and never darken my bed again.' Hardly the best way to cope with a sexual failure

with their relationship generally, are sexually bored, are going through a patch when they are trying to de-love each other to clear the decks for another relationship and so on. To some extent all marriages change for better or worse as the years go by but usually the failures that occur are a result of neglect rather than actual ill will. A man often becomes lazier about pleasing his wife and she in turn is less stimulating to her husband as the years advance so that sex becomes less frequent and the occasional failure much more obvious as a result. Young marrieds who are making love every day can weather sexual failure from time to time because their level of sexual activity is so high that the good times far outweigh the bad but for a couple in their 50s and 60s this is not nearly as true and 'failures' often stand out as milestones. To a great extent older couples are in a better position to weather these storms because they have been through them before and survived and because they have a deeper understanding and knowledge of each other's personality. So it's swings and roundabouts as in so many sexual matters.

What to do:

Prevent situations in which failures occur

This is mostly a matter of common sense but it's amazing how many couples just don't think of simple things before jumping to false conclusions or even going for professional help. Professional help *may* be necassary if a problem persistently produces sex failures. A good example is the man who goes out to the pub, drinks too much, comes home late the worse for drink and can't or won't make love, much to his wife's chagrin. Such a couple may need help because the man is clearly using drink to avoid sex. On the other hand there are those men who need a drink to get over their inhibitions so that they can summon up the courage to have sex at all. This can be a problem if the woman can't bear the smell of alcohol on his breath yet without it he couldn't function at all. Many sexually anxious men especially use drink, work or other outside pursuits to excuse their sexual failures but they unconciously actually produce the situations simply because they need such excuses to avoid sex and to explain their poor performance.

● *If you are a failed partner – don't be over-interpretative*

We discuss this above.

● *If you are the failing partner offer alternative satisfaction to your partner*

Just because you don't feel like sex or can't manage intercourse for some reason don't throw in the sponge and make out that the whole event is a disaster. There are plenty of alternatives. A man who can't maintain an erection, for example, need not leave his wife high and dry but can cuddle her, masturbate her or perform cunnilingus on her to bring her to orgasm. This is often highly arousing for him and intercourse becomes possible *after* her orgasm. How much better for the whole relationship than rolling over in a huff and feeling bad.

Failure in the context that we're discussing here is a failure to have intercourse. This doesn't necessarily mean you have to fail to enjoy yourself. If only more couples realized this the bedrooms of the land wouldn't be filled with harsh thoughts and recriminations.

Doing something is also good do-it-yourself therapy. It's far better than stewing over the problem and neither of you sleeping for ages.

We don't succeed 100% of the time at anything we do so why should sex be any different? We can come to terms with a bad golf shot; dropping the odd note when we play the piano or having a bad crop of vegetables in the garden but when it comes to sex we're often too hard on ourselves.

Nip the problem in the bud

Expecting to fail is likely to produce failure and the male sexual arousal mechanism is so finely set that even deeply-seated unconscious fears and concerns can disrupt it. The problems aren't so great for women when it comes to *performing* because they can lie there and let it happen but if they want to *enjoy* it they too could be in trouble.

It's easy to see that if a couple don't stop the spiral early on either or both could start to avoid sex (see page 234). The secret is to remain optimistic and not to dwell on the occasional failure. Try again.

To many, men especially, the occasional failure is the signal that he should take a break from sex, from that partner and even from some other person in life that could, in his view, be damaging his ability to have sex. Such men often claim that 'impotence is now coming upon me' as if it were an inevitable plague. Most men over 40 or 50 begin to attribute the occasional failure to their waning prowess and some go off sex altogether and revert to masturbation to build up their sex drives and fantasies.

This is usually not helpful. The thing to do is to go straight back to intercourse as soon as possible. Don't get out of the habit by talking yourself into a situation that doesn't exist.

Failure to get the best out of sex

Although no definite or serious sex problems may be present many people feel that their sex life is letting them down. The act of intercourse is less pleasurable than it should be, and isn't as exciting as it *could* be.

Anti-sexual attitudes acquired during childhood, the effects on present relationships of past experience, inhibitions, relationship difficulties, latent deviancy, and poor factual knowledge are all covered by other sections, but these influences may not be strong enough to account for the humdrum nature of your present sex life.

Experimentation, the use of erotica, a return to courtship, a sensual holiday and so on may have been tried without benefit, even in a good, harmonious relationship between people with well-matched personalities and sexualities.

So what is wrong? The real problem is sometimes found to be that following the first flush of emotion and interest in one another the couple have re-focussed their priorities. For example, there are those couples who think that making friends and having lots of social contacts are the most important things in life. Perhaps without even realizing it, they have put other people at the top of their list. This is very subtle, rarely as obvious as it sounds, and it can be a deeply hidden form of sex-avoidance; an unconscious strategy that prevents them from facing up to the real difficulty in their relationship which, to the outside world, continues happily.

In other cases the couple are avoiding each other in other ways. They spend time with one another and seem to communicate very well. But in fact one or both cannot sustain a truly close relationship with another human being, and they use words as a substitute for true intimacy.

In other cases the situation is more obvious. Familiarity over the years has dulled their eyes, and they see one another as very much the same people they were when they met. The exciting differences that gave the relationship its spark early on have long since faded; perhaps working together and the inclination to choose similar lifestyles result in a lack of sexual excitement that can be very difficult to appreciate. Sometimes this occurs simply because the fun has gone out of sex, but in other couples the loss comes about because neither pays nearly enough attention to the other as a unique individual. This partly accounts for the attractions of affairs, in which such freshness can be recaptured.

A similar problem is the gradual shift in the perceptions of one partner for the other as less of a lover and sexual partner than before. The easiest example to understand is a man who identifies his lover as a mother when she starts to have babies.

The subtleties of these situations can baffle all but the most expert professional, and these few examples can be mutiplied by hundreds.

So the basic problem can only be solved by finding the cause and trying to put it right. This section might just give the reader enough insight, along with the rest of the book, to be able to sit down and reappraise things with his or her partner, or to appreciate they may need one of the professionals described in the following pages. The problems won't just go away. Neither is there any magical therapy that will help everyone. Each couple has to find their own way to salvation.

It's also important to remember not to develop unrealistic expectations of our partner or the relationship. This is just destructive, and it can drive him or her to the point at which they can never hope to meet our needs. Rather than looking at things negatively how about turning the subject round? Instead of worrying about the imperfections, think about how much you have.

An appreciation of each other, and the insights gained from reading a book such as this, can be a firm foundation to build on, but even then things might not be easy and you may need the disinterested advice of a professional outsider.

IF YOU HEAR A CLATTER ITS THE SCALES FALLING FROM MY EYES

When to go for help

There can be no hard and fast rule about this because we all have such different tolerance levels to failure. The time to seek help is when either partner becomes distressed and all attempts at self-help have failed.

Getting help and helping yourself

Ideally it would be best if couples with sex and relationship problems could sort them out between themselves, if only because it would save time and money and keep the problem 'in the family'. However, many couples find that they *can't* sort things out between them when it comes to sexual problems because both are so intensely involved that they can't see the wood for the trees. An outsider, especially a trained one can often see a way through to an answer simply because he or she is an outsider.

There is no shortage of outside help even though sex therapists and other 'specialists' are few and far between in the UK. There is such a range of possible helpers that the first thing to decide is what exactly you want or need.

Do you want:
◆ Simply to have a shoulder on which to cry or a willing ear to listen to your moans?

◆ To sort out your feelings within one particular area of your relationship?

◆ To find out pure factual information?

◆ To look at basic and fundamental problems within your partnership such as the inability to communicate with each other?

◆ To find an ally to be on your side 'against' your partner?

◆ To reassure yourself that you aren't mentally or physically ill?

◆ To find out if you are unique with your problem?

◆ To get practical help and advice as to what to do about your problem?

◆ To have a long, deep, look at yourself as a whole person with sex as part of that exploration?

Sorting out which of the many helping agencies are just right for your particular problem may not be easy but commonsense, as always, helps at first. For example, your best friend won't be able to tell

you if you are depressed or suffering from a medical conditon that's causing your pain on intercourse but your GP probably won't be as expert on women's feelings after the birth of a baby.

When it comes to choosing a helper then it makes sense to decide from the above list exactly which (and there may be more than one) area most concerns you and what you most need. Then seek out someone after reading this section and after one get-together ask yourself the following questions:

◆ Is the person sufficiently well qualified professionally to be able to give me the help I need?

◆ Does he or she really seem to understand me? Get the person to summarize the problem as he or she sees it at the end of the first visit as a starting point.

◆ Does the person have any special interest in my response or decision to take up therapy? Some female therapists are ardent feminists, for example, whose motives must be questioned if you have a problem with a man. Similarly, a priest or vicar may have religious axes to grind that might not be in your best interest. Go to someone who is neutral and whose training enables them to stand back from the problem on a personal level.

Whether or not to choose a therapist or helper who you know has personal marriage, sex or relationship problems is a difficult one. Some individuals go into this kind of work as a result of their own distressing experiences in the hopes of preventing others from making the same mistakes and because they have 'inside knowledge' of the problems. However, many people are wary of such therapists and feel that if they can't sort out their own lives they have no right to be advising others how to do so. After all, how seriously do you take anti-smoking advice from a doctor whom you know smokes?

What to do when you have a sexual or marital problem

Probably about two out of three marriages have serious problems at some time although, as we have seen, only half of these will end in divorce. Many more will have sex or relationship problems from time to time. So what can someone who is worried about his or her marriage, or who has sex problems, do?

Talk it over between yourselves

If you have bought this book and read this far you will already have learned enough to have answered some of your main problems (we hope!) and throughout the rest of the book you will find answers to many others, which you will be able to discuss with your partner. Ignorance of the facts is only one area of trouble, albeit an important one. Feelings are the biggest problem when things go wrong and often one cannot share one's feelings about someone else with them. At this point a third party becomes almost essential. The problem is who to turn to.

Talk to a close, loving friend or to a member of your family

Many people turn to a family member when times get tough and this has several advantages. It means you can let off steam in confidence yet not involve the serious step of involving a professional. If you simply want to have a moan this could be all you need, provided you have a family member or close relative you can trust. Unfortunately, family members, whilst they know you, may not offer good advice, often because they too are involved in the problem, even if they don't realize it. This is especially true of mothers and daughters.

When it comes to talking to friends don't go around sharing your marital and relationship problems with just anybody or you will receive so much conflicting and unprofessional advice that you will be even more confused. Also, it will be humiliating for you and your partner when things improve, if your friends and acquaintances know all your business. Seek out a trustworthy friend and talk things over rationally and confidentially. Bear in mind that by definition a friend will tend to take your side because he or she likes you and will not want to offend you. A true friend will tell you the bad news along with the good, but such discussions can put intolerable stresses on the friendship and can even kill it completely.

This is in no way comparable to what therapists do because they don't *tell* you what is wrong they lead you to an understanding of what's wrong and are skilled enough to help you modify your behaviour and thoughts so as to improve your life and that of those around you. Because there are so many problems with all this, lots of people do not confide their marital problems to friends or family but go straight to

When women are far away from their original home, friendship and an extended family life become vital and important support systems

professionals, however reluctantly. When real friends *are* useful is when the therapy is getting tough.

Talk to a professional

Unfortunately, in the UK we do not have a tradition of specialist medical care for marital and sex problems although to be fair, increasing numbers of family planning doctors are becoming well trained in sexual medicine. Those who can help professionally are:

Your general practitioner He or she may have no specialist training in this field but should be quite helpful as a result of dealing with similar problems time and again. A general practitioner can rarely spare much time but he can refer you to other people who are more expert and have more time. A marriage that has been going wrong for years before help is sought (which is usually the case) cannot be sorted out in a few minutes but often needs hours spread over several months. People cannot change their ideas and feelings quickly, and glib answers, however well meaning, are nearly always useless and often fuel the fire rather than quench it.

One reason for starting with your GP is that so many people with sexual and relationship problems have physical and mental symptoms which are very real to

TELL ME
ABOUT YOUR
SEXUAL
INHIBITIONS.
I LOVE A
GOOD
CHALLENGE

them. The fact that sexual and inter-relationship problems produce a lot of psychosomatic illness is little known, and far too often people make endless rounds of doctors and specialists seeking the elusive physical cause for symptoms which are in fact caused by their emotional state. A GP will be able to rule out physical causes for sexual and other symptoms. There is no excuse for suffering from symptoms caused by real illness just because you feel that your sex problem has made you so stressed that the ailment is 'all in the mind'. Sorting out all the tiredness, headaches, sleeplessness and so on can be a very good starting point for dealing with any sexual and marital problem, if only because an underlying physical or emotional conditon can either be at the heart of the sex problem or could make its treatment difficult.

If your emotional state is affecting your life or that of those around you, then you really should seek help from your doctor. We are all neurotic to some extent, but can usually function perfectly well in spite of our neuroses. The line between this level of neurotic behaviour and frank psychological illness is often difficult to draw even for a professional.

Most GPs have little or no training in counselling or psychology but a few are very skilled from clinical experience alone.

If you go to a practice in which the doctors are not expert in these areas, or do not have the time to talk with you in the way you'd like, then ask you family doctor about the availability and suitability of some of the other sources of help listed below. He will probably know someone locally. Increasing numbers of general practitioners have a counsellor or psychologist attached to their practice and this can be comforting as the referral is kept within the practice. The reverse of this is the fact that many patients don't want their general practitioners or any of his staff involved because they see him for too many other things all the time. Such people prefer to go to a complete outsider they'll never see again.

Marriage guidance counsellors The worst thing about these otherwise helpful people is their name. The word 'guidance' is a historical quirk, but today they do little 'guiding' in the old-fashioned sense, they are not in business to save marriages come what may, but offer a realistic service to the married, the single, the divorced and separated, homosexuals, and anyone who needs personal counselling. These counsellors are all trained but are not specialists in the medical sense of the word. Their training is by definition fairly restricted, and they are taught not to tell clients what to do. They work in forty-to-fifty minute time slots, which many people find too short to be really useful. Most marriage guidance counsellors are middle-class women and this puts some people off going to them. Having said this they do see every class of society, and nearly as many men as women. Many of the more common and uncomplicated marital and sexual problems can be dealt with by these counsellors, and the Marriage Guidance Council now has special centres which can offer specialist sex therapy sessions. Marriage guidance counsellors charge very modest fees indeed. The address of the National Marriage Guidance Council is given under Useful Addresses on pages 346–7.

Psychosexually trained doctors and psychiatrists Psychosexual medicine is a new branch of the medical profession in the UK and at the moment has attracted very few practitioners full-time. Having said this, there is a considerable number of Marital and Sexual Clinics within the National Health Service. The majority of 'experts' working in this field are consultant psychiatrists who, because of their understanding of psychological and emotional problems, tend to deal with sexual and relationship problems too. Many do not particularly want to deal with sexual problems and their patients share their reluctance. Few people with sexual or marital problems are mentally ill, and psychiatrists are by definition doctors who deal with mental illness. Going to a psychiatrist still has something of a stigma attached to it and there is always the suggestion (not from the doctor, of course) that one might actually have something 'wrong' with one's personality. The burden of sexual and marital problems is so enormous that the number of psychiatrists who deal with this area is small in comparison and help can be difficult to find. A few psychiatrists offer psychoanalysis for such problems but only a tiny fraction of 1 per cent of all marital problems need or receive true psychoanalysis.

The lay psychotherapist

Anyone can set him or herself up as a psychotherapist – there are no qualifications to be obtained before putting up a plate (though a few UK universities now offer diplomas in psychotherapy) or advertizing in the health press or the local papers. Of all those who set themselves up in this way some are charlatans and cranks and others excellent, yet they often have no formal training in psychotherapy. The best way to find such a person is to ask your GP or your friends. Personal recommendation is usually safest in a field in which feelings run high and in which people are exceptionally vulnerable to weird therapists.

This might be the time to point out that caution is essential when choosing any sex or marital therapist. Some have questionable notions and methods. Be wary of bogus 'clinics' that want a lot of money from you or who offer wonder-cures. If you are at all doubtful try to find out more before even going at all and if anything happens with which you aren't totally happy, don't go again.

Group therapy

Although most people would ideally like to have one-to-one therapy for their personal or sexual problems this is often unavailable or too expensive. Group therapy is a serious and valuable alternative with several advantages over one-to-one therapy. First, it helps people realize that they are not alone with their problems and that others have even worse ones. Second, by looking at your relationship with the others within a group a good therapist can learn a lot about your relationship within your marriage. Third, those in the group who know you very little may give honest feedback about the way you behave and

I LOST MY LIBIDO IN.. 1947

think – and this can be very valuable, especially if many of the others agree with each other because nowhere else will you find outsiders willing to be so open and frank about the effects you have on them. Fourth, by hearing about other people's problems and even helping them you can find answers to your own situation and thoughts, and finally the whole process is less 'you' centred which gives you time to reflect on your problems as others talk about theirs. Obviously, if you are really shy group therapy won't be for you but if you can brave the first few sessions you might well find that a controlled situation led by a professional person might just be the right place to overcome some of the problems.

Family planning clinics

Many people feel happiest going to a family planning clinic for help with sex and relationship problems, if only because it is familiar and less threatening than a 'real' sex clinic. They can also go there under the pretext of a contraception problem yet unbeknown to friends, relatives or even their partner, take the opportunity of discussing sex problems.

Of course there are real sex problems that can arise with contraception itself and contraceptive difficulties can be an expression of a sex problem. Contraceptive methods can be blamed for all kinds of sexual 'ills' and it takes a professional who really knows the facts to sort things out. Perhaps the most obvious example is the woman who goes off sex on the Pill. Some doctors think that this is a real, pharmacological side effect of the Pill and so ignore the psychosexual dimensions underlying the problem. Such a doctor may advise endless pill-switching but the woman's underlying sexual problem will go undetected.

Increasing numbers of family planning clinics now have true expertise in sex therapy too so perhaps your clinic would be a good starting point.

Samaritans

If you can't take your problem to someone face to face the Samaritans offer a telephone counselling service.

Gynaecologists and urologists

Increasing numbers of these doctors are taking an interest in sex therapy and are becoming more interested in the 'non-plumbing' aspect of sexual problems. Urologists end up seeing a lot of impotent men who think their trouble is in their lap when in fact it is between their ears but they can be very helpful with men with 'medical' sexual conditions. A man with a tight foreskin that is producing problems can be circumsized; penile splints can be inserted in those men who have physical reasons for not being able to erect; abnormalities of the penis can be treated surgically and so on.

You get to see a urologist or a gynaecologist by referral from your GP.

Gynaecologists have little or no specialized training in sexual and psychosexual matters yet understandably sometimes become embroiled in such things, often under the guise of physical illness. Increasing numbers of gynaecologists are now interesting themselves in the sex problem area. As with urologists you may have to wait a long time before you get an appointment on the NHS and this delay leads many women to seek private treatment for which they pay.

Self-help and voluntary organizations

Self-help is becoming an increasingly popular way of dealing with problems in many areas of medicine and sex problems are no exception. Dissatisfaction with what is available, its expense or its unavailability when you want it make people seek things they can do for themselves. In the US this has gone much further than in most other countries and there are now many American self-help set-ups often based on feminist groups. Such groups teach each other in pre-orgasmic classes, help each other to become familiar with their normal sexual anatomy and physiology and even diagnose and cure simple complaints such as thrush.

Many millions of women the world over suffer from cystitis linked to sex and for years in the UK a self-help group, the U & I Club, helped thousands of women to cope with this annoying and painful problem. The club is now no longer functioning but there are several books and leaflets written by Angela Kilmartin who started the club still available.

On pages 346–7 we have listed many of the self-help organizations that offer counselling services. You will see that many of these specialize in specific areas so be careful which one you contact so as to be sure of getting the best help possible. Many such organisations have trained psychologists (who are not doctors but are trained in the normal workings of the mind) on hand. Psychologists can actually be more helpful than doctors in many cases because more often than not people with sexual or relationship problems are not 'ill' and do not need a medical mind to sort them out. The strength of the non-medical specialist is that the patient does not go along thinking that there is a magic operation or bottle of pills to answer his problems.

Sex therapists

These are rare creatures in the UK although some of the above groups offer some kind of sex therapy in a very limited way, the vast majority of the 'treatment' of marital and sexual problems is done by talking and listening and by the partners discussing things they have learned when they go home. Most of the real work a couple does happens in between consultations. All professionals can hope to do is dispel some ignorance, get the couple talking again, help give them insight into their problems, show that they are not alone with their problems (millions of others have been down the same path before) and that they, the professionals, care enough to listen and to really try to help. Once they have recognized at least some of these things most couples are ready to work hard between consultations to build up their marriage again.

A small percentage of couples (or individuals) need more specific physical help with sexual problems. A woman who has never had an orgasm, for example, can, by having the blocking anxieties instilled in childhood removed, have her inherent capacity to do so restored to her; premature ejaculation can be helped; and couples with similar problems can be shown how to overcome them. Sex therapy is often highly effective and results can be obtained remarkably quickly for most problems.

None of these helpers can work miracles for a marriage. The couple has to want the treatment or counselling to work and they have to be prepared to put a lot of themselves into it. Results can be quick but rarely are – it usually takes several sessions to make any impact on the problem and progress is then dependent upon the ability of the parties to change and adapt to the suggestions made by the counsellor. The best time to catch any marital or sex problem is early, preferably in the twenties or thirties when the couple are still emotionally and intellectually flexible enough to be able to change their behaviour and their ideas.

Given that the vast majority of young couples are sexually active before they marry we would like to see more care being given to good foundation-stones being laid at this stage. Many a couple can see later in their marriage that it was during their formative years (probably even as late as their engagement and in the early married years) that their troubles started – in fact many say that they knew very early on that they had made a mistake. One survey found that of those couples getting divorced the majority knew the marriage wouldn't work within its first year. It is then, in the early years, that unrealistic expectations fade and the marriage begins to falter. With a little help at this stage it need not do so.

Things you can do for yourself

This book is full of things you can do to help yourself. The main ones are:

1 Learn to communicate better (see page 173)

2 Improve your knowledge of the structure and function of your sex organs (page 23)

3 Understand the normal sexual organs of the opposite sex (page 23)

4 Understand the underlying causes of your problem (page 59)

5 Learn how to deal with specific sexual problems (page 89)

6 Learn how to desensitize yourself to things that make you fearful or anxious (page 148)

7 Learn how to perform sensual massage (page 194)

8 Learn about sensual holidays (page 189)

9 Learn how to cope with sexual boredom (page 238)

10 Overcome your inhibitions (page 225)

11 Learn to enjoy life and sex

12 Change from copulation to intercourse (page 200)

Sex aids

First of all let's be perfectly honest. The vast majority of those with a sex problem don't need any overpriced gadgetry from Japan – they need to talk to someone.

To be fair though some even quite silly sex toys found in sex shops are worth buying for a giggle or as a jokey present. The majority of the sex aid business is now done by mail order, mainly because most women wouldn't be seen dead going into a sex shop and many men are too shy. The catalogues such companies send can be a hilarious read – if you're not offended by them.

So are there are any sex aids that are worth spending money on? There probably are and as previously said, a sex aid or toy doesn't have to have a 'medical' use or value in order to give pleasure or a laugh to the couple who uses it.

There is no sex aid that is more valuable than a *vibrator*. Over the last 15 years countless millions of vibrators have been sold around the world and presumably they have all been used at one time or another even though the majority spend most of their lives collecting dust.

A vibrator is an electrical device that has a high speed electric unit inside that causes the body of the thing to vibrate and so stimulate the area on which it is placed. They come in two versions, battery or mains operated. Obviously battery operated ones cost quite a lot to run but mains operated ones cost more to buy in the first place. Mains varieties are best because the quality of the vibration is always the same. Most battery-operated vibrators are poor simply because most people are using them with run-down batteries.

Vibrators come in all shapes and sizes but the most popular by far is penis-shaped and is made of plastic. They are hard, cold, and noisy and most women find them unpleasant physically to use,

however pleasant the sensation in the area they are stimulating. Better quality, less noisy, vibrators made of soft flesh-like rubber are much more pleasant to use but are more expensive to buy.

A vibrator can be used anywhere on the body that gives rise to pleasant sensations but the vast majority are used by women on or around the clitoris to help them have an orgasm or to enjoy better ones. Those women who enjoy something in their vagina whilst masturbating often insert the vibrator inside themselves at a particular point in the proceedings but millions of others never use it in their vaginas at all.

So what are vibrators useful for? Obviously the main use is for the woman who finds that she cannot get an orgasm without the additional, powerful sensations produced by a vibrator. Some women learn to have an orgasm with a vibrator and then wean themselves off it and use their fingers from then on. A woman without a current sex partner may well find a vibrator pleasant either for clitoral or vaginal stimulation. A few women enjoy the sensations produced by two vibrators at the same time, one inside the vagina and the other on the clitoris. Vibrators can also be useful if the man is handicapped or has something wrong with his hands or fingers and can't help her by stimulating her clitoris. Many couples simply use a vibrator from time to time as part of their foreplay by way of a change.

Some men also use a vibrator applied to their sex organs and, as do some women, to the anus. The only dangers are of inserting it too far so it is 'lost', and the transfer of germs from the bowel to the vagina.

Clitoral stimulators are rings that fit around the penis with protruding knobs that stimulate the clitoris as the man thrusts in and out. Many women find these things unpleasant and even painful and few enjoy their clitoris being rhythmically bashed by a chunk of rubber. They are, by and large, a waste of time and money.

Penile rings fit around the base of the penis, and the scrotum too in some cases, and some men find they have easier and/or harder erections when they use them. On no account should you ever use a home-made ring – there have been medical calamities with men whose penises swelled up so much that solid rings couldn't be removed. Women can help men with erective difficulties during intercourse by holding the base of the penis as if her fingers were a ring.

Virility enhancers

Most sex shops sell sex sugar or virility-enhancing tablets. It's difficult to know what to say about these because they don't contain anything that could possibly have a positive effect on a man's virility and so must be a waste of money. However, to be fair, if a man takes something *believing* it to be of value it could just help his ardour or his willpower to have sex which might just do the trick. So far there are no known aphrodisiacs, so don't be fooled.

Creams and oils are widely available and are of several kinds. Massage oils are, of course, useful for sensual massage but the sex shop offerings are usually overpriced versions of products available at your local chemist shop. Ordinary skin care products and baby oils are good, cheap things to use and more ambitious couples can buy really expensive scented oils from specialist shops if they want to.

Rub-in erection-enhancing creams are popular. They work like the rub-in creams produced for rheumatism (by stimulating the area to produce more blood by creating a slight irritation locally). Some men say that these creams work, but don't expect miracles. For the man who comes too quickly local anaesthetic creams certainly can help when put on the penis. Real premature ejaculation needs proper treatment of course.

Artificial penises (dildoes)

These are rubber or plastic replicas of the penis available in many different sizes. There is a heavy demand for them, mostly from men who buy them to use on their partners. Obviously they have a place if the man has erection problems or is handicapped and so can't satisfy his wife but the sales can't be accounted for on this basis alone. Probably most are never or only rarely used. They are bought by men (who, understandably buy too large a size for their woman to use comfortably) and probably spend most of their lives unused. Some women who enjoy vaginal stimulation while they masturbate like to have a dildo for the purpose but as most women use their fingers inside their vaginas while masturbating this again doesn't explain why so many are bought. A few men greatly enjoy a dildo in their anus as they masturbate or while they are having sex but this is a fairly exotic pursuit.

Artificial vaginas

These usually contain a vibrator and can be useful as training aids, especially in those men who have a fear of the vagina. A more expensive extension of these are:

Sex dolls

These are very expensive, reasonably un-life-like blow-up women. They have a vagina, and some have a mouth and anus as well, all of which can be penetrated by a man. The more sophisticated ones have vibrators built in too.

Quite who buys these dolls is not known but there are some lonely, handicapped and socially disadvantaged men who can and do get sexual pleasure with such a doll. Proprietors of marital aids shops say that a few men buy them when their wives are unavailable sexually for some reason rather than resort to an affair or to a prostitute. It is a sad fact that there are surprising numbers of men who could never hope to attract a woman of any kind and perhaps these dolls provide a valuable function in such cases.

Male dolls for use by women are also available but they have no advantage over an ordinary vibrator and have not caught on.

Fun and novelty items

Willy warmers; erotic but 'silly' under-wear for both sexes, funny shaped soaps, fun condoms, love eggs, frank sex toys and so on are all popular items in sex shops. They are, of course, perfectly harmless fun and if people are prepared to spend money on them – why shouldn't they? Such sex toys can make an amusing present that is then used probably only once or twice a year but if it adds ardour or

enjoyment even on a couple of occasions it's more than worth the money.

Most people have never been in a marital aids or sex shop yet quite wrongly condemn what they sell. The majority of customers buy perfectly harmless, over-priced, gadgets usually in the full knowledge that they won't work miracles for their sex-lives.

Erotica

Many sex shops sell erotic magazines, books, films, video films and audio tapes which can be of value to couples with problems. Some also sell instructional books, whilst others have literature to cater to more peverse tastes. It is probably the last type of sale which causes most condemnation of sex shops but it is unfair, and, perhaps, socially unwise, to deprive the sexual casualties of our community of material which they find erotic even if 'normal' individuals find it disgusting.

Masks

Some sex shop proprietors claim that couples who don't like each other very much, can, by the use of suitable masks return to a vigorous sex-life. This claim could be true, at least for some people, because the partner wearing a mask does seem to alter the perception of their personality. Perhaps this 'new' personality afforded by the mask explains at least some of the attraction of the masked balls so beloved of the gentry of yesteryear.

Seizing a chance opportunity to fondle your partner, even if it doesn't necessarily lead to immediate intercourse, raises tensions and expectations

SUMMING UP

In this section we pull together various themes from the rest of the book which lurk in the background of most, if not all sexual relationships, predisposing to problems of various kinds and especially to a reduced capacity for sexual fulfilment.

Sexual pleasure and inhibitions

For the inhibited person the greatest problem is to accept sexual pleasure. Incredible though it may seem millions of women still believe that the main function of intercourse is to please their man and that any pleasure they get is a bonus. Many so-called liberated women are keen to have sex, may well be exhibitionist about sexual matters and say 'fuck me' at the drop of a hat but their *pleasure* from sex is often very poor – as they admit in therapy. They are simply going through the motions for the sake of what they presume to be expected of them in the 1980s, yet in reality they find little joy.

On the other side of the coin is the woman who will never initiate any form of sexual activity. Such a woman will do as she's told because then the responsibility for the outcome is taken out of her hands. The man may be prepared to go along with the 'game' but on some occasions for all men, and on all occasions for some, he can't or won't be prepared to be the sexual initiator all the time. An inhibited man married to such an inhibited woman will have a very quiet sex life. All may be well until one or the other meets someone else and realizes how life could really be.

Overcoming inhibitions

We are all inhibited at least to some degree. Most couples, though, have levels of inhibition that are somewhat different and it is this that produces many of the most common barriers to sexual fulfilment. The first step to understanding no matter what stage your relationship – courtship or 20 years married – is first to identify the problem and then to discuss it to see what you both really think.

Next, make a positive effort to overcome your inhibitions with the help of your partner. Most couples greatly enjoy this if they do it step by step in a gradual way (see page 148).

Go out of your way to understand and then reverse your learned inhibitions – for that's exactly what they are – learned ways of behaving and thinking that are disadvantageous to you in your sex life.

Discuss with each other your perceptions of love in your relationship. Frank discussion about what love means to each of you can clear this subject once and for all. A man will then see, for example, that his wife really does love him in every way that she can but still, for example, can't tolerate sex in the woman-on-top position. Just because she can't go along with something or can't perform in a particular way doesn't mean that she doesn't love him yet many such men put performance 'conditions' on their love. We discuss how sex *can* be used as a weapon and how it can become a battleground on page 169.

Of course, there are those women who, encouraged by the increasing awareness of female sexuality would really like to make their desires known but fear that they will lose their partner's love if he thought she were a fast woman or a 'sex maniac'. All this needs discussing, perhaps with the help of a professional. Many men do think badly of a woman who takes the lead sexually and who, for example, masturbates in front of him, but the problem is with them and not with their woman.

Such discussions often lead to the 'totally normal' partner realizing that he or she is at least 50% to blame for their joint problems. Experience suggests that it is the one who *complains* about the other being inhibited that is sometimes the more inhibited of the two!

As recommended earlier, take specific words and tell your partner exactly what you believe and feel about them. Most couples rarely or never do this but those that do so enjoy an improvement in their relationship as a result. It shows just how similar we are and how we often share the same fears and misunderstandings. Suitable subjects are breast size; semen; penis size; nipple sensitivity; periods; pre-menstrual tension; premature ejaculation; occasional impotence; what you say during intercourse; love; who initiates sex and why; unusual wishes/desires; masturbation of self and partner; affairs; sexual fantasies; and so on.

Couples, can see such subjects as taboo, even within a committed relationship, and as a result worry and feel bad about all kinds of things. It may not be easy to discuss such things 'cold' so ensure that you choose the right time, get the atmosphere right and perhaps have a drink or two. These will help you relax together. Perhaps even massage each other while you share your innermost thoughts. Some

couples find that going to a pub, on a walk or even during a long car journey gives the the right kind of setting. Be as open-minded as possible and use the discussion to learn about each other, not to re-inforce your prejudices and inhibitions. Be positive and joyful about areas on which you agree and when you don't, give each other an undertaking seriously to take the other point of view into account.

Talk to your parents if you have that sort of relationship with them. It's surprising how much you can learn. They have, after all, invested an enormous amount of time, emotion and energy in you over the years and now, as an adult, you can go back to them on your terms. Many an individual has understood, for the first time, just why things were said or done the way they were during their childhood – understandings that could never have been possible when they were a child. Things you may never have been able to forgive or understand in the past may suddenly fit into place, especially if you are now a parent yourself. Understanding your parents as sexual

In spite of her very obvious 'showing off' her man is studiously ignoring her as he listens to his hi-fi. How else does he ignore her both in and out of bed?

beings who had their problems which influenced your upbringing can greatly help your overall understanding of *your* inhibitions.

Remember during any discussions with your partner never to attack each other's personalities. Marriages are made between personalities *not* genitals and few people can stand character assasination. For more about this, see page 183.

Learn to have really good intercourse – don't copulate. For guidelines on what goes to make good intercourse see page 200. Perfect intercourse occurs only between two uninhibited people and surprisingly, learning to stop copulating can help shed inhibitions.

Remember to make a positive effort to act more sexually and in a less inhibited way. An example may help here. Women who have trouble enjoying orgasms during intercourse are greatly helped by pretending that they are voluptuously enjoying an orgasm, if they *act* in a frankly sexy way and throw themselves into the act wholeheartedly. What starts off as an act often becomes normal and natural behaviour for them. This technique can be used to overcome all kinds of inhibitions – give it a try.

Remember that inhibitions are also subject to fashion. Fifty years ago oral sex was considered a perversion, and to be inhibited about it quite acceptable. The 'semen is good for you' fashion is very recent and many couples have quite understandably not taken the message on board. Having said this, there are women who really are inhibited but greatly enjoy some particular sexual activity to the exclusion of all other sexual activities. Such women are apparently very sexy but in fact are inhibited by our definition because they veer away from intercourse to another activity.

Think positively about at least some of your inhibitions. Once we accept that we are a mixture of desires and inhibitions all we can do is to quietly work at those inhibitions that are disadvantagous to us and to accept certain others. Life, after all, is about coping with things we cannot change and some inhibitions will be unchangeable even with professional help.

A certain degree of *pro*hibition could be said to be necessary to make sex pleasurable. Freud said that we need to see sex as naughty in order to be able to enjoy it and it is certainly true that pornography, for example, is the gift of the moralist.

Start to change your fantasies while you masturbate or make love. In doing this you start off with your usual impoverished fantasy but consciously change the fantasy

Is he undressing her because it turns him on, or because he knows she's too inhibited to make the first move herself?

Sex Games

Many couples like to add to their excitement and anticipation by adding in sex games of various kinds to their lovemaking sessions. Provided that they aren't dangerous in any way there's no harm at all in such games if both parties agree to them. If the game itself becomes perpetually the way satisfaction is obtained and intercourse is thereby avoided then the pastime could be said to have become a deviation and the couple may need professional help. For most couples though these games are simply used to enhance their enjoyment of the sex act occasionally.

Baby games

Most of us use baby games far more than we realize. We cuddle up to each other and revert to child-like or even baby-like behaviour during sex and this is quite natural and enjoyable. Other baby games some couples enjoy are:

◆   Making love on rubber sheets

◆   The man being dressed in a nappy

◆   The man breastfeeding (or pretending to if the woman isn't actually lactating)

◆   The man being her baby as she mothers him

◆   Bathing each other like babies

Dressing-up games

Dressing-up plays a very important part in most social and sexual activities and most of us dress up when we know that the occasion demands it. To some extent at least we all play dressing-up games most of our lives, and especially so when we are trying to capture the heart or eye of the opposite sex. In a settled sexual relationship though dressing-up games can take many forms.

◆   Displaying the body partly undressed. Women like prancing about with few clothes on quite 'accidentally' displaying themselves to their man to turn him on.

◆   Sexy underwear is very commonly used. This doesn't have to be tarty . . . though many women enjoy wearing such things . . . it can be expensive and classy

◆   More specialist couples go in for nurse outfits or dress as nuns, prostitutes or schoolgirls. This is often not just for the benefit of the man . . . the woman in such couples likes the build-up to sex the dressing and undressing gives her and the powerful effect it has on her man

◆   Men usually want their women to dress up but sometimes a woman will ask her man to put on something in which she thinks he looks particularly hunky or sexy. Some women like to see their men in their best business suit and then slowly to strip him. Others are very excited if he keeps all his clothes on and strips her

Medical games

Many couples play some form of medical game some of which are simply an advanced form of doctors and nurses that they played as children . . . and for the

same reason. The commonest forms of medical games are:

◆ Intimate inspection of the partner's genitals. This can involve internal examinations on the woman. There is no danger in this if the man is careful and knows what he's doing

◆ Medical games that involve some kind of humiliation. In this type of game the man gets the woman to come into the room fully dressed and then takes off her pants (or gets her to) and then bends her over to touch her toes with her skirt pulled up to expose her bottom. He then 'examines' her insides at length until they are both so excited that they make love

◆ Nurse games are closely related to this. The woman either dresses as a nurse or pretends to be one and then tells the man what to do in great detail or carries out some 'nursing procedures' on him

◆ Sex clinic games. In these either partner makes the other do what he or she wants as they pretends to be sex experts giving instructions about love-making

Seduction games

These all involve driving the partner wild with anticipation whilst not allowing any touching. Variations include:

◆ Slave games in which the woman uses the man as her slave to do whatever she likes and then lets him have sex with her if he has done them well enough. She makes herself irresistable and rewards him with sex

◆ Sultana games in which the roles are reversed and the woman is the sex slave

Restraint games

These all involve tying up or otherwise restraining the partner in some way. In these games the one who is restrained is helpless by agreement and the other can do what he or she likes to please themselves. These games can involve:

◆ Tying the hands and feet to the bed so that the person is spreadeagled and helpless to resist

◆ Tying the person to a chair

◆ Using special leather restraints (a specialist pursuit)

There are no dangers to these kinds of games provided the basic rules are set:

◆ Only do these things if both of you agree

◆ Never put anything round the neck

◆ Never restrict breathing in any way

◆ Never use hot or cold things that might burn the skin

◆ Never go off and leave anyone tied up

◆ Avoid all such games unless you are totally sober

◆ Agree beforehand a release signal that is always honoured without hesitation

Sado-masochistic games

In moderation these can be fun but need to be played with caution. Common ones are:

◆ Smacking the partner's bottom before sex

◆ Not allowing the woman to urinate when she wants to. Some women have an orgasm during this game

◆ She makes him masturbate in front of her or vice versa

◆ She makes him do whatever she wants (rather like a slave game) or vice versa, and smacks him for disobedience

◆ In extreme cases some couples enjoy whipping and being whipped

Urinary games

◆ Some people enjoy the differences between the sexes in urination and incorporate them into a game which they enjoy to a more *un*inhibited one that you'd really enjoy more. Gradually over several occasions increase the previously unacceptable content of sexually fulfilling activity until the whole of the fantasy is filled with material you were previously too inhibited to accept.

As the years go by, the slow and progressive revealing of one's self in trust to one's partner results in a loosening of the prohibitions we call inhibitions and as a couple relaxes more in each other's company sex becomes more pleasurable. This is especially true for many women who, relax more and feel more confident about initiating sex and asking for what they want. So it is that by their late 30s most women are enjoying sex games they never did before and communication is at an all-time high within the marriage. Unfortunately, just as this happens many men find themselves at the peak of pressure both at work and within the family. As a result, intercourse rates fall at around the time when the woman with her new-found skills and pleasures from sex is blossoming. The secret of success then is to ensure by careful observation and encouragement that you grow together as you shed your inhibitions.

Avoidance of one another

There are two basic avoidance patterns, one based on avoiding a particular individual, and another which avoids sex in general, so to speak.

This is a common but subtle problem which can begin early. Certain teenage boys and young men are so anxious about how women will react to them that they avoid all contact with girls. They aren't gay or disinterested in sex – on the contrary, they think about it and even talk about it a lot. The trouble is that they don't know how to *do* anything about it, so they avoid situations which might lead to sex. They avoid gatherings and activities with girls; later in life, older men with the same problem often fear women of their own age because they are relatively more demanding sexually at a time when *their* physical prowess is waning. A fear of failure in such men leads to sex avoidance fairly commonly.

Another very common group of sex avoiders are those who have experienced some kind of sexual failure. After three bad experiences why put your emotions and sexuality on the line for the fourth time? This becomes a common reason for avoiding sex altogether. Such people, of either sex, channel their sexual energies into other areas of their lives, often with very positive results.

Other sex avoiders unconsciously choose a partner who will be unavailable or a least undemanding sexually. Such a man will choose an inhibited girl and a woman with this problem tends to involve herself with married men who are largely 'unavailable'. At the unconscious level there are reasons why such women don't really want sex and these powerful unconscious brakes totally influence her 'choice', even though she strongly denies it. Often, sex avoiders of this kind are desperately insecure and can't bear rejection. By choosing the unavailable they always have the alibi that things could never have developed to a serious sexual or personal relationship, and so they repeatedly let themselves off the hook. To form a deep relationship with someone who *was* available would be to court disaster.

More subtle methods of sex avoidance abound. An apparently normally sex-centred man can avoid *sex* even though he has a lot of contact with women, often in sexual settings. He is fine until it comes to real intimacy or intercourse, when he opts out. He can't cope with a perfectly normal and good woman. He is put off by her sexual interest and advances and says she is a 'sex maniac'. Once again he avoids sex. There are female versions of this type of sex avoider too. Such individuals avoid any form of sexual courtship, and if pushed will go straight from normal social encounters to copulation.

Then there is the person who, though apparently very liberated and able to 'do anything' sexually avoids certain genital activities (including intercourse) almost entirely. Such a woman for example, will be crazy about oral sex . When it comes to penis-in-vagina sex, she backs off. Other couples indulge in sex games that involve bondage or sex in weird situations to avoid straight genital-to-genital sex for unconscious reasons which only come to light in therapy.

There are, of course, degrees of this kind of avoidance. Most people are able to have sex, at least from time to time, though certain genital pursuits are unacceptable (oral sex, for example) and for a few all genital contact is stressful, only to be undertaken in the dark, possibly while fantasizing about someone else in a nongenital situation. All shades in between are common and produce endless marital disagreements, battles and all too often, divorce.

Signs of sex avoidance

- Not having sex at all or as often as you used to, but still being interested in sex with others

- Sex has become humdrum and boring

- Sex rarely produces a sense of satisfaction or fulfilment

- Too tired, too overworked

- Repeated pelvic complaints in women (vaginal itching, low back pain, vaginal discharge, pain on intercourse, cystitis, painful periods, etc)

What can you do

Recognize the problem: The first thing is to be able to recognize sex avoidance for what it is – and often this will need professional help. Not infrequently the sex avoider's partner is the one who comes to the doctor with the problem. A man may go for help with an impotence problem yet it is his wife's sex avoidance that has produced it. Cure the sex avoider and the impotence 'magically' disappears.

Look for the cause: Once you realize that you might be avoiding sex look carefully at the background factors that could be playing a part in your problem. Think through your own family background to see if there could be any clues that would help you understand. A 25 year old woman with a classical story of sex avoidance couldn't find any explanation until it was discovered that her older sister had had an unwanted pregnancy at the age of 16. This had such (unconscious) negative effects on the younger girl that it put her off sex, against her conscious drives for it. There are many similar examples and if you are a sex avoider you'll probably be able to pinpoint one or more reasons for your problem with the help of the insight you've gained from reading this book. The danger when trying to sort out sex avoidance,

and this is true of most sex problems, is to focus too closely on the current troubles rather than taking the longterm view of the past events that contributed to the current problems.

Talk it over: Once you've found the possible cause for your sex avoidance discuss it with your partner – no matter how painful it is at first. Try professional help and then jointly with your counsellor or therapist discuss things with your partner. A couple who have lived together for any reasonable length of time presumably had a fund of goodwill at some time, even it if is currently impoverished. This gives the average couple a pretty good start. One partner's insights and knowledge of the other other can often be the most helpful thing and an honest and loving appraisal can lead to a strengthening of the relationship – not a weakening of it. The secret of such talks is to gain insights into each other and discussing a problem can be a wonderful way of achieving this.

Taking the pressure off: Stop having intercourse and go back to courtship. This takes the pressure off both partners to perform.

Romantic games:

- Take every opportunity to show your love to each other in non-genital ways

- Give each other presents

- Increase your physical closeness short of genital contact

- Kiss more

- Do more things together and share in each other's hobbies and interests

Flirting is part of the romance of courtship, which needs to be constantly renewed

- Phone up 'for no reason' just to tell each other that you love one another

- Leave little love notes around the house where they'll be found

- Go out with each other as if you were on an early date, taking care to be extra courteous, caring and sympathetic

- See how you could improve your personal appearance and so on – according to your own particular ways of pleasing one another

All this might sound rather corny but it works very well in practice. It's surprising that many young couples so short-circuit their courtship during their teens that they never really learn how to court one another. They often greatly enjoy this courtship 'game' for its novelty value alone – let alone for the results it can bring.

Take a sensual holiday (see page 189)
Massage each other (see page 194)
Eroticize sex For many couples who have been together for some years sex can become dull and strangely unerotic. The man may have slowly come to see his wife as a kind of mother figure and the woman to look to a man as the provider of everyday living. A period of banned intercourse is a good time to re-eroticize sex. Start reading erotic books or magazines. Share your fantasies and act them out when possible. Teach each other what you'd really like, use the current crisis to re-educate each other.

Have intercourse, don't copulate

Slowly, after a few weeks of courtship, and non-genital behaviour you'll be ready for intercourse. Many couples who have problems have never had intercourse – they have been copulating year after year. For the difference between the two, and a look at the elements of good intercourse see page 200.

All of these things can be done by the average, intelligent couple. You don't need a degree in psychology or even necessarily the help of a therapist to go through the steps we've outlined. Give yourself a chance.

Sexual boredom

Sexual boredom is one of the commonest complaints about sex. It can be simply annoying, sexually frustrating or a real sex 'problem'. In all major surveys of people's sex lives boredom comes very near the top of the list of complaints and dissatisfactions yet sexual boredom is a preventable condition given a little imagination and goodwill on both sides. The main thing that people complain of is that sex has lost its savour – that they no longer feel the same about each other as they did in the heady, early days of the relationship.

But the problem isn't as simple as it first appears because it's rarely a matter of being bored with what the other *does* (or doesn't do). Apart from the individual being an actual bore sexual boredom arises from three interlocking problems.

1 'We never seem to have enough time for each other'
2 'We don't communicate'
3 'Our sex life isn't exciting any more'

At the heart of these problems is the long-held myth that once you are married you'll automatically know how to live happily every after. The facts are very different. Most couples know each other rather badly the day they get married and

are in fact entering on a long journey of discovery – a journey which requires maintenance skills if it is to be successful.

Let's look at each of these in turn:

'No time for each other'

This is always something of a cop-out because we can all make time for things that are really important to us. Outside interests are important in any healthy relationship but they're no excuse for not being with each other. Indeed, couples who are always doing things apart even with the best of 'excuses' are ready candidates for sexual boredom if only because they leave themselves so little time to spend communicating and exploring – the two greatest antidotes to boredom.

Men all too often use work as the excuse but do so at their peril because it is only when their marriage is on the rocks that they begin to see things in perspective. They'll happily spend 80 hours a week seeing to and maintaining their jobs or careers but don't spend a hundredth of this time on doing the same for their relationship. The business may go well but the relationship often goes sour and they have no one with whom to share the fruits of their efforts. Many busy men take their marriage for granted – then moan that their wives are so boring sexually that the only answer is to look for sex elsewhere. Marriage, like almost any other human pursuit repays the investment made in it and if you invest little, you get little back.

Having said this, it's not a question of the time you spend together that's so important but the quality of your shared time. An hour in which you really enjoy each other and answer each other's needs for love, closeness, sex and companionship is more valuable than many hours simply spent together for the sake of it, wondering what he or she should or should not be doing instead of being there.

In a busy world making time for one another is a skill that needs planning for. If you leave it to happen, it won't, and you and your relationship will be crowded out by apparently more important things. Also, there's a deep-seated part of all of us that is afraid of the intimacy we so need. This small voice then tells us that intimacy is better avoided.

When it comes to making time here are some simple guidlines that work. You'll find more of your own once you get into the swing of it.

1⁻ Plan something pleasant just for the two of you. A sensual holiday (see page 189) can be at home, you don't need to go away and spend a lot of money. It might be a long weekend break in a nice hotel; a meal in a restaurant or a country walk together. Sensual holidays needn't cost money. The idea is to relax and experience each other in a new situation or location. Seeing each other in a new setting has a powerful effect on combatting boredom with one's partner.

2   Plan some time together (make dates in your diaries, if you have them) in which you *don't* talk about children, the mortgage, the leaking roof or whatever. Focus your attention on each other and do something totally neutral together. Talk about the way you feel, the person you are and the way you see yourself and the relationship. Use these opportunities to go back to courtship behaviour and try to recapture the joys of your early days together.

3   When you are together think only of today and how you both are now. Don't look back to the past and to how you both were then. Just enjoy '*being*' together rather than having to be 'doing' all the time. Learn or re-learn the pleasures of companionship.

Couples who follow these guidelines are amazed at what it does for their relationship and say how they haven't really been alone together for years of marriage. Being together and enjoying it is a skill they have lost and most greatly enjoy re-capturing it. A couple who previously got on each other's nerves often say how surprised they are that they *can* spend so much time together and enjoy it. Once you get into this way of thinking you'll soon start planning time to be alone, to have a sensual holiday or simply to be together. Any effort you put in will be well worth while.

'We don't communicate'

Far too many couples say something like 'He's not the man I married and although we both try, we seem to be miles apart' or 'She has such different interests now and we don't seem to agree on anything much, so why talk?'

We look at communication within relationships on page 173 in more detail. Here though just let's point out a couple of valuable principles. In our relationships we want to represent ourselves as having ideas, emotions and personality traits that are desirable and appreciated for what they are. We all want to declare ourselves and be understood by our partner.

But if this is the starting point, the

Boredom is the greatest enemy of any mature couple. These tourists are so lost in their separate worlds that they may not have said a word to each other for hours

This couple, however, are completely alive to each other, their surroundings and the new *experiences to be found with shared laughter and good humour*

natural follow-on is our responsibility to listen and to take the other person seriously. Far too often individuals hear what they want or expect to hear and not what their partner is really saying. Once we clear away old preconceptions it's surprising what we discover even if the words are the same.

But each has to accept the other for what he or she is – not on any special terms or with pre-conditions. 'I love you because you are you' should be the underlying principle – not 'I'll love if you do/don't do. . .'

Unfortunately, many people talk in a roundabout way which they imagine will be correctly interpreted by their partner. When this doesn't happen one gets huffy and 'can't communicate'. The answer is to be direct. Don't say 'Do you want to go out tonight?' or 'Would you like to make love?', but say 'I'd like to go out tonight' or 'I'd like to make love'. By making 'I' statements you take responsibility for the communication and actually stand the chance of making something happen. Expressing your wishes and needs in this way

is not being demanding or whining; in a loving relationship it produces results.

'Sex is a bore'

Many couples see sexual boredom as their main problem. Let's look now at some of the reasons for sexual boredom:

Being bored with yourself It's amazing that most people with sexual boredom problems don't think of this. If you feel boring yourself or don't much enjoy life it's hardly surprising that you'll find sex boring too. Hasn't it dawned on you that you might be so boring that you bore your partner . . . and not just in bed?

One answer is to start a new interest, not necessarily with your partner. Develop new attitudes, take up a new hobby, go to an evening class, do something you've always wanted to, something that gives you a kick and makes you feel more interesting to yourself. You should even think about your job, and what you are getting out of it, and what you are putting into it. The effect will be that you'll become more interesting to your partner!

More fundamental aspects of feeling – or being – boring are a lack of spontaneity and naturalness. Excessive self-consciousness, undue fears of being found wrong, an inability to laugh at yourself, more or less permanent attitudes of criticism and hostility towards others, eternal predictability, and a lack of occasional access to the child that resides deep down in everyone, all contribute towards being a boring person. Many such aspects of ourselves are acquired during growing-up and can be detected and dealt with by self-scrutiny.

Are you a sexual bore? Do you do the same old things and respond in the same predictable way day after day – year after year? This is a common criticism women make of men. When did you last explore some entirely different aspect of your sexual relationship? Have you ever thought that although your relationship is good you may simply have settled for something less than the best of which you and your partner are capable?

Have you just slowly let things slip? Most couples aren't terrible bores but have let things slip, become casual and generally uninteresting. We advise a positive policy of continuous improvement. If you innovate sexually, trying something new, every few months, sexual boredom will never be a problem. There are positive tips below on what to do.

Successful sex is a trade off between similarity and difference – knowing and understanding each other yet experimenting with new things. No couple is happy with endless change and experimentation – life becomes too hectic and unpredictable in bed for either to relax and even to enjoy those things they know they like. But all human beings enjoy novelty – and not just in bed. The secret is maintaining a balance between what you know and enjoy and doing new things without producing too much anxiety.

Laziness One of the biggest causes for sexual boredom! Most people settle for the least sexual activity they can get away with within their relationship and then wonder why they are bored. The parallels are similar to people who complain about meals being boring. A good meal that stands out as being especially enjoyable doesn't just happen – it needs planning for, shopping for, careful preparation and the right atmosphere in which to enjoy it. Just look at the time we spend doing this and then compare the lack of thought, preparation, shopping and presentation we put into our sex lives. Is it any wonder so many people are bored?

Sexual boredom isn't the inevitable fate of all relationships. Some couples have superb sex but not much of a relationship otherwise. This might be the only way that they can survive as a couple. Their needs for friendship, companionship, being wanted and needed and so on are fulfilled in other ways and they come together mainly as sex partners. This is fine as long as it works for both of them, and has the advantage of not having all one's emotional and personality eggs in one basket. Nonetheless most people would still rather try to find answers to all their needs in their one-to-one relationship if possible.

Poor observation Notice what your partner does to you and bear in mind that it might be what they want you to do to them.

What you can do about sexual boredom

Be yourself Far too many people spend

much of their married lives being (or trying to be) something they are not. Pretending to be what your partner likes is dangerous for two reasons. First, you are closing the door on your own pleasures and putting yourself down. This is obviously not in your best interests. Second, your partner may wonder what is going on and may even see through your deception. Even worse they may not. The false perception you are projecting *must* make your whole relationship false.

Why try to hide your real feelings and needs when it's far more sexy to reveal them and for your lover to indulge you. However, if the partner is very 'nice' and inhibited it's sensible to proceed with caution, so as to avoid shocking her, or more usually, him. An element of selfishness thus helps the relationship. The person we prize most is the one who in spite of differences and disagreements still loves us anyway. Our cultural conditioning in childhood makes us reticent to say what we'd really like sexually or to ask what our partner would most enjoy.

Longterm relationships are especially likely to fall into this trap because a tolerable way of sexual life is developed and the couple simply (unspoken, of course) agree not to rock the boat by making demands for themselves or of the other. Far too many individuals end up looking outside for sex when what they want is there all the time – it has simply never been disclosed. This leads on to the second valuable thing you can do:

Share your fantasies Sex isn't just a medical plumbing job – it's in the mind

Even the most tedious domestic chores can be made interesting and stimulating in a loving relationship

too. Yet for all this most couples are too inhibited to discuss their fantasies.

Perhaps one of the greatest misconceptions about fantasies is that they are all suppressed wishes or desires. Some are more a form of exploration. Many people have fantasies that they enjoy at the personal level (either during masturbation or intercourse), yet they have no intention of acting them out, nor do they necessarily even have a need to do so. Many couples are confused on the subject – if they have an honest and close relationship they often feel, 'Since this is how I really am, I'd feel better if he/she knew'. This attitude is, alas, self-centred rather than partner-centred and may well clear your conscience but do untold harm to your partner. Sharing fantasies is therefore not always a good idea and needs to be done carefully.

The problem is how to decide which fantasies to share and which to keep to yourself. This involves a deep knowledge and understanding of your partner. Be careful. If you declare your fantasy it puts tremendous pressure on your partner to accept it, with all that may entail. The knowledge that one's partner really wants something one can't or won't supply can niggle away in the back of one's mind. A man might be able to say 'If you really loved me you'd do such and such', but a woman may feel that the idea that her love should be equated with her willingness to dress up as a nurse to have intercourse, is outrageous. Some women see their man's fantasies as threatening, and to be discouraged. Even fewer women want to hear about their man's dreams of the girl next door; fact and fiction might just become the same, given half a chance. However, an increasing proportion of younger couples tell everything to each other and it gives them a sense of security because they feel that in such a relationship if anything should start to go wrong for the partner they would be told in good time, and could take corrective action. This may be ideal.

The secret of sharing fantasies is to be sure that you both really want to indulge – coercion plays no part in this game! Take it gently and raise the subject indirectly. If your partner seems willing and is not getting edgy, then start off by discussing pleasant fantasies that involve him or her. If this goes down well, you could cautiously proceed to declaring other areas.

A good way to begin is to encourage your partner to read a book or see a film which may reflect your fantasies, and watch the response; if it causes anxiety or anger, perhaps you should keep the fantasies to yourself.

People in a good, satisfying relationship often also use fantasies which don't involve their partner. The people in the fantasy are film stars, friends, acquaintances, or even strangers. This, along with occasional flirting, can be protective to the marital relationship because it is less threatening than actually having sex with others. Although some couples can discuss these 'other' fantasies, not everyone is sufficiently secure to appreciate the difference, so it may be wiser not to mention them. However, they can serve to put a lazy or neglectful partner on his or her toes. One snag is that if things have gone too far the other may say 'I wish you would go out and do it and leave me alone'.

Some people have been brought up to be so inhibited and ashamed about sex that they consciously restrict their fantasies to passivity or even abolish them from their consciousness altogether. Some men's fantasies are perpetually passive – the woman always takes charge of them. This is a form of masochism, not necessarily because they want to be sexually hurt but because they need to surrender the initiative. Obviously, if both partners fantasize passively they cannot really satisfy each other. If they *can* talk about it, they might try taking it in turns to have their fantasy indulged.

A similar difficulty can arise when one partner, often the man, always has fantasies of activities that do not culminate in intercourse. Their most arousing fantasies are about, or example, dressing in women's clothing, or the woman being tied up and/or beaten. Such fantasies may be repugnant to a man's partner but can be modified with goodwill into forms that indulge the need gradually, and brings it closer and closer to something exciting yet acceptable to both.

The best result With these difficulties in mind, the sharing of fantasies can give maximal pleasure to both partners, so that their lovemaking becomes unique to them and adds to their sense of private adventure – and this is true romance. It also, makes it less likely that either partner will seek sexual and romantic outlets elsewhere, because they are totally pleased and catered for within their sharing relationship. Without this, the experience of intercourse can be impoverished. When a couple with a good relationship begin to share their fantasies, they frequently discover that they are remarkably well-matched. It helps to explain all sorts of things about each other's desires. Explaining and working out the fantasies together, can provide a considerable array of sexual games and behaviour. This stock can be added to as new fantasies occur and the partner's fantasies are stored away for further use when the circumstances seem suitable. Women frequently say that if they have to tell their man what to do during sex it reduces their pleasure. This problem is solved if the man reserves some of her fantasies for occasional and unexpected use, especially if he adds a few variations of his own.

Talk to each other

Learn to please your partner   The cycle of sexual boredom has to be broken somewhere – why not start with yourself?

By talking more, by sharing your fantasies and by being yourself you'll be ready to start *doing* more interesting and pleasurable things. And there's nothing like receiving sexual goodies to make your partner more willing to give in return.

When your partner is doing something nice, let him or her know and reinforce it afterwards, later on in the day, or even the day after!

Really personalize your love play together so that your partner doesn't just get adequately aroused but maximally aroused every time. Of course, this won't always happen but it's worth aiming for even if you only score 8 out of 10 each time.

Improve your surroundings   Make your bedroom more cosy – more sexy. Comfort, warmth and security are almost essential for really enjoyable sex. Atmosphere, lights, paintings, erotica, sex aids and toys, what you wear and so on can all play a part in making the setting just right for lovemaking.

Overcome your feelings of being trapped by marriage   Many of us feel trapped and emotionally hemmed in by monogomy as if it were a life sentence of sexual sameness and boredom. Those of us who are older look around and see all the things the young seem to be getting up to and feel we are missing out.

There are several ways around this feeling. First, discuss it with your partner; you'll be surprised that he or she will probably have had similar thoughts at least at one time or another.

Why not discuss together the value of flirting with other people and agree on stopping points that are acceptable to you both? Flirting is a useful safety valve and if it can stop at an agreed point your relationship should not be at risk because of your jealousy. We all need to be reassured that we are still attractive to members of the opposite sex – and they don't go away just because we're married. The answer is to find a way of dealing with the situation.

Share your thoughts about the opposite sex and say what you find turns you on. A couple in a good relationship can use this in their own sex lives and make it a positive feature rather than a cause for a row or jealousy.

The answer must be to take these few sources of potential boredom within a relationship and by indulging them and building on them within a relationship, ensure that you don't have to be unfaithful to enjoy them.

Forget about being 'in the mood'   Monotony also arises because too many people believe that they have to be 'in the mood' for sex to be enjoyable. But there is no one mood. There's angry sex, tender sex, wild sex, solemn sex, romantic sex, dirty sex, playful sex and so on, and real lovers enjoy them all from time to time. If you narrow down your definition of acceptable and successful sex to only one or two moods then unless you are in that particular mood you won't have sex at all.

Try having sex when you are bored, sad, worried, quiet, or angry. Be aware of the different feelings – be aware of the new emotions and releases. It'll open new doors for you.

Don't have sex for a while If sex bores you, abstain. Go back to courtship behaviour and stop being frustrated lovers. Learn to be friends again, and enjoy each other in non-sexual ways. Trying too hard is a problem in itself. Stop searching quite so hard and the problem may even resolve itself as you take the pressure off boring sex.

Loss of sex drive

We all have a drive to have sex or some kind of sexual outlet, even if it only amounts to masturbation a few times a year. Our libido (sex drive) is influenced by the levels of the circulating male hormone testosterone – the natural chemical substance that enhances the urges of both men and women to want and need sex (see page 52).

Theoretically it would make sense to suggest that we all have biologically different sex drives, but clincal experience suggests this might not be the case; it is more probably that we all have much the same level, but repress or inhibit it in varying degrees according to our circumstances at the time and our upbringing. Even the so-called under-sexed are in fact often not so – they may have a vigorous dream and fantasy life but their upbringing so rules their conscious desires that they never get around to acting them out.

However, it is true that we are all basically interested in sex, and this, coupled with our inhibitions, determines how much sex we want. Our culture also puts on breaks in varying degrees, and some prohibitions and inhibitions are necessary if society is to run smoothly. A few people do seem to be genuinely sexless for some or all of their lives, but this is rare. A study in the US of 100 married couples (mostly middle class, Christian and under 35) found that while 75% of the women and 50% of the men claimed to have had a sex problem and 35% admitted to a total lack of interest in sex, they thought their marriages were perfectly satisfactory. For the other results of this survey see page 70. As one leading expert at the National Marriage Guidance Council recently said 'There are far more marriages without sex than most of us think, not just couples who have simply lost their appetite for sex as they've grown older but young couples'.

So any discussion of a loss of sex drive is difficult because it can be tricky knowing what you are comparing yourself with! If, as most people do, you are comparing yourself with some mythical norm, then you could be doing yourself a great disfavour, if only because you may not really know what the norm is. And are you statistically 'normal' in other ways? Probably not, so why should you be sexually?

It could be argued that so-called norms should never be discussed when it comes to sexual performance because by doing so people will wrongly assume they are odd. Fixed ideas about what the 'norms' are for intercourse frequency; time to orgasm, number of orgasms in a woman or whatever, are not only misleading but dangerous. 'Normal' for any given couple is what is normal and acceptable for *them*.

It's certainly reasonable to compare yourself *with yourself* over a period of time – especially if it's a short time-span, because at least you should know what *your* normal is.

'Normal' in the context of human sexuality is a range not a point. So if you think

you or your partner has lost or is losing their interest in sex, it's important to start with the question 'What in fact has been lost?' A person who wants sex less often with a partner may simply be enjoying it less with that particular person. Perhaps sex has become boring or uninteresting. Perhaps they have fallen out of love or don't want each other any more. They may be masturbating more than usual because the relationship is just not working well. Genital sex is usually the innocent by-stander that gets knocked down once the relationship runs out of control. So before we decide what is the cause of the lack of sex drive, let's look at the main reasons.

Normal variations

Males are at their peak in their late teens. At this time they can manage up to six orgasms a day. Few ever do so and even then they are not sustained over more than a few days. A very few young men say they can ejaculate up to ten times a day but even the thought of doing so would make the average man feel exhausted. This illustrates a point about all human sexual anatomy and performance; whatever is being considered there will alway be some people who are bigger, longer, quicker, slower or whatever than the average.

The male's capacity for sex falls from the late teens onwards but even this is a statement about the average and isn't universal. Some men of 50 are having as many sexual outlets as they were at 20 but other men virtually close down on inter-course and masturbation at 40. Some men, and women for that matter, are still seek-ing active sex partners well into their 70s.

When it comes to discussing average or

normal sex drives in women the subject is even more fraught. Some, who don't seem to be particularly neurotic, say they have 20 orgasms a day by one means or another whilst others have only one every 10 or 20 days. Something like one or two sex acts every day or every other day seems to cover the majority of women and these acts can of course be intercourse or masturbation. The numbers of orgasms in each varies from one to three on average. Some, and perhaps even most, women become more proficient at getting orgasms as they mature. Such women may have sex and masturbate less often but still end up having more orgasms overall than they used to when young. Some women have more intercourse as they get older and enjoy their orgasms more as their earlier inhibitions fade and release their innate sexual appetites that were previously held in check.

Reducing female sexual behaviour to averages is even more misleading than doing the same for men because women's *capacity* for sexual pleasure is almost limitless. Her ability to *exploit* this capacity is almost entirely governed by her upbringing, her emotions, education, her man and her circumstances.

Medical reasons

Drugs The commonest supposed culprit is the contraceptive Pill but there is no evidence that the Pill actually makes women less sexy and many say that because of the contraceptive security they enjoy they feel more, not less, sexy. Research with dummy tablets in controlled trials to look at the supposed anti-sex drive effect of the Pill has found that women taking them were just as likely to be depressed and suffer a loss of sex drive as those on the 'real' Pill. To be fair, some women do seem to get their sex drive back when they change to a different brand of Pill. Tranquillizers in most medium to high doses can cause indifference, and given that 1 in 5 women take them in some form, at some time, this could be an enormous hidden problem. The table below shows the main drugs that cause a loss of sex drive.

Psychological illness The most common by far is depression. One of the earliest signs of depression is a loss of interest in sex. Other signs are feeling and looking miserable; having odd and inexplicable physical symptoms; waking early in the morning and finding it difficult to get to sleep at night; crying for no apparent reason; looking sad; a poor appetite; poor concentration; a loss of interest in things that used to give pleasure; feeling fearful; self neglect and a loss of confidence. If you have any of these problems *and* a loss of sex drive, see your doctor at once.

Drugs that can affect your sex life

- ◆ Any sleeping tablets can put a person off sex
- ◆ Steroids (cortisone-like drugs) in high doses
- ◆ Some anti-high blood pressure drugs
- ◆ Some diuretics (water tablets)
- ◆ Some angina drugs

Serious physical disease Many long-standing diseases such as rheumatoid or osteoarthritis; chronic anaemia; some cancers; any longstanding painful illness (such as chronic backache); kidney failure; breast disease; and many others can reduce a person's interest in sex. Also the cocktail of drugs such people take can add to their problems as many of the drugs themselves can actually produce a chemically-induced lack of sex-drive.

Physical and mental exhaustion Even normal people go off sex when they are exhausted from illness, lack of sleep or prolonged heavy work. Such people quickly recover their sex drive once the underlying cause is remedied. Many people complain of a lack of sex drive for some days or even weeks after an operation and many women go off sex after having a baby. A sense of debility, though, can also come from inner, unconscious anxieties and conflicts which are often to do with love and sex.

It is helpful to remember that quite a lot of people with physical and emotional medical problems use their diagnosed condition as an excuse to retreat from sexual activity that they perhaps didn't really relish anyway. Someone 'going along with sex' for the sake of their partner, once given the excuse of a *real* illness, retreats from sexual activity on the slightest pretext. Such a person for example will have the kind of backache which gives no trouble at all when doing things in the garden or around the house but it becomes intensely painful at the mere suggestion of sex.

Psychological reasons

Stress Most people's sex life is reduced at times of stress. The man recently made redundant or the woman who has just moved house may be too stressed to seek or enjoy sex. Any life crisis such as bereavement can produce stress and reduce sexual drives.

Work as stress This is a far more common cause of loss of sex drive than is generally realized, even by doctors. The man or woman who is working too hard at home or the office, is simply so exhausted and their mind so preoccupied that there seems no energy or enthusiasm to have sex. The person who is perpetually over-stretched simply can't unwind enough to break the cycle. It's the reverse of people who retreat from sex and an unsatisfactory relationship into overwork. Sorting out which is the 'chicken' and which the 'egg' can need professional help.

A bad experience Some individuals have had such a rotten sex life that they say 'I wish sex didn't exist' or 'I don't care if I never have sex again'. For these people sex is unacceptably stressful, and they need help if this bothers them. A few may be truly happy remaining sexless, but most are not. Predictably a previous rape attempt, a sexual assault, or an incestuous experience can have disastrous effects on a person's desire and professional help may be necessary.

251

Inhibitions Sexually inhibited people often have a poor interest in sex and enjoy it very little when they do do it.

Guilt We look at the whole subject of guilt on page 150 but here let's just point out that guilt about what one is about to do or would like to do can be an unconscious turn-off sexually. Guilt about something one *has* already done (such as had extramarital sex, or even fantasized about it) can be a killer. Some people's sex drives disappear as soon as they begin to have an extramarital dalliance. Even the thought of the infidelity turns them off their partner and eventually may even make them unable to perform with their new lover.

Ascetic personality types A very few people believe that anything that's as nice as sex should be denied on the basis that it might control their lives if they were to give into it. Such asceticism is, fortunately, uncommon today but is not rare.

The sleeping beauty syndrome Many a young woman, even today, believes that somewhere in the big blue beyond is Mr Right just waiting to awaken her sleeping sex drive. In the meantime such a sleeping beauty remains sexless or nearly so (even in marriage) in order to 'save herself' for Mr Right. Sadly, most such beauties lie dormant for years and some never marry because they are never asked and do nothing to interest or entice a man. There is a male version of the sleeping beauty syndrome too.

The young, pre-maritally Whatever the current norms of sexual activity in the young our cultural conditioning tells us that sex begins on our wedding night. Many, if not most young people, suffer from a loss of sex drive or sexual repression if only because the culture makes pre-marital sex taboo. A book such as this is no place to discuss the pros and cons of early or late marriage but suffice it to say that most girls have been sexually mature for a decade before they get married in our society. This must bring stresses and strains to the sex lives of the young and many fight daily battles to control their sex drives and some renounce the whole business on the grounds that it is so hazardous. An interesting example of such cultural messages is seen in those young women who have been active sexually, but give it up in the last few days of their engagement, especially if there's to be a white wedding. It may make them feel 'more virginal' whereas in fact there are no degrees of virginity – it's rather like pregnancy, you can't have 'a touch of it'.

Relationship causes

Falling out of love One in three marriages goes sufficiently badly wrong to end in divorce but far more often and possibly at some stage or another (if only for a while) in every marriage, the couple fall out of love. There may well be no treatment for this if it is caused by badly matched personalities but in many cases removing prohibitions on sex and love enable the relationship to take on a new value.

In affairs Here guilt plays an important part in the loss of sex drive as does the fear of transmitting VD to the innocent partner. Some people, when they are actually having an affair, become disinterested in sex with their partner because they fear that he or she will be able to tell they're having sex with someone else. They fear that a new sexual technique (even a different sort of kiss) or a word out of place in the heat of the moment could give the game away. Also, many people say that they have fallen in love with their new partner and feel unfaithful when making love with their husband or wife. With well over half of both sexes *admitting* to at least one affair extramaritally this must be a fairly common cause for a loss of sex drive.

After a bad lovemaking episode A sexual failure or a serious turn down can lead to a loss of sex drive. A man who, for example, pushes his wife too hard on oral sex may put her off sex altogether for some time. Similarly the man whose wife repeatedly refuses him or is capricious about sex to the point where he says 'To hell with this' may go off sex with her. A fear of what each might ask the other to do can also be a turn-off. The woman who enjoys sex but knows that her husband will try some form of sex with her against her will, is unlikely to feel sexy.

Letting oneself go to seed Many a failed sex drive can be traced to a disenchantment with the partner because of his or her appearance and social behaviour. Men lose interest in having sex with their overweight wives and women in their smelling-of-drink husbands. People tell of the most 'trivial' things that put them off sex. Some women, for example, can't bear to have their vaginas touched by a man with long or dirty fingernails or nicotine-stained fingers. Others are turned off by smoker's breath or certain sorts of kissing. There is a tendency for long-married couples to let themselve go to seed and the pot-bellied man is just as much at fault as is his over-eating wife. Being insufficiently attractive, seductive or considerate is one cause of mismatched desires.

Failure with another partner People within and outside marriage can suffer from a loss of sex drive within one relationship if they are having a bad time in another sexual relationship. They often carry their sexual problems or simply their disappointments and failures from bed to bed.

Dirty old man syndrome Many older people believe that sex is for the young and feel bad about being sexually active or even wanting to be. An older woman married to such a man may feel that 'he should be past all that by now' or an older man may think that his wife shouldn't be interested and so smothers his sex drive. This harmful myth should have been dead by now but is not.

Shame Many people are ashamed, rather than guilty, about a particular desire, which they have been brought up to think of as shameful, and therefore dare not reveal to their partner for fear of rejection and condemnation. Only communication can resolve this problem.

What can be done

From the above far from exhaustive list it can be seen that there are some obviously curable causes of a loss of sex drive and others that will need professional help to be reversed or coped with. This particularly applies to medical or relationship problems. For most people a loss of sex drive will be caused by an emotional or relationship problem but if the trouble has been there has for some weeks or months it's probably worth discussing it with a doctor just in case there's something more serious going on.

Let's assume that you have seen a doctor to rule out 'medical' causes then you'd probably do best to try some do-it-yourself therapy before going for professional help with the marital or relationship problems that may well underlie your loss of sex drive. All but the most complex of problems can be sorted out using this book generally and by following the list below.

Stage 1. Stop having sex

Give intercourse a rest and take the pressure off the situation.

Stage 2. Restore your sex drive

1 Treat the underlying cause if you possibly can – discuss the whole thing with your partner and seek help from a trained professional if you can't sort things out between you.

2 Make your lives more erotic Increase the level of sexual awareness in your life by reading erotic books or magazines; watching sexy videos or films; sharing your fantasies with one another; increasing the erotic potential of your bedroom; learning sensual massage (see page 194) or taking a sensual holiday (see page 189).

3 Step up your masturbation rate This is one of the surest ways to get back your drive, especially for women, that can then be shared with your partner.

By deliberately or 'accidentally' exposing herself this woman is certainly making his life more erotic. Incidentally it'll also ensure that he will open the car door for her in the future

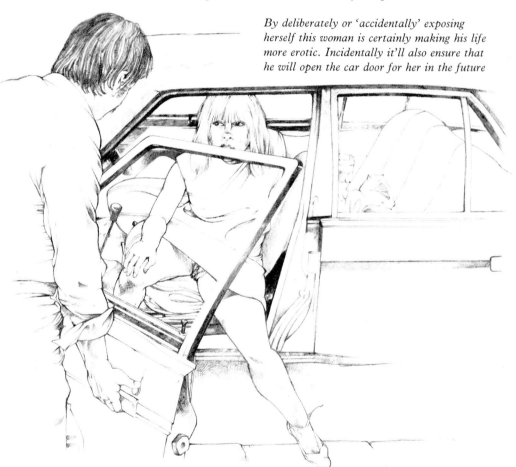

4 Return to courtship behaviour See page 237 for more details.

5 Get your confidence back in your genitals By using sex aids if necessary and by learning to please each other genitally in many ways *other than* by intercourse, build up your genital repertoire but don't have intercourse yet.

6 Study pages 200–207 to learn about good intercourse so that when you start having sex again after 4–6 weeks of doing 1–5 above you won't be copulating but enjoying true intercourse.

All of this could take weeks to practise and will mean dipping into the book to pull out the particular things you'll need to know. If at any stage you get stuck and don't seem to be progressing go back to the beginning and start again. If you get really stuck – see a professional.

Mismatched sex drives

Surprisingly, evidence suggests that the average person, without realizing it, settles for the *minimum* amount of sex that he or she can manage with. The reasons for this are complex but almost certainly stem from our cultural attitudes to sex which are mainly negative.

Most of us consider it a waste of talent not to encourage a child in a sport for which he or she shows an aptitude; we enjoy and encourage musical abilities and put a great value on academic prowess. When it comes to sex, though, things are very different. We reward emotional and sexual abilities and skills very poorly. The idea that one might enjoy sexual activity for itself, that it is worth practising and perfecting like any skilful pleasure and that it is pleasant to try for something above the minimum is all

considered to be beyond the pale, if it is considered at all. Certain other cultures have often elevated sex to a prominent role in society but in the West we have seen it as a rather unfortunate necessity either to answer our animal cravings or to have babies.

All this means that most of us rarely enjoy sex to the full, that we have sex hastily in a stereotyped way or don't have it at all.

Yet as mammals we all have a sex drive. Let's think of this as 100% available in a balanced, healthy, uninhibited person. He or she will be able to enjoy sexual activity most days of their adult lives well into old age. Of course this waxes and wanes with health changes, tiredness, worries, and so on but everything else being equal, a normal person will have 100% of his or her sex drive available to be expressed in various ways including sublimations (see page 15).

But given that people are inhibited sexually in varying degrees, real problems of mismatching can indeed occur. Several surveys have found that the biggest single complaint about intercourse is its lack of frequency. Both men and women complain that they have sex too infrequently. It could be that such couples are truly mismatched (though this is rare) but a far more likely explanation is that one has inhibitions that are acting as a brake on his or her sexual expression. Of course, some couples are perfectly matched as a result of their compatible levels of inhibition. Many such people are happy to make love once or twice a month and then in a very unadventurous way. If this suits both partners who is to say that they are under-sexed or abnormal? It's fascinating that research shows that people make near-instant judgements about a person's sex drive and act accordingly in mate selection. But this is matching – not mismatching. After all, we are all looking for a mate that matches and complements our inhibitions and not one who will make us feel inferior or threatened all the time.

Major mismatching as a result of grossly imbalanced levels of inhibition shouldn't occur in a good relationship because the couple will have sorted out their sexual preferences, intercourse rates and so on during courtship. A few highly religious couples or individuals will not have allowed themselves to progress this far and will clearly stand a much greater chance of discovering this mismatching later in marriage. The best courtship is a full and frank revelation of all the aspects of one's life and personality at the time. If one or the other partner is really unsuited sexually to that union, they are better off looking elsewhere for a partner with whom they *could* happily live for the rest of their lives.

The ideal loving couple that is tuned into each other's sexuality and emotional needs doesn't have mismatched needs on a day-to-day basis because they sense when each is interested in sex, communicate their mutual interest non-verbally, have no set routine for sex and simply make love when the mood takes them.

As women get older they seem to shed many of their inhibitions so that by 40 or so most modern women are increasingly active and interested sexually. This can, ironically produce a new situation because her man who is usually a little older is beginning to experience at least some degree of reduced interest as he ages and may also be at a very busy and exhausting phase of his career. So the tables are turned in middle age. This is usually a vulnerable time for women, who sometimes go out to look for extramarital sex and such a couple could end up being unhappy for a long time.

What to do if you think you are sexually mismatched

First, you need to answer the question, 'Were you ever really well matched?'

If you think you were never really well matched, there are several ways round this. Either the partner who is getting less sex than he or she needs can seek sexual outlets elsewhere in various ways (see the discussion about sexual deprivation, page 9); the couple can seek professional help to see if the inhibitions causing the mismatching can be removed; or they can agree to part and look for more suitable partners. A lot of good work can be done between the couple themselves if they share their inhibitions freely and then try to find ways of accommodating each other's wishes. This is often very much more easily done with a professionally trained third party. Unfortunately, current conventional wisdom sees this kind of mismatching as the end of the relationship mainly because they see the mismatched sex drives as unchangeable. This is not true and if someone tells you that you should get divorced on this score search around for an insight-trained counsellor (preferably with a psychosexual training) who *can* handle the situation. It is only very rarely that inhibitions can't be removed, at least enough to enable the couple to function well again provided that they genuinely *want* to do so.

Coitus reservatus ('non-come' intercourse, see page 104). Can be of help when the woman needs more sex than she is getting.

Apparent mismatching

Couples sometimes seek help because they are sure they are mismatched, yet they haven't made the effort to make sex a priority in their lives. This then produces apparent mismatching. They will always rush sex (to get it over with); put sex lowest on their list of priorities; avoid opportunities for sex by doing other things and so on.

They will need to treat sex seriously by committing themselves to spending time and effort if this is their problem. Here are a few hints to work on:

1 Take a sensual holiday (see page 189)

2 Re-arrange your lifestyle so that you go to bed early enough to have time to be together before you are too tired to do anything sexually.

3 Avoid being capricious about sex – your partner has to be able to rely on your response or he or she'll never know what

the response will be when he or she approaches you. A totally unpredictable sex partner can be very destructive to a relationship.

4 Make your bedroom a sexy place – and a place that reflects your personalities. Most women see the bedroom as their territory – the place where they have control over what goes on at least to some extent. Take a small TV to bed with you if that helps you relax together (but beware that it doesn't take over your sex life); make the room attractive; have a locked drawer in which you can keep sex aids or erotica away from the prying eyes of the children and so on.

5 Seduce your man from time to time.

6 Practise stripping for him to some music you both enjoy on a tape machine in your bedroom. (See page 340.)

7 Get some erotic literature or videos to enjoy together.

8 Get used to making love at unusual times of day – don't stick to predictable routines.

9 Make a real effort to go back to courtship behaviour (see page 237), touch each other frequently; phone up to say you love each other; give little gifts for no reason, praise each other and so on.

A couple who follow even half of these suggestions will soon have a blooming sex life irrespective of their apparent mismatching. It's then simply a matter of keeping the momentum going – never becoming complacent or boring. Above every marital bed should be the slogan of a well known airline 'We never forget you have a choice'. Unfortunately, too many couples work on the assumption that once they're married and have a contract that ties them together they can let their relationship go to seed. As a result one or other often becomes dissatisfied and may look elsewhere for emotional or sexual satisfaction and fulfilment. Then the other partner suddenly realizes that there are other men and women in the world, some at least of whom are prepared to put more effort into a relationship with their partner than they have been. Marriage shouldn't be seen as a passport to laziness and taking one's partner for granted but all too often this is what happens. Often the marriage shuffles along amicably enough but a mismatched sex drive is frequently the first cry for help.

Many individuals, unable to face up to the straight biological act of intercourse end up getting as close as they can to it compatible with finding it pleasurable. Fear, shame and guilt are the three biggest brakes on normal sexual enjoyment and everyone who has deviant needs however undramatic, will develop a style of intercourse or lovemaking that stops short of activities that produce these destructive and alarming emotions. Two common examples are the woman who gets orgasms from oral sex (cunnilingus) but can't have an orgasm any other way and the man who enjoys being masturbated but finds intercourse unpleasurable and unacceptable.

Mismatched enhancers

Probably the most commonly complained-of form of deviancy or mismatching of aims is the couple who finds that one or other absolutely refuses to do what the other wants. Such heartfelt difficulties can't easily be ignored. The main problem here is to distinguish between what is a sex enhancer and what is a perverse act. A true perversion is compulsive (the person can't have satisfactory sex unless that particular condition is present – be it black underwear; spanking; oral sex etc) and the person can't do without it. In therapy many of these individuals turn out to have deep 'needs' which were unsatisfied in childhood and which they are now acting out. Such people need professional help. There is nothing much that can be done on a self-help basis apart from adjusting to the need and gradually trying to modify it step-by-step. The individual can try thought stopping (see page 149) to eliminate the pertinent thought or he or she can retrain their fantasies.

On the other hand sex enhancement is a transitory phenomenon which is almost always totally harmless. We all need sex enhancers from time to time if only to ring the changes on sex with the same individual over many years. Anything that makes sex more enjoyable for one or both partners, should be accepted and gone along with wholeheartedly. The problem comes when the sex enhancing technique used by one partner induces so much anxiety in the other that he or she can't function well. This can be difficult but shouldn't be impossible. There are almost always ways of sorting out such disagreements, perhaps by finding a way of gratifying the one who wants the enhancers in a slightly different and more acceptable (to the other partner) way. Sexy underwear, vibrators, dildoes, erotic literature and videos, unusual lovemaking positions or places and

Ardour and passion can be greatly increased by such things as sexy underwear, watching oneself in a mirror or unusual positions

Shared happy times are like money in the bank for a relationship. With a little effort and imagination most couples could find more opportunities to enrich their lives in this way

many many others are all examples of enhancement techniques. The interesting thing about sex enhancers is that they change frequently (unlike perversions which are fixed) and that they soon lose their attraction and so need to be replaced by other enhancers. This can lead the spouse of such a person to become disenchanted with such endless variations and to long for 'normal' sex. Many sex books and girlie magazines have made people feel that if they are simply having straight sex on a regular basis they must be rather conventional and unadventurous but nothing could be further from the truth. On the contrary, an obsession with endless sex enhancers can be a form of inhibition. Very often the individual is too intimidated by normal sex to enjoy it unadorned by 'extras'. This kind of problem needs professional help. However the

vast majority of us don't come into this category – we simply enjoy the variation it gives.

The commonest complaint that women have against men sexually is that they are boring and predictable in bed.

This is a cruel irony because these very same men often complain that their partners are too inhibited and wouldn't want to experiment with sex enhancers. The two have seldom talked about the subject and often in therapy are found to have exactly parallel sexual fantasies! What a tragedy then to find the man going off to a prostitute and the woman having an extramarital affair to fulfil a fantasy that they could easily have enjoyed together.

A loving individual comfortable in his or her own body will at least *try* any reasonable suggestion that enhances the partner's sex life. Of course there are limits to what any of us can do without destroying our own enjoyment of sex and a loving acceptance of one's partner's deeply felt concerns in this area are part of a caring relationship.

Foreplay

Foreplay is the highly personalized and enjoyable behaviour that takes place between a couple before penetration. Every couple is by definition unique in what they most enjoy but here are a few tips that could be helpful:

Set the scene

◆ For all enjoyable sexual activity remember to take the phone off the hook and lock the bedroom door to keep the children out if that's a problem

◆ Take a little alcohol if you like

◆ Make sure the room is warm

◆ Get the lighting right . . . just enough to see clearly but not too bright

◆ Put on some mood music if this is what you like

◆ Strip yourself, or strip each other slowly

Things to do together

◆ Have a bath or shower together

◆ Massage each other (see page 194)

◆ Stimulate each other's erogenous zones, try variations, leave out genitals at first

◆ Kiss and cuddle

◆ Tell each other what you feel – praise little things about one another

◆ Kiss each other's bodies, especially parts that you know the other is sensitive about (a scar perhaps or a fat tummy)

◆ Be unashamedly romantic. Tell each other of your love (if it is true)

◆ Indulge in 'dirty talk' if that turns you on

The idea is to relax completely and to return to child-like loving behaviour between you.

Things that women like

No man knows what any individual woman most likes until she tells him or indicates in other non-verbal ways.

Women are infinitely variable in their tastes. This means that each woman has to be 'discovered' by a man even if he is experienced with many women but, in general, he should be bold.

- Talk to the woman and generally be guided by what you know about her. Romantic and admiring talk goes down well at this stage. Some women at this stage like to tell of their fantasies and like to hear their lover's

- Kissing and caressing is probably the most universally enjoyed pastime. Start furthest away from the sex organs and work slowly and teasingly towards them. Seek out the areas that she most enjoys having stroked and concentrate on them. The feet, behind the knees, the shoulders, the insides of the thighs and the ear lobes are just some of the favourite areas that are often overlooked by men

- Caress her more specifically erotic areas such as her breasts, bottom and mouth

- Kiss her most erotic areas, especially her breasts. Be gentle with the breasts. Most women complain that their men are too rough too early on in their arousal cycle. Be especially sensitive about her breasts just before a period as many women find that almost any stimulation is too much or even frankly unpleasant

- Don't get so carried away that you bite her too hard and leave love bites – at least not where they can be seen and might embarrass her

- Start to run your fingers through her pubic hair and gently caress her vulva

- Find her clitoris. Use fluid from the vaginal entrance and moisten the area or if necessary use saliva or baby oil

- Be guided by your partner as to what she most likes done. Usually this entails repeating what she does when she masturbates and is highly personalized to her. Pay attention to the length of stroke, the speed, the type of movement required; the area to which it is applied; the pressure which you apply and how long you go on for

- If she wants your fingers in her vagina, and many women do, find a position in which you can do this and still carry on with clitoral stimulation using both hands

- Bring her to a climax if she wants to, not forgetting that she might enjoy being stimulated elsewhere at the same time. Many women greatly enjoy having one or even both breasts held, pressed, caressed or sucked as their orgasm grows near. Some women like to take over clitoral stimulation at a certain stage and leave the man to kiss their breasts

- Keep both your hands and your mouth active all the time so as to give the most intense stimulation in several places at once

- Once she has had one orgasm continue to stimulate her in the way she likes to give her the chance to have another (unless she says that one is enough)

- All the time, without being obtrusive, observe her body to try to gauge the point she is at on the arousal response cycle (see pages 25)

Some special variations

◆ Use a vibrator on her vulva and later directly on her clitoris if she likes it

◆ Use the vibrator in her vagina while you (or she) caress the clitoris

◆ Use the vibrator on her anus as you put fingers in her vagina and caress her clitoris. Be very careful not to push it in too far as it can get lost inside

◆ Use several fingers, if she likes it, inside her vagina. Most women who use fingers inside themselves during masturbation insert two. As sexual tension mounts though many women find it exciting to take more than this and any woman who has had a baby can take three or even four fingers. Be careful to do what she most likes with them

◆ Early in the proceedings tell (rather than ask, because this helps the woman) her to masturbate herself and be sure that she knows how much you enjoy watching. Help her while she does this by caressing other parts of her body

◆ Sometimes it helps, at least some women in certain moods, not to bother with any of the above but to more or less force her to have intercourse. Many women greatly enjoy being pushed down, having their knickers pulled off and their legs forcibly opened – all perhaps accompanied by some wrestling or rough stripping off of the rest of her clothes. The level of ardour the man shows by doing this can be a real turn-on for many women. Some women greatly enjoy being told in advance that all this will soon happen to them and by the time the man gets her knickers off she is already highly aroused

Don't get stuck in a rut. Experiment with new types of foreplay. There is no need to be bored or boring.

Things that men like

Men are much simpler creatures than women when it comes to foreplay and their repertoire of likes and dislikes correspondingly smaller and less sophisticated. Once again though it makes sense to be guided by what the particular man wants and not to assume that because you know what one man likes that it necessarily makes you an expert on all men.

◆ A man's erotic areas are few compared with women (whose whole bodies are erotic zones) but even so men are not solely penis-centred, as many women believe. Other areas that greatly turn some men on are their nipples, their scrotum, the area between scrotum and anus, their anus itself and their feet

◆ Just as with exciting a woman a man has to be given a chance to say what he most enjoys

◆ Kissing and cuddling is greatly enjoyed by many men. Men like to be told they are loved and wanted and some like to hear their woman use crude language. Things such as 'I want to you to fuck my cunt in a minute' or 'what a super prick you've got' are a real turn-on for many men but nauseating to others

◆ Start with areas of his body far away from his genitals and drive him to ecstasy by kissing, nibbling, sucking and running your hands and hair all over him lightly. Ignore his genitals to tease him for as long as he (or you) can stand it. Alternatively touch them gently in passing as a tease

◆ Caress his genitals more specifically. Be careful not to overdo this though if you aim to make love or he might lose control. The squeeze technique (see page 105) is useful in slowing down his progress to orgasm. Bring him to an erection then tease him by stopping it and then resume until he can't bear it any longer and begs to make love to you

◆ Use both hands and mouth to stimulate several areas of his body at once. Stroke his hair or other parts of his body while you kiss his penis, for example, and at the same time squeeze his scrotum gently with your free hand

CASE STUDIES

Over the years various explanations and theories have been put forward to help people understand the barriers to sexual fulfilment. These are valuable not only in helping with the understanding of problems but also in treatment itself. Clinical experience shows that today more than ever people want to understand rather than simply to be told. This applies to many areas of life but especially so to the field of interpersonal and sexual problems.

The first and most prominent name in the field of sexual theories was Freud but he has since had many challengers and other schools of thought have built on his work and some have contradicted it. No single theory explains all human behaviour but they all add something to the jig-saw puzzle. Most therapists use a combination of the theories that they find work best in their hands.

A book like this is no place to go into all the relevant theories in detail but some understanding of them can give insights into an individual's problems. Of all the weapons in the therapists armoury the giving of insight must be the most powerful. Without at least some insights few people can make much progress with their relationship and sexual problems.

The brief case histories that follow are intended, albeit inadequately, to illustrate theories about psychosexual development, the unconscious mind, the conflict between desire and inhibition, the importance of experience and most important of all the development of the personality and the capacity to love.

The Unconscious

Mr A, a 42 year old psychologist, attended with his affectionate, older, matronly and Catholic wife, to state calmly that he had been impotent for 14 years. He was curiously unconcerned about the problem and had sought the consultation, he said, only to please his wife. They had been married for 16 years and had started intercourse, according to her, at her insistence, about a year before the ceremony. After a shaky start, he, having had no previous experience, became moderately proficient but never obtained as much pleasure from intercourse as from self-masturbation. In the second year of marriage he started a relationship with a younger married woman pharmacist and had enjoyed sex with her more than with his wife until one day, when she requested an encore, he became impotent.

Thereafter, with his wife's full knowledge and implied consent, he started to acquire a series of lovers. He adored and was devoted to women, he said; he loved their minds, their bodies and their genitals. He had become expert at pleasing them emotionally, romantically, physically and sexually by all and every means except the use of his penis. His pleasure was to please them and this was all he wanted. No matter what the woman did to him he never erected. He frequently masturbated himself, sometimes two or three times a day, but could do so only as long as he visualized foreplay and not penetration.

He had no interest in men, and wasn't homosexual, genuinely delighting in the love and companionship of his wife; his willingness to come for treatment was a sign of how far he would go to make her happy, even though he himself seemed content with the situation.

From this and much else he and his wife

said, it became clear that he feared women – regarding them as dangerous and powerful, and he especially feared emotional rejection by them if he wanted intercourse. His behaviour met both his heterosexual needs for physical contact with women and his need to be loved by them whilst avoiding his fear of intercourse. He had unconsciously chosen his easy-going wife to love him, and in the hope she would make no sexual demands.

He disagreed violently with this explanation, saying the exact opposite was the truth, but gradually through a number of consultations he developed much more insight into his own behaviour, and realized that his whole sexual and emotional life had been governed by these fears. With the help of his wife, who was encouraged to speak openly to him about her own sexual interests, needs and practices, the realization dawned deep-down that women are not really vestal virgins, and that they desire sex as much, or more, than men do. Eventually, he said that his penis eagerly erected to meet his wife's hand whenever she moved in that directon.

___

Discussion

___

Although the patient consciously knew of the nature of female sexuality and accepted it with enthusiasm, the knowledge exerted no effect on his behaviour, which was ruled by his unconscious beliefs. These had evidently been acquired in childhood from a sexually repressive mother, who punished him for his sexual interests. He had managed to function with his wife and the pharmacist because his desires, at that time, had marginally exceeded his fears. When confronted by her desires immediately after his own had been satisfied, the balance was upset and the impotence started.

The content of the unconscious mind is not known to the conscious one and can only be deduced by 'reading between the lines' of what an individual says and does. The unconscious mind largely controls the penis; if making it erect were under the control of the conscious will, impotence would never be a problem.

Against this it could be argued that, for example, a man can consciously decide to rub his own penis, think about a woman, and it will erect. However, the original impulse to obtain genital pleasure probably originated in the unconscious and was facilitated by conscious activity.

A man who is able to masturbate perfectly well on his own may be unable to do so if, say, a woman is watching him in spite of a wish to do so. The unconscious is preventing the act perhaps because of painful reproaches from the mother in childhood for being seen to be touching his genitals. Although not remembered by the conscious memory, the 'lesson' has been stored in the unconscious.

In this case the patient was not knowingly aware, in spite of his training, of either his desires for intercourse, or his fears of it and his conflicts about it. He had no conscious memory of punishment for his sexual behaviour in childhood, although in therapy some of these returned from the unconscious to the conscious and he recounted them as if they had happened yesterday, saying 'I never thought of it from that day to this'. He was unaware of his false notions about women, his tendency to regard them as he regarded his mother in childhood, or of the reason why he was so preoccupied with pleasing them.

The Mouth and Love

Miss B, 24 years old and shapely but plump, complained of recurrent bouts of unhappiness and depression. She said at first she had no idea of their cause but eventually began to cry and said no one liked her, including her parents. She felt they had always been reluctant to provide her with anything she needed. This was not attributable to jealousy of a brother or sister as she was an only child.

As she talked about her past and present it emerged that she felt insecure in relation to others. She always felt an outsider and was unsure whether others really liked her. Without realizing it, she responded to this situation by endeavouring to involve others in interactions with her to an excessive degree. Her basically demanding attitudes were designed to test the esteem in which others held her. The effect was clearly to make her a bit of a nuisance to most of her acquaintances and their withdrawal seemed to confirm her fears and repeatedly led to depression.

When asked about men and sex she said she was sure this was not the problem, as she had been to bed with dozens! Apart from trying to avoid them seeing her naked, especially when standing up, there were no difficulties. Her behaviour towards men was sexually provocative, again a form of demand, and she usually had intercourse with them on the first night. Such relationships were usually short but, she said, this was the way she wanted it since she did not wish to marry at the moment.

However, eventually a different pattern emerged. She obtained little genital pleasure from intercourse and never reached orgasm by this means. Her greatest satisfaction came from fellating men and swallowing the semen. She interacted intensely with them and wanted them to love her. Even if they had, she would not have known due to her basic distrust of others. Her tendency to over-burden relationships led to those with men collapsing and to her depression mingled with rage.

She responded to all her emotional and other setbacks with excessive eating and alcohol. She comforted, babied, loved, reassured and masturbated herself through her mouth. She greedily ate all and any food available in a way that indicated she unconsciously felt she must eat *now* because she could not trust her environment to provide more later.

Although she obtained some pleasure from her vulva and frequently rubbed it, she said she had never had an orgasm from it and did not regard the activity as important or as amounting to masturbation.

She made excellent progress in psychotherapy, controlling her oral drives and losing weight, enhancing her genital pleasures and behaving less neurotically with others, especially men. Better attitudes led to better behaviour and this in turn to better experiences resulting in improving self-esteem and self-confidence. As genital pleasures became more important to her she valued them more and ceased to be 'promiscuous'. Her parents and acquaintances perceived her as being a totally changed person and began to like her. She eventually established a good relationship and is now happily married.

Discussion

The two greatest body zones of physical pleasure are the mouth and the genitals. The former keeps the individual alive and the second the species. For the newborn child the mouth is of primary importance. Feeding offers the pleasures of being close to the mother and being cuddled by her, the stimulation of the mouth and the satisfaction of hunger. This stage is the oral stage of psychosexual development.

Excessive satisfactions or frustrations at the oral, or any other stage of psychosexual development, tend to make it difficult for the child to proceed to the next stage and, furthermore, to have a tendency to revert back to that stage in the face of any adversity later in life.

Miss B had been breast-fed but presumably this had not been satisfactory for one reason or another. Perhaps too she had not been fully wanted and perhaps her mother had encountered some difficulty in being fully affectionate and demonstrative. The response of Miss B to these frustrations may have alienated her mother even further and Miss B was continuing to display this pattern throughout life.

When the stages of development which succeed the oral stage occur they do not destroy the previous oral pleasures but they simply downgrade them. Thus, adults use the mouth to get and to give pleasure as part of lovemaking, in the form of kissing, licking, nibbling, biting and oral sex. However, these pleasures, in normal people, are subordinate to genital pleasures. One way of thinking of growing up is to view it as the gradual transfer of the primary pleasures of the mouth in childhood to the primary pleasures of the genitals in adulthood.

Miss B failed to make the transfer effectively. Unconsciously, for her, sucking the tip of the penis was sucking the nipple and semen was milk.

Although this fixation at the oral stage was only part of her overall problem it was basic. Her depression, her demands, her distrust, her over-eating and her genital inefficiency were attributable to it but it only partly explained her difficulty in loving herself and loving others. There were other facets of this case, not mentioned here, which were of importance.

The potty training stage

After years of investigation and treatment for a variety of complaints which her doctors eventually regarded as being mainly psychosomatic in origin, Mrs C, a 38 year old civil servant, was referred for psychosexual assessment. She turned out to be an extremely 'nice' if somewhat puritanically educated lady who had obviously preferred to make complaints about her physical health rather than about her husband. It distressed her to say anything about him which could be construed as being in the slightest critical.

This was understandable because he was also extremely 'nice' and a civil servant. He was tall, good-looking, amusing, attentive and evidently a model husband in every way. Superficially he was adaptable and easy-going but he turned out to be hard to influence and very obstinate even over trivial things he thought were important.

Nevertheless he was miserly and restricted her expenditure. Their combined income was high, and she earned very nearly as much as he did. Her dress allowance, for example, for a year would have been spent by many women in a week. They had all they needed but if she broke anything that had to be replaced he made her feel guilty about the consequences of her clumsiness. In spite of their affluence and both being in full-time employment, she had no help in the home (apart from his considerable contribution). All tasks in the house and garden had to be undertaken by the couple themselves and everything had to be perfect and tidy. She liked to go out occasionally to parties or to the theatre but such activities were limited because of their expense.

He loved and cared for her and mothered her in respect of her symptoms. However, demonstrations of physical appreciation and attraction were rare as were displays of adult heterosexual love, as opposed to concern. He had no sexual interest in any other women, but only rarely paid her any sexual attention in spite of her considerable attractiveness and somewhat coy attempts at seduction. He had no difficulty in erecting and claimed to enjoy intercourse but very often he could not ejaculate in the vagina no matter how long he tried.

Realizing the true nature of her situation, which had previously puzzled her, reduced Mrs C's distress and her symptoms. Having located the real origins of her problems she began to seek alternative satisfactions to meet her deprivations. His attitudes also became more relaxed and more sexually and emotionally generous.

Discussion

In the second year of life, a child's primary preoccupation turns from the pleasure of taking things in through the mouth to elimination through the anus. Not everyone agrees that this stage genuinely exists but in our culture the mother's concentration on potty training, if for no other reason, turns the child's attention to elimination and its pleasures. Faeces become a gift the child can give or with-hold. The child is being taught to retain faeces until their production is convenient and it may over-learn the lesson deriving pleasure from, and even punishing the mother, by retaining them.

Conflicts at this stage are thought to affect a child greatly. Certainly, anal pleasures can become over-valued and may be excessively retained in later life. Many individuals find some stimulation of the anus somewhat sexually arousing but for others it has to be present for full satisfaction, even in self-masturbation. Some women can only have orgasms in anal intercourse and similar desires in some men is a possible cause of them wanting to be penetrated homosexually. Excessive reactions against anal pleasures and interests can also lead to trouble.

One way of thinking of Mr C, who had a very upright, strict mother, was that although he had no great desires for anal stimulation his personality had been affected by the anal stage. He wished to store and retain money, love and semen. Whilst not being actually stingy he resented demands for supplies of any of these, leading to deprivation in his unhappy wife. Due to her own rearing Mrs C had not perceived any fault in her husband and had assumed that anything which was wrong must have been caused by herself.

The Phallic Stage

The life of a 30 year old solicitor, Mr D, was disintegrating. His wife of five years standing was leaving him, his boy-friend was giving him up, his senior partners were increasingly critical of his work, he was finding his religious beliefs less and less satisfactory, and the ever-present sensations of tension within him, when he felt he was going mad, were becoming stronger. Although very distressed he was not as depressed as might have been expected and he continued to function – albeit not too satisfactorily.

His wife had been his only female sex partner, and he rarely had intercourse with her. In fact, from the beginning, she had been compelled to force the pace, or intercourse never occurred. He also did not like her very much, and often complained of her to anyone who would listen.

He found himself much more concerned with his status in the eyes of men, rather than women, and in the third year of the marriage had acquired a young male friend with whom anal intercourse was undertaken. At first, he preferred to take the active role and penetrate his friend, but gradually the passive role gave him pleasure which became greater with time. He also enjoyed the odour of the anus and liked to lick his friend.

In spite of all this they were in frequent emotional conflict, and he was very jealous. This led to the deterioration of the relationship which was unfortunate since he derived much more sexual satisfaction from his friend than from his wife.

He had always had a poor relationship with his father and was much closer to his mother but was also sharply critical of her, her behaviour and her personality. He had always felt she preferred his younger brother to him. Whilst under treatment he began to have dreams that he was having intercourse with his mother and his rate of masturbation, which had previously been low since it was 'wrong', rose to around ten times a day. This rate, especially when sustained, is abnormally high for a male beyond puberty (when very young some men possess an almost unlimited capacity for orgasm).

Although he had not matured very far beyond the phallic stage, under the stresses he was encountering he had gradually gone into reverse, regressed as it is called, and returned to the phallic stage of intense masturbation and unconscious thoughts of sex with his mother which emerged in dreams. In fact he had partly returned to the even younger anal stage since his masturbation was accompanied by manipulations such as the insertion of fingers into his anus. He did not attempt to find a partner to replace his boy-friend.

Under treatment, the seriousness of his difficulties made it clear to him that he needed help. Gradually he began to understand his situation and his intense anal drives subsided. After a period of indecision he spontaneously started to develop an interest in heterosexual sex; although his marriage did not recover, his professional life did, and he developed a reasonably satisfactory relationship with another young woman which may yet end in a more adult attempt at marriage, with a good sexual life for both of them.

Discussion

Although not everyone, including some psychoanalysts, agrees with the notion that psychosexual development proceeds by stages in which one area of the body after another becomes the principal focus of interest and pleasure, it is possible to make some sense of what happened to Mr D on this basis. The anal stage is succeeded by the phallic stage, around the age of two to three years, in which the penis in a boy and the clitoris in a girl take over from the anus. The child, of course, handles the genitals from long before the phallic stage and the signs of genital excitement are present from early on. For example, a boy may erect when cuddled or a girl may roll her thighs together whilst breast feeding. Even true masturbation may be present and the youngest child to be observed reaching orgasm by this means was, Kinsey records, a girl of seven months.

During the phallic stage the character of the little boy's love for his mother changes and becomes more intense. Although the idea is offensive to some people, perhaps for reasons to do with their own child-hood, the boy may be said in some sense to have instated his mother as his lover in a way which is not too different from the type of love relationship he will, hopefully, enjoy with a woman in adulthood. An inaccurate but short-hand way of putting it is to say that his mother is his first girl-friend and the first woman he wants. The same condition applies to a girl in respect of her father. The difference is that children of both sexes first love the mother, but with the onset of her phallic stage the girl turns towards her father.

Mr D had difficulty negotiating this stage of development as a child. Undue jealousy of his brother was one reason. This start to life remained an important force as was shown by the dreams of intercourse with his mother. For reasons to be explained, such wishes, although unconscious, provoked anxiety, from which he had always suffered, and feelings of being different to others. He felt inferior to other men. Unconsciously he identified his wife with his mother and intercourse with his wife provoked anxiety which reduced both its occurrence and the pleasure. He was less tense with men and so enjoyed sex with his boy-friend more.

Our first love affair

Miss E was 23 years old, a clever PhD student and very attractive. In spite of all her advantages she was miserable most of the time and for weeks at a time could not get on with her work because of her emotional disturbances.

The basic trouble was her perception of herself as being a failure with men. Her father, a plumber, was evidently ambitious for her academically and she had worked so hard at school (unconsciously to please him) that she had never had time for boys. This continued at University, but in her second year she began to feel increasingly discontented, and had felt jealous of her friends who had boyfriends and sex. She started a relationship and began to have intercourse but without enjoying it much. She was baffled by her feelings of uncertainty as to whether she loved the man or even had any affection for him.

To reassure herself she behaved in an attentive and loving way, telling him how much she adored him. However, she was annoyed when he spoke about any technical matter she knew well, such as car mechanics. She would think 'bloody fool' but say nothing.

Inseparable from her father when small, as she grew up, she had spent a lot of time with him. He, presumably having wanted a son, had involved her in car and house maintenance, football, fishing and so on. She had regarded him as a genius and still did so, comparing the academic staff at the University unfavourably with him. Although the family was a peaceable one she and her father jointly regarded her mother as a bit of a fool and she had unresentfully fallen into this role. As far as the daughter was concerned the mother was almost a nonentity.

Eventually her boy-friend gave her up, and although she found it easy to establish new relationships, she had no success at maintaining them, in spite of her total willingness to do anything to please her partners. She went on to establish relationships with men who were clearly less educated or sophisticated, but this only aggravated the problem.

These bare-bones of the story took a lot of uncovering because they were well concealed under masses of incidental detail. Once she understood the underlying nature of the problem she adjusted well and successfully resumed her studies, leaving boys alone for a while. She finally established a more satisfactory and mature pattern of relating to men.

As she developed insight and began to mature, so her sexual capacities rapidly increased. She began to feel she knew what love was and who to love. She even loved herself more. She became much more stable, predominantly happy instead of unhappy, and finally married a professional man, incidentally to the great delight of her father.

Discussion

Although a satisfactory relationship with her father during childhood is crucial to the future welfare of a girl, this patient's father was unwisely over-close to his daughter. In a sense she displaced her mother as his partner. The cause may have been an immaturity in the father which encouraged him to relate better to a little girl than to an adult woman, or possibly defects in the mother had prevented him establishing an enduring and satisfying relationship with her, so in effect, the daughter had become his main love-object. In handling, cuddling and playing with her he may also have been somewhat excessive which in turn may have exerted a seductive effect on her.

In growing up the attractions to the opposite sex parent have to be largely abandoned or a transfer of the loving and sexual feelings to another member of that sex is impossible. This girl was still locked into her loving relationship with her father to a large extent and had insufficient 'space' left to love and make love to another man. To her, all men were inferior to her father and were contemptible. Consciously, this view was deeply concealed from her and she was unaware of any sexual attraction to her father or any older man. Her masturbation fantasies were of no help in this direction since she thought only of what she was doing and was unaware of having any fantasies. In any case she was deeply ashamed of masturbation and it was rare. Her struggle was not only against the act but also against the fantasies about her father which she repressed into her unconscious mind.

Other women patients with similar backgrounds are affected in other ways. For example, some have become trans-sexual, some lesbians, some promiscuous and some mentally ill. 'Mild' cases are common and manifest themselves in an intense attraction to much older men (a phase which commonly passes), sexual problems such as lack of orgasm in intercourse, and abnormal relationships with the mother. Although they may horrify a feminist, many mild cases seem almost to enjoy the problem since they, in effect, install their husband in the role of father, yielding dominance to him, and happily resume the status of the beloved and adoring little girl themselves.

This can be conflict-free and utterly successful even when children arrive, because the mother frequently interacts with her children, not as may be expected with jealousy, but almost as a delighted and deeply involved older sister i.e. she tends to make friends of her children.

Women, too, seem to be less disabled sexually than their male counter-parts with similar problems. For mechanical reasons a woman can, as did this patient, have intercourse whilst her male equivalent would probably have been impotent. Her sexual distress showed up in her inadequate masturbation and her lack of response and pleasure in intercourse - which she concealed from her partners by pretending to have orgasms.

The Unresolved Oedipus Complex

Mr F was unmarried, handsome, 29 years of age and a teacher. In addition he was amusing and witty.

He taught mixed classes in a senior school and frequently volunteered to accompany school trips abroad as a supervisor. He was the object of much attention from his mid-adolescent girl pupils, some of whom told him they loved him. While on school trips, out of the country, several girls found opportunities to make provocative displays in his presence. On two occasions, he had attempted to have intercourse with them, but he had been totally impotent. This puzzled him because, unlike almost all parents and fellow teachers, he had no professional objections to sex between teachers and pupils and regarded morality as a matter of inconvenience to be overcome. There had been no risk of detection and he trusted the girls not to discuss the relationship with others. In masturbation he often envisaged intercourse with the girls and far from inhibiting erection, thoughts of it facilitated the act.

In general, his attitudes towards discipline were rebellious and he sided with the pupils. With the girls he was somewhat intimate and flirtatious, inviting them to confide in him about their problems. Any control he exerted over his pupils was by appeal and not authority. Although he appeared mature in his manner and behaviour he was, in effect, an ageing school-boy himself.

He was much less open with women of his own age, and even when in relationships with them, he was reserved. He was always unsure about his emotional feelings towards them. He had managed to undertake fairly unenjoyable intercourse with one or two but with most he had finally decided that their bodies or personalities were such that he did not really 'fancy them'. However, he would undertake mutual masturbation and oral sex with them. His tentativeness finally resulted in several of his previous girl-friends becoming angry and when this happened he would sulk and thank his lucky stars that he had avoided 'getting in too deep with an absolute bitch'.

His most marked feature was in relation to his parents. He loved his mother who was a 'good woman' but his hatred of his father was pathological. As far as could be determined his father was inoffensive and long-suffering, although he tended to drown his many sorrows in drink. The patient had changed his name so as not to bear the same one as his elderly father and had ordered him out of the parental home with threats of violence so as to 'protect' his mother. The father lived alone and was forbidden the house even at Christmas when his five children, of whom the patient was the youngest, would congregate. The mother made occasional half-hearted attempts to bring her husband home but was always frightened out of it by the violent threats of the patient.

Discussion

The Oedipal situation is called a complex because there is more to it than just the attraction to the oposite sex parent. The child wants possession of the opposite sex-parent and sees the same-sex parent as a competitor. The child fears the same-sex parent knows of their jealous feelings and consequently fears revenge. Since boys are often teased, reproached or even punished for touching their genitals and for erections they are prone to fear that revenge may take the form of damage to the genitals. The fear is labelled castration anxiety. The conclusion is not unreasonable since boys are very likely by the height of this stage to have seen the genitals of sisters, mother or of female playmates. They may well conclude initially that females are boys who have 'had it cut-off' as a punishment for touching. Many girls arrive at the same conclusion. Some think the mother carried out the act on them but one student, the daughter of a doctor, recollected her infant theory that she and her little girl-friend had been turned into girls due to the carelessness of her father with the hedge-cutter whilst they had been sitting on the garden gate watching him trim the hedge one day.

Boys normally turn away from the mother and the world of women to that of the father and the world of men around five. With this step they also give up masturbation which previously relieved the tensions of the excitements of the Oedipal stage. Theory asserts the change is brought about mainly by castration anxiety. Since he still has his genitals, and can therefore still have them removed, the threat continues giving a big impetus to the development of conscience, guilt, morality and so on. This is discussed later. The same impetus is thought not to be present in girls to the same extent since they have nothing further to lose. The girl therefore does not give up her father at this age in the same way as the boy does the mother. Boys repress their desires for their mother into the unconscious and along with it their recollection of childhood masturbation. The overwhelming majority of men assert masturbation first started at puberty. About a third of all women say they can not recollect a time when they did not do it.

The turn against the Oedipal situation may be influenced by other factors. Many, if not most, mothers are fairly casual about undressing, bathing and even the use of the toilet in front of their small sons. As the intensity of the Oedipal interest in her body rises, the mother probably becomes somewhat alarmed and denounces it as 'dirty'. The underlying thought that they are 'dirty' whilst girls are 'nice' is all but universal amongst men and probably derives from the mother's curtailment of his interest at this stage.

The ending of the Oedipal stage is part of the development programme built into all human beings but it can go awry, as in the case of Mr F, for reasons such as, it is thought an absent, weak, brutal, unfriendly or rejecting Father, which prevents the boy liking him and copying him and thereby beginning to make his way in the world of men, or a domineering, seductive, over-close or unsatisfactory mother who keeps him in the Oedipal relationship with her or who has given him so many problems he can not leave the stage due to the need to try to solve them. Mr F's mother was clearly a rather weak and confused woman who probably doted on him as her love-child. He was much younger than the other children which didn't help matters.

In spite of much therapy designed to give him insight into the nature of his problem he made little progress. In the end his activities were detected and he was dismissed.

Parents and the Oedipus Complex

Mrs G, an attractive and intelligent divorcée of 32 years, had two sons of eleven and eight years old.

She had become concerned about their development and her influence upon it. Her feelings for the older boy were not hostile but neither were they, she felt, fully maternal and fully loving. The younger one, however, excited her and always had done. She always had him, usually naked, present when she took a bath and allowed or even encouraged him to fondle her breasts. This excited her intensely as did his erections. She particularly admired his 'manly balls'.

Discussion

There is an erotic component to all love and it is not to be doubted that it is important.

Mrs G might seem extraordinary but she simply used her body to express her love although she did derive conscious erotic pleasure from it. Many mothers report similar, if lesser, feelings and it is probably an important component of all maternal love.

She felt more secure loving a child than loving a man. The younger child reminded her of herself when young and so loving him intensely was a way, to some extent, of loving herself. This also expressed her long (consciously) forgotten wishes to be a boy during girlhood.

The longterm outcome of such an involvement with her son is not known but most experts would consider it unwise. Curiously, whereas girls, when adult, often report that the father, or some male relative, interfered with them as a child, men rarely make similar claims against women. Women in society are less criticized for physically loving their children, and hugs and kisses are not only allowed but encouraged. In practice some boys with over-close mothers seem to grow up very self-assured in their subsequent relationships with women, whereas others become shy, guilty, inhibited and frightened of physical contact with them. Some want to instate any woman as a mother, and react accordingly towards her – often, especially after she has had a baby herself. The first group have resolved the Oedipus complex whereas the others have not.

Obviously, our first experiences of the opposite sex, which usually means the opposite-sex parent, profoundly affect subsequent attitudes towards them. However, the situation is intensely complicated and many factors affect the final outcome. So is it not possible to assert that Mrs G was particularly right or particularly wrong or necessarily to attribute any subsequent difficulties the boy might encounter with certainty to her. If her behaviour continued into the time of the boy's puberty then it would definitely be harmful.

In any case, it would be difficult subsequently to disentangle the effects of the mother's behaviour, the divorce, the absence of the father and the jealousy of the older boy, to name only a few factors.

Latency

Miss H, who was 18, was abnormally thin and had not had a period for over four years. She concealed her state under bulky clothes and claimed that she ate adequately. She was a 'nice' and neat girl whose behaviour was impeccable. She was a virgin, having little interest in sex. She had recently done very well in her 'A' level examinations.

She was the older of two sisters and whereas she spoke well of her relationship with her father she said she found her mother fussy, interfering and tiresome.

When she was examined, her bones were easily visible and she had so little fat that all her female curves had disappeared, as had her breasts.

Discussion

The Oedipal phase is followed by a period of relative calm which lasts up to puberty. Children continue to be interested in sex, but not excessively so, and the intense attachment to the opposite sex parent becomes gradually replaced with ordinary affection and love. Heterosexual games of the pre-school years become uncommon. At some stage, usually pre-teens, a girl is likely to banish her previously welcome father from the bathroom. Her interest in girlie magazines can increase as she wonders what it is like to be a woman. She is quite likely to become involved in sex-games with her best girl-friend and may play games like 'kiss me as a boy would'. They may inspect each other's genitals and even smack bottoms but mutual masturbation is very rare. This is curious since, in addition to the girls who have continued to masturbate, some of those who ceased at the end of the Oedipal phase have resumed the activity again towards the end of the latency stage. The interest that girls have in relationships, both their own and others, also increases.

In spite of all this, latency is a fairly quiescent period sexually and, for example, most girls at this stage are unaware of the real significance of their masturbation. It is regarded as naughty and secret but not as sexually sinful. That comes with puberty. Many girls in latency are extremely well balanced and poised but this calm is shattered at puberty and new guilt arises.

Anorexia, which is many times commoner in girls than boys (probably 20 to 1) may possibly be best explained as a retreat or regression towards latency designed to avoid the stresses of full genital sexuality. Many anorexic girls are similar to the junior school girl in latency. Miss H was a perfect example of this. Other explanations of anorexia are put forward but from the psychosexual point of view the loss of breasts, periods and genuine sex interest is very striking.

Some men seem never to acquire much real interest in heterosexuality (or any other form of sexuality) and others lose the interest after a bad experience with a woman. The relative freedom from direct sexual (i.e. genital) needs seems to liberate some of them into the relative calms of latency when they can become intensely creative.

Miss H responded quite well to the type of psychosexual explanation offered above.

Opposing forces

Mrs I was 28 years old and had not had intercourse with her husband for the last six years of her seven year marriage. Her husband, she said, was 'very considerate' and did not complain about her refusal. 'He adores me' she claimed. She had let boys feel her breasts from the time she was 14 years old; but was guilty about this. She had met her future husband at 16. She had 'saved myself for marriage' but did become involved in mutual genital handling with him but never looked at his penis.

On her marriage night she was 'too tight' and saw a gynaecologist who 'stretched' the vagina under an anaesthetic and gave her a series of glass tubes of increasing diameter to insert afterwards. She was repelled and following a few attempts at pleasureless intercourse she gave up sex.

In the third year of marriage they had met another couple. She convinced herself she liked/loved the other man and manoeuvred everyone into a wife swapping episode and became convinced she was pregnant. The man 'was large and tore me inside leading to much bleeding'. However, she was jealous of the other woman with whom her husband had intercourse. Later she felt guilty about the episode. But her interest was aroused and she began to masturbate by rubbing her vulva. (She thought she had never masturbated previously. Presumably she had been using a non-genital indirect method, suppressing the conscious awareness of orgasm, thereby maintaining the denial to herself. Even now she was doubtful if she

obtained orgasms but the act finished in five minutes or so, coming to a definite satisfactory end.)

At this point she became fearful and consulted her local priest in order to make use of religion to curb her sexuality in the way adolescent girls often do. He did not let her down and told her the affair had been 'very wrong' and that 'masturbation is a mortal sin'. This slaked her desires for a time but eventually she became jealous of her women friends talking about their sex lives and determined to seek help.

She accepted she was immature psychosexually. She had difficulty in talking about sex and had come from a strict background where it was never mentioned. She was jealous of her four-years older brother and hated her mother for doting in him. She remembered feeling that you have to be a boy and have a penis if you are to be loved. She became alienated from her genitals as a result and did not want to know about them. The start of menstruation at 12 had disgusted her. Although very intelligent she had not grasped the concepts behind the mechanics of intercourse until 19 (twice the usual age) and had thought pregnancy was possible from standing next to a man until she was 20. She had not used tampons until she was 21. Obviously she had just not wanted to know about sex.

Her treatment was complicted but two factors were of crucial importance. One was satisfying her tremendous curiosity about the sexuality of other women and the second was the discovery of the powers her womanly body held over her husband. She eventually accepted her female role and body with delight and spoke of her orgasms in lyrical terms.

Discussion

Experiences in childhood had, in effect, psychologically castrated Mrs I. She wanted to escape from home and be loved but sex was off the agenda. She did not psychologically accept she had a vagina, or, as it is put, she had not incorporated it into her body image. Hence the tightness, called vaginismus. To dilate it before she had made psychosexual progress was as wrong as doing the same to a five or six year old girl. Her extramarital adventure was not genital in purpose but to discover whether it was she or her husband who was at fault. The resultant bleeding, and fear of pregnancy, were seen as punishments from God which drove her to the priest.

The treatment consisted of taking her through the stages of psychosexual development until she became 'adult'.

Very little of this had passed through her conscious mind and she was not able to account for her behaviour. She simply thought she had a low sex drive but when she thought about it she was dimly aware that, like many women, she had deep and fearful sexual desires which would lead to some disaster if she indulged them. Because the hazy fantasies on which her knowledge of these desires was based could be brought into consciousness in a clinical setting, they are called pre-conscious i.e. by concentrating on them they could be made conscious.

Different mental forces influenced her at different times and her behaviour reflected the interplay between them. Freud labelled these 'the it', or 'the id' as translated into English, 'the I' or 'the ego' and the 'over-I' or 'super-ego'. The id is concerned with instincts and their gratification regardless of circumstances, the ego with external realities, self-control and relationships with others and the super-ego with self-criticism, moralizing and conscience. The id is present at birth but the ego and super-ego develop later.

Mrs B possessed a strong and rigid super-ego, which ruled her much like her parents ruled her as a child. Her jealousy of her brother and her desire for love made her very attentive to her parents' attitudes towards sex and most other things in order to not offend them and lose their love. Like the instinctual needs in her id, much of the content of her super-ego was unknown to her, it simply exerted an effect on her behaviour. She, or rather, her ego, was like a shuttle-cock between the two and in addition had to cope with the realities she faced. Wherever her id managed to influence her ego successfully, as for example, in arranging the wife-swap, her super-ego had its revenge by inducing fear and guilt in her. Her super-ego damaged her capacity to grow up and be a happy woman; it kept her as a perpetual child.

The influence of learning

For reasons which were never adequately explained, the mother of Mrs J had, for as far back as Mrs J could remember, criticized her child for an interest in sex. By junior school age she was being told she was 'tarty' and by adolescence she was being called a 'whore'.

Perhaps the mother had perceived trends in the girl from infancy which she felt should be strictly suppressed for fear of their later expression or she may have been jealous of the affectionate responses the child obtained from her father. To some extent the mother's reproaches must have reflected how she herself had been brought up and her own struggles against *her* sexuality. In any case Mrs J, at 21, had learned the lesson and had suppressed all her interest in sex. Her psychiatrist saw her as a case of absolute frigidity.

This was not unreasonable because although she had intercourse with her husband she derived neither sensation nor pleasure from it; she did not masturbate and never had. any sexual fantasies or dreams. She appeared to be totally sexless in the way that Kinsey, from his research, thought some women are for reasons to do, he suggested, with a defect in their constitution.

After many sessions Mrs J mentioned in passing, as a matter of no importance, that she retained urine until she was nearly bursting. She would roll around on her bed, contracting her muscles to hold back the flow. She agreed this gave her some pleasure and that finally letting go was a pleasure both for the relief it gave and for the sensations in the urethra.

This was her form of masturbation which involved no touching; presumably as a result of fierce prohibitions learned in childhood. Gradually she learned, or rather re-learned, to expand the feelings she experienced and then to substitute normal masturbation for this indirect method. At the end of treatment she was able to experience several orgasms both in masturbation and intercourse. When followed up several years later the capacity had been retained and her marriage was flourishing.

Discussion

Masturbation is a rehearsal or training for intercourse. During their childhood many girls are conditioned out of direct masturbation and out of the pleasures of sex. Muscular contraction methods are the second commonest form of female masturbation. Other methods, as with Mrs J, depend upon unavoidable actions such as urination or washing. Some women can even masturbate solely by fantasy.

A more common response in girls to rebukes for touching themselves is to masturbate face down, perhaps with the legs together and through the knickers. None of these variations are helpful to future intercourse.

Everyone learns – or as in the case of Mrs J, mislearns – from the moment they are born. According to learning theory anything which has been learned and later leads to problems can be unlearned and re-learned in a better way. This theory can be applied in treatment. An example is aversion therapy in which the occurrence of certain behaviour it is desired to eliminate is associated with something painful. For example, a transvestite may wish to break the habit. A simple form of self-treatment is to place a rubber band around the wrist and then when any exciting thoughts of that nature come to mind, or the desire to undertake it, or buy a magazine about it, the band is pulled and allowed to snap-back painfully.

In Mrs J's case she had learned to associate high levels of anxiety with any form of sexual pleasure. Any thoughts she had of inducing such pleasure led to a quick and large rise in anxiety which supressed her desires. She had learned, or been conditioned, out of her sexuality by her mother. As urination is inevitable she made use of that for very mild sexual pleasure, which is not uncommon in women, but was still compelled to deceive herself. Her treatment consisted of taking a little step at a time back to normality so that the amount of anxiety aroused was insufficient to block progress. Combined with encouragement and approval it was successful to a point where she was eventually free of all anxiety arising from her sexual needs and pleasures and was eventually able to function with abandon.

False perception

Mr K was humorous, good looking, well made and well educated. However, at 22 he was contemplating suicide since 'girls never look at me' and obviously 'no girls want me'. The reasons he advanced were that he had a stupid Christian name, poor hair, a misshapen trunk and a fat bottom. All these allegations were manifestly false but he was utterly impervious to any reassurance from anyone. Clearly his fears about himself were defending him from even deeper fears. This was proved by the fact that two years earlier a girl had noticed him and had even ended up in his bed. Intercourse had not occurred, due, he claimed, to his tiredness and drunkenness. The episode was a freak one and no conclusions could be safely drawn from it, he considered.

Going back it appeared his real troubles had started at the age of four with the birth of his sister. He was not jealous of her but rather regarded her with some awe because she, he felt, was a success in life both scholastically and with boys.

It was not that he was tragic about it, but in spite of coming from a secure and loving background he felt he was not really loved or even liked. Because he had reached an age where love and making love are major preoccupations his fear was being applied to his current needs and he particularly saw girls as not wanting either form of involvement with him.

Discussion

Although there was much complicating material which has been omitted, in essence Mr K was still applying a childhood problem to life. Because he had no *recognition* of the real problem he kept on misperceiving himself and others. In fact he found spurious explanations to account for the difficulties.

When a younger child is born the older one loses some of the attention and affection he or she previously received. The effect seems to be greatest when the new child is two to six years younger. The older child sometimes reacts with resentment towards the mother for having produced the competitor. Although he or she may love the new child some jealousy and even hatred is present. They may seek to punish the new rival but this earns sharp rebuke from the parents. This can aggravate the third and commonest reaction which is to regard the self as being inadequate in some way and not fully loveable. Mothers sometimes say there is no reason for such reactions because she shared attention equally between them. Even if this were true the older child loses half of what he or she previously received. Due to differences in personality and such factors as the state of Oedipal relationship at the time, some older children respond with great efforts to achieve, so as to earn back love regarded as lost, and so ultimately first-borns swell the ranks of the successful and famous out of all proportion to their numbers amongst all children in the population. Just as some become over-achievers some become very anxious in competitive situations and so become under-achievers.

Mr K tended to belong to the latter group and although intelligent was not as successful as he could have been. He was unable to overcome the unconscious notion that he was inadequate, different and unloveable/unlikeable and from his earliest days at school had felt uncomfortable with others. Initially he reacted against this and became aggressive towards others but later, especially as his heterosexual needs began to emerge, he felt inferior to other boys. He did not know, and did not want to know, why he felt this way and so developed delusions about his body. He preferred to blame his body rather than his personality and loveability.

The false ideas about himself made him shy and nervous with girls, and, moreover, on social occasions he tended to become drunk to drown the anxiety. The drink gave him a degree of courage but at the same time the girls he then approached, for example to dance, rejected him thus confirming his prejudice against himself.

The alcohol also gave him an excuse to avoid performing sexually if the opportunity arose or an explanation if he was impotent. He was a virgin and was full of performance anxiety. Further still, he boosted his weak ego by drink since he believed that large rates of consumption proved he was a man.

Realizing the true origin of the false perception of himself enabled him to develop more accurate ideas about himself and behave accordingly. He stopped fearing rejection for being unloveable and began to be more active in pursuing girls. Previously he had watched all girls closely, really hoping to see signs that they were overcome with attraction and desire at the mere sight of him. It was because this did not happen that he elected to blame his body.

Adolescence

Mr L was a wealthy and highly successful businessman of 40 who was a model husband and father to his two children. He and his wife were very well matched which was not surprising since they had met through a highly professional marriage bureau. They communicated easily about everything and understood each other perfectly. Intercourse was intensely satisfactory for them both and occurred frequently.

One day Mr L was attending a meeting and saw a woman he had previously seen many times but this time it was different. She was slim, unlike his shapely wife, and when she gave him a long look it seemed to him that there was something special between them. He became more or less obssessed with her. Meetings were arranged at which nothing much occurred but they served to increase the intensity of his feelings. He constructed various fantasies about her and joint activities together but these did not include intercourse. He thought of her as being pure and not to be sullied. Although intercourse continued with his wife his independent masturbation ceased. He lost weight, looked ill, felt he could not cope with his work, had difficulty in sleeping, could not concentrate and was irritable with his wife and children.

His wife, from whom he felt it was useless to conceal anything because she could read him, became upset at his infatuation with the woman. She pointed out how far the woman in actuality departed from his romantic perceptions of her but all to no avail. He did not see his interest in his new-found love to be in the slightest conflict with his interest in his wife. He felt she was simply trying to frustrate him.

He sought advice about his condition. He had always been shy with girls, hence the bureau, and was tense in socializing with them. Prior to his wife he had had only one partner, a divorced older woman with two children whom he had met at the age of 25. When that relationship finished he enrolled with the bureau. His mother had brought him up to be 'nice' and he believed that intercourse was unthinkable in the absence of love. He had never really had an adolescence.

Eventually he became aware that in reality he was simply preoccupied with thoughts of intercourse with many women but that he had fixed on this woman whom he had endowed with romantic fantasies. He eventually accepted that they were fantasies and did not correspond with the actual woman in reality. He rapidly became more realistic about women and sought to solve the problems his delayed adolescence had presented him with in ways less dangerous to his marriage and more acceptable to his wife.

Discussion

Clearly Oedipal factors had some place in this case but its main interest lies in the fact that for no readily apparent reason Mr L suddenly developed all the signs and symptoms of adolescence. His promiscuous urges were concealed under his romantic pre-occupations. His wife safely belonged to some other compartment and was not threatened. In fact the relationship improved because, as his experience of women grew, he had some yardstick with which to measure his wife and the excellent quality of their loving friendship.

Early adolescence in boys is really a homosexual stage whereas girls take a sharp turn towards heterosexuality. In both sexes Oedipal longings repressed in middle childhood threaten to break through again, thereby increasing anxiety. A boy's homosexual stage, in which he is likely to be involved to a greater or lesser degree in masturbation with other boys, marks the separation of the phase in life in which his mother was his sex and love object from the stage in which he will eventually seek a sex and love object of his own. His erotic interest in his opposite sex parent is withdrawn and the drive, called the libido, is invested in himself.

Masturbation rates rise as do self-preoccupation and moods. Romantic thoughts and perverse fantasies may arise and are explored. The consequences of any psychosexual, emotional, social or other disability placed on the child in earlier years now become increasingly manifest. If all goes tolerably well tentative investigations of the opposite sex start in mid-adolescence. Girls at this stage begin to attribute increasing significance to the vagina both in fantasy and masturbation. A sign of this is that tampons start to be used. The stage for both sexes is basically a promiscuous one, emotionally if not genitally, and the self and the opposite sex are explored.

In late adolescence, starting at 18 or 19 in a girl and even later in a boy, the individual becomes much less dependent on parents as adult-type emotional needs begin to emerge. It is the final stage of childhood and the evolution of the complete individual.

As some of the case histories show, late adolescence is a time when changes can still be wrought, old wounds healed and deficiencies repaired with more ease than is ever possible later. Because the individual is still not fully mature change is more easily possible than later in life.

Although Mr L gave everyone involved with him a hard time he was fairly easy to treat and the storm abated in a few weeks. At the end of it he felt much more confident and self-assured. It is open to anyone to say that all this was only his second adolescence but he had never had a first one before he was seen for therapy.

Communicating

Mr and Mrs M were due shortly to take up residence in the Far East so the time available for treatment was short. They were fond of each other but the marriage was not as they would have liked it to be because of rows which were not especially bitter but they never solved anything. Communicating over their real problems never occurred. Very sensibly they wanted a new start in their new life.

He was a 49 year old moderately successful export executive and she was one year his junior. He smiled sadly as she catalogued his failings and agreed ruefully as she repeatedly called on him to affirm the fairness of her account. She complained of his aggressive manner, his lack of enterprise (in terms of ruthlessly seeking worldy success), his expectation that she be home-centred and his reducing their home to 'the place where he died', by which she meant he interacted insufficiently with her. Her frustration was obvious and intense.

He did not fight back. He perhaps felt these frustrations were but another way of complaining about a more important frustration which she did not include in her original list. A year before he had undergone an operation on his back which he said made it painful for him to have intercourse. He functioned satisfactorily in mutual masturbation. As he related this she suddenly said 'I am rather large'. Obviously she recognized he was using his back as an excuse to avoid intercourse but thought it was because her vagina was capacious and unstimulating to his penis which accounted for his preference for masturbation by her. By offering her vagina as the explanation she disguised from herself her real fear that he no longer found her attractive sexually.

In fact her sexual frustration was only a part of her problem. She obviously felt unwanted and unappreciated and was angry about it. He, however, was so civilized, affectionate, reasonable, generous and humorous that she really felt, without realizing it, she must be to blame.

She was the oldest of four girls. Her parents were fairly affluent and her mother was a Catholic. In spite of this the mother had been involved in a number of affairs with other men and had left home for varying periods in connection with these relationships. She had, as a child, lived with her parents jointly, each parent separately, grand-parents, foster-parents, at a convent and in a boarding school. She had hated her mother, she said, until she was 30 years old when they made friends. In contrast she glowed and laughed indulgently when discussing her father. He was clever, talented and full of good ideas but lacked the drive to follow them through.

She said of her sisters 'none of them is my sort of person' and was still jealous of one who behaved in a 'baby-like-way' to attract the father. Although she did not verbally connect the two topics she went on shortly to say she 'always had a father problem' in that she could not fill the 'daughter role'. She had always strived for independence and personal competence she said. Although unaware of it consciously her own days of dependence on her parents had been cut short and she had never adjusted to, or, as it is put, mourned the loss. Her mother was frequently not present and therefore was not available to meet her daughter's dependency needs.

This accounted for her detachment from her mother which was not overcome until she was 30. This increased her dependence on her father but he had used her as a deputy mother to the other girls and had asked her long before she was ready, to be competent and independent. To try to please him and to retain his love (threatened by the arrival of her sisters) she had adopted these requirements as her own aims and was still pursuing them as a plan, or model, for living.

Following the consultation, when her dependency needs were discussed, she had gone away and had cried for several days. Her husband, who had always perceived her as competent and not needing him or anyone else, was astonished because she never cried. He loved her and her distress triggered-off his father-role as he attempted to comfort her. In spite of her previous conscious dislike of being babied she discovered her husband, far from rejecting her for being so helpless, responded as a good father. She found this deeply satisfying and thereafter whenever she felt the need for help, reassurance, loving and cuddling, she could ask for it. A whole new way of relating and communicating became available to the marriage and rows subsided.

Her first intercourse had occurred at the age of 17 and she had had six partners in all. Masturbation had started, she thought, at 13, to weak fantasies. She had recurrent dreams of 'being chased by a Chinaman with a pigtail' but said she did not know of the existence of the penis until she was 15. The denial and inhibition this revealed made it no surprise when she said she was 'not much good at orgasms'. She felt unwilling to have intercourse when it started, and liked to be coaxed, but she was always pleased she had done it when the act was over.

In spite of this, some years before the husband's operation she had, in an attempt to improve the marriage, been through a phase when she often tried to initiate intercourse but he had mostly rejected the advances. This was puzzling since his masturbation fantasies revealed that he wanted the woman to take charge. The explanation he offered was that he did not see her attempts at seduction as being the product of genuine desire but designed to manipulate him. If he responded the offer might be withdrawn to humiliate him and this made him feel vulnerable. Listening to him talk of his fantasies, which they had not previously discussed, led her to the insight that raping him might please him more than masturbating him. She began to do this in the female superior position 'because of his back' and discovered that they both enjoyed it. Later on she said, taking the blame again, that if she 'had not been lazy' or 'had allowed it' or had 'given-in' (actually to her own de–sires) intercourse would have been more frequent.

The husband regarded his own father as being weak for not asserting himself and his rights. His mother he saw as undemonstrative, unsympathetic and prudish. Once, when he was eight, she had, when he was asleep, found a letter in his pocket from a girl asking him to meet her naked. He had been woken up, taken downstairs and made to face the music. He first had intercourse at 23 and had also had six partners in all, most in brief affairs in which he had not done much of the chasing. He had been depressed in the marriage for years and sometimes secretly cried about the rows. They made him feel wounded and rejected. He simply retreated into his own sad inner feelings, rarely arguing, and never considering what the real problem might be. He accepted her hostility as he had accepted his mother's criticisms. At this point his wife said she now withdrew her original complaint that he was aggressive; she realized it was in her and she was attributing it to him, because it was 'not nice to be aggressive'. She added that she often wished she had no tongue.

To blot out the pain of her attacks on him he had taken to alcohol and, more recently, after the most violent episodes, to shop-lifting. In his position the risks were horrific. He denied wanting to be caught, thus punishing her indirectly by saying in effect, 'see what you made me do'.

Much more emerged, such as his notion that he was bad for being sexual, scarcely surprising with such a mother, and that a woman must show unequivocal determination to have intercourse before he could believe he was genuinely desired. To their surprise they discovered they could say anything to each other and that they loved each other. They began to see that their past relationships to their parents in childhood were still haunting them, leading them to damage instead of help each other. Realizing that his wife had only attacked him because she felt frustrated in her love and need for him strengthened his own sense of personal and masculine value. His submissiveness, which had not been abject but had emerged in his apparent reasonableness, was replaced by a much more adult way of relating to her and to women generally. As he grew up she could give up her intense striving and move in the opposite direction of being a securely loved girl.

Matters rapidly improved in all directions, rows ceased, intercourse improved and they became happy. A postcard from the Far East later confirmed their improvement had been sustained and extended.

Discussion

The story of this couple has been given at some length because it encapsulates so much of importance between men and women and parents and children. Disturbances in parental relationships affect the way their children grow up and subsequently relate in *their* marriages. Both these two had so many problems from their own childhoods to solve that neither was adequately prepared. Both had needs they could not express, or even perceive, for fear of rejection by the parent/partner. They could not communicate except in indirect ways, she by her verbal anger and he by behaving, or, as it is called, 'acting out' his distress in drunkenness and shop-lifting. Her anger was the last thing he needed and his retreat the worst response to her. Intercourse, which might have been one route by which communication could have been established, was not utilized in this way due to his fears from childhood and her inhibitions. They both, in their own ways, felt inadequate and bad, but their poor communication prevented them conveying how they felt about the other, which would have helped them both.

These two learned to overcome their fears and become intimate. Furthermore they rapidly learned to understand each other and become capable of working out the motivations of the other, based on childhood experience, rather than to make hostile assumptions about the significance of the behaviour of the other.

Presumably, he had initially seen in her a competent mother who would not make too many sexual demands, or, more hopefully, might take his sexuality in hand so to speak, and she probably saw in him an easily satisfied man who would not expect of her more than she could give. This relationship had endured because, in spite of the difficulties, they were similar, did

love many aspects of the other, and in any case life had taught them both not to expect much better. Both of them, but especially her, finally found it fairly easy to admit fault and accept blame but, they found, they wanted to help each other rather than attribute blame.

Although it may be felt that whereas he grew up under treatment she regressed to dependency and childhood, this conclusion is not valid. Excessive independence is a sign of immaturity and not maturity. They both came in as children and left as adults.

A perverted instinct

Mr N looked, and was, a very respectable trade representative aged 26 years. He was also a practising Christian. He had been married for two years to a highly attractive and uncritical, adoring wife. He liked intercourse frequently and she never refused. However, he soon found her sexually boring and they had sex only once in every four to eight weeks. He then masturbated two to five times a day. In spite of the strictest resolutions not to do so he began to revert to earlier patterns of sexual behaviour. These distressed him but he felt unable to resist them.

Via a contact magazine he found a married woman in her late forties or early fifties who was uneducated, rather unclean personally, forceful and physically unattractive. Once a fortnight, or so, he felt a compelling urge to see her. From the outset she dominated him and he regarded her as would a little boy his mother. She would order him to remove his clothes and when he protested that this was not what he had come for she would tell him peremptorily to 'get them off'. When stripped she would, perhaps, hang weights on his testes so he could scarcely move, give him impossible tasks and then thrash him for failure. She might make him put on stockings and a suspender belt and then taunt him. Sometimes she would tie him up and then masturbate him with linement or one of the gloves used to groom dogs. Sometimes she would make him lie on his back and then crouch over him ordering him to carry out oral sex on her or would urinate on him. She would treat him like this, and often in the presence of her female friends as onlookers, more or less organized as a tea party. Sometimes when he was on the verge of reaching orgasm and requested her permission to 'finish myself off' she would refuse and would make him dress and leave.

The woman required 'presents' from him in return for her valuable services to him, although she was not a professional prostitute. Other costs included a fear of catching VD from her, a terror of being found out by his wife and his employers and anxiety about the possible reactions of the woman's husband. But it was a game and he was ultimately in control of her since little was undertaken which was not in accordance with his wishes. She varied the menu and added only a few variations of her own invention. However, when asked what he did when permission for masturbation was refused he smiled like a deceitful child and brightly said 'I do it when I get home'. With this woman he obtained his firmest erections and his most intense orgasms. After the event he felt guilt and shame and wanted further punishment which the woman sometimes inflicted physically and sometimes by forcing him to lick his own semen from the floor.

Mrs N became involved in her husband's treatment. She had, incorrectly, blamed his troubles on her inhibitions. They, so to speak, grew up sexually together in treatment. They said finally that they had 'gone mad sexually with each other'. His sexuality caught up with his emotional development and he both loved and wanted his wife and only her.

Discussion

Mr N loved his wife but perceived her as 'innocent', unknowledgeable about sex and undertaking intercourse only because she loved him. The other woman, whom he hated and detested most of the time, he regarded as sexually rapacious, unsatisfiable, demanding and oppressive. When small he had always wanted his mother to notice him and love him but she was undemonstrative except in frequently smacking his legs. It was a form of attention and eventually he almost deliberately sought punishment by her. However, he was very upset at 12 when his father found his girly magazines and thrashed him.

Some men regard the woman they love as an untouchable princess – like their mother – and all others as prostitutes. They can only have intercourse with the latter. Mr N had intercourse with his wife but never with the other woman, so this is not the explanation here. Nevertheless she was functioning as a sort of mother and by commanding him she was giving him permission to show his genitals and obtain maximum pleasure from them. The pain she inflicted helped in the process. Pain – emotional and/or physical – is used by parents to deter children from indulging in unacceptable pleasure. In some people the punishment acts as an incentive, not a deterrent, and what happens is that the punishment is seen as wiping the slate clean thereby permitting the sin again.

The woman was repulsive to him, and he finally recalled that his mother's unattractive appearance compared with other mothers had embarrassed him from the age of nine onwards. Although he had never thought of it he quickly accepted that the attraction to the woman was Oedipal. Furthermore, since the woman was in every sense of the word 'dirty' he dared reveal the side of his needs which he had been reared to regard as shameful and dirty. He let go with her, and did not mind what she, and her friends, thought of him, at least sexually. Furthermore, they indulged his need to exhibit himself. Their watching him at the moment of ejaculation was an important part of the pleasure. It was more satisfactory than the other form of indulging his transvestism and exhibitionism which consisted of asking if he could try on clothes in women's shops saying by way of explanation he was the same size as his wife. He would then strip and hope the assistants and other customers would see him before putting on the female clothes.

Mr N's pleasure in intercourse was impaired by the anxiety he had been taught to feel about his genitals and his sexual needs, and the fact they were not 'nice'. The 'games' he played with the woman were as near as he could get to normal sex without so much anxiety that the pleasure was impaired. Much of his sexuality was like that of a child and he had no great interest in pleasing women. His masochistic submission to pain and humiliation removed the responsibility for his sexual pleasures from himself and the guilt of it, at least at the time, resided with the woman.

His sexual instinct was not fully mature in its expression and was 'perverted' from normal intercourse to some extent. The anxiety blocking the instinct diverted sexual energies away from his wife to the other woman, away from intercourse to other sexual acts and partly away from the penis to adjacent parts of the body such as the testes and buttocks.

Instincts are biological urges lying in the unconscious which are stimulated both by internal needs of the body and outside influences. They then create tensions or needs which reach consciousness and influence behaviour. Directly satisfying such a need may be unwise or impossible so it may have to be postponed or met in some modified way – as in the case of Mr N. A further modification is sublimation (See page 15).

The instincts are part of our inborn, genetic inheritance fixed at conception. All that is ever added to the individual thereafter is nutrition and experience. Both influence the ways in which instinctual needs are later met.

There are no doubt many instincts but Freud divided them into the erotic group, which includes love, sex and creativity, and the death group which includes aggression and destruction. The existence of a death instinct is much disputed and the choice of the word 'death' to label the group was probably unwise. The two groups sometimes work together and sometimes in opposition. A man with too much aggression (death) instinct attached to his sexual (erotic) instinct may become a sadistic sex-maniac and one with too little may become a masochist like Mr N. One theory of masochism is that it is a form of sadism turned not towards others but towards the self.

Messages

Pretty Miss O, aged 19, had a boy-friend she felt strongly she loved, but no matter what he did she would scream as his penis approached her vagina. In spite of several months of trying she was still a virgin.

From preliminary discussions it was obvious that this was but one part of a larger rejection of sex – she was a prude. However, under treatment she became able to show her body, including her vulva, and to submit to masturbation and even oral sex by her boy-friend. Masturbating him was more difficult and she did not enjoy touching him. Putting his penis in her mouth was impossible; the thought of it made her heave.

Eventually intercourse was achieved but, as anticipated, she did not enjoy it. In fact she interpreted sensations of deep penetration, enjoyed by nine out of ten women, as pain.

No fantasy material was available from her since, whenever her unconscious mind suggested a sexual theme to consciousness she repressed it. One day, on a train, a fantasy did come to mind. She had her boy-friend naked with his hands and feet tied together behind his back. Arched back in this position his erect penis stuck right out and there was nothing he could do to prevent her interfering with it as she wished. She wrapped toilet paper around it.

Discussion

Submitting to the pleasures of having her vulva stimulated was one thing but to give the penis pleasure was another. Ultimately, Miss O, did not want to accept that there was any difference between the sexes. This was due to having repressed jealousy and envy of a younger brother who she had felt was much better treated than herself. She attributed this to the fact that he had a penis and she had none.

Wrapping the penis in toilet paper (in fantasy) was a way of removing it to be flushed away. Denying, unconsciously, the existence of a penis led to a parallel denial of the existence of the vagina. The prospect of using the vagina was seen as a painful penetration of an area that did not have an orifice and must therefore be painful.

All this is easily comprehensible from some of the cases quoted earlier. More importantly, beyond all this there was a dislike of semen. Not only was masturbating her boy-friend unpleasant, since, in reality, the existence of the penis was being acknowledged, but, worse still, it produced semen, the sight, smell and feel of which she could not bear. She shuddered when talking about semen being on her or in her.

Semen, to her, was an excretion like faeces and therefore requiring toilet paper. Her horror of semen was the same as her horror of faeces and ejaculation was the same act as defaecation, i.e. it derived from the anal stage of development. There were two reasons why semen and faeces were linked in her mind. One was the jealousy already mentioned – that is, rejecting semen assisted in the denial of the genital differences between the sexes. Secondly, she had been prudishly reared and, as most mothers do, helped to bring the various stages of psychosexual development to an end by calling them 'dirty'.

In the oral stage the child eventually explores the world by testing it with his or her mouth as well as sucking the thumb. The mother, fearful of the child taking germs into the mouth, says 'stop it, dirty'. In the anal stage the child is fascinated with the appearance, texture and odour of faeces. He or she may well play games with them. The mother denounces the interest as 'dirty'. In the phallic stage the touching of the genitals is often objected to on the grounds that it is 'dirty'. This is often overdone to the point that the child acquires the same distaste of genitals and genital fluids as was instilled over faeces.

This is an example of a 'message' rather thoughtlessly transmitted from one generation to another. Messages are to do with sex, reproduction, and relationships. Many are unconscious, being learned early in life, whereas others are conscious, when they function like prejudices, or are pre-conscious i.e. they can with a little effort be brought into consciousness. Miss O was an example of this pre-conscious form. Messages often exist in contradiction to the conscious attitude. Messages are reinforced by teachers, peers and other close associates.

The 'sex is dirty' message is soon extended to sex in all forms such as dirty magazine, dirty film, dirty week-end, dirty old man and so on. For Miss O most things to do with sex were dirty.

'Sex is sinful' and therefore must be punished is another example. Pregnancy fears and VD phobias can follow indulgence since the crime has been committed and punishment will surely follow. Religious beliefs, which everyone possesses regardless of their superficial attitudes, are usually involved.

'Sex is very private' is a message which implies that everything to do with sex is a matter of shame and is therefore very private. Women blush more frequently than men over sexual matters not because they have more to blush about but because they suffer more from this message.

'Unmentionable sex' messages are given to children by families who never mention it, switch off the radio or T.V. when any sexual material is mentioned and who fail to give names to the genitals. What is not mentioned in some sense does not exist. Victims of this message deny the importance of sex by saying such things as 'Freud said everything was to do with sex' or 'sex is not everything you know'. Many men will not discuss sex problems with their partner and will not read sex books.

'Nice girls are sexless' messages are universally drummed into girls and although many women believe as adults they do not subscribe to it there is little difficulty in demonstrating that they do. The message is designed to castrate girls so that as women sex turns out to be something a man does *to* them not something they possess of themselves.

'Sex is only for babies' is probably the first message given to every girl. 'One day you will grow up and have a baby like Mummy'. Most women claim not to believe it but starting on effective contraception can destroy sex pleasure as can sterilisation and the menopause. Conversely wanting a baby can increase sex pleasure but a woman who does not want a further pregnancy may accept it because she has had the pleasure. This relates to the 'sex is sin' message and pregnancy is seen as punishment.

These are only a few of the messages in current use. It remains to be seen whether or not Miss N's life will be ruined by them.

Loving

Seven out of 10 members of a ship-wrecked crew finally survived nine days at sea and four more on land before they were rescued. Usually the survivors thought often about intercourse but during their ordeal all such fantasies ceased and were replaced by recurrent thoughts of their partners and children. These thoughts increased the will to survive in order to resume the relationship. Thus they lived and overcame circumstances of great adversity where it would have been all too easy to give up the struggle, give in and die.

The seven were followed-up over the next 12 to 24 months to see what happened to them. The story then became less happy; five of the seven had developed mental disorders for the first time in their lives. Only one considered that his triumph over adversity had enriched him as a man. Of the others one was drinking excessively and rowing a lot with his wife, one had become impotent and two had lost their libido.

Discussion

Perhaps it is because the baby first loves the mother before he or she can speak, that is, since love is a pre-verbal emotion, it makes the subject so difficult to discuss in a meaningful way. Also, since no animal can speak to us it is impossible for us to know what animals feel about love. One way out of the problem is to call love *attachment* and then see what can be discovered by observation rather than trying to talk about complicated inner feelings and mental states. We realise that some people may see this as a dismal and unromantic way of proceeding.

The sailors' ideas during the ordeal were of their attachment to their partners. After disasters such as earthquakes or bombing where everything is in chaos both adults and children display what is called attachment behaviour by ceaselessly searching for each other until they are re-united. This may be basic biological behaviour since in primitive tribes separation from parents or the group could be fatal. Predatory animals often select as prey an animal which is separated from the herd. The need to be attached, children to parents and adults to other adults, is seen as being as important to the survival of both the individual and the species as are feeding and sexual behaviour. If baby monkeys are taken from the mother and are reared in a room containing an artificial mother made of wire but possessing a nipple they will feed from it. If a similar mother is constructed in wire but covered with a terry-towelling exterior and not having a nipple, the baby will cling for hours to such a mother and go to the other only to feed. Attachment, then, is not dependent on feeding. In other words, babies do not simply love the mother because she feeds them but because they have an inborn need to love and be loved.

In human babies, attachment behaviour includes crying, calling, clinging and protesting on being left alone or with strangers. Up to the age of three attachment behaviour can easily be produced by anyone in contact with the child who mothers him or her, but usually attachment to a preferred person (i.e. the mother usually) is in evidence in the first few months of life. The intensity of attachment behaviour becomes less with age but in adulthood it appears when the individual is distressed, ill or afraid. The presence of attachment is thus deduced by attachment behaviour which basically involves getting and staying close to a special and preferred other person. Attachment is not the same as dependency since the latter does not necessarily involve either strong feeling or an enduring bond.

Failures of attachment can later express themselves as personality disturbances, emotional ill-health or psychosomatic illnesses. In other instances, the individual may later, in their own adult relationship, feel insecure and therefore make constant demands for love and care or they may react in the opposite way giving the care they really want to others and thereby become compulsive care-givers. This is one basis of mother love. Anyone who feels poorly attached to a human being may become attached to an animal and may become ill or even kill themselves when the animal dies.

Before leaving the subject of love it may be useful to discuss love objects, or for that matter sex or hate or any other kind of object. As used the word object does not imply that the person who is loved and/or desired sexually is an 'it'. The sentence 'I love you' consists of a subject 'I', a verb 'love' and an object 'you', hence 'you' are my love object. Instincts have an aim and an object. Thus the sex, or more accurately genital, instinct has the aim, for most people most of the time, of achieving intercourse, and the person with whom it is desired or preferred to have intercourse is the object or sex object. The relationship between the subject and his or her object is called the object relationship. As seen in the case of Mr and Mrs M, early object relationships with parents adversely influenced their later object relationships with each other.

Self-love consists of taking the self as the love-object i.e. 'I love myself'. Babies do this before they are sufficiently developed to form proper object relations. This is called narcissism. Freud suggested that some cases of homosexuality may be due to the individual taking him or herself as their own sex object. Originally self-love is seen as proceeding from the id but subsequently the individual can send the love out, or bring it back again, from objects. In consequence, typically in adolescence, the love object this week may not be the same as last.

In growing up, the child, at some stage, forms an object relationship with the mother and endows it with love. Eventually, just as food is taken into the body so a representation, or fantasy, of the mother is taken into the mind. Once the mother and her loving and caring functions have been taken in, (incorporated, internalized or introjected) in this way, the child can bear physical separation from the mother without feeling anxious or abandoned. Self-sufficiency then increases since the mother is not 'out there' but 'inside'.

Other objects are later introjected and once this has happened the individual may identify himself or herself with it. In this way, some or all the aspects of the object may be assimilated by the subject and become his or her own. Thereafter the subject can love him or herself for being like the loved object. This is the secondary form of narcissism. This is important. For example, as the Oedipal stage in a boy declines and he gives up his mother he introjects his father and identifies with him. This allows Oedipal hostility to decline and allows the boy to love himself for being like his loved father. It can also be argued that he wants to be like his father, that is, identify with him, in order that a woman like his mother, who he has now relinquished to his father, will eventually love him in the same way his mother loves his father. Thus faults in either or both parents can disrupt this solution to the Oedipal complex.

Love consists of some balance between self-love, or narcissism and the love of the other or object love. If self-love is totally extinguished in the furtherance of object-love then the condition is not love but infatuation. Without some self-love, loving another is impossible.

Everyone, or nearly everyone, has some notion about how an ideal partner would be and behave. Many relationships are spoiled by unrealistic partner ideals. The partner may seem bit by bit to be so far from an ideal partner that love declines, leading to indifference or hostility.

Although five out of seven is only a small number on which to generalize it is possible that the shipwrecked sailors idealized their partners during their phase of attachment thinking whilst marooned. The notions of their partners may have become somewhat detached from the reality of how their partners actually were and they may have endowed them in fantasy with features of the ideal partner they had in their minds. The reality of return may have disrupted the ideal rudely suddenly leading to the mental illnesses, loss of libido and so on. Perhaps after diasters of this type both the victims and their partners need counselling to avoid future harm.

YOUR TOP 50 QUESTIONS ANSWERED

Q1 *I very much love my wife but still often masturbate; is this alright?*

Most men continue to masturbate occasionally throughout their sex lives although they are frequently ashamed to admit it; this happens even in totally sexually fulfilled relationships. Masturbation after marriage is also very common indeed in women and contrary to what most men imagine, is frequently a sign of a very good sex life with her husband. This is usually not so true for men who tend to masturbate *less* the more intercourse they have.

Some people feel that they shouldn't *need* to masturbate after marriage and so feel guilty and secretive. On the other hand some men and women say that the sexual experience of masturbating is different and even more pleasurable than shared sex and feel that at least occasional masturbation provides something they don't get in even their satisfactory man-woman encounters.

Q2 *My nipples are sexually sensitive. Is this normal for a man?*

After puberty a male's nipples are less sensitive than a female's but some men experience nipple stimulation as arousing just as do many women. A very few men can be brought to orgasm by nipple stimulation alone.

Q3 *I am very keen on oral sex and wondered whether it is all right to swallow semen?*

The vast majority of couples who practice oral sex do so as a part of foreplay to excite them both to greater heights. Others sometimes have oral intercourse with the man ejaculating in his partner's mouth.

Semen varies considerably in taste, smell and consistency from man to man and even in any one man from day to day. Many women don't like the taste and smell of semen at all and others greatly enjoy it. It is made of protein, which like other proteins, is digested along with food. It also contains substances called prostaglandins, which have well-known actions on the body, one of which is to make the uterus contract.

Women in the last few weeks of pregnancy have been known to go into labour prematurely after swallowing semen, but this could be the result of the sexual excitement they experience at the same time. Some women claim that when they are swallowing semen frequently, their breasts slowly enlarge. Whether this could be explained on the basis of prostaglandin intake or whether it's all in the mind (it is proven that women can be trained by self-hypnosis to enlarge their breasts) is as yet unknown.

Because it can be so intensely exciting for a man to have his penis sucked and stimulated orally and because many men see the swallowing of their semen as the ultimate sign that their woman loves them enough to do anything for them – oral intercourse has become something of a battleground in many relationships. Many women find even the sensation of semen in their mouths quite revolting, and some *men* don't want to ejaculate in a woman's mouth because they see it as defiling her (by equating semen with excretion, which, of course, it is not).

Sometimes the man very much wants his partner to have oral intercourse with him, if only very occasionally. If she does not agree, he may interpret her reaction as un-loving rather than simply accepting it for what it is, a simple dislike of a particular practice. As with many other unfamiliar sexual practices it helps to talk things over and then to take it gently. Some women 'gag' with anything in their mouths, but this can be overcome if both partners are patient and gradually try to enjoy each other's pleasure.

$Q4$ *Can I catch VD in my mouth by having oral sex?*

Yes you can, if the man is suffering from a venereal disease. But there's no reason to believe that you'll do so any more readily than catching it genitally. It makes sense not to have oral sex with any man you don't know if only because he may well have caught something from another woman –

you can be more protected in genital sex by using a condom. Casual sex is hazardous enough emotionally for many people, so to add this health danger to the act would seem unwise. If you get a painless sore or ulcer in the mouth, always see a doctor. It could be serious.

The signs and symptoms of oral VD are usually of an ordinary sore throat which doesn't get better but the diagnosis will have to be sorted out by your doctor at a VD clinic. Oral sex with your regular faithful, partner carries no infection danger, of course.

$Q5$ *Why does my fiancé still read girlie magazines even though we have a vigorous sex life? Why does he need such things – aren't I enough for him?*

Don't worry, it is perfectly normal male behaviour to want to look at women with no clothes on. Remember that generally speaking men are turned on by visual images and women more by feelings and emotions but none of this means that your man finds you insufficient for him. Many men are simply curious about other women's bodies.

It is also true that men can be sexually aroused by the explicitly erotic poses of women who behave in a way they'd like their partner to. It could help if you took notice of the sorts of pictures that turned him on because it could be that he would like you to do whatever she is doing. His interest in such nude females is arguably no more harmful than bodice-ripping yarns of romance and forceful passion so

commonly read by women. Both are ways of encouraging fantasies. In an ideal world neither would be necessary because each individual would be totally and maximally fulfilled within his or her relationship.

Clinical experience shows that the woman who most objects to such magazines in her husband's hands is likely to be somewhat underconfident. In her mind the women in the magazine become competitors, and some women even see the reading of such material as a form of mental adultery – which in a sense it is. But unless it becomes an important part of his sexual life, then it should not be troublesome. Many men in relationships use nude material to increase their ardour and this usually benefits their woman. If your man rejects you for such fantasy material then you have a real problem that could require professional help.

If you react too negatively, he might feel like a little boy being told off by his mother and this is likely to spoil your relationship.

Q6 *My husband has just told me that he went to a prostitute a few days ago. Am I to blame?*

The very fact that he has told you of this episode suggests that you have a comfortable relationship with him. Perhaps he is hinting that he went to the prostitute to do something that he'd ideally have rather done with you. He may not really know why he did so.

Many men perceive their wives as being so sexless and 'pure' that they wouldn't dream of asking them to do anything that they felt might be objectionable to them. The sadness is that women are often more

than delighted to go along with what their man wants, and perhaps have even had fantasies of exactly the same thing.

When you can't, or won't, answer each other's sexual needs in this way, prostitution still offers a solution. There are several ways of handling this problem.

First, a number of women will understand that on the odd occasion (say a couple of times a year) her husband wants to indulge in a particular practice which she really objects to, and that he's best off going to a prostitute. The alternative, finding a woman friend who will do what he wants, is too drastic a solution and is fraught with potential problems for the relationship.

Second, she could make an effort to go along with his requests now and then. Unfortunately, some women take offence at their partner even *wanting* such things and make it a point of issue and even divorce. Most couples fall between the two extremes. They can use fantasy and masturbation to protect their otherwise good relationship and still enjoy certain practices they'd really like.

It is unthinkable to throw out a good relationship because a man wants something his wife can't or won't provide, but if the request is reasonable then her refusal is often deeply rooted in other relationship and personality problems the couple have.

Q7 *I am 32 and when I am making love with my wife I often fantasize about other women. Is this alright?*

Yes, you are perfectly normal. Most people fantasize about a member of the opposite sex or about a sexy subject at least on some occasions during sex. A recent survey found that just over half of all women fantasize about a man other than their husband when making love and other surveys have put the figure at over 60%. Men are not likely to be very different. Most people can't bring themselves to admit to such fantasies to their partner because they think they'll be seen as unfaithful. However, the best way of looking at it is to simply treat such fantasies as sexual enhancers. Certainly a very perverse sexual fantasy might need professional help to sort out but this is uncommon.

For some people who are anxious and inhibited about intercourse, these fantasies can enable them to function sexually. The fantasy tips the balance from impotence (in a man) or non-arousal (in a woman) to full and enjoyable functioning.

Q8 *My girlfriend seems to make a mess in the bed when we have sex. Is she abnormal?*

First, why are you so concerned about what is probably your partner's normal secretions?

There may be several reasons for wetness. Some women produce a very large amount of normal lubrication when they are sexually excited. Usually this is no problem at all, and simply means protecting the bed with a towel.

Of course it could also be you rather than her; semen always leaks out of the vagina after sex. This can be simply overcome by placing a couple of tissues between her legs over the vulval area, or gentle washing with a damp cloth.

A few women actually urinate during the peak of sexual excitement and this can be messy. If it happens in any quantity you can make love on a rubber sheet or in places where the urine doesn't matter – such as out of doors or in the bath. Even more women let go a tiny amount of urine as a part of the total letting go at orgasm. Emptying the bladder before sex is the way around this for most women.

Recent research has suggested that some women actually ejaculate a kind of colourless fluid from their urinary passage. Historical evidence for female ejaculation goes back into antiquity yet modern doctors repeatedly refuse to believe that it occurs.

The fluid is released from the urinary passage but is *not* urine. It has been shown to be very similar in chemical content to male prostatic fluid. It is colourless, odourless and taste-free and seems to be produced most plentifully when the sensitive front wall of the woman's vagina (the G-spot) is stimulated. It is thought that the fluid comes from a kind of prostate-like structure in women at the base of the bladder – a structure which only becomes apparent on specific sexual stimulation. It can be felt as the G-spot near the top end of the front vaginal wall and can be as large as a small walnut if the woman is very aroused.

So many women report the presence of an exceptionally exciting spot on their front vaginal wall and others talk of wetting themselves during sex, but not with urine, that the phenomenon of female ejaculation must be taken seriously. Certainly not all women have a prominent G-spot and only a very few ejaculate on orgasm but both are still very real phenomena.

Q9
I feel very sexy during my periods but don't like to ask my boyfriend to make love because of the mess. He says I am silly. What do you think?

Ask him anyway, especially if you are one of the many women who feel exceptionally sexy during a period, but make it as unmessy as possible. There are several ways of doing this. First, avoid intercourse on the two heaviest days and you'll have less of a problem. Second, you can put in a diaphragm and then wash yourself well. The small amount of blood that dams up behind the diaphragm for a few hours won't do any harm and then you can take it out and wash as normal. Third, you can simply put a towel underneath your bottom to protect the bed and then both wash at once afterwards. Paper towels and tissues have made all this a lot easier. A woman who is on the Pill has much lighter and shorter periods; and a wet flannel kept handy is another simple answer.

Q10
I am worried because I have been faking orgasms during intercourse for years. I now realize that the situation will never change unless I talk about it. I don't want to hurt my husband so what should I do?

The main problem is that you have probably now gone some way down the path of what could be called sexual dishonesty. You have started a lie and have now trapped yourself into living it out. The worst thing you can possibly do at this stage is to 'come clean' about your deception because your husband will be deeply hurt and may never believe you when you really do have an orgasm. The answer is to start exploring ways of ensuring that you

do have more orgasms in intercourse and slowly to change your husband's views so that he can enjoy himself and *not* see it as a slight on his sexual prowess if you don't have an orgasm. It's a shame that you've got into a rut of deception but it's not incurable. If your husband has read page 25 your days of fooling him are numbered because he'll know the real signs of a woman having an orgasm – signs you won't be able to fake.

When you fake orgasm, by concentrating on your acting 'performance', you miss what's happening to your body and miss all the *real* sensations which you could and should be building on to really enjoy *yourself*. It's all very well being selfless for the sake of your man but perhaps you should take stock of why you are doing this rather than concentrating on getting pleasure for yourself. This would make your partner feel much happier and fulfilled. An important part of sexual loving is freedom but sexual dishonesty impairs this.

First, you need to go through the relevant parts of the book and ask yourself why you don't often feel like it bearing in mind that some women enjoy sex a lot yet never have an orgasm during intercourse. It could be that with some small changes in technique on your's or your lover's part that you could climax in this way whenever you wanted to. If you don't want to then you shouldn't feel you have to and a loving and caring man will understand perfectly and still enjoy sex without you climaxing. Unfortunately, a lot of men feel 'at fault' if they can't bring their partner to orgasm during intercourse.

Some women, because of their upbringing or the faulty technique of their partners, can come perfectly well during masturbation but never during intercourse. A very few don't want to give their man the pleasure of having his woman enjoy an orgasm while he makes love to her, and this is harder to face up to, and may need professional help.

Have you started to worry because you know that it means telling your husband he'll have to change his technique, and you're not looking forward to it? Unless you are very shy it should be easy to get him to try something new for the excitement of it. For example, you could produce a vibrator and play with it in a way that gives you an orgasm during intercourse. From this it should be a short step to masturbating yourself while you make love and slowly you can get him in on the act. Many women need extra stimulation if they are to have orgasms during intercourse, so it is quite wrong to think of yourself as somehow inferior if you don't have an orgasm spontaneously.

Perhaps the answer is that you are too self-conscious when you are with your husband and can never let go sufficiently to have an orgasm. Unfortunately, this situation feeds on itself with more worry producing more tension. Setting the mood, teaching your husband to do exactly what you most like and practising yourself with really powerful fantasies during masturbation will all greatly increase your chances.

recent years and for many women involved in such relationships it often amounts to little more than high spirits or a form of curiosity. Don't forget that in certain cultures such relationships between women are not at all uncommon, in parallel with a normal heterosexual marital life. So if it's 'fun' at this level you would probably be best to ignore it if you can and accept it for what it is.

If, however, your wife is turning her sexuality towards other women you have a real problem, especially if she prefers her homosexual relationship to the one with you. You need to reassess your emotional relationship and seek professional help if you can't sort things out between you.

A few married women who really want sex with another man find the problems of an affair too much, and turn to a close girl friend who may feel the same way. They thus both indulge their sexual appetites for sex outside their marriage but with each other rather than with men. If this is the case then you need to ask yourself all the questions about your relationship that you would if your wife were to be having an affair with a man.

A few women, like some men, are genuinely bisexual – able to enjoy sex with members of both sexes – and if this is the case here with love, understanding and communication you might be able to come to terms with this, especially with help.

Q11 *At a party recently an attractive woman seduced my wife. My wife says she was curious. Do you think she is a lesbian?*

Not necessarily, though your fear is understandable enough. Lesbianism has become fashionable in certain circles in

Q12 *We have been happily married for 30 years but recently I have wanted to try anal sex with my wife. The trouble is I dare not even ask. What should I do?*

Realizations like this are often disturbing, and all the more so after many years together but it doesn't necessarily mean that your sex life has somehow been lacking all these years.

Some women greatly enjoy anal sex (about 1 in 7 according to a recent US survey) even though (or even because) it is prohibited (and illegal) so don't automatically assume you'll be turned down. You could be surprised that your wife might be more ready than you had imagined.

If you wait until your wife is very aroused one day and then start with some gentle anal stimulation you can slowly build up to more anal activity and at the same time tell her of your wishes. Of course there's always a real chance that she'll be disinterested or frankly turned off by the idea. If this happens it's best not to force the matter because she'll be rejecting what she sees as an unacceptable practice, *not* you. Don't let yourself become worked up by the whole subject so that it becomes a major disaster area. After all, anal sex is, like all sexual activity, very much a matter of personal preference and you're unlikely to do much to change your wife's sexual preferences at her age.

There are a few practical tips worth mentioning, First, you could use a sheath if the practicalities of anal penetration upset you and as long as you go gently and use plenty of lubricant all should be well. Start off by using a single finger and then insert two or three until she feels happy with the sensation. Only once you have got through this stage is it wise to try penile penetration.

A few women have their best orgasms when being penetrated anally and some men prefer anal intercourse to vaginal on the basis that the anus is tighter and so offers more stimulation to the penis.

The only hazards occur if once you've put your penis in her anus you then also put it in her vagina. This can cause troublesome infections so don't do it.

Q13

My husband and I have been married for two years and our second child is due in four months' time. Our sex life in the past has been pretty satisfactory but since I've been carrying this baby I've lost all pleasure in sex. I go cold whenever my husband tries to make love to me. I can't understand why I'm like this, it was just the same in my first pregnancy. Can you tell me if this is natural?

Many women go off sex when they are pregnant but there is no real reason why they should do so. Until a short while ago many doctors felt that intercourse might do harm to the unborn child and often advised against it. It is now recognized that this was over-cautious advice.

In the absence of purely physical difficulties the cause is psychological. For some reason you are unconsciously opposed to intercourse during pregnancy. A common fear is that it might hurt the baby but more basically it is probably just part of the largely unconscious cultural attitude that sex is for getting pregnant and is therefore 'wrong' when you cannot become pregnant. Some women also become psychologically tuned in to motherhood in a big way and their whole being is centred around the growing new life. If this is so for you then you may need to make a very deliberate effort to reach out sexually to your husband.

All we can say is that gentle intercourse during pregnancy can be very pleasant for both partners. It helps to prevent the husband seeking an outlet elsewhere, and it possibly even helps with the progress of pregnancy in several ways.

Attitudes can be hard to change but you should perhaps try.

Q14 *I am 20 and have been engaged for 18 months. My problem is that during or directly after intercourse, my vagina makes alarming noises, especially if I draw my knees up suddenly. What frightens me is the thought that the air being sucked in and blown out after intercourse could have some terrible internal affect. My fiancé has tried to reassure me that all will be well, but I'm very worried.*

Your fiancé is right – the air moving in and out of your vagina will do you no harm.

Most of the time the walls of the vagina are in contact and it is a potential rather than an actual cavity. When the walls separate air enters and then by shortening the vagina, as when drawing up the legs, the air is ejected. The air is not under any great pressure and can easily leave via the vaginal entrance. If air is actually blown into the vagina during oral sex it cannot escape and 'blows-up' the vagina like a balloon. This air is then under pressure. Under these circumstances it can occassionally enter the blood stream through the vessels in the walls of the uterus. This is why it is dangerous to blow into the vagina during oral sex.

The way around your problem is to find lovemaking positions that don't suck air into your vagina or alternatively to come to terms with these harmless noises and have a laugh about them.

Sex in Pregnancy

Pregnancy can be a good time for a couple sexually, especially after the first 12 weeks during which pregnancy symptoms, if any, are usually at their worst.

Points to bear in mind

◆ No contraceptive worries gives a degree of freedom you may not have experienced for some time

◆ Research shows that most women like to be cuddled and stroked a lot, especially from the third month onwards

◆ There is no evidence that masturbation or orgasms of any kind do harm to the baby though it makes sense not to have an orgasm late in pregnancy if you have a history of early labours. It's also sensible to go easy around the time of any previous miscarriages

◆ Pregnancy is an opportunity to enrich your sex life and to lay foundations to cope with the changes which will occur in your life

The best positions

◆ Any position that's comfortable will do but as the months go by rear entry positions are best because they put no weight on the woman's enlarging tummy

◆ The best positions are the doggy position (see right); spoons; standing up; (with the woman leaning forward onto something); woman lying on bed or low table and man kneeling between her legs; or the couple embracing on a chair as she sits on his legs to control penetration

Preparation for the birth

◆ Research shows that women who are at ease with their sexuality and who are orgasmic during pregnancy have easier births than do their 'uptight' sisters. This is a good argument for keeping up an active sex life during pregnancy – if one were needed

◆ *Learn sensual massage* (see page 194) and practise it so that you can give your partner pain relief during labour. Very gentle butterfly massage (effleurage) can be an effective pain-reliever when things get tough and the time to learn is during pregnancy

◆ *Perineal massage* is worth learning too; Here's what to do:
1 Cuddle up together and get sexually aroused
2 The man then uses well lubricated fingers (two at first) in the woman's vagina to massage the whole interior

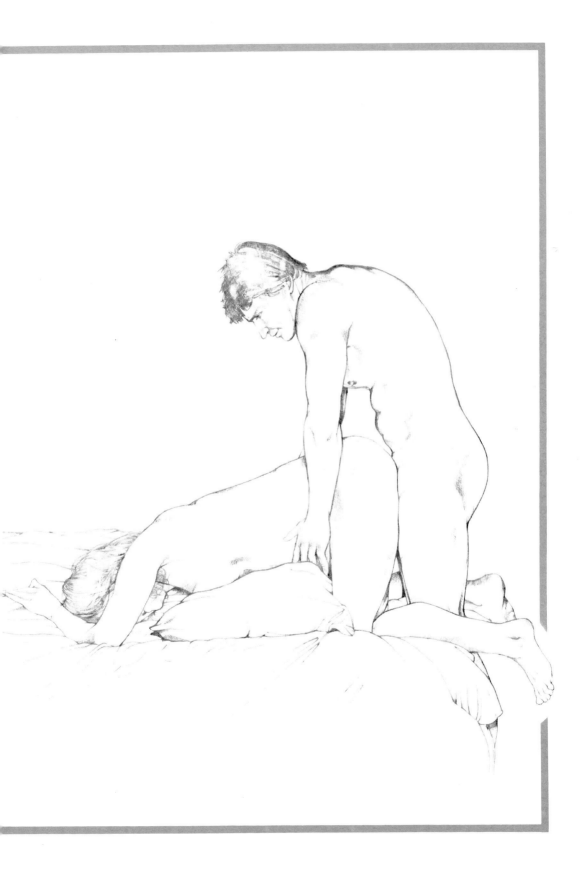

◆ As she relaxes he inserts more fingers
until she can't bear the sensations and asks
him to stop. He then keeps his fingers still
until the intense stretching feeling wears
off

◆ Over the months the man can easily
and painlessly stretch the vaginal opening
to accept four fingers. By 12 weeks the
average woman will easily take three fingers and the vagina naturally loosens further as the months go by

◆ This form of perineal massage can
easily develop into foreplay and there's no
reason why it shouldn't lead onto to intercourse too if the couple wants

◆ A woman prepared in this way should
almost certainly not need to have an

episiotomy and this is a real bonus to the
couple's sex life afterwards. American
midwives who teach this form of ante-
natal massage almost never need to do an
episiotomy and rarely see perineal tears

◆ Practice pelvic muscle exercises (see
page 36) – this not only helps with the
labour but also in your subsequent sex life

◆ *Breast preparation* is not essential
during pregnancy but it helps to ensure
that breast feeding proceeds smoothly.
The only form of breast preparation that's
worth doing though is for the man to play
with his partner's breasts in a way that
gives her pleasure. Taking the nipples into
his mouth, rolling them around and drawing them out by hard sucking does won-

ders for the flat-nippled woman (and is greatly enjoyed by many others) and with this kind of ante-natal preparation she'll have no troubles getting her baby to suck and she herself will be interested in and enjoy breastfeeding more than she otherwise would. Remember after the birth that your partner might want to share your breasts with the baby.

◆ Many women go off actual intercourse for a time during pregnancy but yet want to continue with physical closeness and cuddling. This can be a very good opportunity for a couple to re-learn (or learn or the first time in many cases) lots of other ways of giving and receiving physical pleasure. Go to page 201 and follow through steps 1–20 as a guide.

Q15
The inner lips of my vagina protrude outside. This makes me feel ugly and although we have two lovely children, I just don't want my husband to touch me and our relationship is suffering.

It is common for some women to have protuberant inner lips of their vulvas (which you have called your vagina). Vulvas, like feet and faces, come in different shapes and sizes. Some women have scarcely any inner lips at all while others have well developed ones. Since these lips are sensitive, large ones may help the woman to have orgasms more easily and thereby make her desirable as a sex partner.

Apart from coming in different sizes anyway there are two theories as to how the inner lips can come to be enlarged. Pulling the lips, as in certain types of masturbation, can, if done around puberty, cause them to get bigger. Some tribes around the world do this to their girls ritually. The other theory is exactly the opposite and points to the fact that if, when young, a girl doesn't relieve the congestion which occurs when she becomes sexually aroused (by masturbating to orgasm), the swelling of the vulva will persist for hours and such episodes repeated over a period of time will eventually lead to the lips becoming permanently enlarged.

You should try to think of your vulva as being like a very nice flower. Look at it yourself, show it to your husband and let him play with it. As you become excited you will see that it swells and opens up like a bud coming into bloom. The fact that the tips of the petals stick out a bit before you start is simply a promise of what is in store!

Q16
Before the birth of our only daughter, now three months old, my husband and I had a perfect sex life. The baby's delivery was normal and I only had four stitches, but since then I have found intercourse very uncomfortable. I love my husband very much but sometimes I can't bear him caressing me or even kissing me.

I am unable to produce any lubrication, so intercourse is painful. I can also feel pressure where the stitches were and I feel that I'm going to tear.

Since you were responsive before the baby and are so again now occasionally, it shows that some special and recent factor is at work which you fear is harming you.

You may have had only four stitches but even this number could be the cause of your discomfort, especially if they were inserted badly and have pulled the tissues too firmly together. Forty-five per cent of women still have pain from their episiotomies months after resuming sexual activity and 1 in 3 women who have had an episiotomy seek medical advice about it for one reason or another. One study found that only one half of all episiotomy women had even attempted intercourse by the time of their 6 week post-natal checkup.

The reasons for your not becoming sexually aroused are many and could lie with the baby, with your husband, with the relationship or with yourself. Your little girl may distract you; your husband's attitude may be different because, for example, he has a fear of hurting you; there may be underlying resentments in the relationship, for example, you perhaps feeling your husband does not help you enough or that he is jealous of your relationship with the child; or in you yourself, for example, you may believe that unless you want another baby you have no further justification for sexual pleasure. Some women who in childhood thought of their own mother as being against sex can become sexless on becoming mothers themselves and so on.

Disliking kissing and breast stimulation may be caused by a fear that if you accept such attentions you are committing yourelf to intercourse. Your anxieties about being torn in intercourse may be more of an exuse rather than anything structurally wrong in the area. First make sure that your GP has examined you and found everything to be in order.

The best way of coping is probably for you and your husband to agree to maintain plenty of physical contact but to drop intercourse for a time. Concentrating on 'courting' behaviour might restore your confidence as might the regular insertion of a suitable object, such as a vibrator, into your vagina under your own control, perhaps while you masturbate. Then you could wean yourself off the vibrator and slowly resume intercourse again. As with so many of these sexual problems after birth the causes are complex and often involve many factors. You might need some professional help to sort them out.

Q17 *I am a 59 year old married woman and have had 3 children. Recently my orgasms have become painful. Should I see my doctor?*

As women get older they can begin to experience a certain amount of pain with orgasm.

At orgasm, the uterus repeatedly contracts – or to be more exact, the periodic contractions of the uterus, which occur constantly, increase in force and in frequency. The contractions are similar to those which occur in labour, although they are less forceful. In the older woman, these contractions can be painful.

If an older woman feels, even unconsciouly, that she should have lost her sex drive by her age, she may be even more predisposed to a painful reaction.

In some women who have reached or passed the menopause, hormone replacement therapy may remove the pain and restore them to a pleasurable sex life.

Are you also, perhaps, trying to limit your sexual needs? If this is the case, having more and more frequent orgasms, by whatever means, might help you. Women can experience pelvic pain if they have prolonged spells of sexual excitation without orgasm.

If you were a younger woman, the last suggestion might have accounted for the problem. You could ask your doctor for a gynaecological check, in any case. Some of the contraceptive pills, containing the newer protestogens, also seem to lead to occasional uterine pains in a few women.

Q18 *I'm seven months pregnant with my second child and I wonder if my occasional masturbation could harm the baby? I always have an orgasm when I masturbate and I have read articles saying that sex is not harmful during pregnancy but nothing that indicates whether orgasms in themselves are.*

Whether a woman is pregnant or not, the only harm that can come from masturbation is the guilt that she has been taught to feel about it.

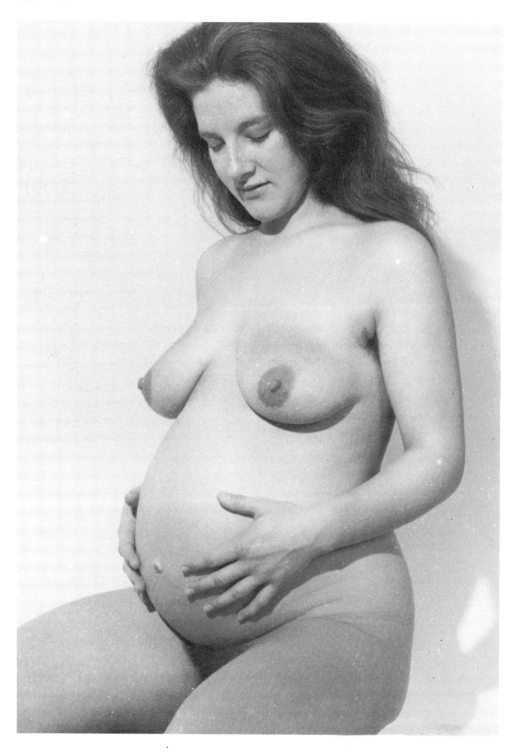

Your fear that the baby might be hurt as a result of your orgasms reflects the parental punishment or rebuke you experienced for touching your vulva when you were very young. You unconsciously expect punishment for sex.

All that happens to the womb when a woman has an orgasm is that it undergoes a few contractions. Since it is continually contracting and relaxing anyway, this does not disturb or distress the baby. As you become bigger you'll notice that your orgasmic contractions seem to come from all over your tummy as the uterus enlarges. Many women say they greatly enjoy this widespread orgasm and some masturbate right up to and even during labour. Some women knowing about the contractions believe that they might go into premature labour and lose the baby. This very rarely happens but if you have ever had a premature labour it makes sense not to masturbate in the last month or so. The other possible 'danger' time is around the timing of any previous miscarriages.

It appears that an orgasm can start off labour if the cervix is 'ripe' and the baby ready to come out and some couples say that they have used this as a way of starting the woman off when she is overdue. Orgasms during labour actually reduce the pains and hasten the progress of the labour.

However, your real concern may be that your feelings of guilt could affect the baby. Maternal emotions can indeed affect an unborn child but your distress about masturbation would be too short-lived to be of any significance. If anything, masturbation could have a good effect as orgasm usually releases tension.

Your only problem is your guilt. Do try and free yourself from the effects of your upbringing and particularly try not to transmit such attitudes to your children in the future.

Q19 *My husband always says that he prefers me to wear a rubber or plastic mac when we have sex and it has become almost an obsession with him. I'm afraid I can't understand this desire at all, and I'm not very keen on the idea myself. However I comply with his wishes most of the time – around three or four times out of five. Have you any explanation of why he should have such a strange desire?*

There have been a number of theories put forward to explain such behaviour but none is really satisfactory. It may well be that there are pleasant sexual associations at an unconscious level for your husband – associated from good bodily feelings from babyhood and early childhood when rubber sheets or pants were used. This can cause a 'link up' or association in the mind.

Most of us have all kinds of good and

bad associations aroused by objects, sights and smells. The same applies to good sexual feelings. But repeated use of these objects to enhance present feelings can lead to a dependency on them. We suggest you talk about this with your husband and plan ways of reducing his reliance on them. Also, you need to find ways of increasing their pleasure for you.

One theory of how they arise is that the fetish object – in this case a raincoat – in some ways represents a desired, but prohibited woman, that is the mother. Since the object is not actually the mother, it can be used to arouse the man sexually and give a high level of satisfaction. In some cases, the man loses interest in the actual woman he's having sex with and all his sexual energy becomes directed at the object instead. In most cases, however, the object simply enhances his enjoyment of intercourse.

None of the theories adequately explains all the features shown by men like your husband. Everyone has a different sexual personality with some of us finding certain things more acceptable and exciting than others. In mild cases – and your husband is a 'mild case' – the best attitude to adopt is probably that if it turns him on, so much the better. If you indulge him willingly, and even happily, it could improve your relationship which would, presumably, be a good thing.

You could also look on it another way and that is to realize that intercourse without the raincoat leads to anxiety, which makes sex less enjoyable for your husband. This can be interpreted as a form of psychosexual immaturity, and it could be this which has impaired your relationship. If you continue to indulge him in this and in any other way he wants, his anxi-

eties may slacken, normal intercourse may become more satisfactory for him and his maturity could be helped. That again would help you. In other words, you could try to see the situation as more of an opportunity for growth than a bore, a threat or a misuse of yourself.

Q20

We have been married for three years, and during this time I have never experienced an orgasm. I was brought up in a very strict household. I was always told by my parents that 'nice' girls don't touch themselves 'down there'. My husband had a similar upbringing. Part of my problem, which may seem silly in this day an age, is that I really don't know how to masturbate. Do you think learning about it would help me?

Attitudes unfavourable to sex are often laid in the unconscious mind of a child, both by directly forbidding sexual activity and punishing it, and also more subtly, by creating an anti-sex atmosphere, whereby sex is not mentioned, or is associated with dirt, illness or sin. Girls probably suffer more from this phenomenon than do boys.

Sex interest in boys is regarded as normal, up to a certain point, in our culture, but – as you were told – it's not considered 'nice' in a girl.

Some girls respond by becoming secretive about self-stimulation. Others find non-obvious ways of doing it and they can in this way deny to themselves, and others, that what they do is the same as masturbation. This partly accounts for the large variety of ways in which women in general masturbate.

You probably fall into the group which

finds indirect ways of masturbating which don't involve touching the vulva. It's difficult to be sure just how women like you masturbate, and it's made even more difficult by the fact that women do not visibly erect or ejaculate like men. Some women have the bodily responses of orgasm, but they can't actually 'feel' they are having one because their mind blocks it, and the orgasm fails to develop properly.

Effective masturbation is like learning to talk, whereas intercourse is like conversation. Masturbation is basic to enjoyable intercourse.

If you and your husband have both been brought up to feel inhibited over expressing yourselves sexually then you both have a wonderful opportunity of building up a good healthy sexual life together, to explore and build up your knowledge and interest in sex. Part of a reliable knowledge of one's own sexual and emotional feelings is to 'backtrack' and learn to discover in a relaxed and positive way how to masturbate. This is the way most of us learn about ourselves sexually in the first place. Decide to do this for your own self knowledge, and gain experience which you will then share with and teach your husband and he you.

Is your husband ignorant of the existence of the clitoris, perhaps? Even if you felt too inhibited or anxious to stimulate your clitoris yourself, he could do so for you, and in this way teach you to masturbate. You could buy a vibrator. This is often a great help. After a while, as your anxiety falls you will be able to take over from the vibrator and rub your clitoris with your fingers.

Good masturbation also involves fantasy. If you fantasized, your attention would be drawn away from what you are doing to your vulva, which would help reduce your anxiety. If you find you're unable consciously to create fantasies, you could get hold of some erotic books, or persuade your husband to tell you his masturbation fantasies while you masturbate. If you do have fantasies yourself, tell your husband about them, and he can try to enact them so as to arouse you. Similarly, concentrating on thoughts or situations you know turn you on will help, as may watching erotic films, taking a little alcohol or talking frankly to a woman friend who masturbates easily.

When you can masturbate, or can be masturbated, then the next step is to find positions for intercourse which allow you or your husband to continue to stimulate your clitoris while you learn to have orgasms with his penis in your vagina. With a little effort, and a lot of encouragement from your husband, you will soon make progress.

Q21
We have been married for nearly four years, and we have a five-month-old son whom we adore. In all our marriage I have never had an orgasm when we have intercourse, although I do when we have sex play. Our marriage is very happy but it is upsetting when my husband tries so hard to satisfy me and we get nowhere. Am I normal or is something wrong with me?

You and your husband are worrying too much about your orgasms. Women need to relax if they are to have orgasms. When they learn to do so they can usually have them easily and in abundance.

The fact you can have orgasms from 'sex play' shows there is nothing wrong with you physically and that everything 'works'. It is only the tension in your mind which prevents you having them during intercourse.

We suggest that you work out a 'programme' together. It seems that foreplay is working well for you so put some effort into developing this – read pages 262–267. The first step is to use your present sexual knowledge of what works for both of you and then to get used to having an orgasm with something in your vagina. Try to fantasize about being penetrated and build it up into an exciting thought. When you masturbate – which you should do fairly frequently – in addition to rubbing your vulva use your fingers to pretend you have a penis in your vagina. Put them inside as you fantasize penentration. Use masturbation to train yourself to relax. When you have intercourse either get your husband to stimulate your clitoris at the same time or perhaps better in your case, do it yourself.

Finally, stop worrying about your orgasms during intercourse and instead think of all the pleasure your vagina is giving to your husband's penis. If you do this you could soon find that his orgasm makes yours come too.

Orgasms during intercourse have become a quite unnecessarily important subject anyway. Certainly men greatly enjoy intercourse with a woman who climaxes with his penis inside her but for some couples this takes too much time and effort to achieve and simply isn't worth it. A very

few women climax immediately a man's penis enters them and others do so only with a lot of clitoral stimulation by themselves or their partner.

Q22 *My wife is keen to make up a sexual foursome with some close friends but I am not keen. What do you think, I am very wary about it.*

Usually the woman who is making the suggestion wants to have sex with the man of the other couple but is reluctant to come clean about this and so suggests a foursome. There is absolutely no reason to suppose that the other pair will fancy each other so the whole thing is usually somewhat selfish. What your wife may be trying to do is to involve you in her affair and so legitimize it. It may also be that she is bored with your love life and that you both need to put more effort into it.

The classic dangers with swapping like this are that you'll be interested in what the other man is like and will ask about his penis and his abilities to excite her. If she says he's useless you'll feel bad on her behalf if only because you probably still fancy her and find her sexy) and if she says he's terrific you'll be jealous because she seems to be better satisfied by him than you. In practical terms you may also have to be lumbered with the other man's wife for whom you may feel nothing

and not even want to have any kind of relationship with. Of course, you could end up liking her more and then you're in trouble that way round.

The main problem with swapping, though countless couples about to embark on it all deny it will happen to them, are the dangers of emotional involvement. This is especially likely in your case because you know the couple. A friendship could easily be struck up with sex at the heart and this

can strain or break all but the strongest of marriages.

Q23 *Does the position in which we make love make any difference to the chances of my wife having an orgasm during sex?*

Coital position isn't a crucial factor in a woman's ability to have an orgasm but

some women who have a well developed G-spot (see page 26) claim that rear entry positions in which the penis stimulates the front wall of the vagina around the G-spot are exceptionally pleasant for them. Positions in which the man can easily and tirelessly stimulate the clitoris are obviously very good to ensure that she has an orgasm and you can experiment to find positions in which you can achieve this. A man on his back has a slower progress towards orgasm and this can delay things long enough to let the woman come to orgasm before or as he does. Some women come more easily in woman-on-top positions because they feel they are more in control and can angle the vagina to get the best stimulation for themselves.

The length of time a couple devote to foreplay and the way it is done are probably much more important than anything done during intercourse itself.

Q24 *Does penis size have anything to do with a woman's satisfaction in intercourse?*

Not really, although some women are psychologically turned on by the sight of a 'well-hung' man. Certainly it isn't true that men with bigger penises are any more virile, fertile or more likely to please a woman and those women who have experience of lots of men say that penis size is of no importance whatsoever. 'It's not what you've got – it's the way that you use it'.

Extremes of penis size can cause problems but these are very rare.

Q25 *Can vaginal size affect a man's pleasure in intercourse?*

Yes – a very small or a very flabby vagina can be unpleasant but these are very rare indeed. A young woman who has never put her fingers or a tampon inside her vagina may well be tight but the hymen usually breaks or stretches with little discomfort and there's nothing to worry about.

Too flabby a vagina after repeated childbirth is more of a problem because it doesn't give the penis a feeling of snugness which men so enjoy. Pelvic exercises (see page 36) can be of enormous help to get the vaginal muscles back into trim. If you have any lumps in your vagina or anything bulging when you feel inside, tell your doctor; you could have a prolapse. Many women find that training their pelvic muscles has another benefit – it can be an exciting variation to their lovemaking as they alternately contract and relax them with their partner's penis inside them. Most men greatly enjoy this too.

A change in position can be very helpful if a woman has a very stretched vagina. Some women find that closing their legs after insertion of the penis makes it nicer for both of them. Any position in which the penis goes in at an angle can also be pleasant.

Some women fear that their vagina is at fault if their partner cannot come or if he loses his erection but the trouble is rarely with the vagina in such cases. The entrance to the vagina can seem to be tight and difficult to negotiate if the woman is nervous and is involuntarily contracting her surrounding muscles. This can also happen if the woman has never stretched her vaginal entrance with her fingers, has never used a tampon and sometimes if the man is not skillful at inserting his penis.

Q26 *Does a hysterectomy impair a woman's ability to enjoy sex?*

Not usually although many women say they feel 'less of a woman' or 'mutilated' by the operation and so enjoy sex less if only for a few months. To be fair some women never come to terms with the psychological wound. A hysterectomy is a very major event in the life of a couple, as is a prostate operation in a man, and the resuming of sexual activity needs to be thoughtful and gradual. Often couples say they enjoy sex more as the fear of unwanted pregnancy is removed. In the earliest few weeks it makes sense to go very gently as the vaginal area heals but most couples feel confident about getting back to sex within 6–8 weeks of the operation.

Vaginal lubrication usually continues exactly as before and orgasms are felt much as before. Some women claim that their orgasms are felt just like they were before. Others claim that their orgasms feel different because there is no uterus to contract during orgasm and a few surgeons, realizing this, perform a partial hysterectomy if at all possible so as to leave the cervix intact. Undoubtedly some women experience uterine contractions on orgasm just as if they had a uterus still there. Recent research suggests that some women go into a kind of 'ovarian shock' even if their ovaries were not touched at the hysterectomy. This produces a short-lived depression of ovarian hormone secretions which can cause gynaecological and emotional symptoms.

Q27 *Is there any harm if a woman is repeatedly sexually aroused and not brought to an orgasm?*

Yes. Every time a woman becomes sexually aroused blood builds up in her pelvic organs including her uterus, vulva, clitoris and all the surrounding tissues. Short-lived stimulation causes congestion which soon disperses but prolonged stimulation causes a considerable pooling of stagnant blood which may take many hours to decongest. Some women remain permanently congested and feel very unsatisfactory with backaches, irritability, sleeplessness, itching of the vulva and a sense of pelvic fullness. A constant vaginal discharge can also be a sign of this problem.

The answer is to try not to get to the point where you are really sexually excited and aroused unless you go on to orgasm. If your man doesn't bring you to a climax,

then do so yourself or you could be building up quite unnecessary problems for yourself over the years.

Many women, even in the absence of genital stimulation by themselves or their partners, complain of the symptoms of pelvic congestion and have found (especially pre-menstrually) that an orgasm produces a wonderful sense of relief. Both sexes probably do best if they have orgasms fairly regularly and thankfully today most women are confident enough to ask their men to satisfy them or masturbate themselves so that they don't suffer from the symptoms of pelvic congestion.

Q28 *After 15 years of marriage I am sick to death of my husband always doing the same things to me sexually. It's just like having a robot in bed with me. What can I do to improve things before I go off with someone else or just walk out?*

This is a common criticism of men and indeed women but to be fair, sexual practices do tend to become somewhat stereotyped after 15 years of marriage. Most couples have found what they best enjoy (or at least they think they have) and tend to stick to it. The problem arises when one of them (you in this case) becomes dissatisfied with this pattern out of boredom more than anything else. We discuss all this more on page 238.

The main problem in your case is almost certainly one of communication and in this the fault is as much with you as with him. You almost certainly have not told your husband everything about your sexual needs, fantasies and desires and we suggest you do so gradually over the next few weeks. Few men, once they know such

'secrets' are unwilling to indulge their women in what they want sexually. Those that are unwilling usually have much deeper relationship problems and need professional help.

Has it dawned on you that you might be as boring to your husband as he is to you but that he just hasn't told you so? All this needs some soul-searching honesty. After all it takes two to keep marital sex enjoyable and exciting year after year.

Q29
I like normal intercourse but my husband is forever going on about new positions, new sex games, aids and so on. I love him a lot but find all these demands perverted. Am I being unreasonable?

We tackle mismatched aims and desires on page 255, but it could be that your husband is immature and possibly even somewhat inhibited. It could be that, as in so many cases, he can't get his best enjoyment from intercourse alone for one of many reasons and so needs these other activities to turn him on. Going along with his reasonable wishes isn't too much to ask, if only because you both will soon become bored by these games, sex aids and so on, yet he will feel cheated if he hasn't had a chance to try.

But if you find that going along with these ideas produces less acceptable and even more unreasonable demands, then it may well be that your husband needs some professional help.

It could just be that at least some of the

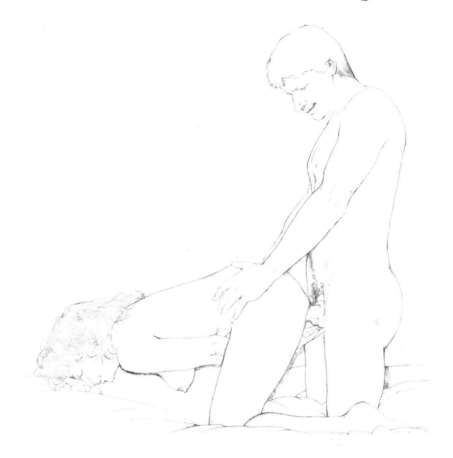

In this form of the doggy position the woman can stimulate the man's scrotum

Q30
My boyfriend likes the all-fours (doggy) position when we have sex but I feel degraded and ashamed. What can I do about this?

things he wants to do could be pleasant for you too, so be sure that you aren't simply being a killjoy by refusing to try anything new. Most couples settle down to a pretty routine sex life after a few years together and one partner who is more innovative and extrovert than the other might well find this boring and so want to introduce sex enhancers.

The 'doggy' position in which the man enters the vagina from behind with the woman on all fours was especially condemned by the mediaeval church because of the intensely pleasurable sensations it produced for both sexes. Some women can only climax during intercourse in this position as the penis stimulates the front wall of their vagina.

Your objections to this position are based on your views that it is animal-like and in this you are right because all animals except Man copulate in rear-entry positions. Perhaps you feel that the position is unloving (facing away from your partner as you do) or you don't like your bottom or anus being seen during sex. All of these are common complaints about this position. You need to work out what it is about the position which makes you react so strongly against it.

The advantages far outweigh these disadvantages and you should, perhaps with professional help, be able to discuss with your boyfriend why it is that this position, which is so pleasurable for him, is so revolting to you. After all, if you are ashamed of your buttocks being seen, you could make love in the dark when you use this position.

Penetration *is* exceptionally deep in this position (which is why it *is* so pleasurable for men) that it could cause pain in a few women. This can usually be solved by reducing the depth of penetration. A more 'loving' rear-entry position is the 'spoons' in which the man lies around the woman's body as she moulds her back into his front. Penetration isn't quite so deep but many of the advantages of rear-entry positions in general are still there. In this rear-entry position air is less likely to get trapped in the vagina and then escape making the alarming noises which so often occur in the doggy position.

Because all our animal ancestors use this position there are those biologists who maintain that it is *the* normal position for intercourse. Certainly it enables a man to caress his woman's clitoris and breasts and generally to stroke and cuddle her. It also makes anal stimulation easy, which some women greatly enjoy, and at the same time allows extremely deep penetration, again a real source of pleasure to many women. Many women like the fact that they aren't facing the man and find it easier to climax when their face can't be seen and in those women who have a well-developed G-spot it is *the* position that best stimulates it in intercourse. Some women say that because they expose their vulva, bottom, and anus in this position they feel terribly vulnerable to the man who could penetrate them vaginally or anally and that this greatly turns them on.

Q31 *A woman I have sex with from time to time likes me to use crude language when I am having sex with her. I am quite put off by this and I am shocked that she should even ask me. Should I give her up?*

The fact that your relationship with this woman is very casual may mean that the woman involved can afford to be herself with you – if only because losing you would be no great loss to her life. If this is so, she is at least paying you the compliment of being frank and uninhibited – what she may not feel free to be with her regular sex partner. If a woman or a man is turned on, or has his or her sexual pleasure increased by hearing crude things, only a fool would refuse to oblige. You like her enough to want to continue having sex with her so you should be prepared to make the experience as good as possible for her. Perhaps you are not enjoying sex as much as you could – partly because you unconsciously think women should be 'nice' like your mother.

Q32 *My little boy of 3 sometimes plays with his penis and often gets erections. Is this normal or will he grow up to be sex-mad?*

This is perfectly normal behaviour and is best ignored. Few parents can put a brave face on such behaviour when it occurs in front of friends or relations but simply asking the boy not to do it in public is usually enough. Certainly don't smack him or make him feel bad; he'll soon grow out of the stage and no harm will be done. Teach him that playing with his penis is a private thing but not a wrong or bad thing.

Q33 *I like using a vibrator on my clitoris and have wonderful orgasms in this way. Could this damage my capacity to have orgasms with men?*

A vibrator is a very powerful stimulus to the clitoris and you may be one of the many women who get their best orgasms from a vibrator. The majority of women soon find that even if they have been using a vibrator as a training aid they soon prefer orgasms produced by their own fingers and that the vibrator collects dust in a cupboard from then on. Some women worry that they'll become addicted to their vibrator because of its powerful orgasm-inducing properties but this is extremely rare.

A few women are so inhibited that they can *only* have an orgasm with a vibrator. They should be pleased that there is at least one way in which they an have orgasms. If you need to, seek professional help to disentangle your inhibitions so as to enable you to have orgasms with a vibrator and eventually with a man.

Q34 *My husband has to go away from home for a week or so at a time with his work and when he returns we usually have rows because he wants to maul me and have sex but I usually don't feel at all like it on the first day or so. What can we do?*

This is a very common problem in couples who don't have sex regularly. Women who use the rhythm method and girls who see their boyfriends every other weekend, for example, often say that things are rather strained on the first night and the following day that they are together.

The man in such situations often doesn't masturbate for several days beforehand (sometimes because he thinks he should 'save himself' for his partner) and so is rearing to go like a bull at a gate on his return. The woman, however, being based on a more emotional and psychological plane wants to reassure herself that the man still wants and loves *her* and isn't especially flattered at the thought that he simply wants to jump on her.

The best way round your problem is to encourage your husband to masturbate the day before he comes home and to be especially pleased if he brings you gifts, flowers or a present. Courtship behaviour is what is needed, if only for 24 hours while the relationship gets back onto an even keel again. A sensible plan is to set up a candle-lit dinner and make obivous efforts to court each other rather than rushing straight into sex. No woman wants to be used only as a sex object – she wants to be wanted as a love object.

Managing a One Night Stand

Although not recommended as a way of life it is an undeniable fact that very many people have experienced a one night stand at some time in their lives. The aims of a one night stand are totally different from intercourse between regular lovers and the rules too are different.

The top three rules

● Beware of VD . . . use a sheath

● Beware of unwanted pregnancy . . . use a sheath (even if the woman says she's on the Pill)

● Don't tell your regular partner

How to prepare

● Don't dress to kill. You could be in danger as a woman if you give out too many or too powerful signals of availability because it could then be difficult or even impossible to switch off the man or men you have switched on

● Don't drink too much or it'll ruin your pleasure

● Be prepared with a sheath (whether you are a man or a woman)

Making a choice

● Keep out of your own area. It's no surprise that the vast majority of one night stands among men occur when they are away from home. Women too have most one night stands on holiday or when travelling

● Go to the best places where you are likely to meet the right kinds of people. Parties, discos and dances are good places . . . pubs are not

● Watch the sign language and be sensible about other people's partners . . . you don't want to offend or end up causing a fight

● Obviously promiscuous people are best avoided – they often have problems and may give you VD or even AIDS

● Avoid anyone who drinks heavily, is obviously disturbed emotionally or is at all odd. Such people can be dangerous

Getting to bed

● Those who are involved in one night stands know the score and are looking for straight intercourse (or more likely copulation)

• Most women can't directly ask for sex even if they have gone out that evening looking for it. Such women usually start kissing and cuddling and 'get carried away'! The result is sex. More advanced individuals can come straight out with 'where are you sleeping tonight?' or something similar

Some Dos and Don'ts

• Don't expect meaningful intercourse . . . settle for pleasant copulation

• Don't expect lots of foreplay . . . enjoy the copulation for its own sake

• Do beware of any man who says he wants to do unusual things to you. You might be in real danger so play safe and keep away

• A cautious man in this situation makes his intentions absolutely clear, possibly even in front of witnesses if the circumstances permit. This can prevent a charge of rape being brought by a guilty woman who regrets the episode. Some men resort to professionals rather than run this risk

• Do expect the man to have sexual problems, even if he never usually does. Many a one night stander loses his erection or ejaculates prematurely even if he is a great performer with his regular woman

• Don't be surprised if you feel terribly guilty afterwards. Many men fear they have caught VD and many women that they have got pregnant. Both may have real symptoms that convince them and some end up in VD clinics and on the doctor's couch quite unnecessarily. Don't have one night stands if you can't stand the guilt

• Do expect to go off sex if you are worried about being found out, possibly by your usual partner. Some women go off sex for ages and some even have their hair cut off as a form of self-induced punishment for their wrong-doings

• If the woman is known to mutual friends never ever let her down by boasting (or even talking) about the episode. Leave the talking to her and be prepared to lie on her behalf if necessary

• Don't fall in love with the partner

• If you are really looking for a long-term relationship and the partner seems a possibility don't short circuit things by going straight to intercourse on the first night. Take time to court each other

• Avoid the very young, especially if you are a male, because the courts are very hard if you get caught

• Do be wary of teasers of either sex. A man should never tease a woman that he intends to have sex with her yet won't when it comes to it and the newspapers are littered with stories of men who have killed women who refuse to have sex with them after leading them right up the starting gate. It's a dangerous game

• Lastly, if you find yourself perpetually on one night stands, get professional help because it's a lonely and destructive road and one which makes it increasingly unlikely that you'll meet anyone who'll be a good one-to-one partner for you

It is probably worth pointing out that many women tied to the home with children and leading a fairly hum-drum life often resent their husband's gay-abandon life style when he's away and free from domestic and family responsibilities. On occasions this latent aggression and even frank jealousy shows itself as a ban on or an unwillingness to have sex as an unconscious form of punishment for his high-living. Such a wife has power over at least one area of her husband's life and may unconsciously wield it to show him that life doesn't always favour him. If this is done consciously the relationship is in bad trouble but usually it is much more subtle, coming as it does from the unconscious of the woman. A part of this dissatisfaction is often tied up with even so much as a hint that another woman might be involved in his time away from her. Even the most platonic of business relationships can be used as a weapon to punish either herself or her husband.

At a less dramatic level some couples have a similar problem when the man comes home from work in the evening. The fact that each have had different stimuli during the day – some exciting and satisfying and others negative and emotionally wearing, doesn't help. If the man's work has been intellectually tiring this might have exhausted him and he'll need to relax. So too will the housewife whose children have drained her in quite another way. Many men on their home-coming are met by a list of the day's problems that have arisen out of a frustrating day at home with the family. He too may have had a 'bad day' and the children will be tired. Tea time in many homes is a disaster area and a sensible couple will try to work out the best way of dealing with it.

As with almost all sexual and relationship problems the answer is often highly complex and can involve many or all of the possibilities we've outlined. Such problems can only really be sorted out by discussion. If this doesn't produce results most couples will benefit from a professional outsider's help.

Q35

My wife and I are in our late 30s and we are satisfied that our family is complete. We do not think that if we had the misfortune to lose them, we would wish to start a family again. I would like to have a vasectomy. I accept that I should regard it as final, although I know in theory at least it might prove reversible and also that there is no change in the sensations during intercourse. These I accept, but two other points, which I have discussed with my doctor, I am still not happy about.

Firstly I wonder whether psychologically, because I know I should not be able to be a father, I should feel less of a man in my mind, and secondly, whether the removal of all possibility of pregnancy would make intercourse too easy and less exciting. I may add that our married life has of late been much less happy and satisfying, due in the main to dissatisfaction with our sexual relations owing to a lack of a mutually acceptable form of contraception. My wife is not at all happy about being on the Pill any longer and I don't trust any other method totally.

In theory at least, vasectomy is a very sensible operation. It is the cheapest and one of the most effective methods of contraception. Although precautions are taken to detect cases where the operation is a failure before any harm is done it is perhaps worth pointing out that as a method it is not always as efficient as the Pill. Also, as you realize, it must, unlike the Pill, be regarded as irreversible even though a small percentage of men have an operation successfully to reverse the procedure.

Your wife's adverse reaction to the Pill could be a dislike of the hormone content, an adverse reaction to the side effects, the result of underlying and unreasonable misapprehension about it or to an unconscious desire to produce more children. In a similar way it may be that your wife still feels unconsciously guilty about intercourse unless it carries the risk of pregnancy. This aspect should be investigated because a vasectomy could put her off sex altogether.

In most cases vasectomy is a success but some men who have had the operation never stop talking about it, which suggests they are uneasy about it. If such men subsequently become ill or some disaster overtakes them they are likely to blame the operation!

In any direct sense this is nonsense but if a man is not fully secure in his male ego (for example if he has any considerable doubts about his maleness and his ability to fulfil the male role) then the operation can tip the balance against him and he becomes 'unmanly'. He can then be troubled with impotence or loss of desire. However, this only really happens with men who might have found the same problem occurring in other circumstances. Nevertheless, every man who wants a vasectomy should be properly and professionally assessed by a doctor or similar person with the necessary training to detect the presence of such a condition

before the operation is carried out.

So the answer to both your questions is that there is something in both of them. Your wife, yourself and your relationship need proper assessment before a decision is taken. Whether vasectomy is the best answer or not would then depend on the outcome. The best vasectomy services do have proper assessing doctors skilled in this work but some cheap services ignore these factors or assess them in an unsatisfactory or unprofessional manner. It's worth spending time and money.

Q36 *My friend and I were discussing sex recently and she told me that when her husband has a climax in her vagina she can feel the liquid spurting against her. I have always felt the spasm of climax, but never the actual semen. I wonder now if my vagina is unusually insensitive.*

A number of women make the same claim as your friend. It is true that some men ejaculate with force but even so, it is hard to envisage that it could be sufficient to result in a detectable feeling for the woman. If the vagina were a tight fit over the penis it might be possible but during sexual excitement the inner end tends to balloon outwards. It might also be possible if the semen were at a considerable temperature difference, but it is not.

The only likely explanation, is that the semen might be deposited on, say, the front wall of the vagina, with the woman on her back, and then drips or runs over the cervix to the back wall. The vagina might detect the movement involved; however, even this seems somewhat unlikely, and in any case the penis would be in the way. Also the women who make the claim say they feel the actual ejaculatory spurts and not movement afterwards.

Another possibility is that what such women are really describing is the very real sensation of the man's penis throbbing repeatedly at ejaculation. Perhaps they misinterpret this as feeling the semen.

One contraceptive manual, written by several authors, asserts that men can blow a sheath off the penis by the force of their ejaculation. Perhaps a woman like your friend wrote that!

Q37

My attitude to sex has changed since I was sterilized six months ago, I just cannot let myself go. I've always enjoyed sex and my husband is an excellent lover and will spend hours on foreplay. I'd like to enjoy the same happiness we had before but I feel that I'm turned off because I know I can't get pregnant. My husband has been very patient and says I'll get over it. I only wish I could see it that way.

It is true that some women react to sterilization with a decline in sex drive but this is least likely when the woman herself wanted to be sterilized and suggested it herself.

Sterilizations performed at the time of a Caesarean section or abortion are much more likely to be regretted than those done 'cold' after careful consideration.

Problems arise when one partner (often the husband) definitely wants no more children and the couple don't want him to have a vasectomy. A woman who is steril-

ized in these circumstances may well feel that the operation has ruined her unconscious or even conscious desire to have another baby.

The trouble with sterilization procedures either in men or women is that they are so final and for those women who see their sexuality and even their whole being as linked to the producing and nuturing of babies this can be a terrible blow. In a sense it is like an early menopause – a time when many women feel their 'true' role in life is over because they can no longer have babies.

Although you may be able to come to terms with your condition, you may nevertheless always regret the fact, at least to some extent. Time is the great healer and at 6 weeks it is quite normal to feel the way you do. To you sex and babies were probably very closely linked and it could be that you are so inhibited about the pleasure of sex that you can only enjoy it if there is the possibility of a pregnancy (a baby) hanging over you all the time and find sex for pleasure alone difficult to come to terms with.

If you were uninhibited and sexy before the sterilization the chances are that you'll go back to a normal sex life pretty soon.

Sometimes the sterilized woman worries about her ability to keep her partner on the grounds that he might some day want to prove he is still able to father a child. Or the unsterilized partner may envy the sterilized one his or her freedom to have sex with no danger of conception.

Give your husband a chance to woo you out of these situations and with time your normal feelings will return and even blossom as you come to enjoy sex for its own sake and have the problems of contraception removed from your shoulders.

Q38 *My wife is 62 and I am 64 and she only wants to make love about once a month. This is too infrequent for me so what can I do? She used to be very sexy until the menopause and has slowly become less interested.*

Many women become less interested in sex after the menopause and this can occur for several reasons. Some think that sex is for the young and that now they are no longer fertile that they don't 'deserve' sex for pleasure. Women, and especially those whose sex life has become infrequent, experience soreness or dryness of the vagina which makes intercourse painful. This is to be expected and can be helped by osterogen creams or by taking oral oestrogen. Husbands also become less interested in sex as they age and perhaps have erection difficulties, but it is the woman who goes to a doctor for her own lagging sex life. There could be a medical reason why she finds sex unpleasant.

Many couples find that their sexual rhythms and appetites gradually lessen. There are no rules about frequency of intercourse any more than there are rules about eating meals. The important question is – do you really enjoy it? It's the quality of the experience, not the frequency which matters. Some middle-aged people get very set into routines and may be sex needs to be planned into a more flexible life-style. For many people in your age group there is more time to relax – or does your wife seem to be too busy? Does she try to do too much in an attempt to reassure herself that she isn't getting old. Unfortunately this is common, especially in an inhibited woman who doesn't much want sex anyway. As a result sex often gets crowded out.

So the problem could be complex, and yet your wife may well see no need to do anything at all!

If she refuses to seek help you could try masturbation to fill your sexual needs. You could also ask your wife if she would masturbate you, even if she didn't want to go on to have intercourse. For many older people to whom masturbation doesn't come easily this can be the first stepping stone back to a rich and fulfilling sex life.

Many older people say that they enjoy sex more than ever, without the pressures of contraception and a family, and with time to spend together perhaps for the first time in 30 or more years. Perhaps just knowing this could help your wife.

Q39 *Since I have been using a diaphragm all the pleasure has gone out of sex. Could it be that this method simply doesn't suit me?*

The diaphragm is a very good contraceptive method when used properly with a spermicidal jelly. But many women see a diaphragm as unromantic because they haven't yet learnt the art of putting it in place regularly like 'cleaning their teeth'. Others find the jelly itself has an unpleasant odour.

One disadvantage to this otherwise reliable method is to the woman who can't bear touching her genitals and so simply dislikes inserting the diaphragm in the first place. Such a woman will put off using the device whenever possible.

Some men find that sex is less pleasant with a diaphragm because about half of the vagina and all of the cervix are covered with rubber. This leaves only the back wall of the vagina in its natural state and some men find this relatively unstimulating. If this comes across to the woman she'll enjoy sex less, even if he doesn't or can't say why.

Lastly, the diaphragm covers over the G-spot and so reduces the chances of stimulating what is for many woman their most sensitive vaginal area. Perhaps this is why you don't enjoy sex as much now. Try another method.

Q40 *My penis is only 4 inches long when erect and I wonder if there's any way I can enlarge it.*

The subject of penis enlargement is a vexed one. The majority of men who think they have a small penis have, in fact, a perfectly normal-sized one when it erects though it may indeed be on the small size when limp. A very small percentage of men with small penises have a shortage of the male hormone testosterone (they also have very slow-growing beards and sparse body hair). Replacement of the missing hormone can increase their penis size but this has to be supervised by a specialist in the subject.

Assuming that this is not the case, and that you simply have a small penis for genetic reasons (just as some people have small feet) the most important thing to bear in mind is that by no means all women like large penises, or even know the difference!

Obviously your question is aimed at the possibility of using some kind of penis enlarger which is available at a sex shop. It is current medical wisdom that if your penis is fully grown and you are not short of testosterone no further enlargement is

possible. However, owners of sex shops claim that men return telling of great results with penis enlargers. No controlled trials have been done on this subject and anyway they would be extremely difficult to do if only because the size of a man's penis varies considerably according to his state of sexual arousal.

One theory that could explain the apparent increase in size obtained with such gadgets is as follows. The penis is at its largest immediately before an uninhibited orgasm and some inhibited men never fully erect neither do they have a full orgasm. If these devices make it easier for the man to relax or to be confident about his penis size then they might just enable him to have a fuller erection which is interpreted as a bigger penis.

Confidence about one's genitals usually reflects confidence in other areas of life.

Q41 *I am uncircumcised and wonder what effects this could have when I get married. Are there any dangers to it and will I be able to enjoy sex as much as circumcised men?*

The main question is whether or not your foreskin can be pulled back completely and easily. If it can then you will be able to enjoy sex just as well as any circumcised man and might even enjoy it more because the sensitivity of your penis tip will be greater because it will not be rubbing against underpants all day. If your foreskin won't pull back completely you probably masturbate with it forwards and will have intercourse with it forwards. Some men with this condition say that they get very little sensation in their penis tip (the most sensitive part) and that they even experience pain as the foreskin is stretched. You might try using a sheath.

If you have either of these problems you should consult your doctor. He will teach you to stretch your foreskin slowly over several weeks or might suggest circumcision.

It is said, since you ask about 'dangers' that the partners of men who are uncircumcised are more likely to get cervical cancer. This is very unlikely at the best of times but is almost certainly completely abolished if the foreskin doesn't trap any white matter (smegma). So as you are not circumcised do ensure that your penis is kept clean by regular (daily) washing with soap and water especially under the foreskin. If this is difficult and you suffer from inflammation and itching of the penis head, a simple circumision operations would cure it.

Q42 *My penis has a bend in it when it erects and my doctor says it is called Peyronie's disease. Could this have been brought on by masturbation?*

You are unlucky to have this uncommon condition but you are in good company . . . for some reason it is more common in clergymen! For reasons which are unknown, a patch of fibrous tissue develops in the penis causing it to bend towards that side on erection. The condition is initially painful but tends to get less so. Various treatments have been tried, mostly unsuccessfully, and the best thing to do is to adapt your style of intercourse to accommodate the defect.

Although the cause is unknown there is

no reason to believe that masturbation could have anything to do with it, if only because if masturbation were the cause then every man would suffer from Peyronie's disease!

Q43 *I can only really enjoy sex after my husband has spanked me. Is this normal or am I a pervert?*

This is not uncommon. Obviously sex is a guilty activity for you, although you may not realize it and at the unconscious level you have to be punished (if only symbolically) before allowing yourself to be 'naughty' and have sex. You may also long to be the passive victim and to be led to sexual 'heights' beyond yourself. A lot depends on how serious the spanking has to be and if your partner can enter into the spirit of it freely and be relied on not to let things get out of hand. The fact that you ask if you are a pervert suggests that it does worry you a bit. Many men are in exactly the same position but this is usually less apparent, except perhaps to prostitutes who are often asked to beat men before or after sex.

If the smacking simply enhances your pleasure and doesn't *replace* intercourse, in no way could you be considered a pervert.

Q44 *I hear a lot about other women having multiple orgasms, but can men have them too? Incidentally, I only have one orgasm – and I'm none too sure about that. Am I defective as a woman?*

To answer the first part of your question – yes, pre-adolescent boys and some young

How to Strip

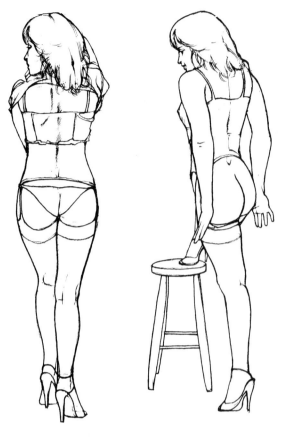

Strip tease for women

Even quite 'together' women find stripping a little embarrassing so if you decide
to try it have a small drink beforehand and
get the music and the lighting right.

The basic principle is to reveal the
obvious first and to save the best bits till
last.

Here's how to do it:

◆ Choose the clothes carefully. Avoid
things with fiddly fastenings. Stick to
small numbers of clothes and things that
are sexily removed. It's probably best to
wear a dress (or blouse and skirt), bra and
pants, suspender belt and stockings, high-
heeled shoes and some body jewellery.

◆ Make up to look sexy and get your
man on the bed or relaxed on a chair.

◆ Start by dancing around to the music
(which should have a strong beat).

◆ When moving emphasize your
breasts, legs, bottom.

◆ Undo your blouse slowly in a teasing
way and gradually remove it and then
cover the front of your chest with it so that
it looks as though you aren't wearing a bra
underneath. Toss is over to him.

◆ Undo the waistband of your skirt and
wriggle out of it letting it fall around your
ankles to the floor. Kick it over to him. Be
sure to remove it slowly edging it down
over your hips and showing him first your
front view and then your bottom as you do
so. Take your shoes off sexily.

◆ Sit down on a chair or high stool and
slowly undo the stockings from their suspenders one at a time. Roll down one
stocking at a time to the toe and flick it off
your foot. Be sure to keep the toe pointed
as you do so as this greatly enhances the
shape of your leg. Once your stockings are
off put the shoes back on if it makes your
legs look glamourous.

◆ Show off your breasts and slowly and
teasingly remove your bra. Start with one
shoulder strap and then the other and
finally undo the back clasps with your back
to your man. Hold the bra to your chest as
you turn around to face him. Reveal your
breasts with a flourish or do a peep-bo
with each nipple.

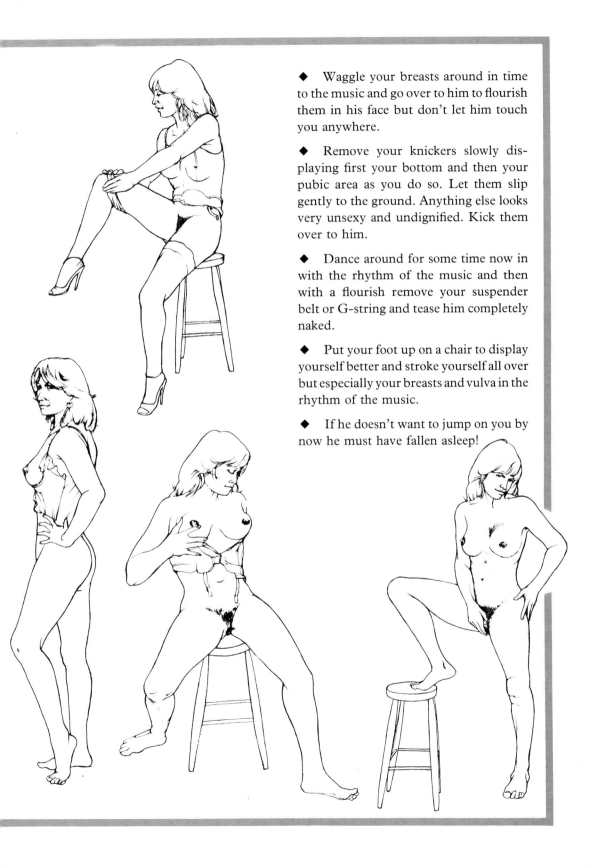

◆ Waggle your breasts around in time to the music and go over to him to flourish them in his face but don't let him touch you anywhere.

◆ Remove your knickers slowly displaying first your bottom and then your pubic area as you do so. Let them slip gently to the ground. Anything else looks very unsexy and undignified. Kick them over to him.

◆ Dance around for some time now in with the rhythm of the music and then with a flourish remove your suspender belt or G-string and tease him completely naked.

◆ Put your foot up on a chair to display yourself better and stroke yourself all over but especially your breasts and vulva in the rhythm of the music.

◆ If he doesn't want to jump on you by now he must have fallen asleep!

men can indeed have repeated orgasms in very quick succession. But very few men over the age of about 20 can do so. According to Kinsey between 8 and 15% of his younger men had experienced multiple orgasms.

On the subject of multiple orgasms for women, things are fairly complicated. It is probably true that all women are naturally orgasmic from early on in life and are conditioned out of their capacities by negative events and attitudes in their upbringing. Obviously some women are more sexually responsive than others just as some are more ticklish than others.

A small percentage have several orgasms all the time, and a few more experience them from time to time, especially when they are highly aroused. Some women claim that their first orgasm is the best, and others say that they build up to their keenest sensations as they have more orgasms one after the other.

If you relax, you will enjoy whatever you have and stop worrying about how things could be better. As you grow within a sexual relationship, you may find that

one day when you are highly aroused you could ask your partner to re-stimulate you (or you could do it yourself). If you achieve this easily, well and good but don't let it take away from your enjoyment of your first orgasm. Many women who try this approach do find that 'more means better'.

Q45 *I sometimes have trouble keeping an erection and have tried putting a rubber ring around my penis. This gives me enormous and sustained erections, but I am worried it might be dangerous.*

You're right to be worried because such bands can become very difficult to remove if the penis becomes extremely swollen as it can do. Never ever put a ring of solid, rigid material around your penis, and never use anything if you are unable to ensure that it can be released easily.

Although many members of the medical profession are against their use, special bands can be helpful to men with erection difficulties, even if they only act as a kind of talisman that brings them erectile 'luck' on that occasion.

For how to increase erectile staying power, see on page 330.

Q46

My girlfriend worries me because she always wants to get the sex act over with very quickly. From what I read I gather that women like to take things slowly during lovemaking and if anything look down on men who rush along. Is there something wrong with her or am I at fault?

There could be many reasons why your girlfriend is in such a hurry. The place you make love could be unsatisfactory for her, and she may be frightened of discovery. For some this can mean added excitement, but for others it is a complete turn off, and they rush the whole thing through as quickly as possible. This is particularly true if she is inhibited or scared to begin with.

She could simply find sex too upsetting and wants more time with you exploring your emotional relationship first.

Perhaps she doesn't really like you much yet needs some sort of sexual release. Or it could be that your technique just doesn't please her but she's 'too nice' or shy to tell you. She then rushes into sex without spending time getting warmed up.

Not all women want to spend time on sexual enjoyment; or she may have a private fantasy which she prefers to you. If this latter is the case you can't be said to be making love – you are copulating using each others' genitals.

Talk this all over with your girl and tell her that it would be nicer for you to take things more slowly and savour it all. If she doesn't want to you'll have to think again about the whole relationship.

Q47

I have a lovely girlfriend but when we are having sex she talks all the time and this puts me off my stroke. She says it's all part of the togetherness. Is she right?

There are two views about this common problem. Some couples appear to enjoy keeping rational and conscious control over themselves and each other through-out intercourse and others go for complete abandonment. In the former group quite a lot of people actually fear letting go and keep a hold on reality and protect their vulnerability by talking all the time. They usually do this quite unconsciously. This is clearly a form of inhibition. For the partner who wants to lose him or herself in a fantasy a talking lover is a real nuisance because it brings him or her down to earth. This can often be of greater importance that it at first seems because for such a person sex may only be acceptable or enjoyable if the fantasy is just right. In a sense such a person is inhibited and is using their lover as a tool for indulging their fantasy. Most people do this some of the time during sex but if it becomes a habit and the person's partner 'intrudes' very easily onto the sexual scene then it's time to get professional help unless you want the relationship to falter. Most partners of such people are very aware that they are being left out and it hurts.

The commonest reason for talking all the time during sex though is the fear of total abandonment. True intercourse involves a regression to baby-like vulnerability. Unselfconscious abandonment is the secret of perfect intercourse – and for many people this will include some talking especially the use of crude language or loving praise for their partner.

Q48

When I was spring cleaning I had a dreadful shock when I found a box of women's clothes and realized that they belonged to my husband. Does he need psychiatric or medical help?

It must indeed have been a shock for you. Some men find cross-dressing, as it is called, very sexually exciting. This often dates back to their childhood when they might have received confusing messages about whether they were boys or girls. Some such men even say that their mother wanted a girl and even treated them as a girl.

First you and your husband need to talk about the situation to see if he dresses and stays in the house or if he has the need to go outside and pass off as a woman. If the latter is the case then you both need to talk this through with a professional counsellor. If your husband's dressing is confined to the house then perhaps you can co-operate with him over it by recognizing and indulging his need to cross-dress. You may even be able to incorporate it into your sex play and this could help your husband to 'work it out of his system'.

Because he is a cross-dresser does *not* mean that he is homosexual or bisexual. It may be that he is acting out some sexual fantasy or exploring part of his emotional or sexual self that has become very important to him. He needs your love, support and insight but this may be very difficult for you to give without professional help. Get help as soon as possible because the

sooner you can start to sort it all out the better. Some women can never come to terms with the problem.

Q49

I don't always feel like sex and sometimes want to refuse my wife. I also get approaches from other women from time to time. How can I turn down sex nicely and not hurt the woman?

This can be very tricky because it is often difficult to put off one's partner or indeed any member of the opposite sex who wants to have intercourse – when we feel unwilling for some reason. The situation divides fairly easily into two distinct areas. If your relationship is a strong one based on love and respect for each other a 'refusal' to have sex now and again can hardly be seen as a cause for serious concern. If sex refusal has become part of your life, however, then you may need to re-appraise your whole relationship and not just the sexual side, to see why it is that you don't seem to want one another as much.

If the relationship is a casual one which you'd nevertheless describe as 'good' then perhaps refusal to have sex means that you are trying to wean yourself off the relationship or indeed that you unconsciously want to free yourself of it because you have become bored or have someone else in mind. This can, of course, also occur within a stable relationship.

When it comes to refusing to have sex then the only overriding principle must be to be gracious and helpful rather than damaging. The approach should be 'I'm flattered you want sex with me but . . I have just masturbated/I'm worried about not being able to keep my erection/my wife would be desperately hurt etc etc. Honesty may or may not be the best policy and considerable tact may be required. How much of the rest of the relationship is based on similar dishonesty? What are you doing about it?

Many couples use their partner's willingness to have sex with them as a test of their love. Men especially do this. Even if they aren't especially interested in having sex at a particular time they often bring up the subject to see how willing their woman is. If she agrees readily they are then secure in their woman's love for them but if she refuses it makes them worry about how much she really loves them. After all every man is brought up in our monogamous culture to believe that a woman who *really* loves him will do anything for him. Similarly, many women believe that if they are *really* attractive a man will be crazy to have sex with them at the slightest provocation.

Lastly, even if you don't want sex whenever they suggest offer to relieve your women by means other than intercourse – don't leave them high and dry!

Q50 *I seem to do an awful lot of daydreaming about sex even though we have a good sex life after 20 years together. Is this something I should curb?*

You'd be surprized how much time people spend thinking about sex in one form or another. Nature obviously intended us to be interested in the subject and few would deny that sex is one of the basic human desires. If thinking about sex is all you ever did about it then you'd need help so that you could put into practice what you so obviously desired but if your thinking adds to your existing sexual life with your partner, whose complaining?

Many individuals complain to therapists that their partner doesn' think *enough* about sex and simply crashes on in the same old boring ways, both in and out of bed, for year after year. Most successful couples are always thinking of new ways to enhance their sexual life together though much of this need not necessarily involve intercourse. Flirting, courtship behaviour and sexual creativity are all helpful in keeping a longterm relationship fresh and this involves at least some thought. Having sexual fantasies is a part of this build-up of excitement and anticipation and sharing your fantasies (see page 245) with your partner could be a way of releasing this bottled-up feeling you are so obviously concerned about. Could it be that you never really talk to your partner or share your sexual thoughts with him? Try to do so the next time you are sexually aroused and see what he says. He'll probably be delighted and will be tempted to share his sexy thoughts and daydreams with you.

Useful addresses

All the addresses and telephone numbers on the following pages were checked at the time of going to press, but it is quite possible that some of them will have changed by the time you read them. If you have difficulty in contacting a particular organisation discuss the matter with your local Citizens Advice Bureau who will be able to suggest an alternative organisation or might even help you with a new address and telephone number.

General help and advice
Association of Sexual & Marital Therapists
c/o Dr C. M. Duddle, Student Health Centre, University of Manchester, Manchester M13 9QS.
A multi-disciplinary professional organisation which, if you send an s.a.e., will tell you the name of your nearest sex therapist or clinic.

British Association for Counselling
37A Sheep Street, Rugby, Warwickshire
Tel 0788 78328
Produces referral directory of counselling agencies and organisation. £4 to non-members.

Citizens Advice Bureaux (CAB)
These can be found in most towns and cities. Telephone numbers in local phone books. They give free, confidential advice on all kinds of subjects and will tell you where to find other specialist organisations in your area.

National Council for Civil Liberties
21 Tabard Street, London SE1
Tel 01 403 3888

A vigorous group that campaigns to safeguard the rights and freedoms of the public. Gives free and confidential advice on many areas including drugs, sex, homosexuality, dealing with the police, legal aid and so on.

National Marriage Guidance Council
Herbert Gray College, Little Church Street, Rugby, Warwickshire CV21 3AP.
Tel 0788 73241

Parents Anonymous for Distressed Parents
(Life Line) 6 Manor Gardens, London N7.
Tel 01 263 9818
A self-help organisation run by parents who have battered their babies, for those who fear they might batter or who actually have battered their babies.

Release
1 Elgin Avenue, London W9.
Tel 01 289 1123
24-hour emergency service 01 603 8654
Provides free advice and information on birth control, abortion, single parents, marriage, legal, personality and personal problems. Can also help with names and addresses of organisations local to you.

Samaritans
An organisation mainly to help the lonely, desperate and suicidal. Look up local branch in telephone directory. Telephone advice and counselling in complete confidence.

Education
Advisory Centre for Education ACE
18 Victoria Park Square, London E2 9PB.
Tel 01 980 4596
A valuable source of information about all educational matters. Will help if you are pregnant and under school-leaving age, if you are expelled from school etc. Advice free. Phone or write.

Health
Committee on Sexual & Personal Relationships of the Disabled (SPOD)
286 Camden Road, London N7 OBJ
Tel 01 607 8851

Community Health Councils (CHCs)

Usually on your local high street in or over a shop. Look up telephone number in local directory. Will advise on your medical rights, how to complain about the Health Service, where to go for help on abortions, contraception, VD and drug problems, among other things.

Health Education Council

78 New Oxford Street, London WC1.
Tel 01 637 1881
The country's main source of health education information, research and materials. Has free leaflets on VD, personal hygiene, sexual development, contraception, drugs and many other interesting areas.
Look up local branch in your local telephone directory or contact the main address above.

Patients' Association

Room 33, 18 Charing Cross Road, London WC2.
Tel 01 240 0671
A pressure group which acts for patients who have complaints against the Health Service or for those who want to know where to get medical treatment for a specific illness. Many useful leaflets and books.

Sexually Transmitted Deseases Special Clinics

For address of local VD clinic talk to your general practitioner; look up in phone book under venereal disease or VD, or phone your local hospital and ask for the Special Clinic. Sometimes these clinics are now called STD clinics.

There is a National Health Service information service (a recorded message on a tape). Tel 01 248 8072

Women's National Cancer Control Campaign (WNCCC)

1 South Audley Street, London W1.
Tel 01 499 7532
Provides information on cancer and its treatment. Free leaflets on checking for breast cancer and other interesting topics.

Vasectomy Advancement Society

1 Ravenscroft Court, 56 Ravenscroft Avenue, London NW11. Tel 01 455 6541

Sex Therapy Clinics in the UK

Many of these clinics are funded by the National Health Service or are supported by charities. A few of them are private clinics, so it is wise to check the fees before making an appointment. Hospital clinics will want a referral letter from your doctor.

London Area

Ante-natal Tower Block, North Middlesex Hospital. Tel 01 807 3071

Caryl Thomas Clinic, Harrow Weald
Tel 01 853 7004

Cassel Hospital, Richmond
Tel 01 940 8181

Charing Cross Hospital, W6.
Tel 01 748 2040

Family Planning Clinic, 8 Stuart Crescent Health Centre, N22 5NJ. Tel 01 889 4311

Hammersmith Hospital, W12.
Tel 01 743 2030

Hampden Wick Clinic, Middlesex
Tel 01 977 6552

The Institute of Behaviour Therapy, W8.
Tel 01 938 1011

King's Family Planning Brook Centre, SE5.
Tel 01 274 7711 ext. 2662

Lincoln Memorial Clinic for Psychotherapy, SE1. Tel 01 928 7211

London Centre for Psychotherapy, NW3.
Tel 01 435 0873

London Hospital, E1. Tel 01 247 5454

London Institute for the Study of Human Sexuality. Tel 01 373 0901

Margaret Pyke Centre, W1.
Tel 01 734 9351

Index

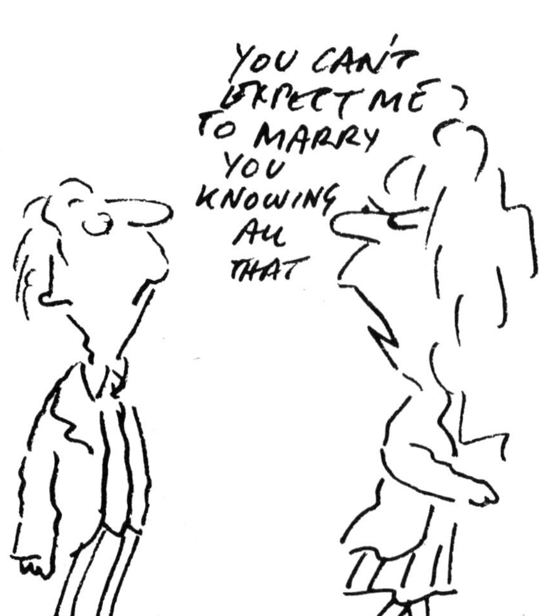
YOU CAN'T EXPECT ME TO MARRY YOU KNOWING ALL THAT